SIGHT

ANTONY GORMLEY ON DELOS

ARCHAEOLOGICAL SITE AND MUSEUM

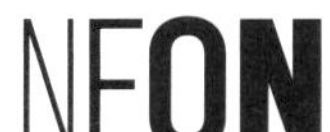

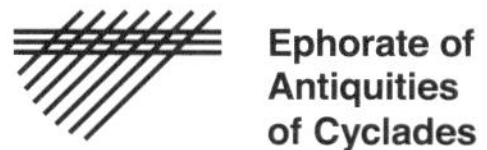

Ephorate of Antiquities of Cyclades

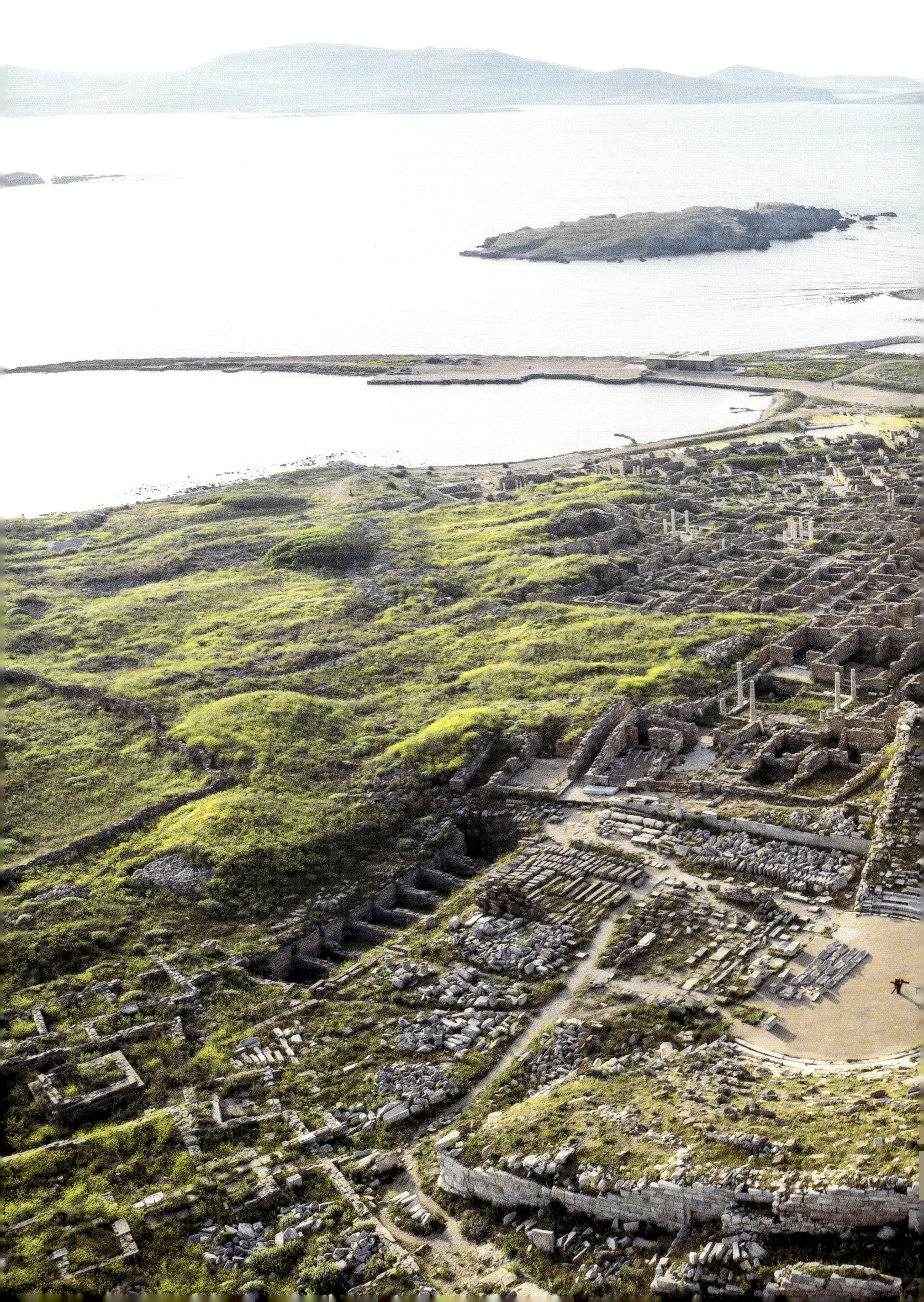

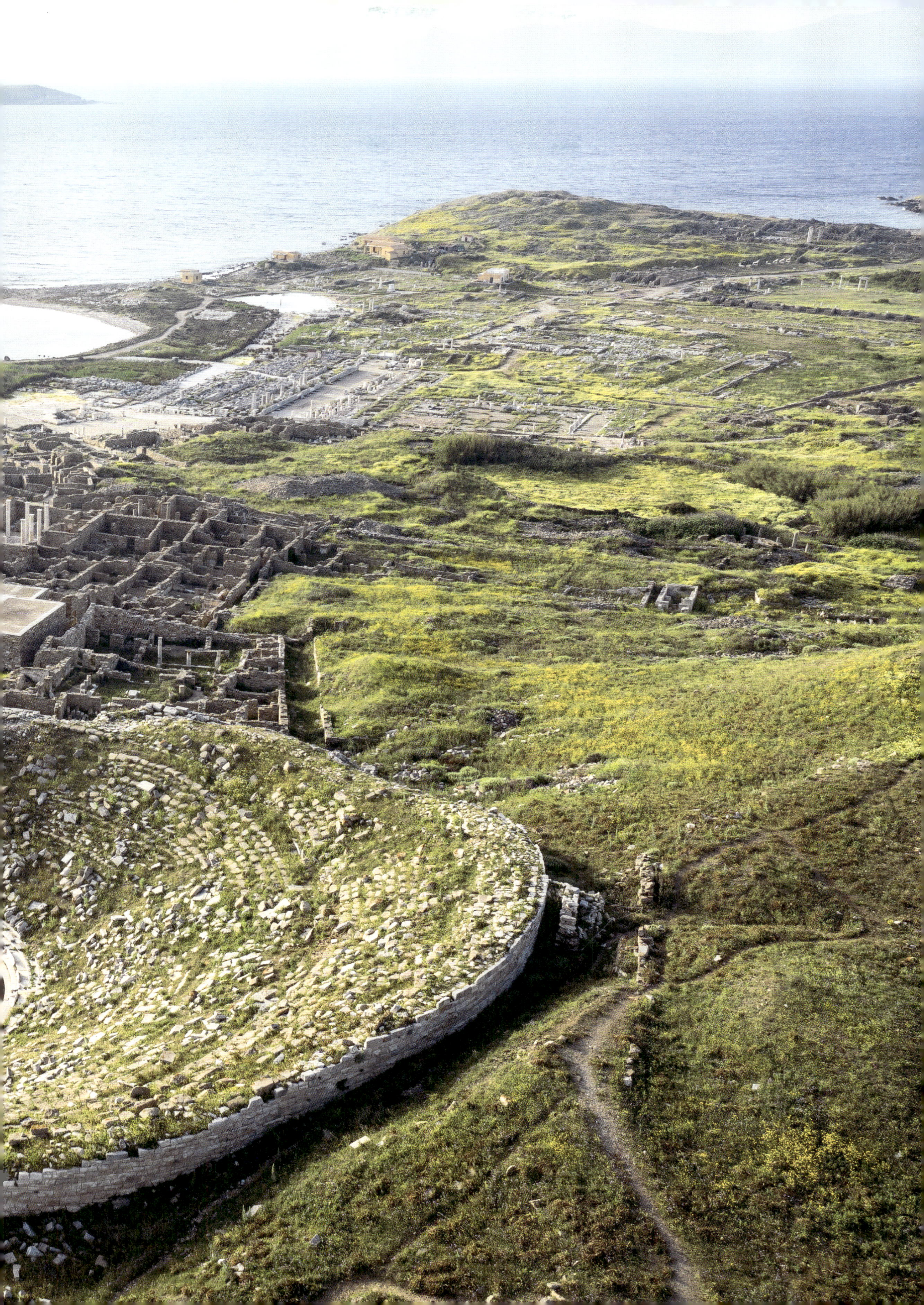

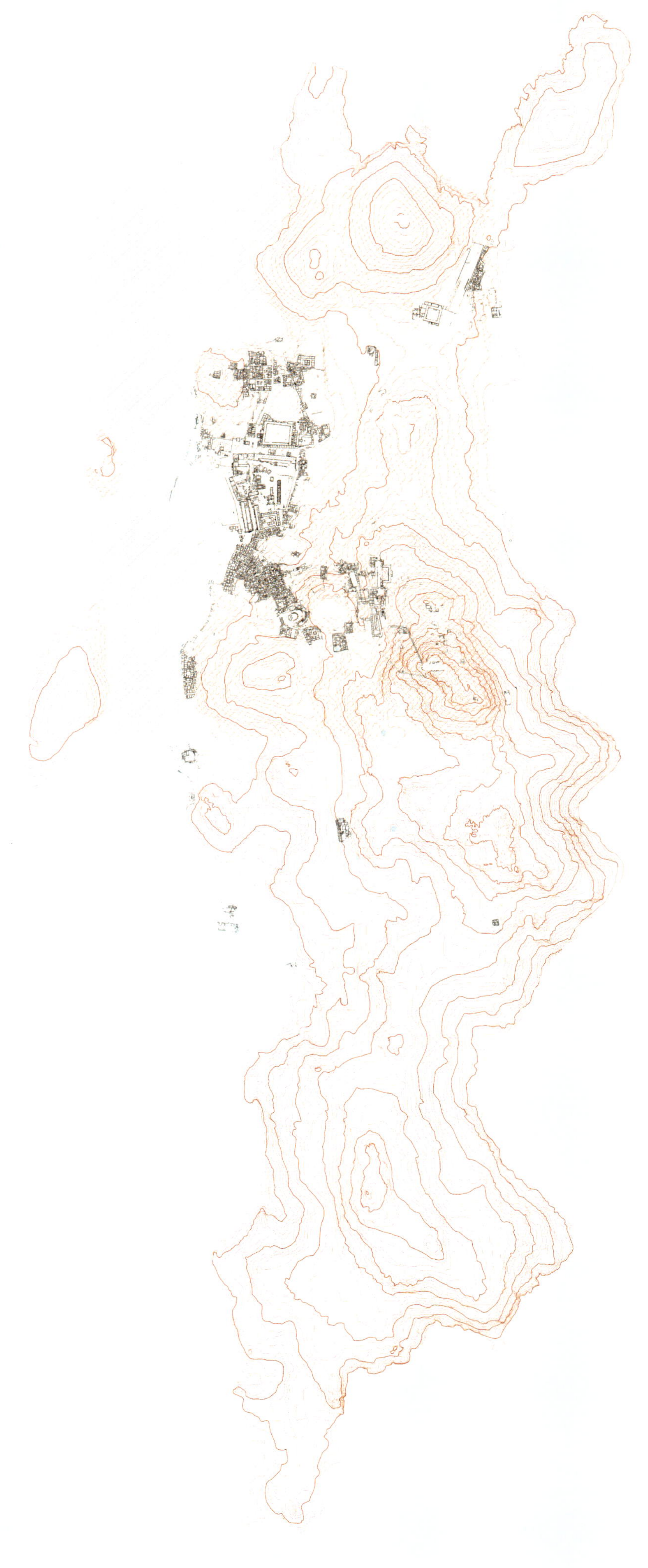

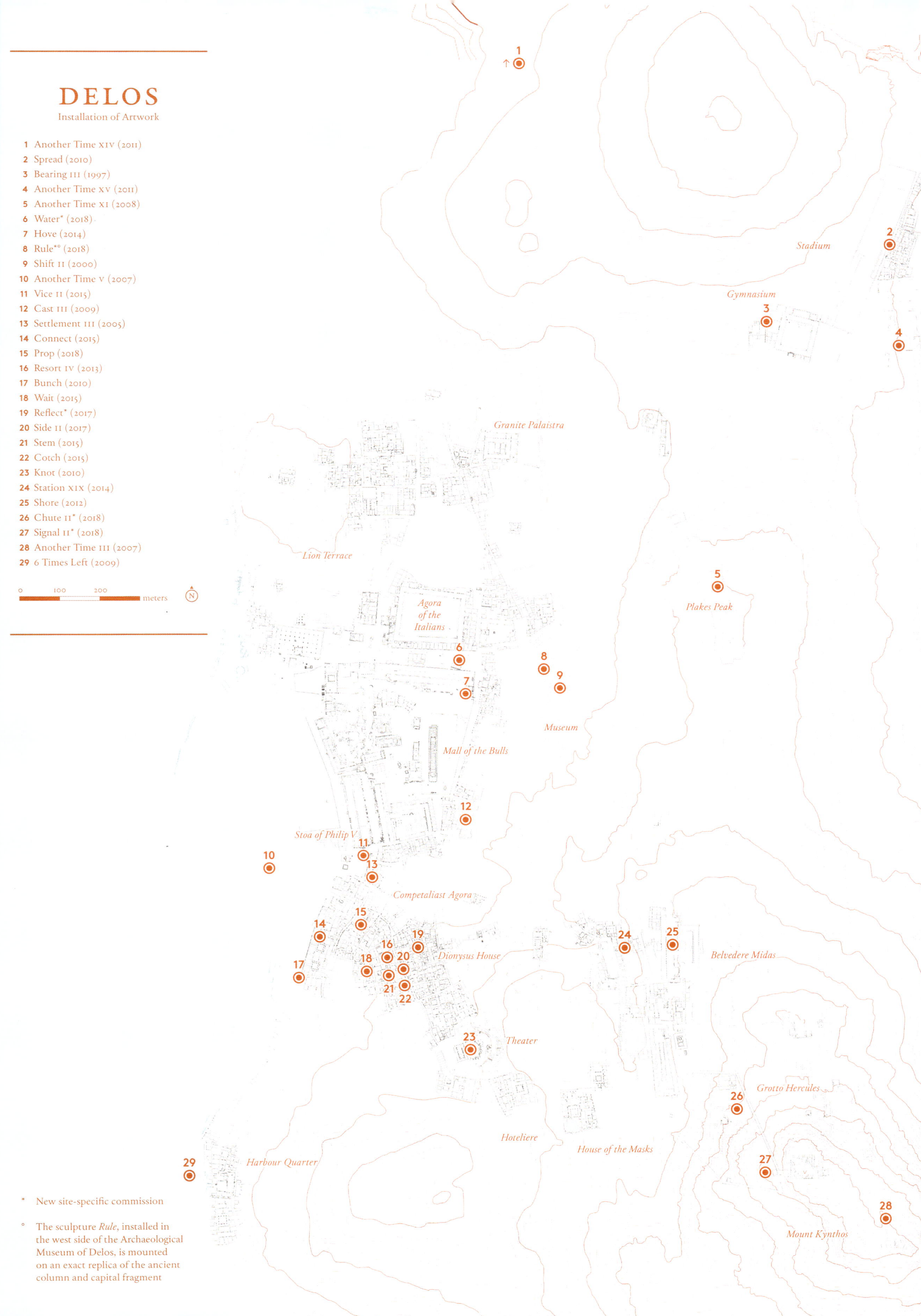
DELOS
Installation of Artwork
1 Another Time XIV (2011)
2 Spread (2010)
3 Bearing III (1997)
4 Another Time XV (2011)
5 Another Time XI (2008)
6 Water* (2018)
7 Hove (2014)
8 Rule*° (2018)
9 Shift II (2000)
10 Another Time V (2007)
11 Vice II (2015)
12 Cast III (2009)
13 Settlement III (2005)
14 Connect (2015)
15 Prop (2018)
16 Resort IV (2013)
17 Bunch (2010)
18 Wait (2015)
19 Reflect* (2017)
20 Side II (2017)
21 Stem (2015)
22 Cotch (2015)
23 Knot (2010)
24 Station XIX (2014)
25 Shore (2012)
26 Chute II* (2018)
27 Signal II* (2018)
28 Another Time III (2007)
29 6 Times Left (2009)
0 100 200 meters
N
Stadium
Gymnasium
Granite Palaistra
Lion Terrace
Agora of the Italians
Plakes Peak
Museum
Mall of the Bulls
Stoa of Philip V
Competaliast Agora
Dionysus House
Belvedere Midas
Theater
Grotto Hercules
Hoteliere
House of the Masks
Harbour Quarter
Mount Kynthos
* New site-specific commission
° The sculpture *Rule*, installed in the west side of the Archaeological Museum of Delos, is mounted on an exact replica of the ancient column and capital fragment

FOREWORD

DIMITRIS DASKALOPOULOS

With this exhibition, we are overjoyed to welcome Antony Gormley to Delos to exhibit a group of 29 sculptures, including five new site-specific commissions, across the whole of the island's archaeological site and within its Museum. Created over a period of 20 years, these sculptures chart a significant and prolific period in Gormley's career as an artist, demonstrating his versatility alongside his steadfastness to his explorations of existence.

For Gormley, his fascination extends beyond the wonders of Hellenistic antiquity to be found on Delos, and into the geological histories present on this magical island. Delving deeper, Gormley expounds the importance of considering quantum time when contemplating our place in the universe, with many of his bodyforms here 'appreciating' the natural world around them as they gaze up to the sky, out to sea or towards the molten interior of the earth.

At NEON, with this exhibition we continue our intertwining of antiquity and the contemporary, stirring once again the solution of their fluid histories, demonstrating, we hope, that they are not immiscible. At the same time, we have worked tirelessly to ensure that the exhibition remains sensitive to and respectful of a place described in the 3rd century BC by the poet Callimachus as 'the most sacred of all islands', while also inviting new perspectives and inspiring innovative creativity.

The unique collaboration between NEON and the Ephorate of Antiquities of Cyclades marks a continued positive shift in the relationship between the public and private sectors in Greece. SIGHT, the product of widespread and lengthy dialogue, demonstrates the change in perception regarding the role of private entities in cultural production, and the willingness of public authorities to be open to such collaborations.

We thank the Greek Ministry of Culture, the Ephorate of Antiquities of Cyclades and the Archaeological Council of Greece for their close and ambitious collaboration with Antony Gormley and NEON, as well as for developing a shared vision for this exceptional exhibition.

Dimitris Daskalopoulos is the Founder of NEON, Athens, Greece

DELIAN SIGHT

DEMETRIS ATHANASOULIS

The mythical birthplace of Apollo and Artemis, Delos bears a historical weight disproportionate to its size. Already inhabited in the Early Cycladic 3rd millennium BC, present during the Mycenaean Age, it evolved into one of the most important sanctuaries of the Ancient Greek world, is fatally associated with Classical Athens and was transformed into a wealthy commercial and urban centre of the Hellenistic Oecumene, before fading irreversibly in the Early Middle Ages, only to be rediscovered when European Modernity and the Modern Greek state began to shape their past, based on the findings of the large-scale 19th-century excavations.

Today, the sprawling ruins within the unspoilt natural beauty of the Cycladic landscape of uninhabited Delos offer the visitor the unique experience of a journey through time. However, the steady increase in visitors recorded at the site is linked to the global trend of transforming the past into an object of pleasure, and to the inclusion of memory in the mechanisms of production and consumption. This phenomenon is observed at all the emblematic archaeological sites and leading museums around the world. The progressive rise in the number of visitors is of little comfort to the Ephorate, as it poses the question of how sustainable a superficial relationship between mass tourism and monumental heritage can be in the long term. During a perfunctory visit to Delos, besides a selfie, what else does the average visitor take away after disembarking for a few hours from the passing cruise ship? What does he or she gain from this unique repository of knowledge and values?

Given the dynamic and ever-changing relationship between the monument and the public, and the integration of cultural heritage into the highly competitive field of leisure and recreation, we consider it necessary to build more substantial links between the monumental reserve and each visitor.

Besides, or rather alongside the academic reading of Delos's historical significance, at a time when the past is not read unambiguously and our acquaintance with it, through its registration in our individual memory, passes through a personal – quasi-unmediated – experience, we encourage visitors to discover their own path; to become individually connected to the space and the countless stories that are recorded in the ruins, in order to finally take away a personal historical, aesthetic, environmental, even emotional experience. For besides being a 'sacred' island and a landmark of Western civilization, Delos was also a melting pot of cultures and religions and a renowned slave market. In addition to masterpieces of art, it produced cheap replicas with which the nouveau riche of antiquity adorned their homes. Besides being a cosmopolitan urban centre, it was also a model in terms of its use of finite natural resources and its functional adaptation to the Cycladic ecosystem.

Through the 'Delos, Open Museum' integrated management programme, the Ephorate of Antiquities of Cyclades has invested in precisely this *in rem* enrichment of the visitor's experience. Thanks to this programme, the first major restoration works of the 21st century of the Stoa of Philip V and the great temple of Apollo will contribute decisively to the unimpeded perception by the public of the values inherent in Delos as a repository of knowledge and symbolic historical weight.

Along with the restorations that improve the reading of the monumental space, new sensory stimuli are offered which enable the visitor to discover the multiple aspects of the island's past as well as the latent islets of memories contained in Delos's monumental reserve, which the visitor may recall based on their own perspective and personal pursuits. However, these multiple and new readings of the past require new, powerful synapses with the present.

One such synapse is Antony Gormley's installation SIGHT. The artist, constantly exploring the relationship between the human body and the environment, installs his anthropomorphic iron sculptures on Delos, redefining space and offering new sensory stimuli to the visitor. Whether as shadows of the people that haunted the once bustling historic harbour, or as dark reminders of the ancient statues that adorned the Delian houses and sanctuaries, Gormley's sculptures are harmoniously contextualised *vis-à-vis* the surrounding antiquities and are absorbed, almost organically, by the ancient landscape. The pleasure of wandering amid this Delian anasynthesis is ideally suited to reflecting on our identity, and cognitive and aesthetic ties to the past.

And while it is well established that the importance of Delian monumental heritage, for the intellectual formation of the contemporary collective and individual subject, is served by policies that deepen the relationship between the monuments and the public (such as the policies cited above), the functional integration of Delian heritage into the 21st century requires a sustained outward-looking attitude and a deconstruction of stereotypes. By going beyond safe entrenchments and self-referencing, we seek for our actions to be inclusive. For example, beyond European or national credit, our Ephorate is also looking for resources from society. Not only because the needs of Delos are enormous, but mainly because we are interested in developing healthy synergies. After the sponsoring of the restoration of the Stoa of Philip V and the involvement of the local community through a contract funded by the Municipality of Mykonos, a major sponsorship was the first outward-looking long-range action to be implemented on the island.

Attempting to introduce new ways of perceiving the values of Delos through contemporary art, the contribution of Dimitris Daskalopoulos's NEON, is exemplary. The consolidation of an entirely successful public-private partnership in the field of culture, without prejudice and, above all, without concessions, is a collateral but equally undisputed gain. In this respect, the medium, i.e. the cooperation between the two bodies, is as important as the message, the installation SIGHT itself.

Dr. Demetris Athanasoulis is the Director of the Ephorate of Antiquities of Cyclades

ANTONY GORMLEY ON THE SACRED ISLAND OF DELOS 02.05 – 31.10.2019

ELINA KOUNTOURI

On the archaeological site and in the Museum of Delos, the non-profit organisation NEON and the Ephorate of Antiquities of Cyclades present an unprecedented exhibition of contemporary sculpture by British artist Antony Gormley.

Gormley is one of the most renowned artists of our time. During the past 40 years, his sculptures and installations have challenged our perception of space and the human body.

As an undergraduate at Trinity College, University of Cambridge, Gormley studied archaeology, anthropology and art history, equipping him with a deep understanding of the diversity of human cultures and their origins. These interests led him to leave England in 1971 and embark on a transformational journey: hitchhiking through Europe, on to Turkey, Syria, Lebanon, Iran, Afghanistan and Pakistan, arriving in India a year later where he lived for two years, studying Buddhist meditation. He returned to London in April 1974, knowing that he would dedicate his life to art. This early expedition has had a defining influence on his sculpture, which focuses on the body, its position in space and its connection to the elements and time.

In his own words, Gormley treats the body as 'a place encouraging empathic occupation of that which lies the other side of appearance: what it feels like'. His works resemble 'black holes in human form that indicate a human presence in space, but in some senses identify a subjective particular body in time that could also be anybody', thus 'making a new relation between the universal and the subjective, between the intimate and the general'. Gormley uses sculpture to 're-position our feelings of being alive from very high ideals and the possibility of perfectability to something felt, bodily, manifest and material'. His sculpture in Delos creates 'a dialogue between History, Geology and now, and allow the far-off things to be seen at one moment on the horizon and then the next moment in proximity, so that you can touch them'. Gormley explains that the relation 'between the revealed and the hidden, between that which can be seen and that which can be touched and that which can be imagined' is a vital element of the project.

In this installation on Delos, Gormley repopulates the island with iron 'bodyforms', restoring a human presence and creating a journey of potential encounters. He has installed 29 sculptures made during the last 20 years, including 5 specially commissioned new works, both at the periphery and integrated amongst Delos's archaeological sites.

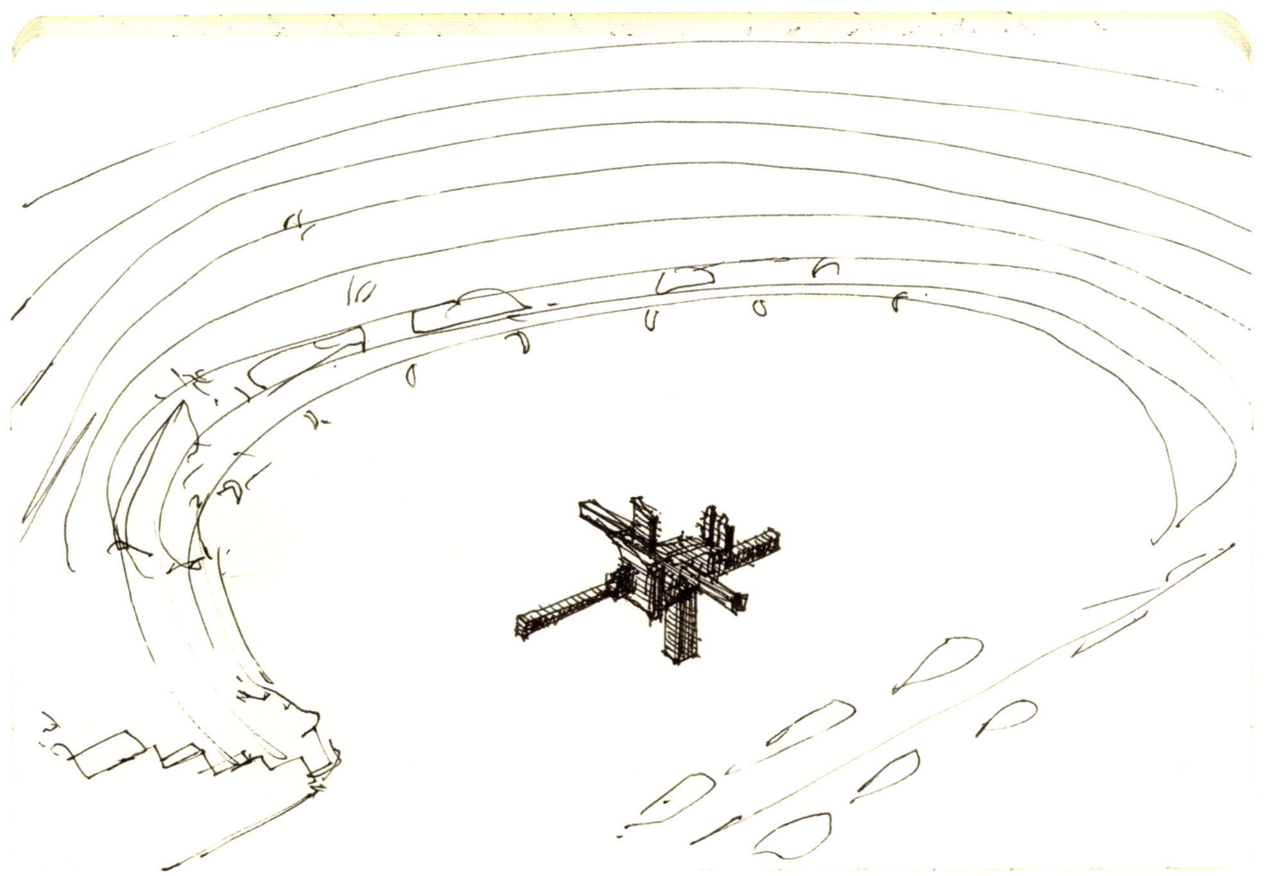

Antony Gormley, sketch for location of *Knot*, 2019

The works animate the geological and archaeological features of the island: a granite rock in the middle of the Cycladic Islands in the Aegean less than 5 kilometres long and 1.5 kilometres wide, which has a past filled with myths, rituals, religions, politics, multiculturalism and trade. Its intertwined and contrasting identities, as both holy place and commercial town, combined with its topography and geographical location, made the island a singular and cosmopolitan Hellenistic town.

Mythology tells us its first name was «Ἄδηλος» (A-Delos), meaning 'the non-visible' – a floating rock with no fixed location. It became «Δήλος» (Delos), 'the visible', when Zeus arranged for Leto, his mortal lover, to find refuge there, safe from the wrath of his wife, the goddess Hera. When Leto gave birth to twins Apollo, god of light, and Artemis, goddess of the hunt, the island's destiny and future prosperity were assured. This unique history is imprinted on Delos's architecture, sanctuaries and houses, and in the past was animated through rituals that celebrated the gods and protected the island. Later, sanctuaries to foreign deities, including Serapis and Isis, were built here.

Historical narratives record that humans occupied Delos at the highest point of the island, Mount Kynthos, during 2500–2000 BC and remained through ancient and classical times up to 69 BC, when the majority of the inhabitants abandoned Delos as it was no longer a vital commercial port on the Mediterranean routes. Today, with the exception of archaeologists safeguarding the island and those undertaking scientific research, Delos is uninhabited. Its ruins, like those at Pompeii, stand devoid of human presence.

Gormley completely reinterprets the function and purpose of sculpture, transforming the traditional statues and totems of the ancient world that once adorned public squares, temples and private dwellings into sites of empathy and imaginative projection. The first connection between visitors and the work is established before they even set foot on Delos. Approaching the rugged northwest coast, they catch sight of a lone figure (from Gormley's series *Another Time*, 1999–2013), standing sentinel on a rocky promontory at the water's edge. Two more works from the same series – also looking towards the distant horizon – stand on Plakes Peak and on Mount Kynthos, and another similar work stands in the waters of the harbour. Further sculptures are integrated with archaeological sites across the island, from the Stadium to the Theatre Quarter and from the merchant stores to the Museum site.

Gormley has studied the temples and the sacred enclosures, the horizon and the topography created by the wind and the salt. His sculptures, taking naturalistic, cuboid and more abstracted forms, either stand or lie on the ground, exposed to the elements. Interacting with the island's topography, the works appear and disappear. They activate the elemental character of the island and its human history, establishing a connection with our collective memory. Gormley respectfully engages the audience in an experience that does not compete with the space or its history, but rather, establishes a physical and intellectual connection with our collective memory. He proposes a radical openness:

'Art is about reasserting our first-hand experience in present time.'

Visitors to Delos are invited to connect with time, space and nature, which inevitably link to our shared future. Gormley on Delos reminds us how central art is to the human story.

Elina Kountouri is the Director of NEON, Athens, Greece

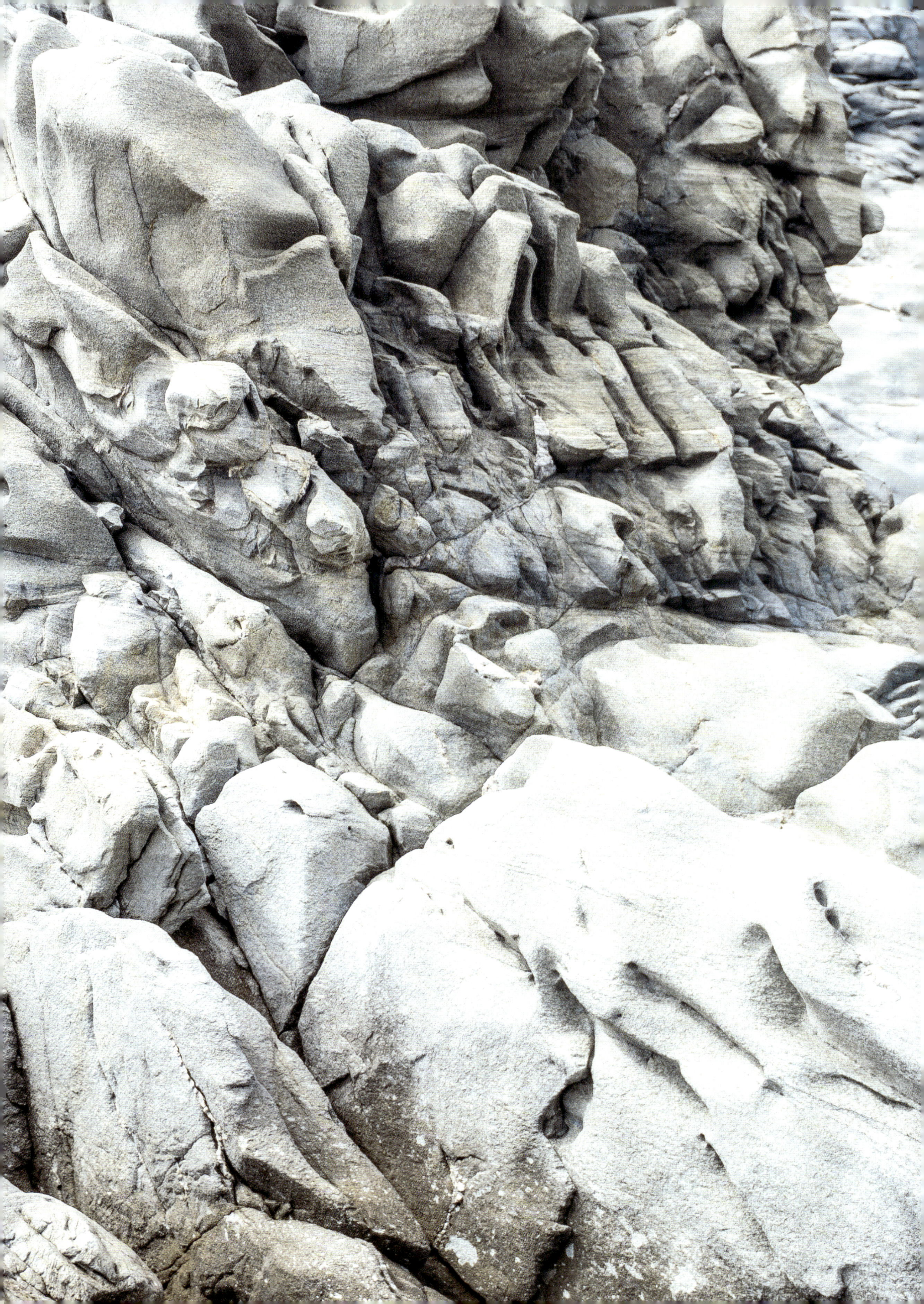

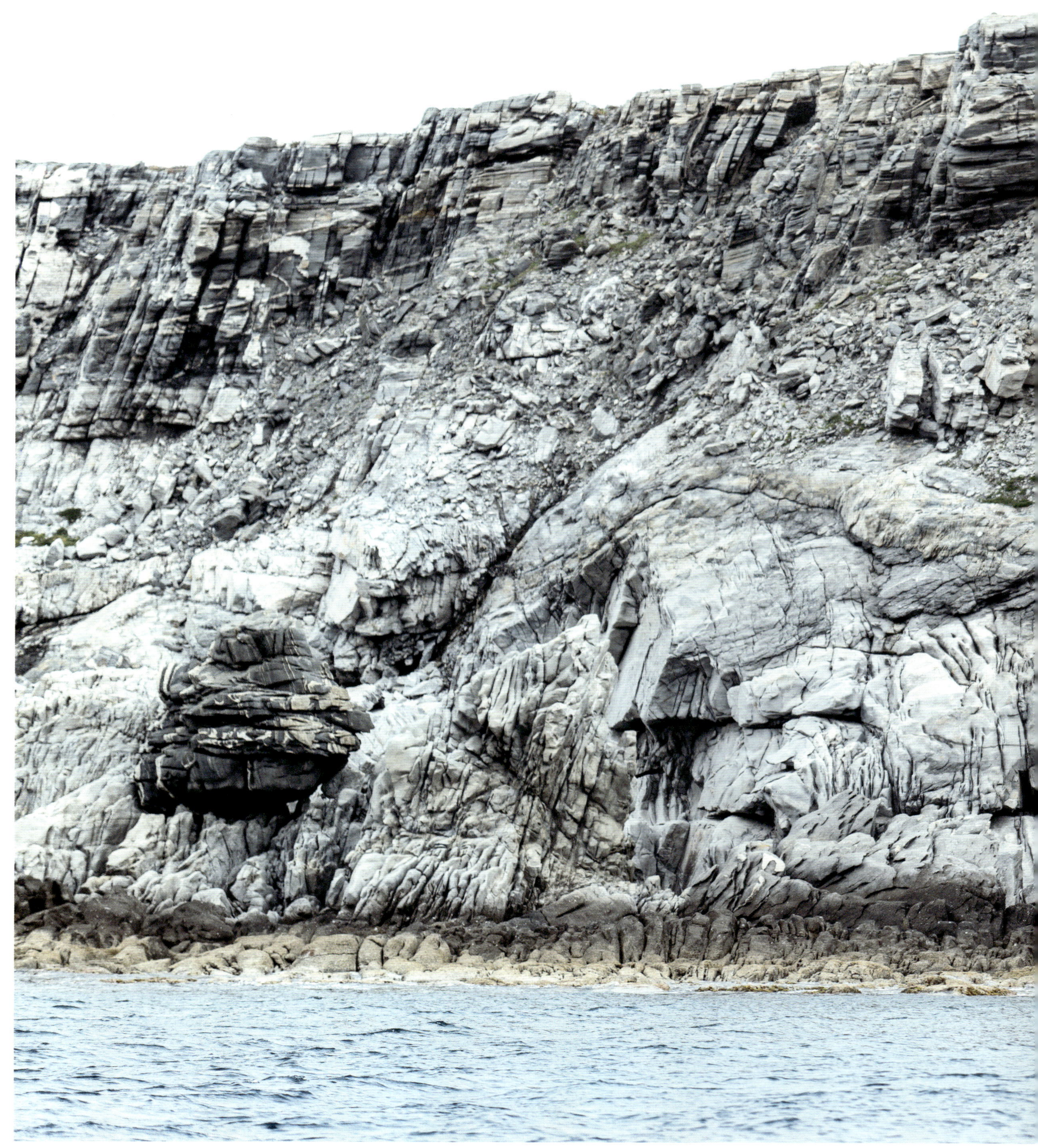

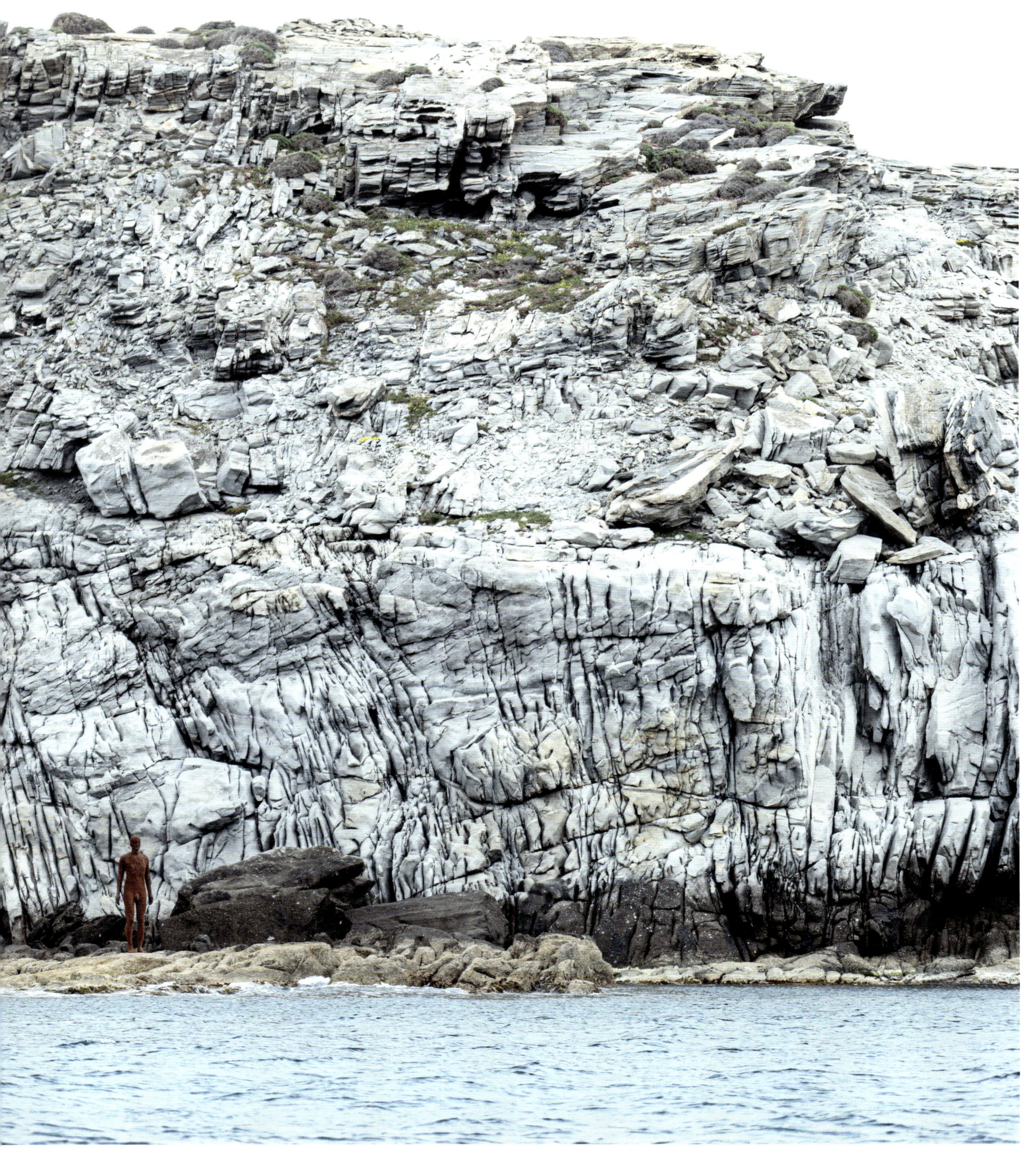

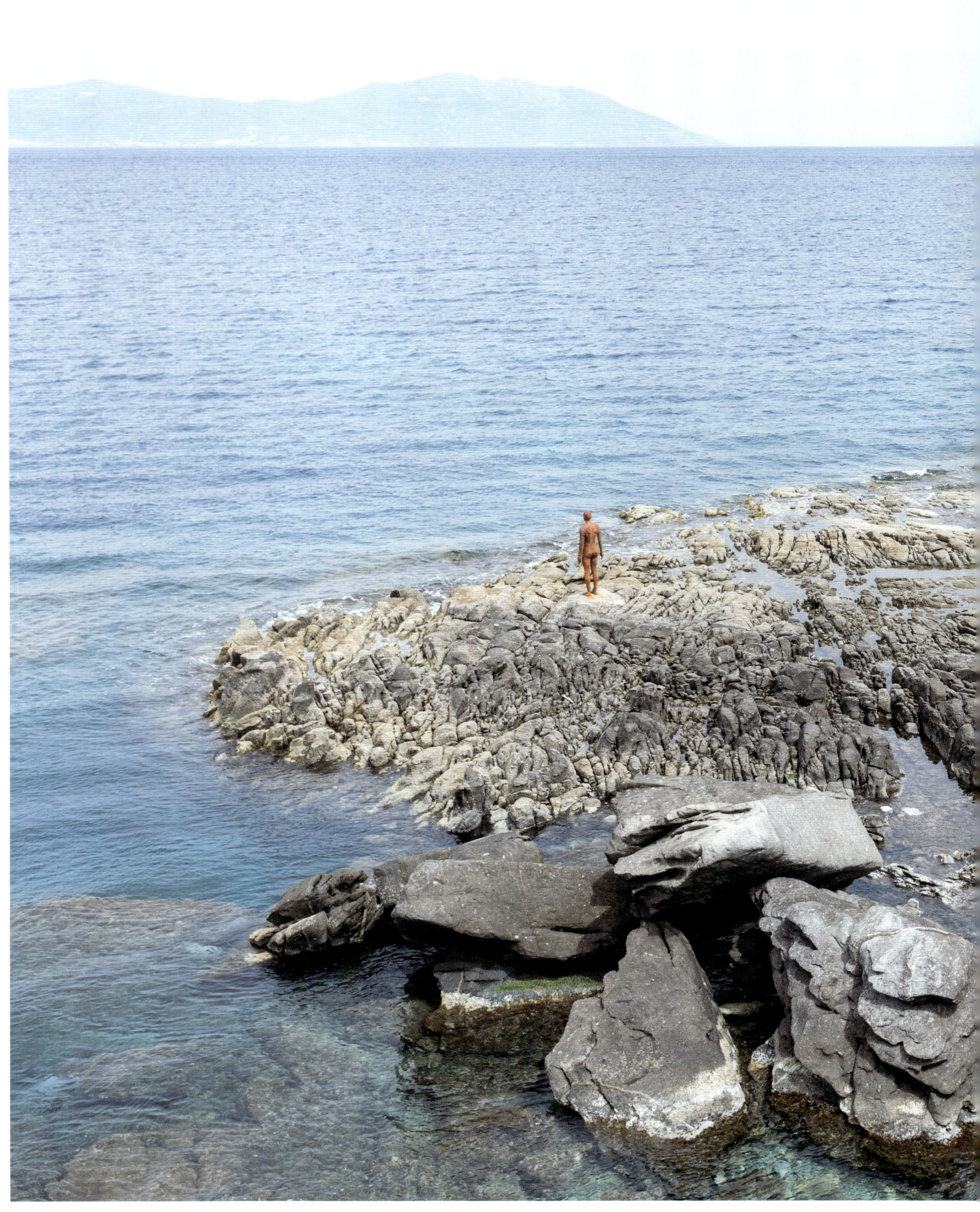

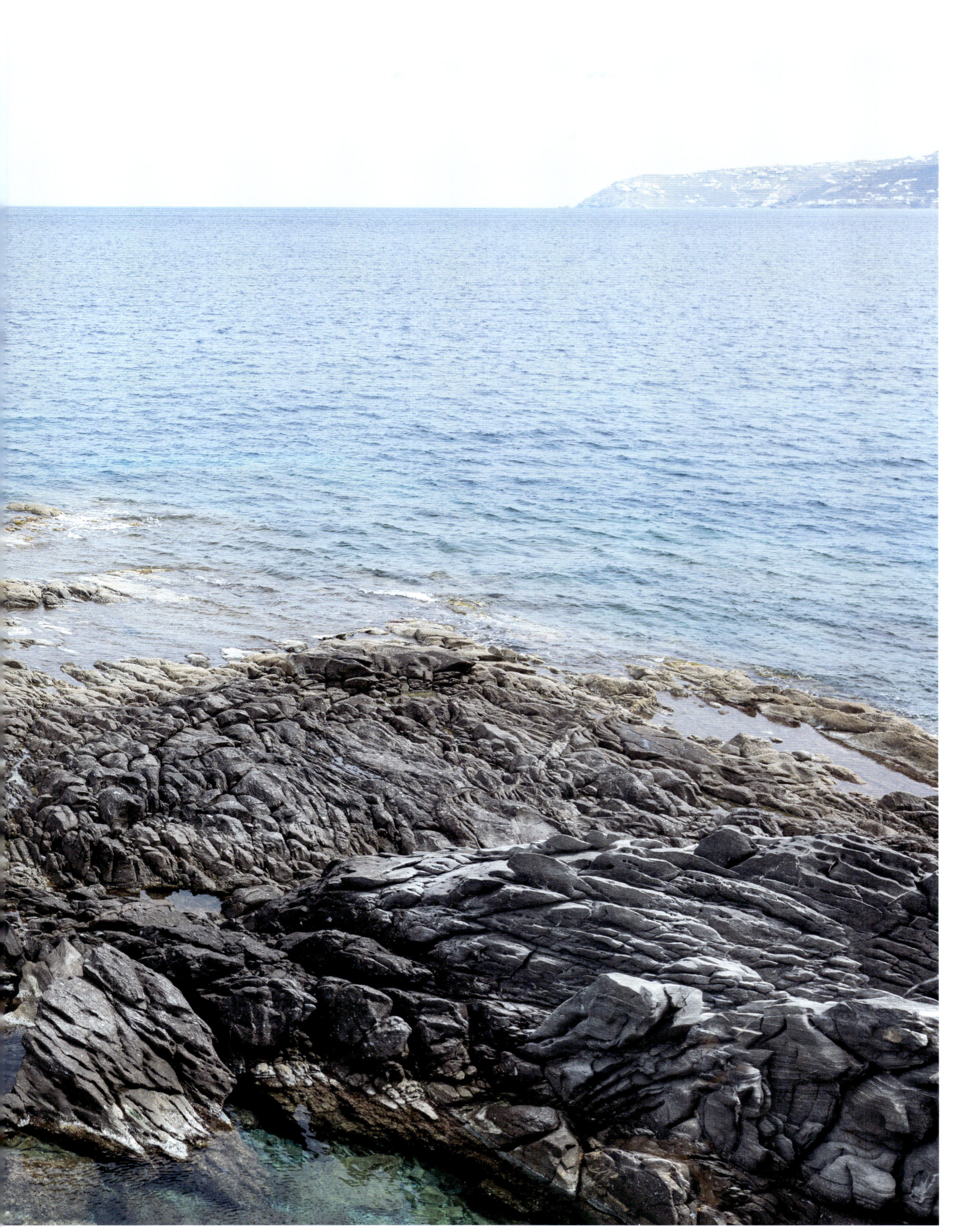

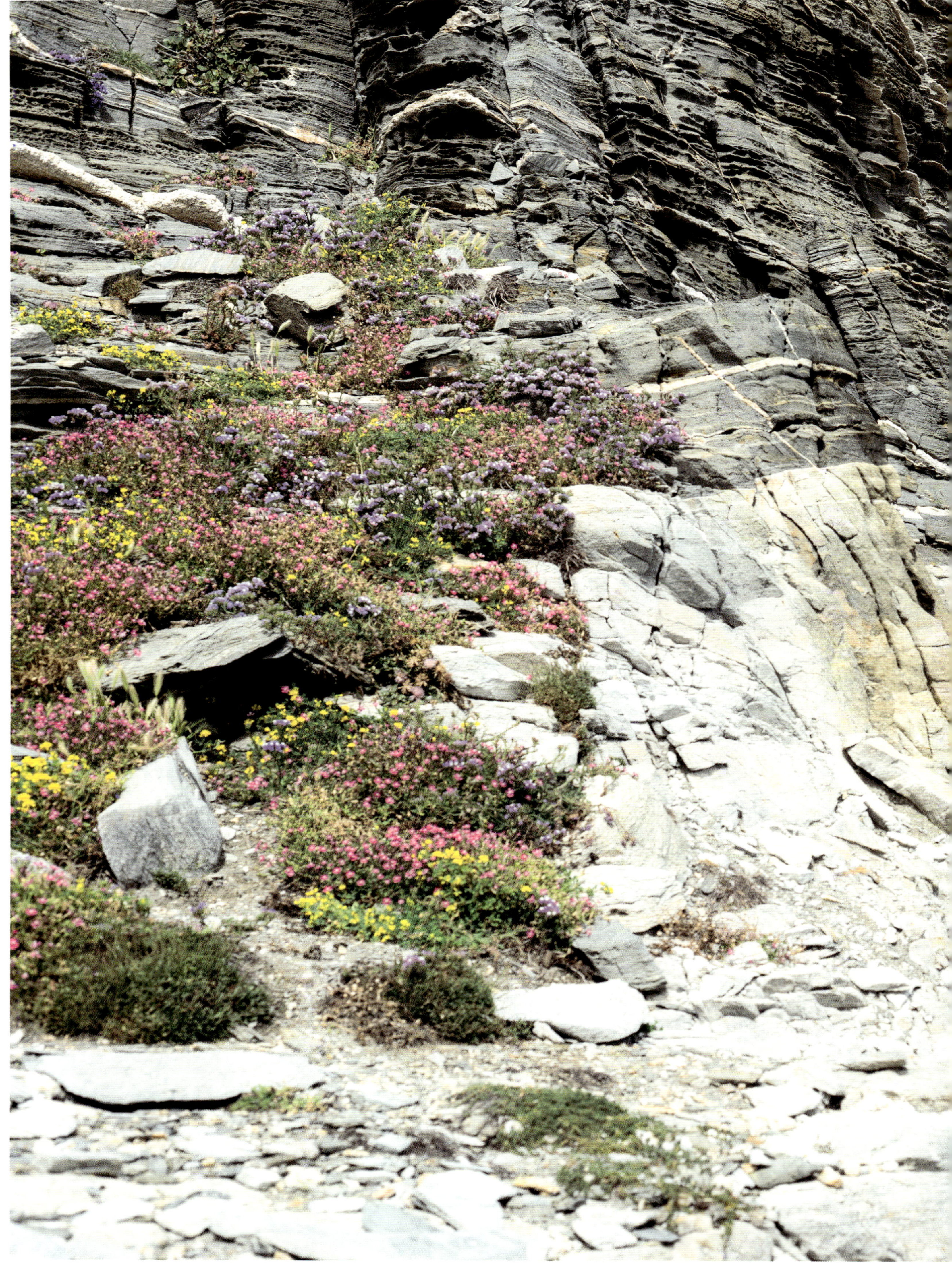

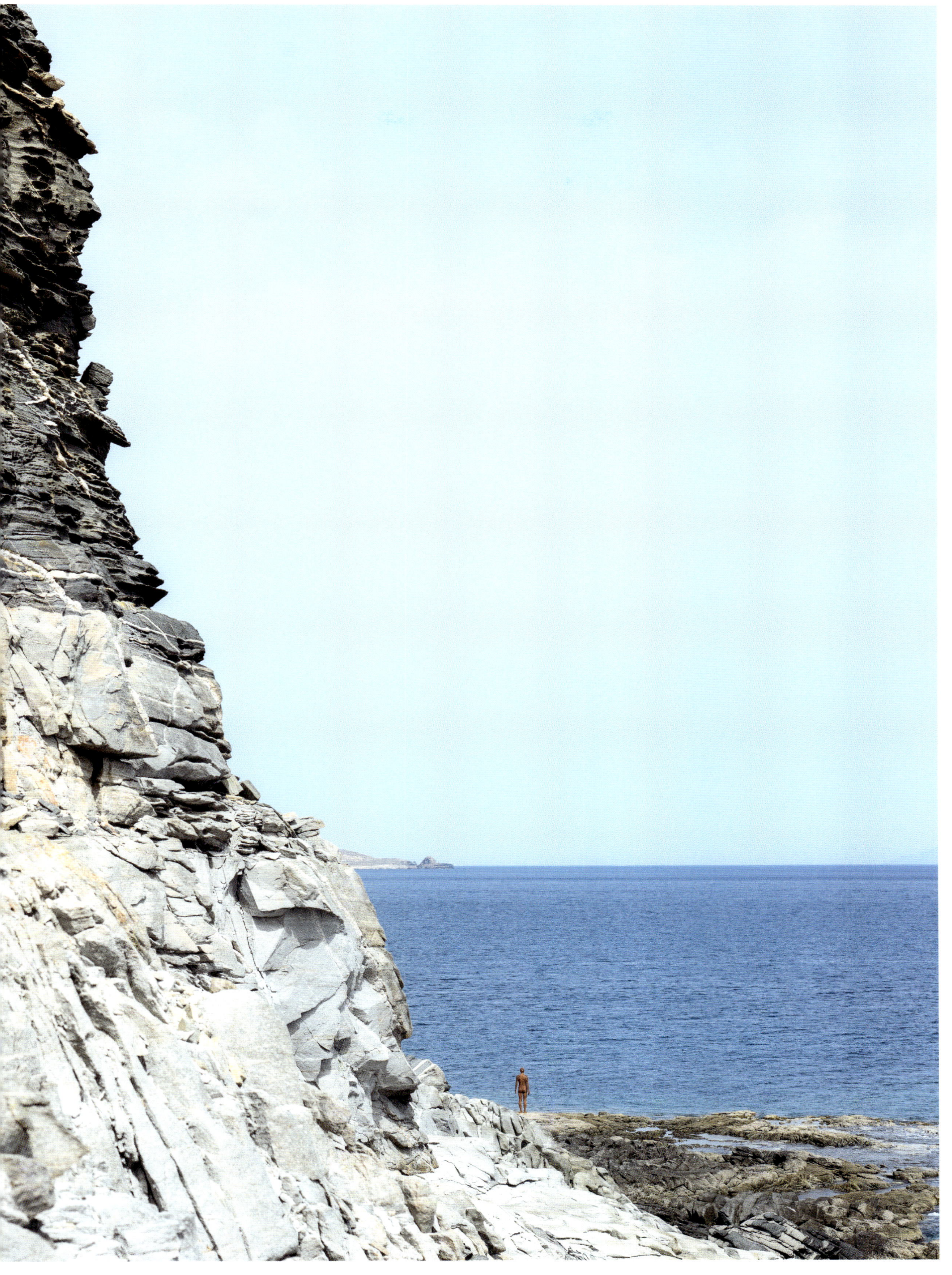

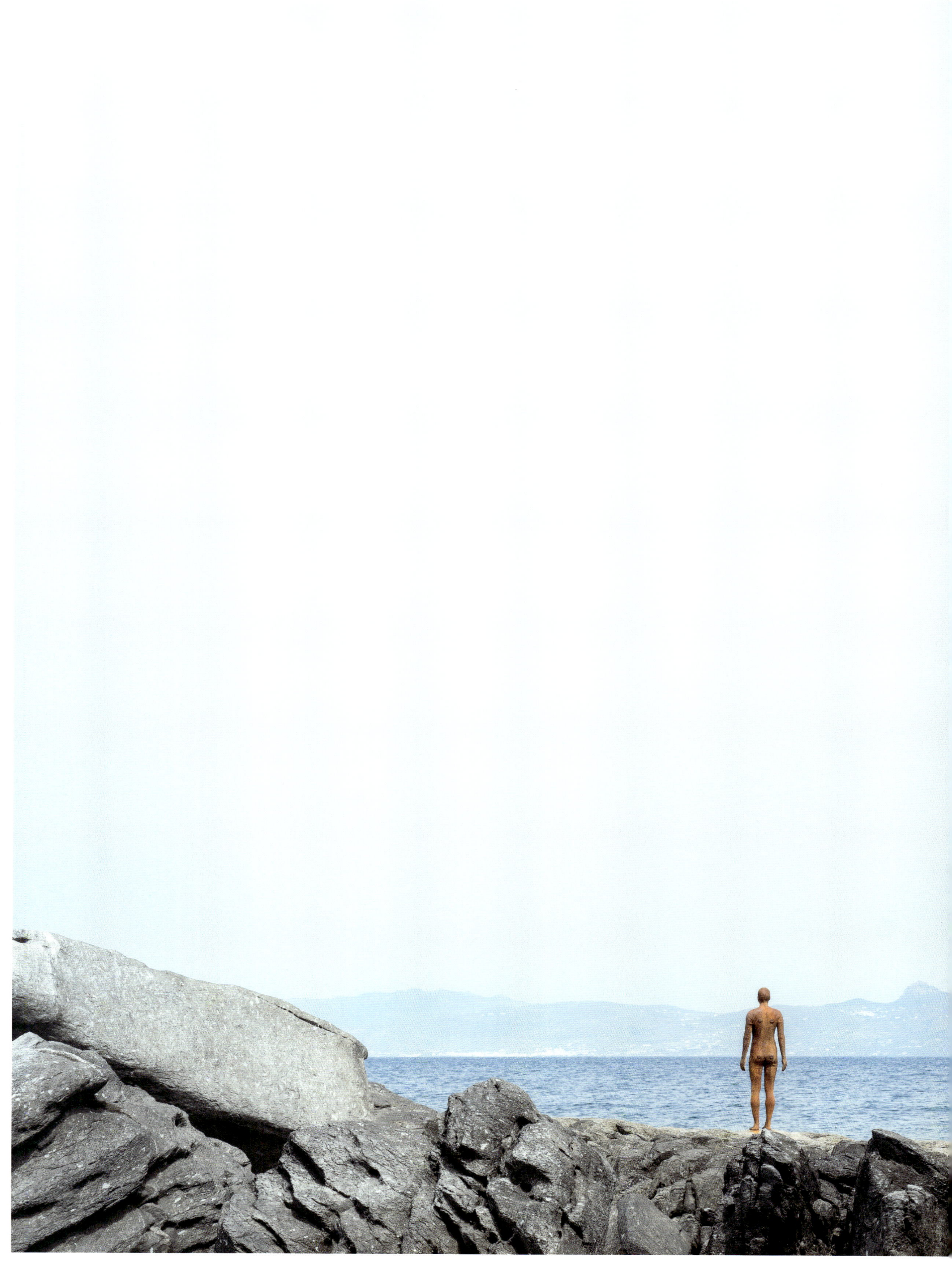

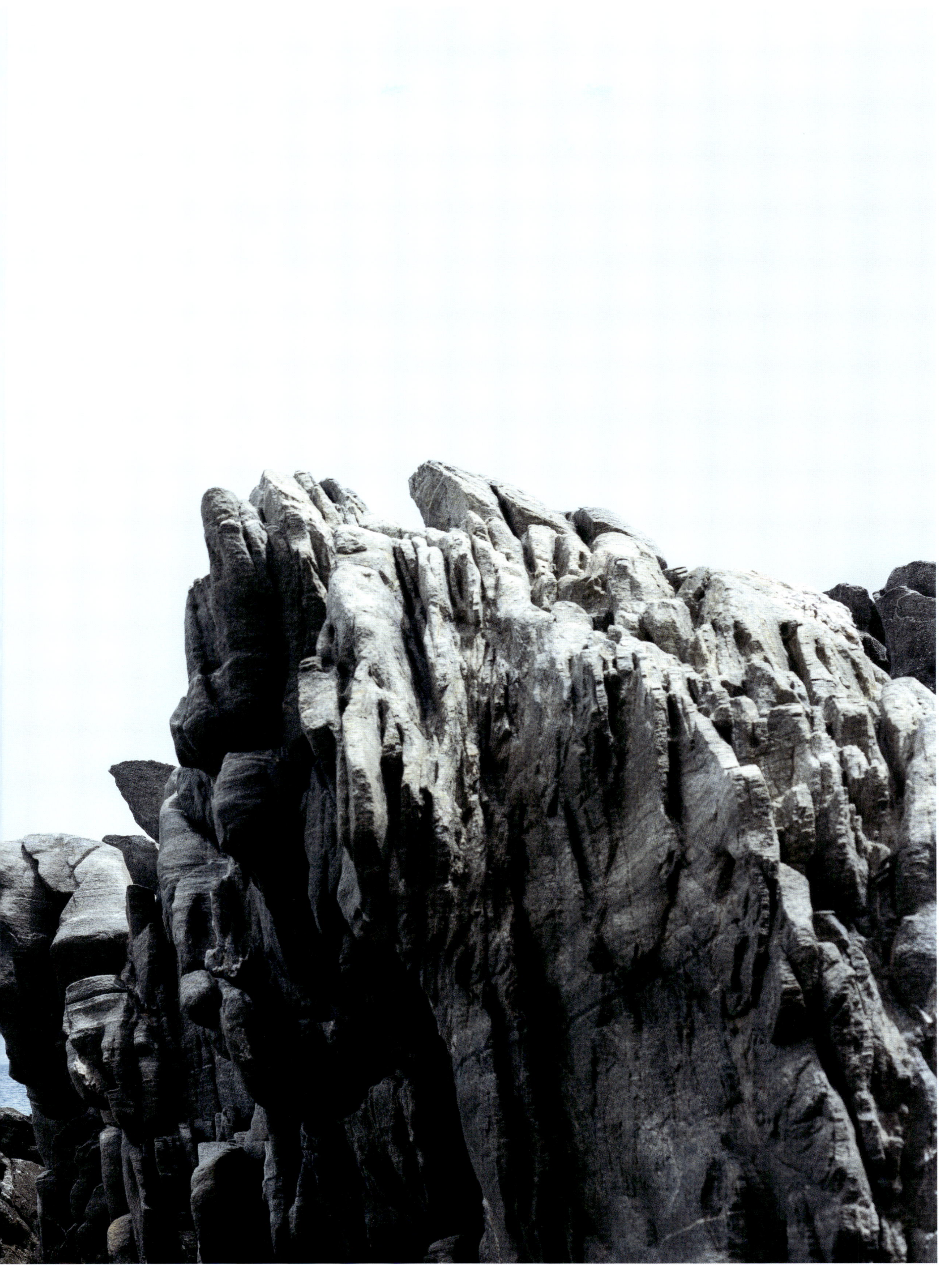

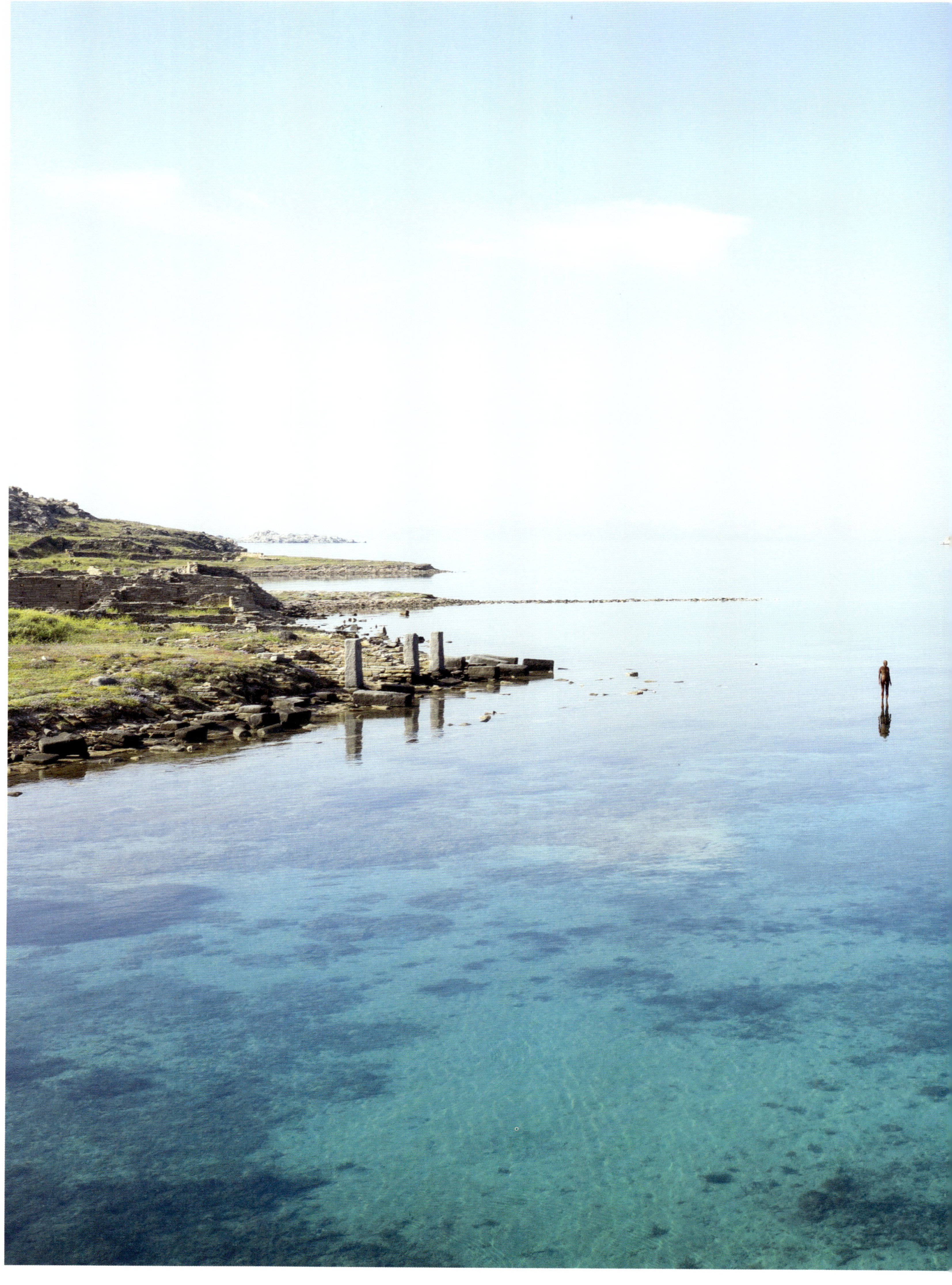

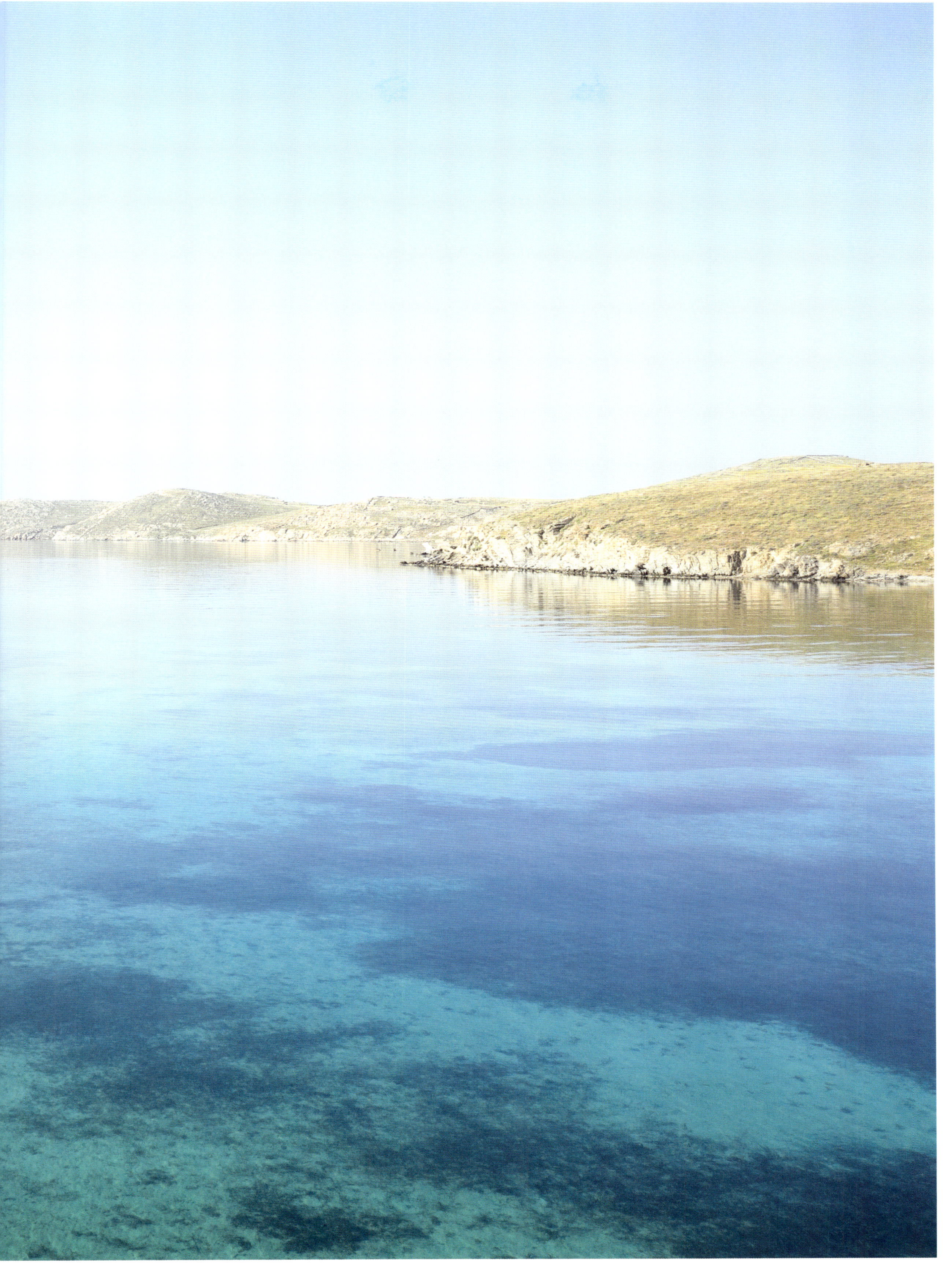

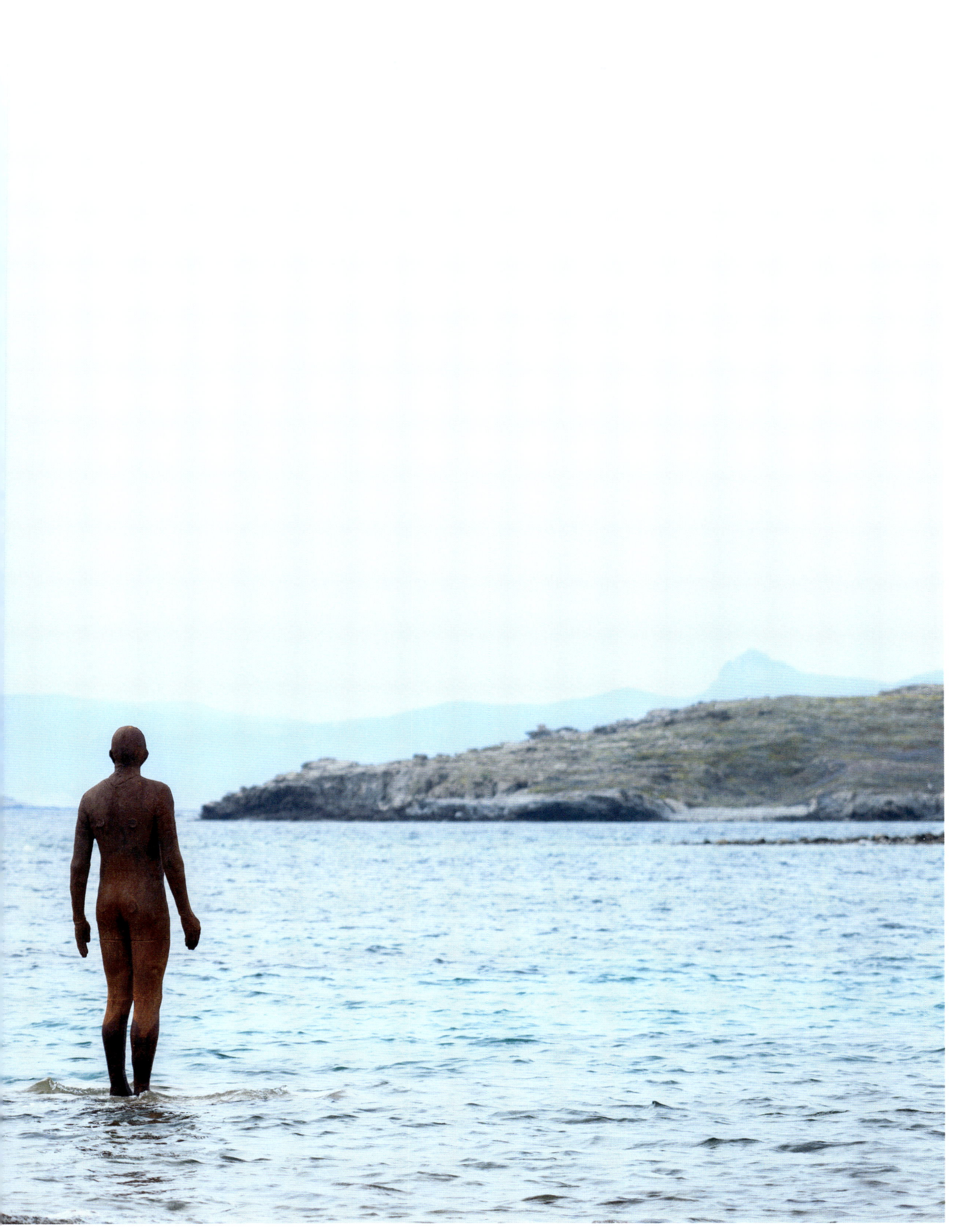

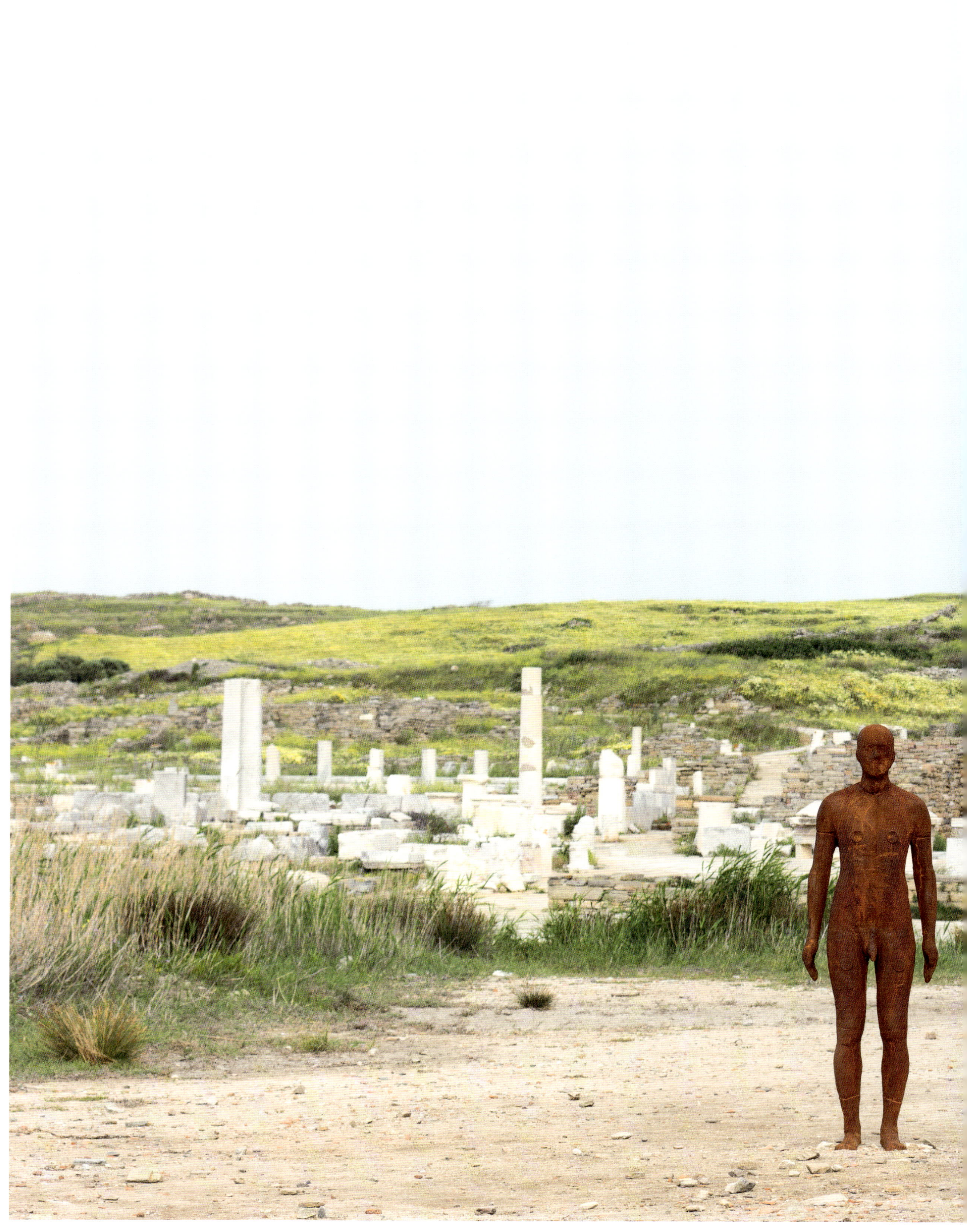

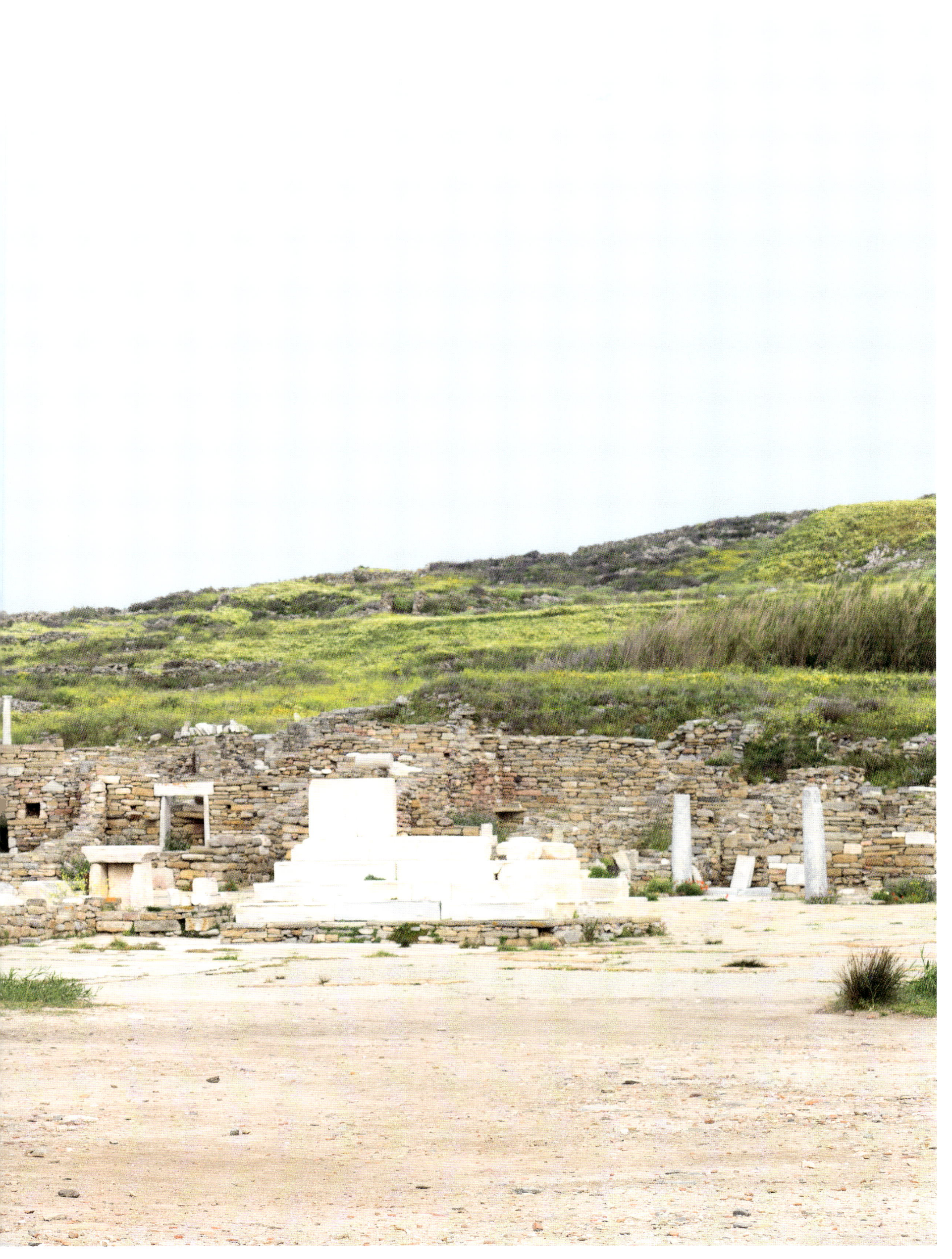

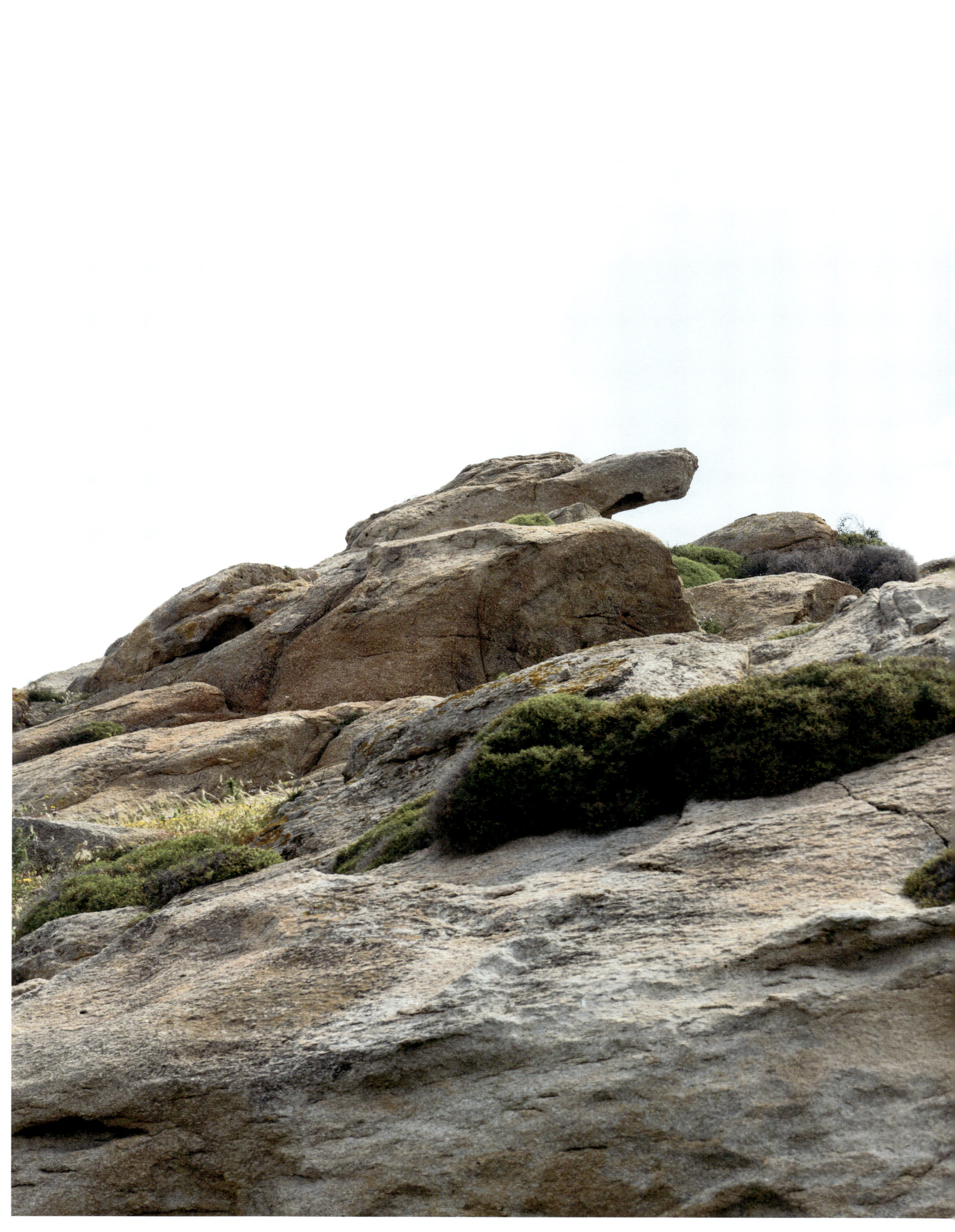

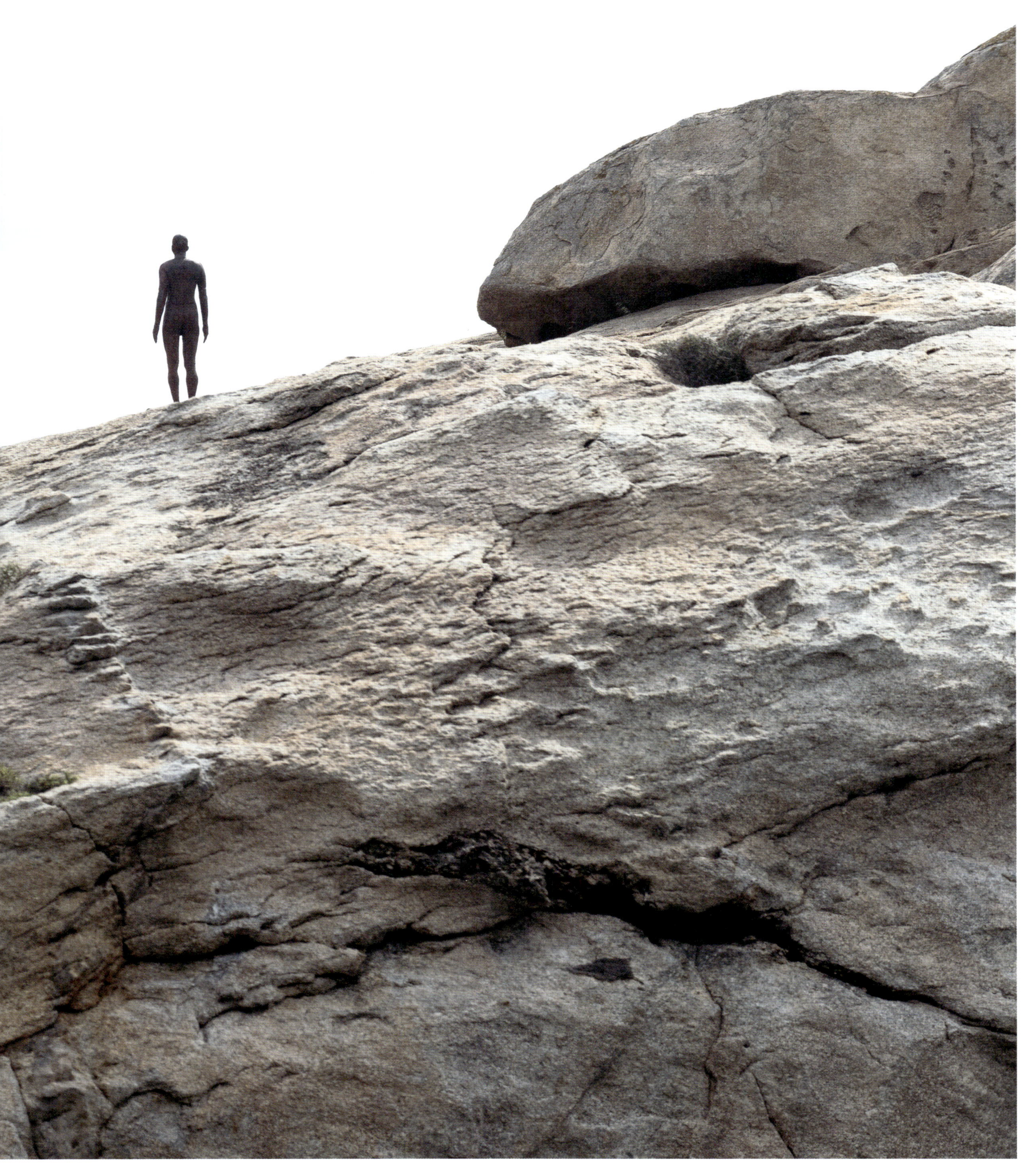

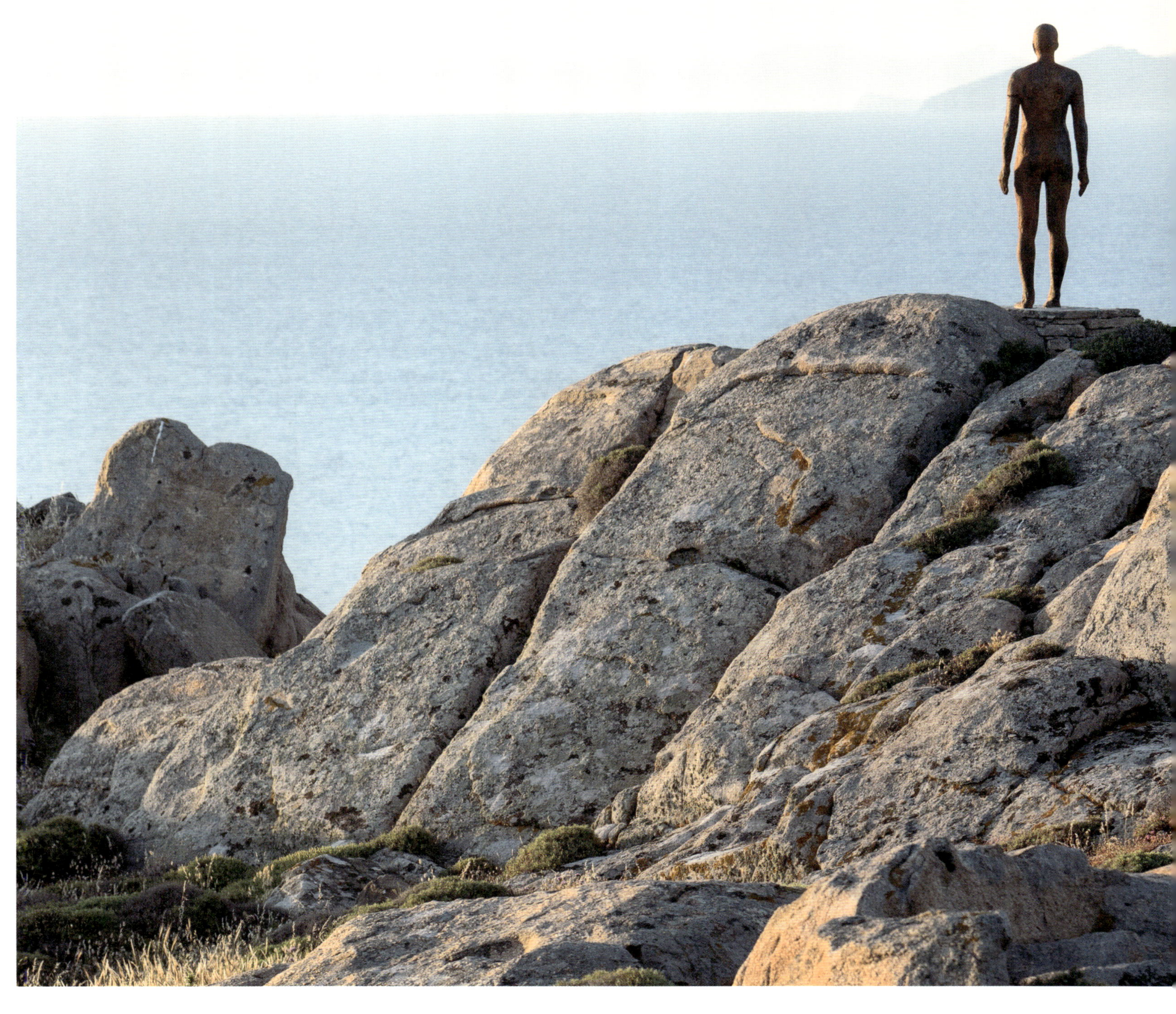

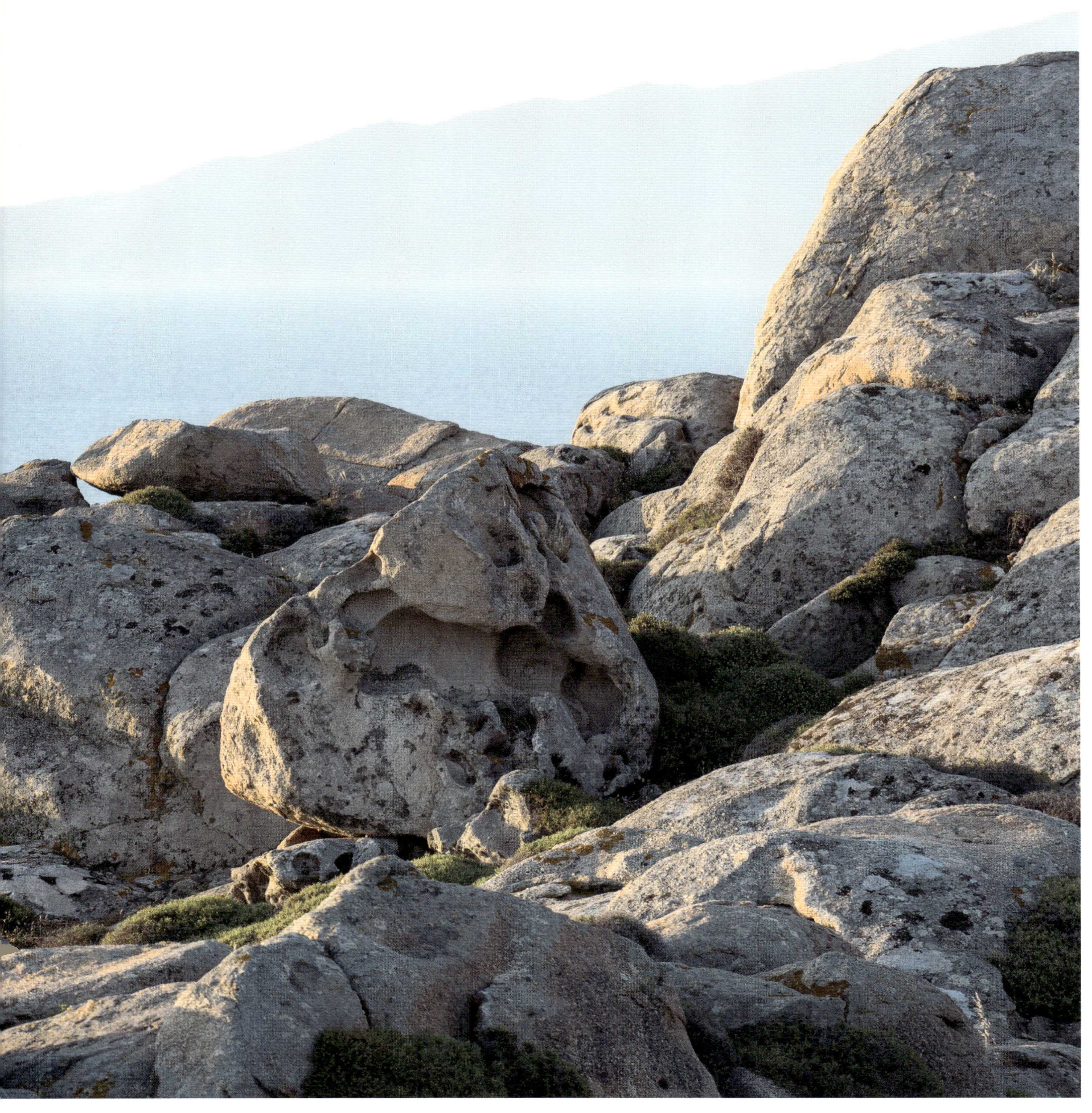

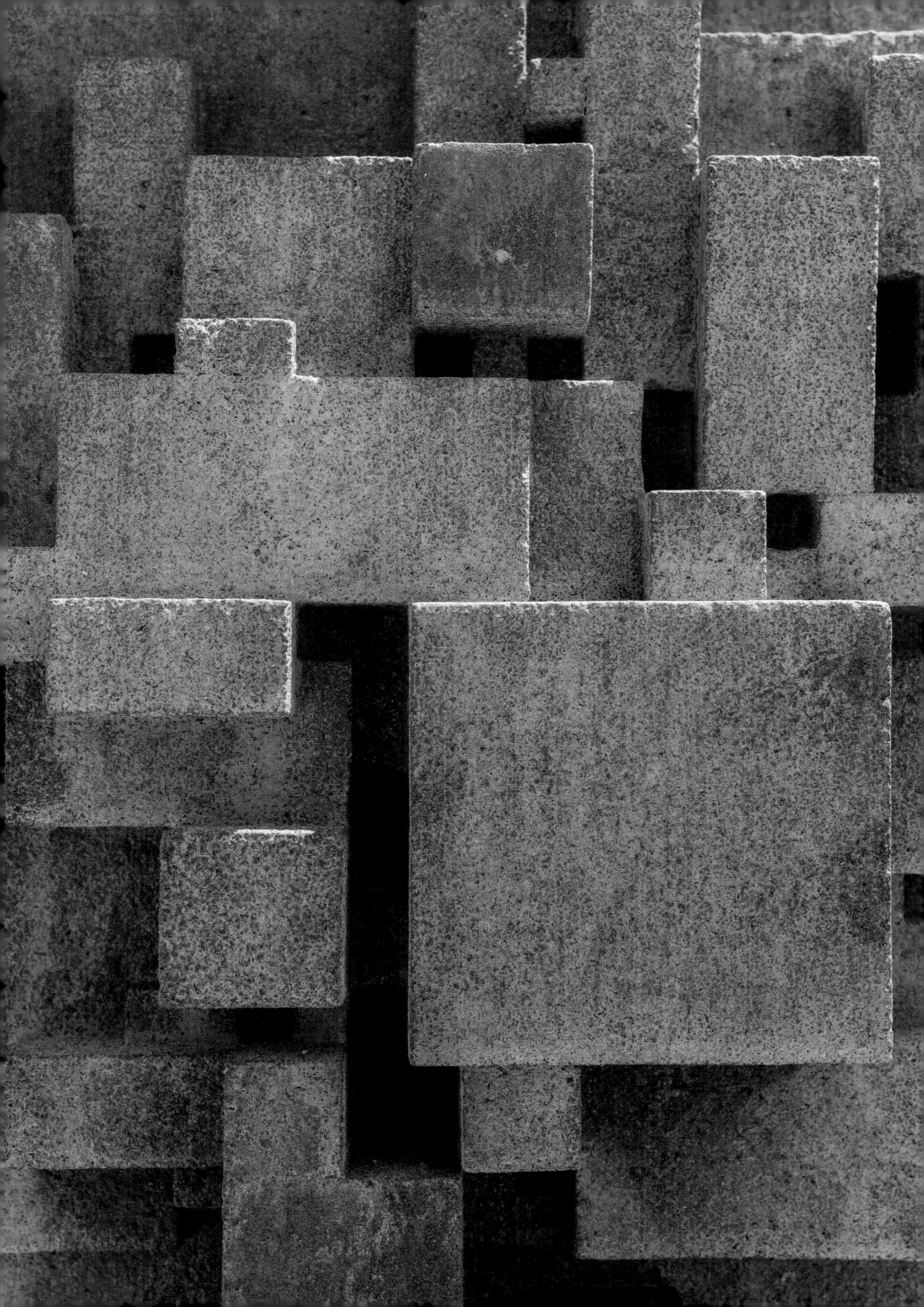

ANTONY GORMLEY – A GLOSSARY

IWONA BLAZWICK

—

ANATOMY

Antony Gormley's sculpture is based on his own anatomy. In the 1970s, when he was an art student in the UK, conventional sculpting of the human figure had given way to artists experimenting with performance, language and film to evoke the body. Emerging from this creative context, Gormley set about reinventing traditional figurative sculpture. For his first public exhibition at London's Whitechapel Gallery in 1981, he cut his clothes into continuous ribbons of fabric and used them to create an enclosure entitled *Room* – a portrait of the artist as an empty room. In the 1980s he began working with his partner, the artist Vicken Parsons. She covered his body all over in wet plaster, leaving a single hole at his mouth so that he could breathe. When the plaster had set, she cut it open, leaving the internal cavities of this mould empty: they had made his first 'body case', which he then covered in thin lead sheet. Later, he filled the moulds and made his first solid iron bodyforms. Almost all his sculptures take his physical proportions as their foundation. Although they are featureless, they are clearly masculine.

—

ANGEL

One of Gormley's most famous sculptures is a monumental figure standing on a man-made hill outside Gateshead in North East Britain. Measuring 20 metres in height and with a wingspan of 54 metres, it is constructed, like a ship, in curved and welded plates of Corten steel. Instead of arms, the body has wings like a plane. Traditional monuments usually feature figures of authority, noted individuals or deities. This sculpture rejects such direct iconography. Its colossal scale is not a representation of power or domination. Neither does it ask to be worshipped. Rather, the body stretches out as if to embrace the northern landscape and its communities. It is an intensification of place.

—

BALANCE

As well as making bodyforms as single casts, Gormley also renders them as rectilinear and biomorphic constructions. Their components are stacked and cantilevered to give them tensile strength and to articulate gesture and poise. Unlike statues from antiquity, these sculptures do not stand on plinths. Balance is implicit not only in their inner structural composition but also in relation to the space around them. A body may lean against a wall, make a head stand from the floor, or crouch in a corner. Gormley's sculptures evoke the experience of being embodied. At the same time, they explore the body's relation to the multi-faceted planes and dimensions of the space it inhabits. They are dependent on their surroundings for both balance and meaning.

—

BUDDHA

Before going to art school in the 1970s at Goldsmiths College and the Slade School of Art in London, Gormley studied anthropology at the University of Cambridge. Inspired by the rituals and material cultures of non-western civilisations, in the late 1960s and early 1970s he travelled to India to explore different systems of belief and how they found visual expression. He was drawn to Buddhism and its emphasis on meditation as a way of intensifying our sense both of our inner selves and of the cosmos.

—

CAST

The sculptures installed across Delos are all made of iron. They are all created either from moulds or digital scans of the artist's body; translated into patterns made in polystyrene.

Unlike the marble or alabaster carvers of antiquity, Gormley favours casting his sculptures, using materials such as iron and concrete. There is a sense of metamorphoses in his work as he turns fluid molten metal into solid form. His work is produced at his studio in London and at a studio and an iron foundry in Northumberland. Here he has developed a radical new casting technique. He has replaced traditional 'lost wax' with 'lost foam'. Traditionally a plaster model would have been moulded and cast in 'resin-set' sand into which molten metal is poured. Today Gormley and his team place a polystyrene pattern in a steel box and use vibration and vacuum to hold the sand in place, a process which is swifter, cleaner and which allows for the most delicate structures to be created.

—

ENERGY

The artist is interested in making the static figure embody dynamic forces of energy such as gravity, mass, velocity or light; also, of human gestural or psychic energy. He has created sculptures that are three dimensional but entirely linear. At their centre is the body; radiating out from its limbs are lines that define a force field of energy. He has also made works of great density and weight that are at once about the tangible world of physics and the metaphysical notion of being.

—

FIELD

The scale of Antony Gormley's work can range from the monumental to the miniature; and its production can involve entire communities. In New York in 1991 he flooded a gallery with tens of thousands of figurines roughly shaped out of raw clay, each no higher than 25 centimetres. *Field* is an epic project that has since been presented in North and South America, Asia and Europe. Each small figure is pared down to essentials – a single totemic body and head with two holes for eyes. As he was invited to remake *Field* in different countries, Gormley invited local communities to make the clay forms with him. Although they are all the same height and proportion, each of the several thousand sculptures is also unique, bearing the handprint of its maker. This cooperative work floods any space within which it is installed, excluding and confronting the body of the viewer, symbolising the collective power of individual gesture.

—

GEOMETRY

Many of the sculptures in Delos translate the human form into angular architectural structures. This enables him to create geometric units that stack on top of one another or extend vertically and horizontally. In this way he makes a visual relation with architecture and with geology. In Delos, the structure of rock and marble combine with the structure of walls and pathways. This geometry of surface and form is echoed in Gormley's sculptures. This method also enables the artist to create bodyforms that are completely transparent – coming across them in the ruins of Delos can be like seeing a mirage.

—

HORIZON

SIGHT, the title of Gormley's installation on Delos, reinforces a fundamental relation his work has with perspective and lines of vision. In a work called *Event Horizon*, he has situated 31 bodyforms across the rooftops of central London, Rotterdam, New York, São Paulo, Rio de Janeiro and Hong Kong. He has also sited his work in deserts, up mountains and on coastlines. We gaze at the bodies who in turn gaze out across the landscape. We can also encounter his work from the back, looking out to a horizon and guiding our own vision beyond the body. In this way his work gives intimations of infinity.

—

ORIENTATION

In 2018, the artist spent time exploring the meeting places, habitats, streets and temples of Delos; and roamed its hillsides and coastline to consider every aspect of its natural and cultural terrain. Every one of the 29 works in this project has been carefully positioned to articulate two perspectives – one is the gaze of the figure that may rest on a floor, a wall or the horizon. The other is of the viewer as we first take a 360 degree walk around the sculpture and then let its point of view guide our own sight lines to the environment beyond. We move back and forth between the appreciation of each sculpture to the way it resonates with its context.

—

PEA

Since the 1990s Gormley has focused exclusively on the body. However, the smallest sculpture he ever made is a pea covered in lead. It is one of a line of found objects wrapped in lead called *Natural Selection* (1981). Placed next to one another on the floor, 24 forms intersperse the organic with the man made. Following the pea is a pencil, a carrot, a chisel, a banana, a vibrator and later a hand grenade in ascending order of size and form until we finally reach a ball. Where the natural objects symbolise growth and nutrition, the examples of human technology include tools, toys and weapons. This linear still life testifies to both the creative and destructive aspects of humanity.

—

RUST

Many of Gormley's sculptures have a deep orange patina. This 'rust' is an iron oxide formed by the reaction of iron, oxygen and water in the air. Although this can be degenerative, the use of alloys in materials such as Corten steel prevents this oxidation compromising the works' structural integrity. We fear the presence of rust in machinery and engineering. However, the artist enjoys this slow entropic process and the sense of immersion in the elements and of time passing that it lends to his sculptures.

—

STATUARY

The statues that still remain on the island of Delos are part of a foundational moment in western civilisation. They represent a tradition in sculpture that has informed approaches to the figure until the 20th century. The past hundred years, however, has seen an unprecedented period of experimentation where every aspect of 'the statue' was interrogated, dismantled and reinvented. Antony Gormley's representations of the body provide the bridge between this formally, politically and philosophical revolutionary era and the great legacies of antiquity.

Iwona Blazwick OBE is the Director of Whitechapel Gallery, London, UK

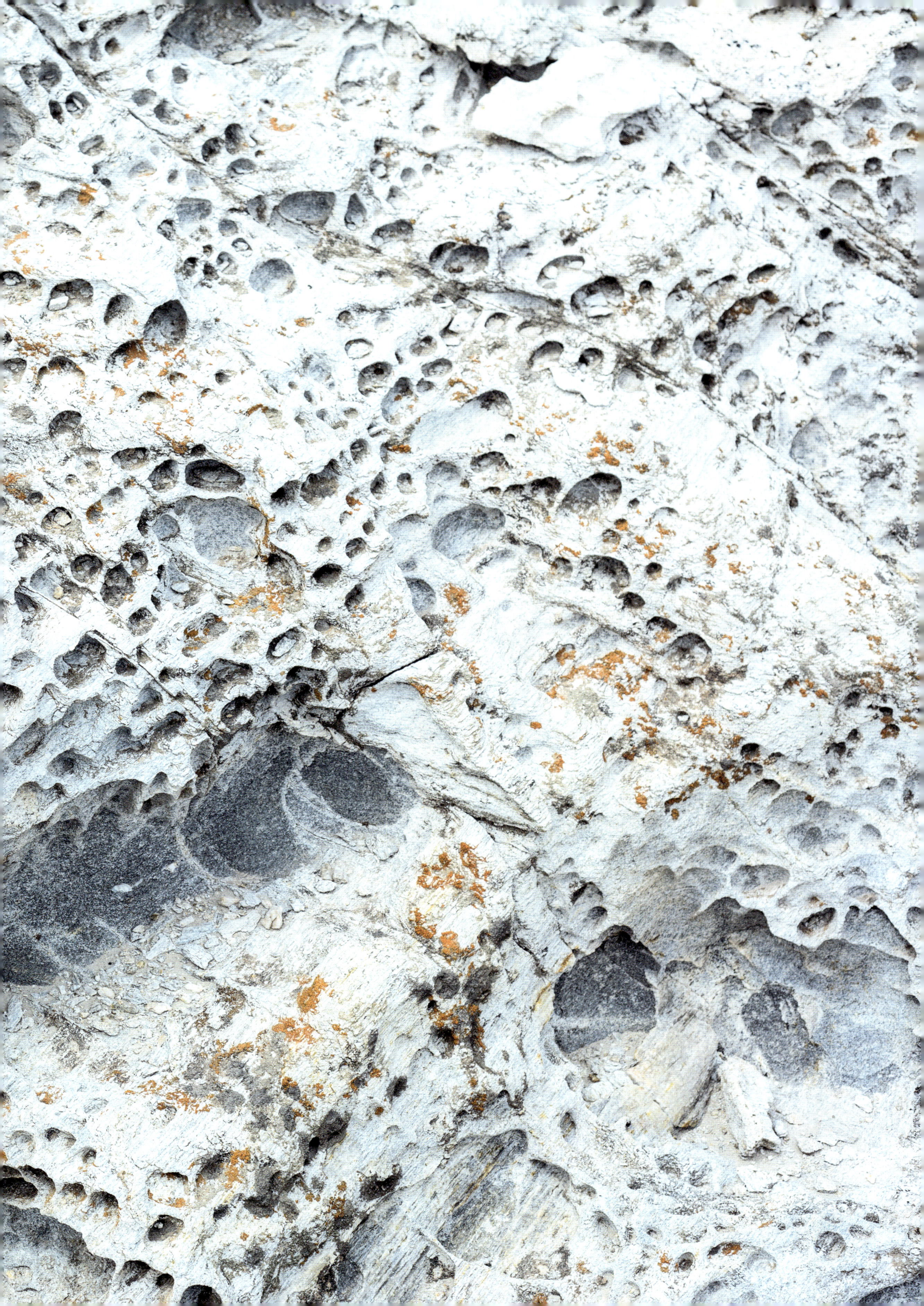

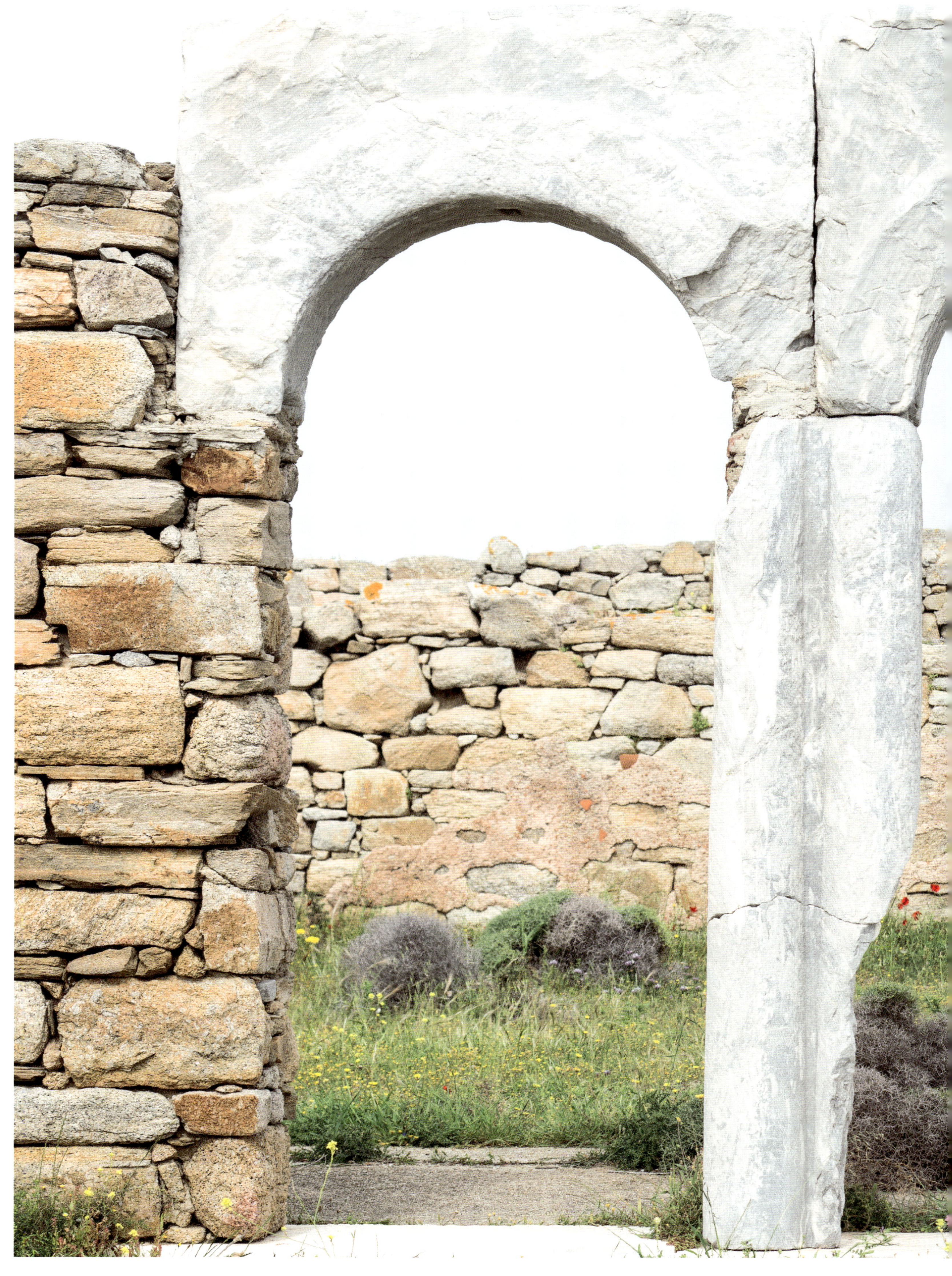

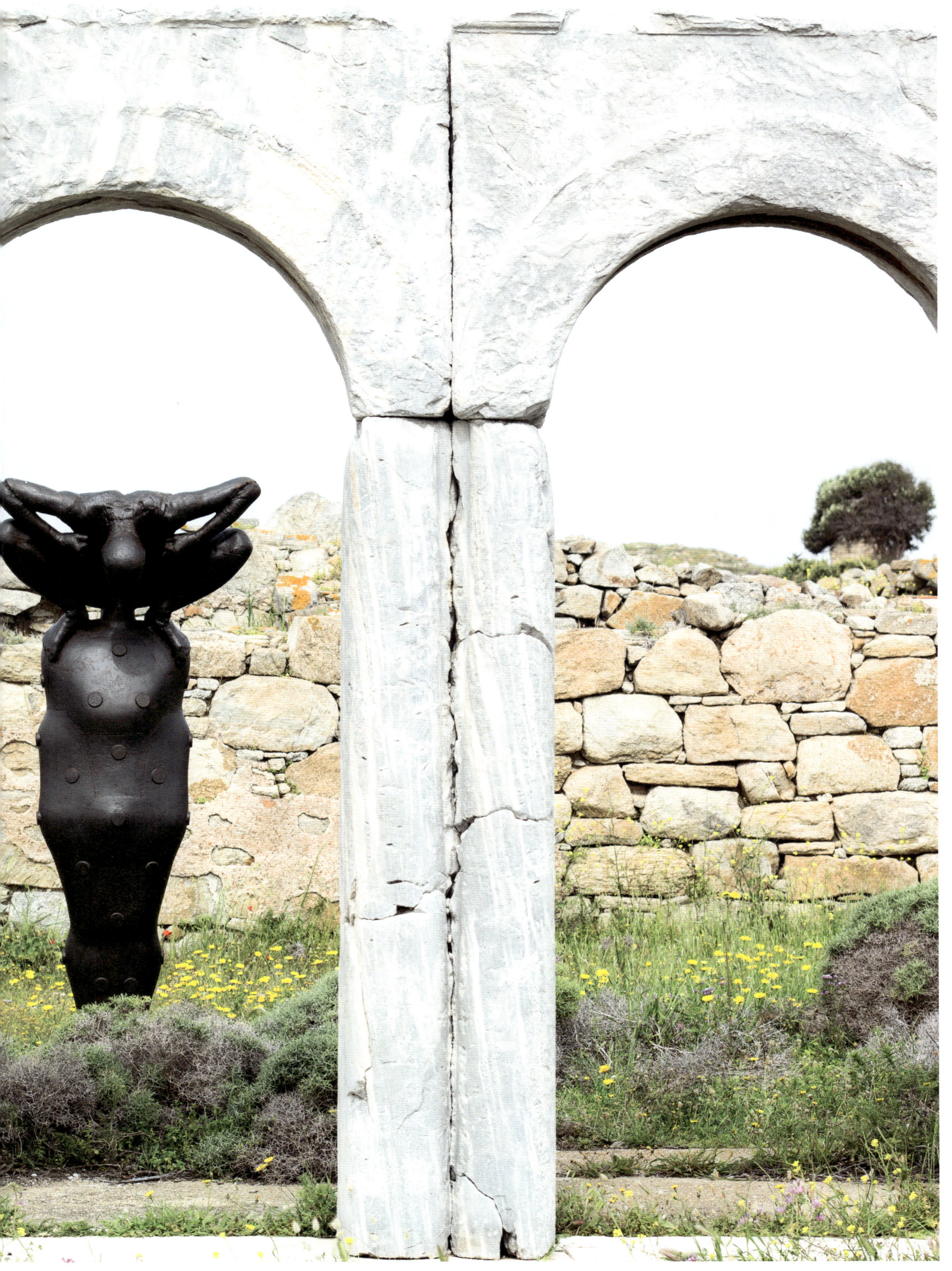

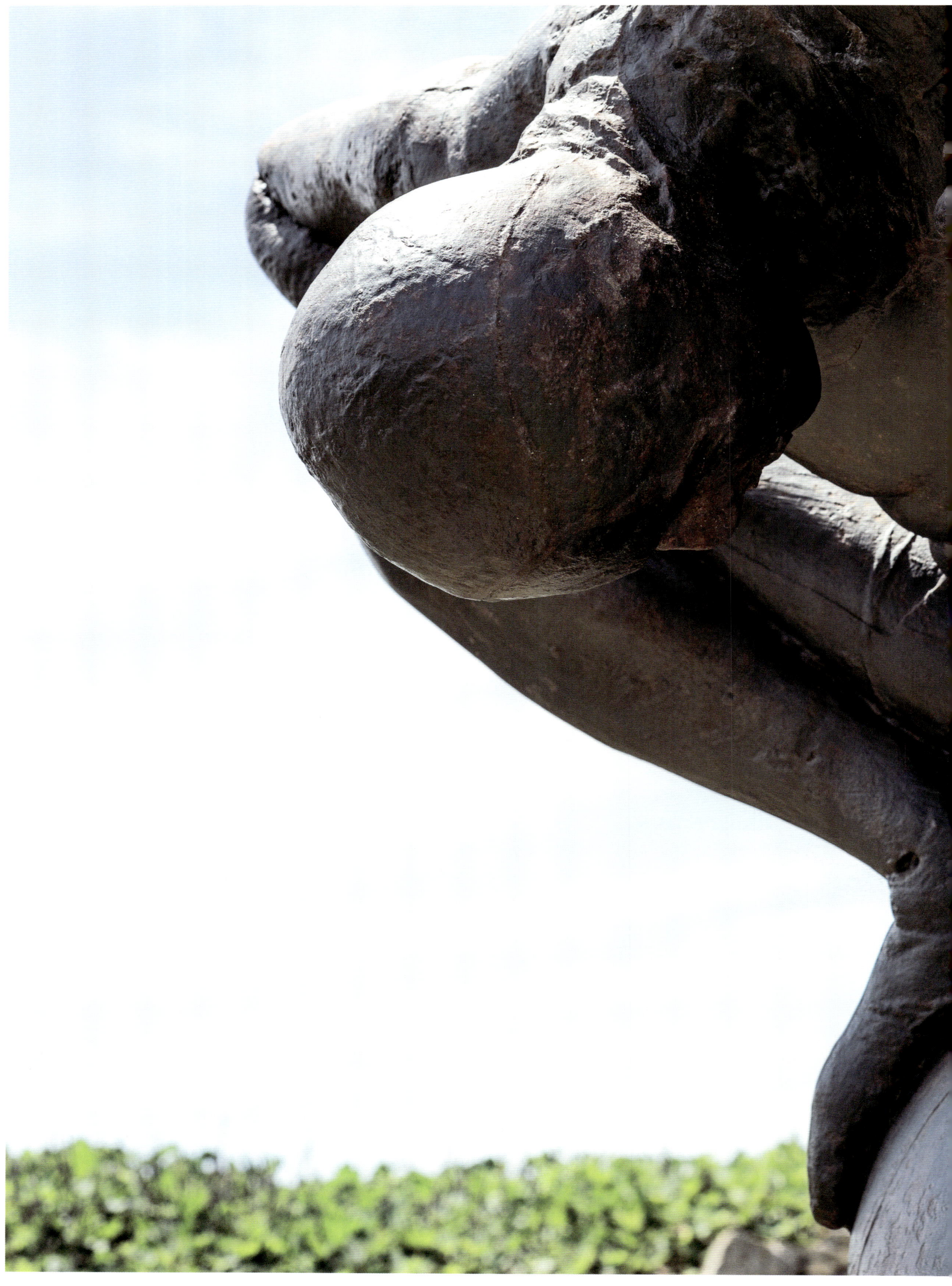

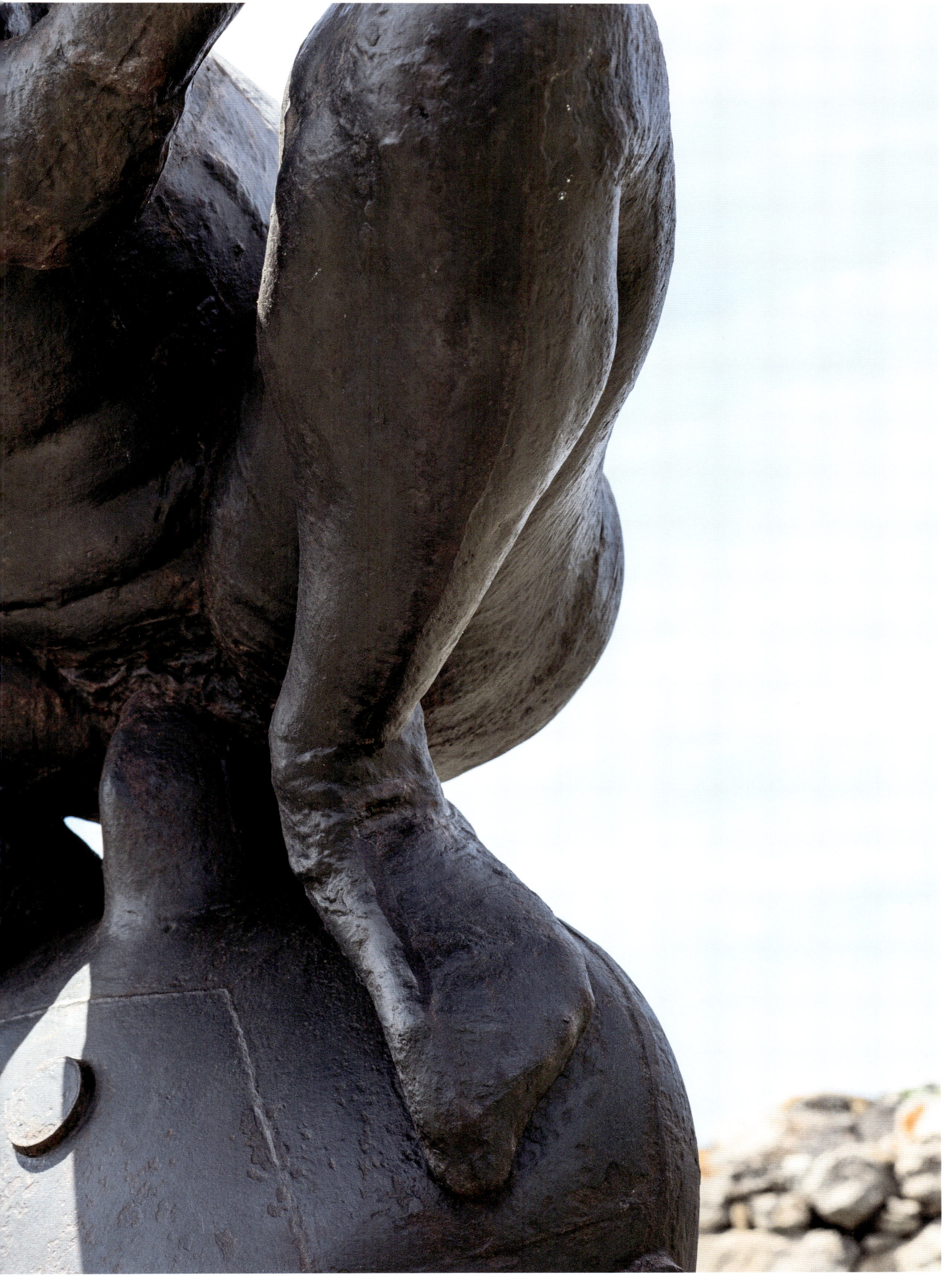

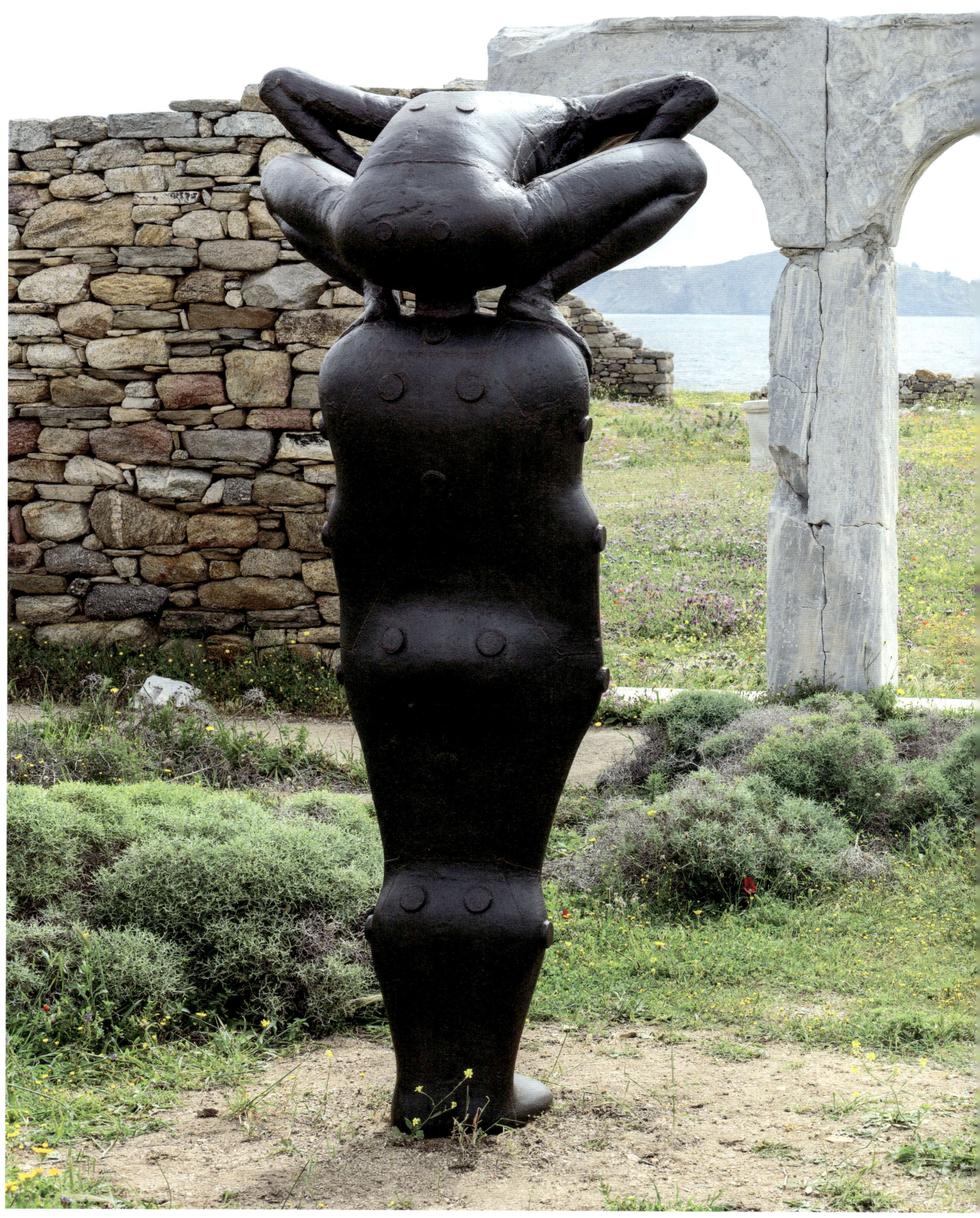

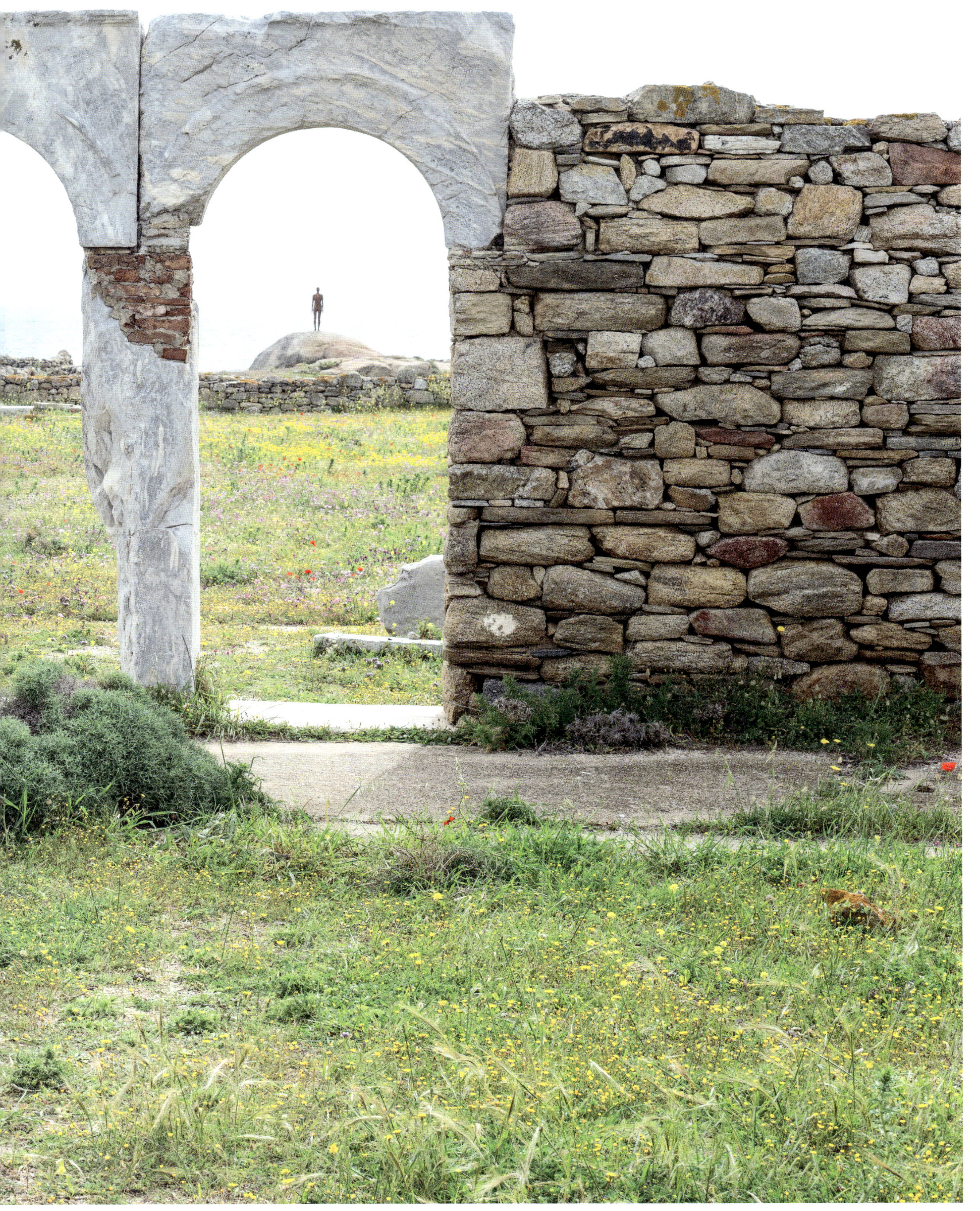

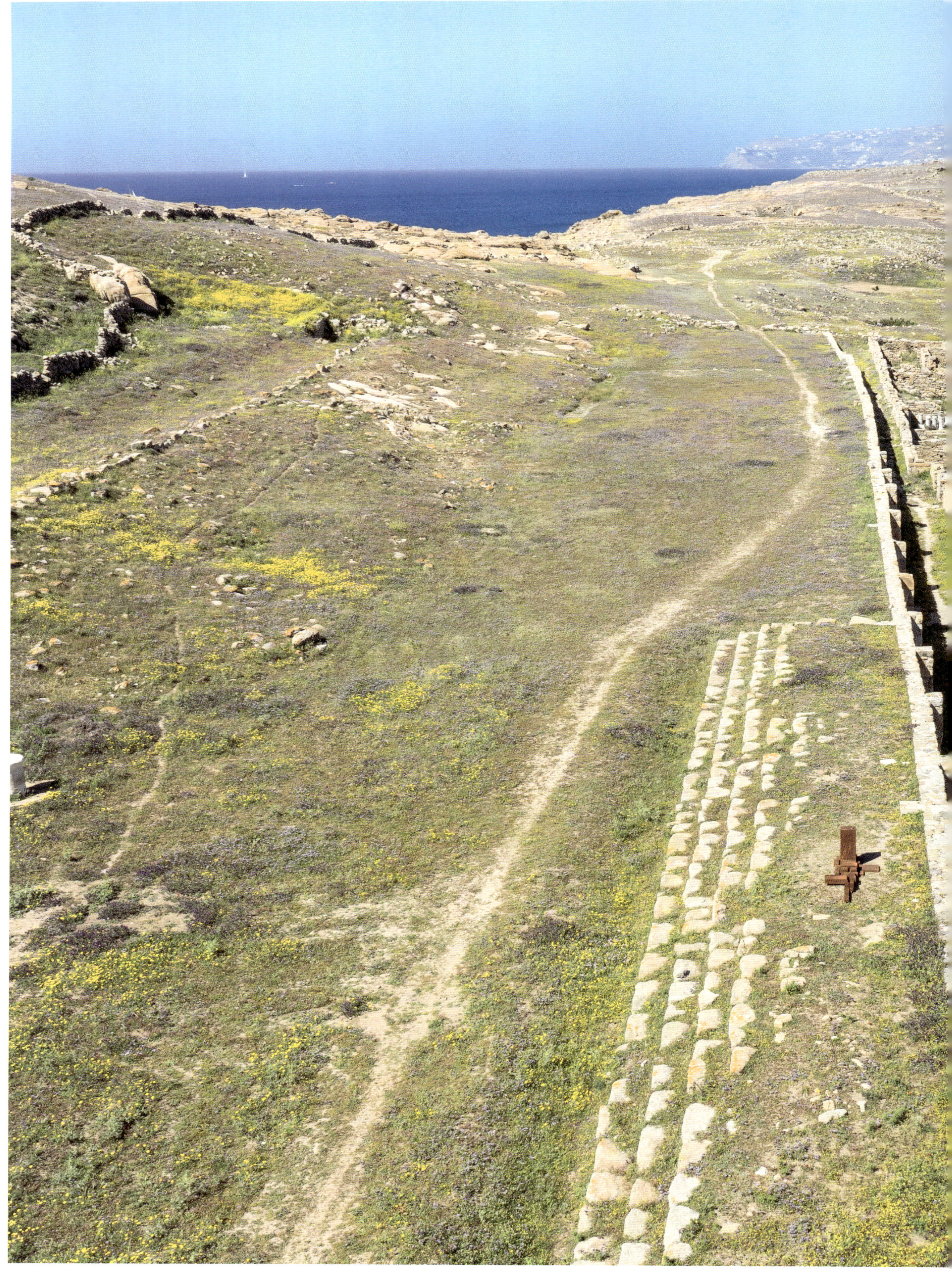

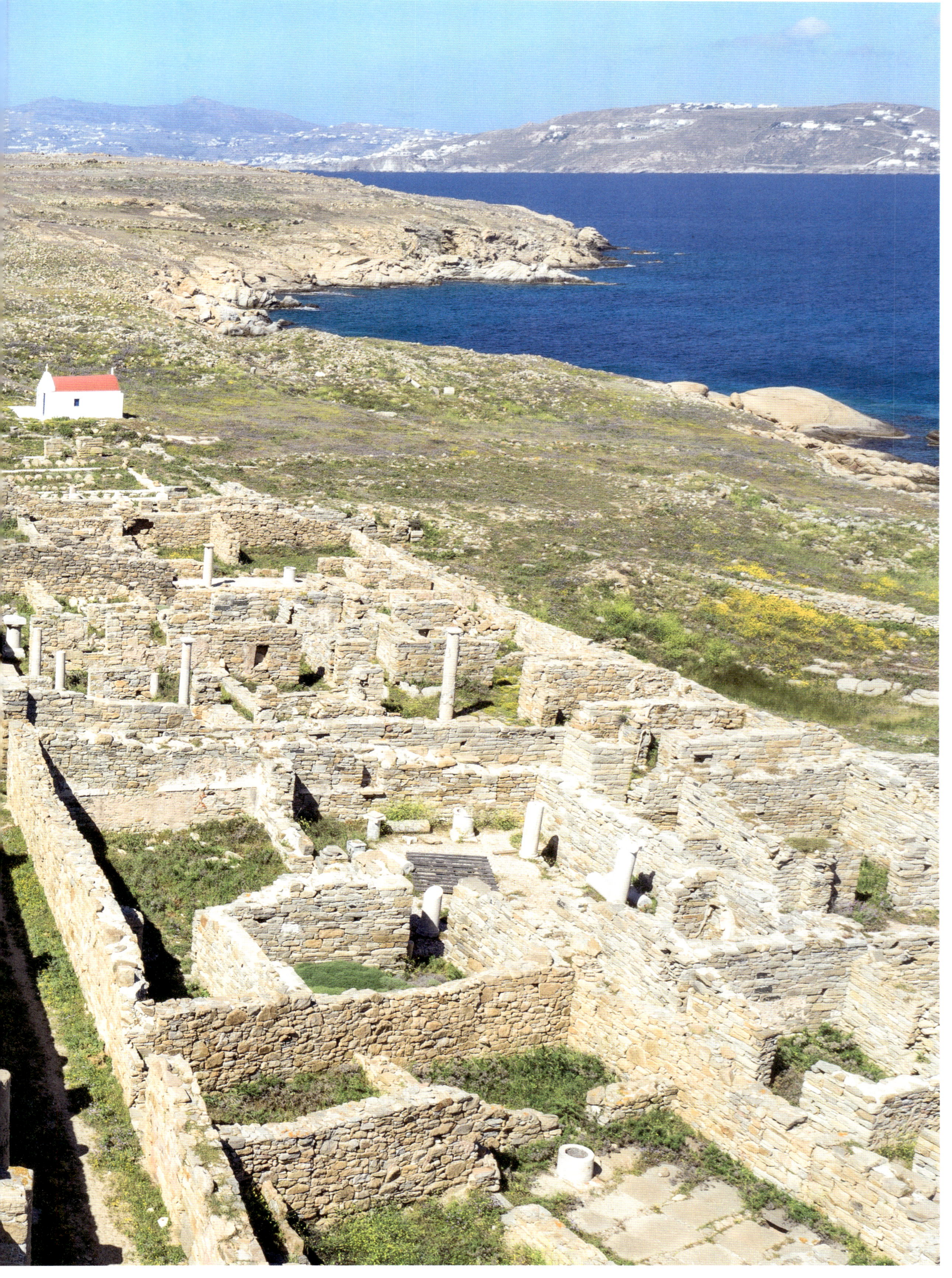

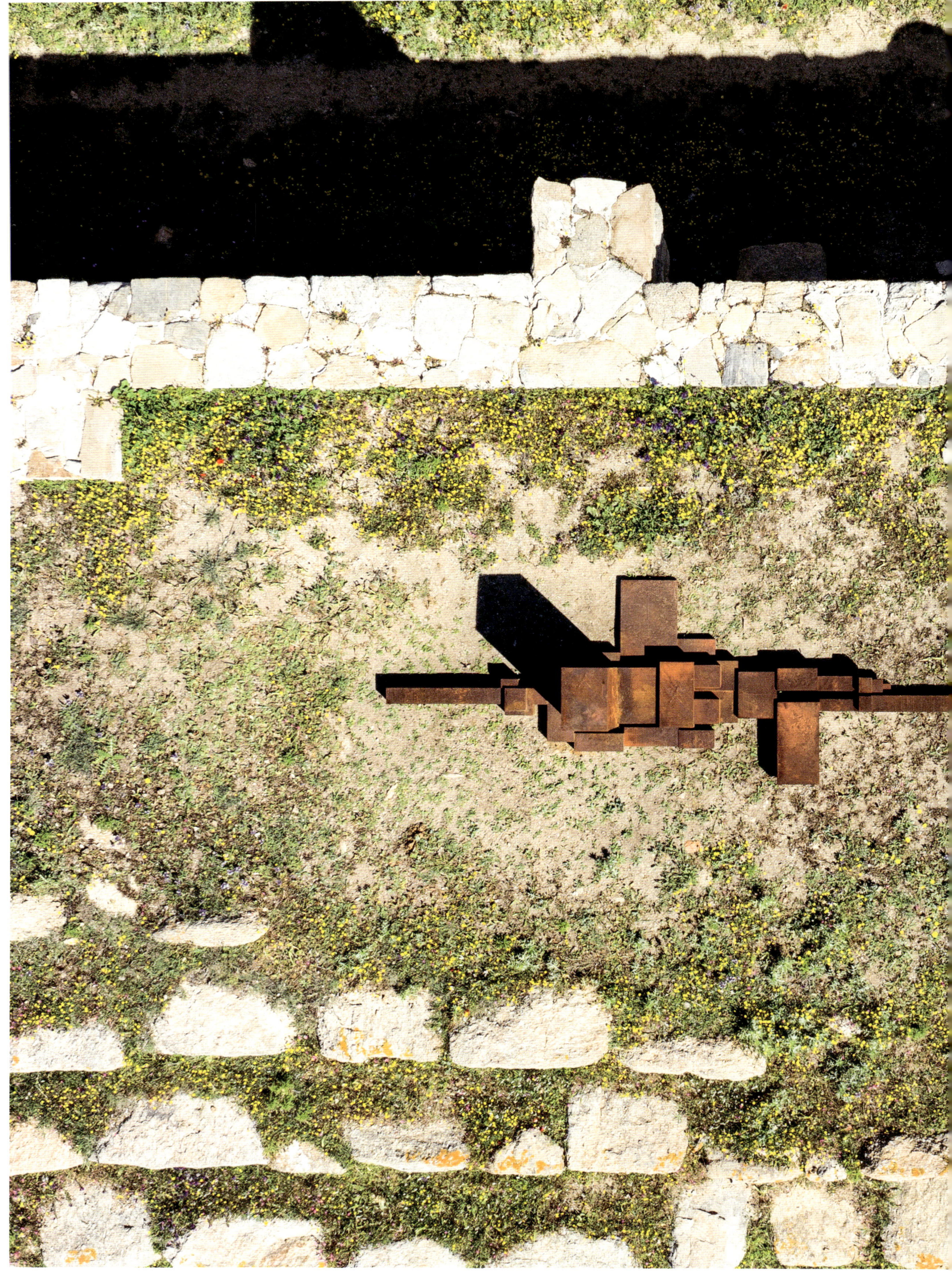

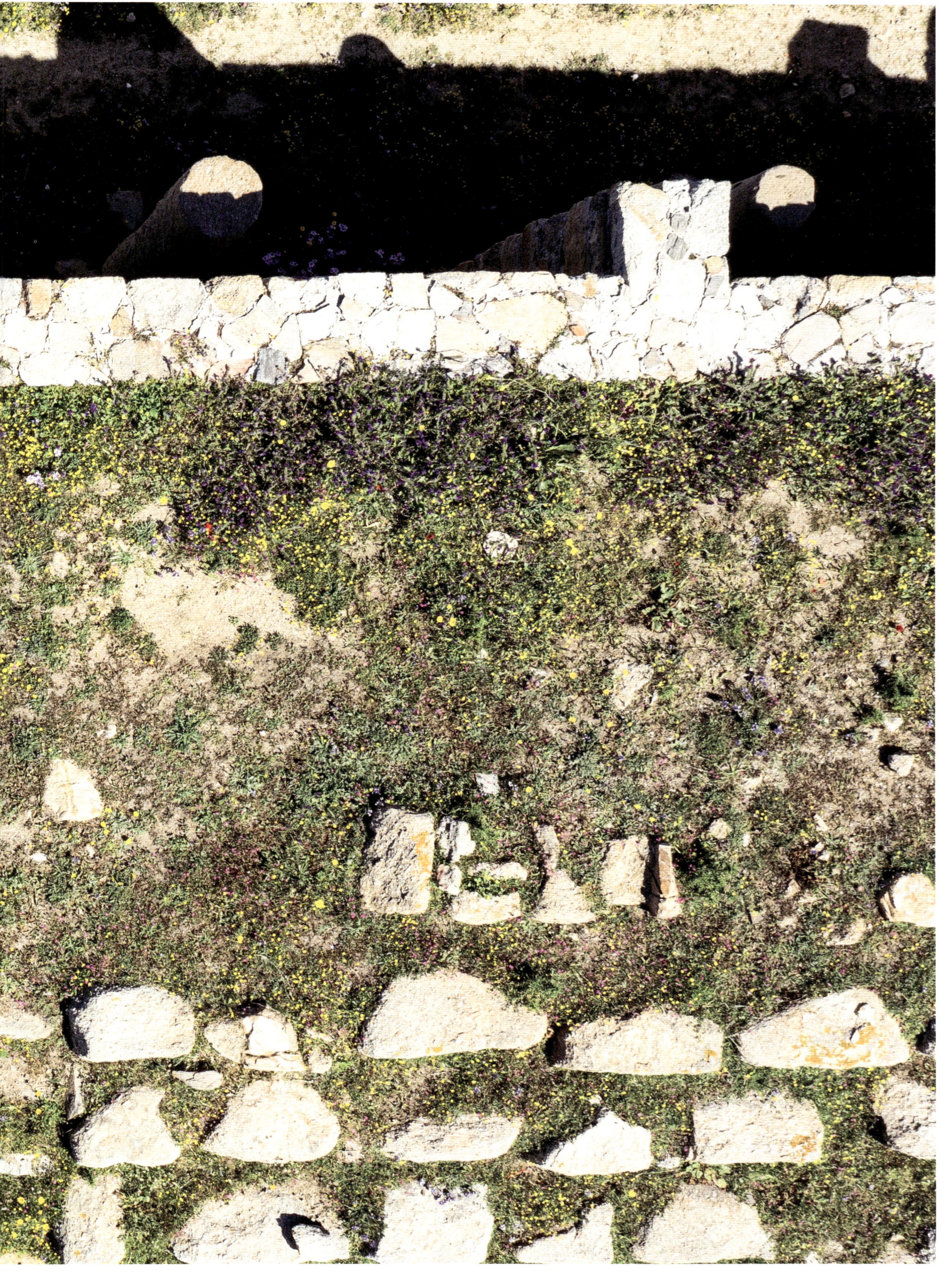

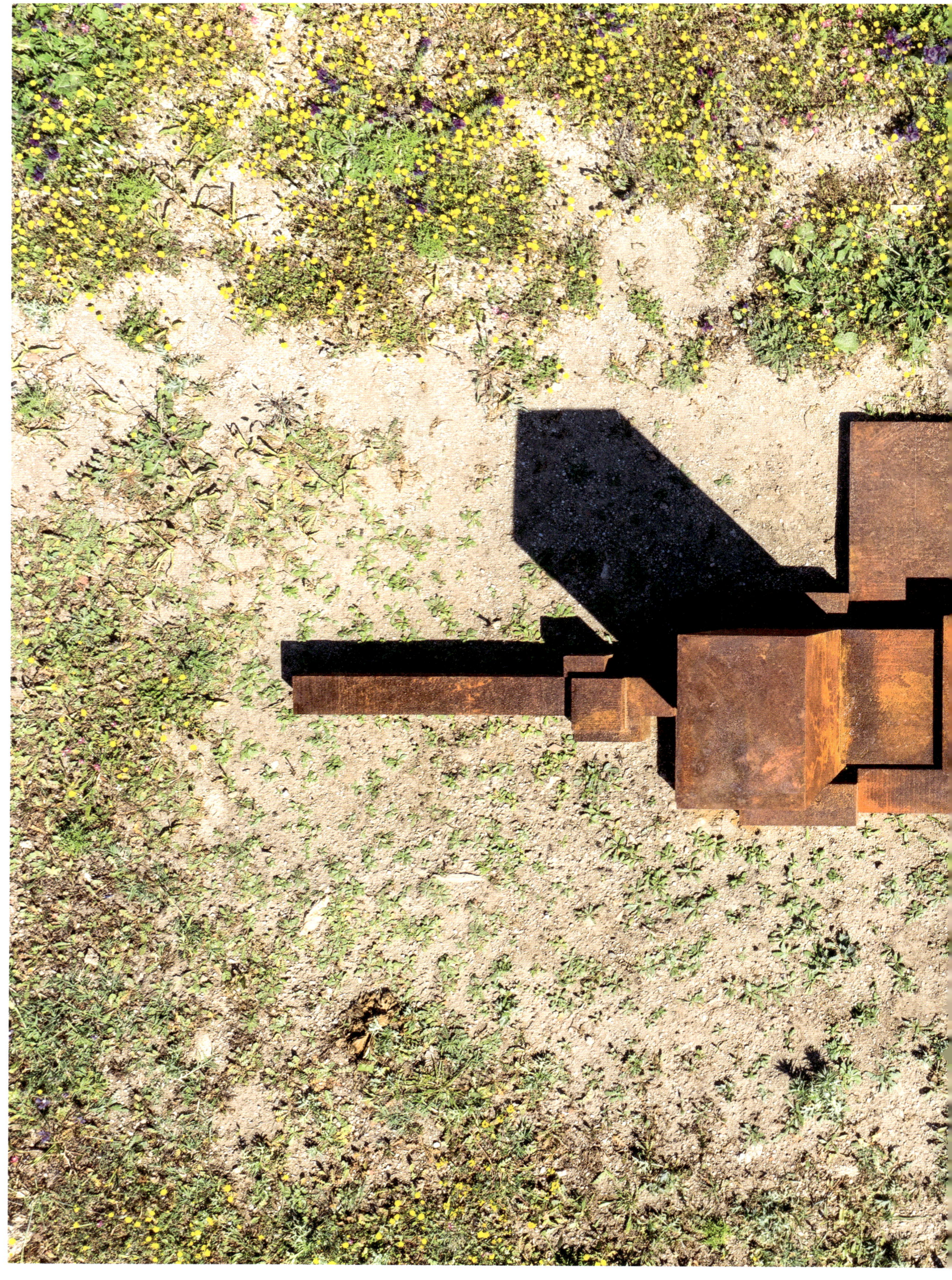

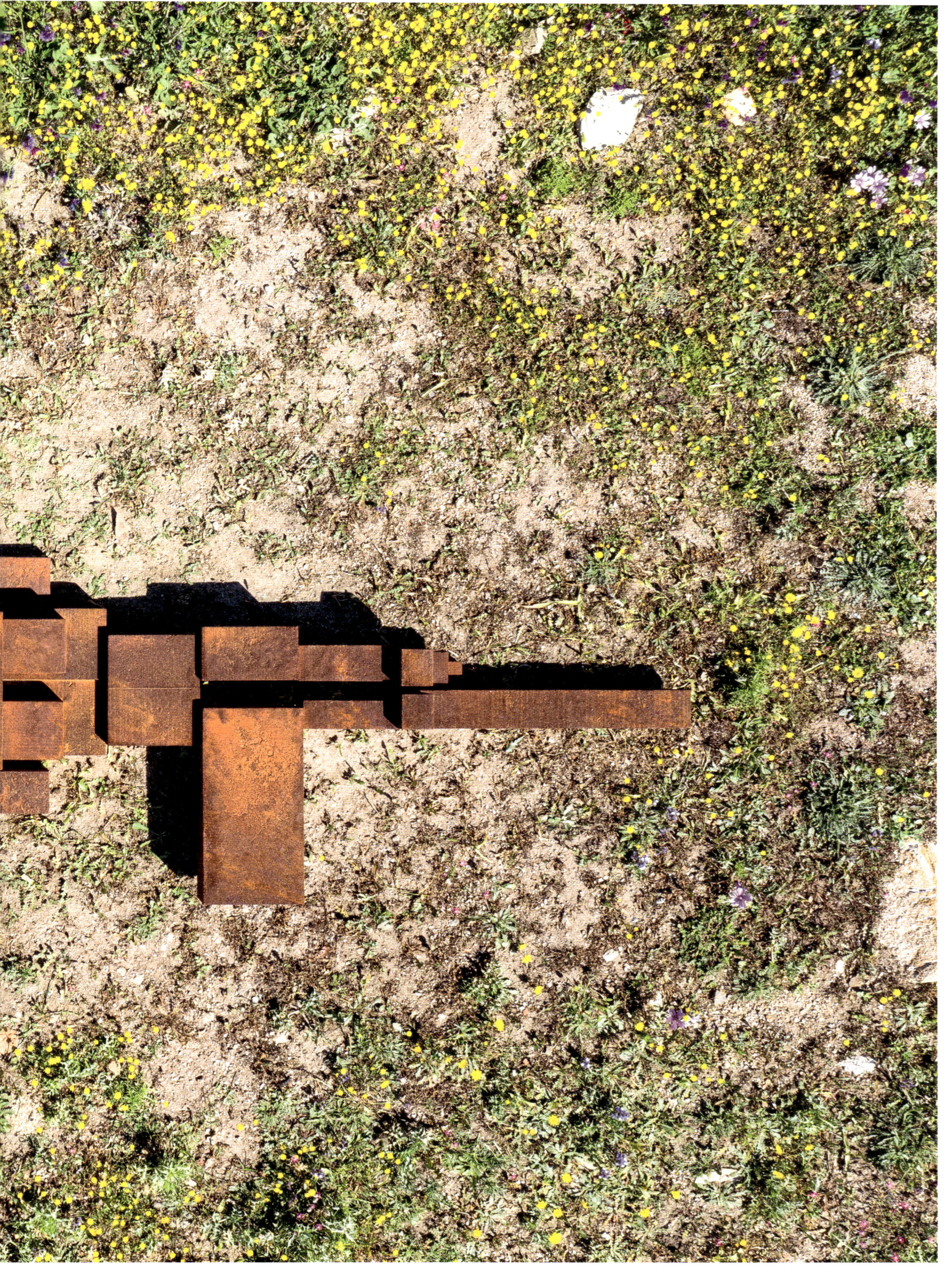

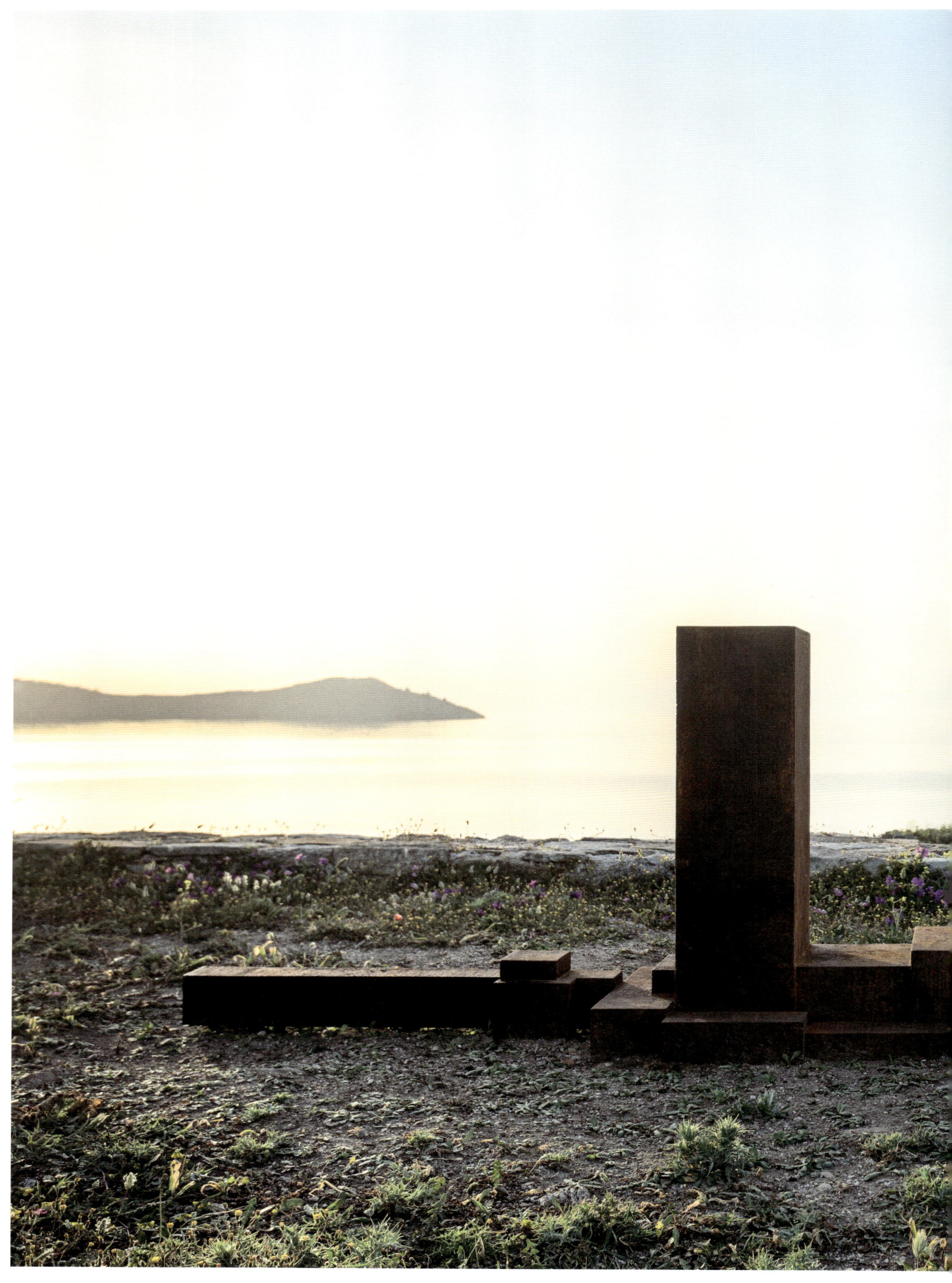

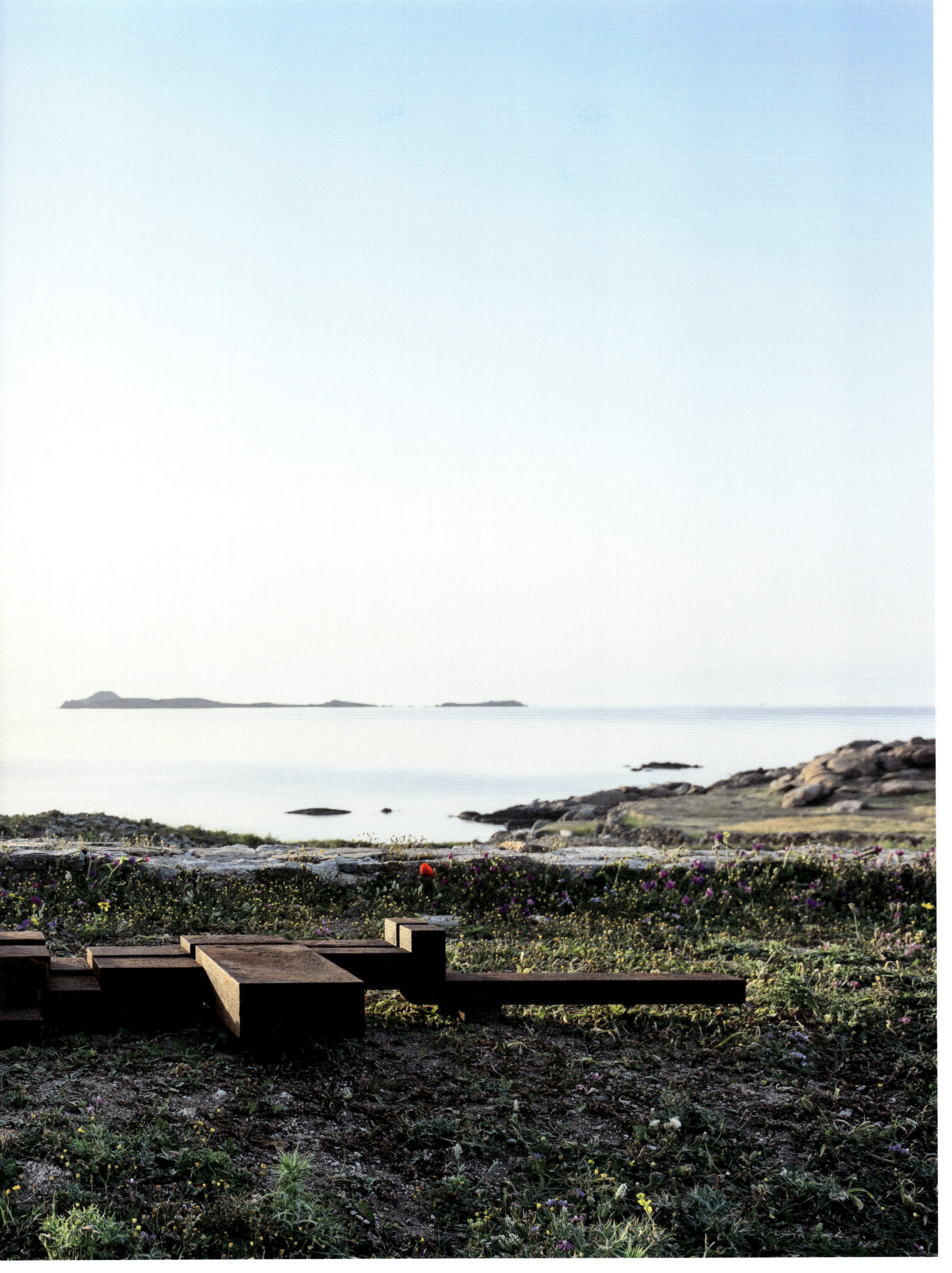

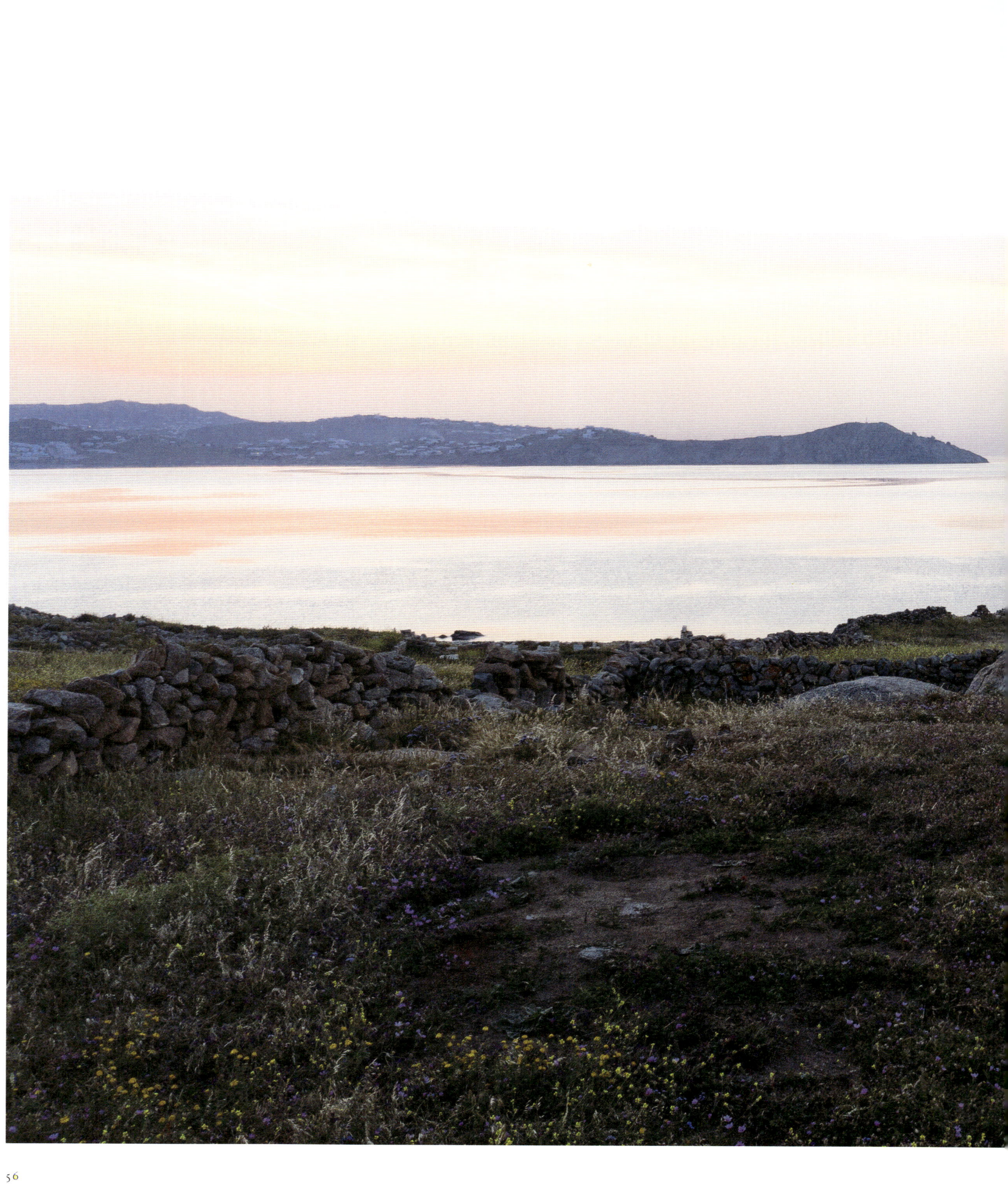

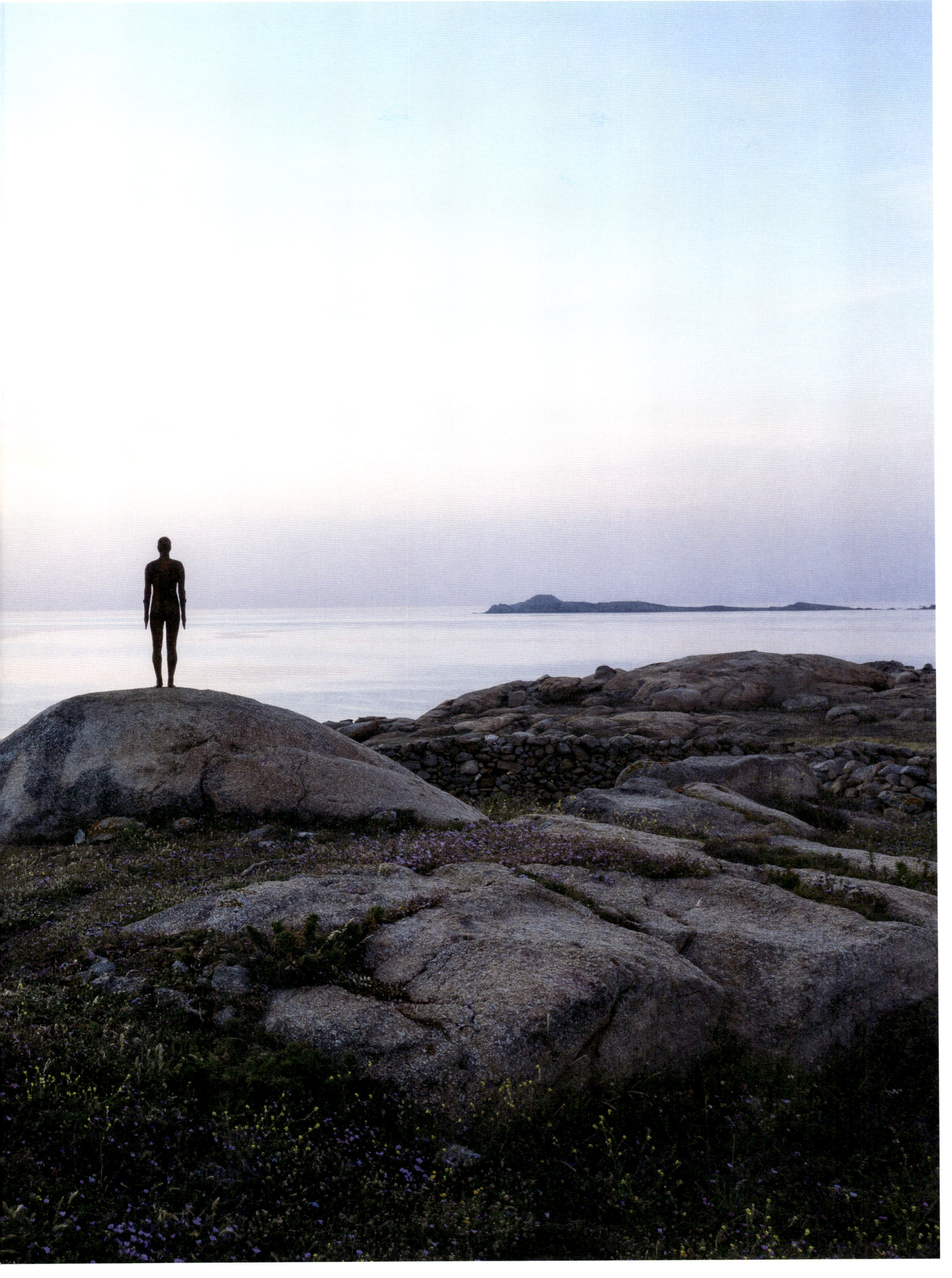

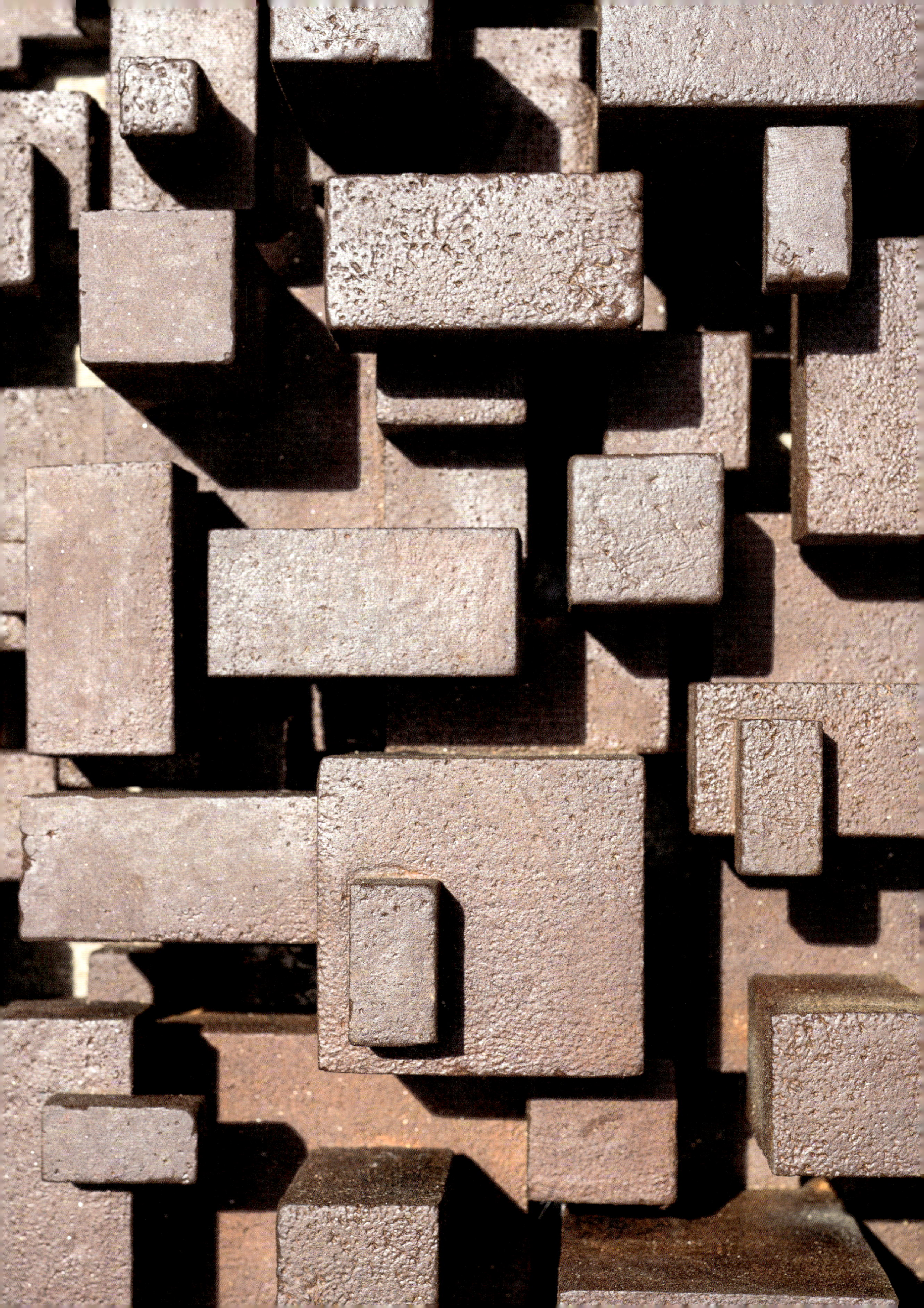

ANTONY GORMLEY: AT THE STILL POINT OF THE TURNING WORLD

EMILY RIDDLE

At the still point of the turning world. Neither flesh nor fleshless;
Neither from nor towards; at the still point, there the dance is,
But neither arrest nor movement. And do not call it fixity,
Where past and future are gathered. Neither movement from nor towards,
Neither ascent nor decline. Except for the point, the still point,
There would be no dance, and there is only dance.

T. S. Eliot, 'Burnt Norton', 1943

In 'Burnt Norton', T. S. Eliot's most sustained exploration of time and transcendence, the poet evokes 'dance' as the source and object of the creative act, at once rooted in the space and time of the corporeal, and disembodied in the realm of the eternal or absolute.[1] In their silent stillness, the sculptures of Antony Gormley seem to act as physical points of access into this metaphysical dimension, probing – even collapsing – our sense of location in time and place, and our condition as self and other. Each 'bodyform' exists as an index of a lived moment, as 'proof of where one body once was and any body could be', the first body acting as an individual marker of the past, the latter a universal possibility in the conditional mood.[2] The present, crucially, is left to the moment of sculptural encounter, neither wholly of the flesh nor wholly fleshless. Concentrated at the interstices between the physical, the mental and the spiritual, Eliot's 'dance' and Gormley's bodyforms seem to locate *and* transcend the present moment – the here-and-now – 'where past and future are gathered'.

Given the rich potential of considering Gormley's sculpture in relation to the corporeal and time-based medium of dance, it is surprising that the subject has, at least to date, been treated only fleetingly in the growing literature about his work. Perhaps the most telling acknowledgement of this relationship lies in the text by dancer and

1 T. S. Eliot, 'Burnt Norton' (1943), in *T. S. Eliot: Collected Poems 1909–62*, London: Faber & Faber, 1974, p. 179.
2 'The Body as Lost Subject: Conversation between Alberto Fiz and Antony Gormley', in *Antony Gormley: Time Horizon*, Milan: Electa, 2006, p. 194.

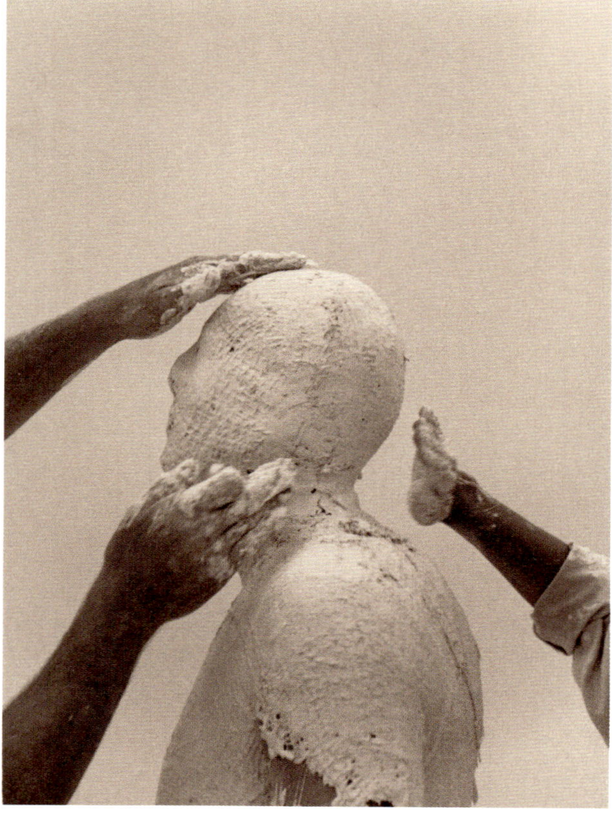

Work in progress for *Critical Mass II*, 1995, casting at Bellenden Road studio, Peckham, London

choreographer William Forsythe commissioned for the exhibition catalogue, *Second Body* (2015), in which he makes the case for the choreographic significance of Gormley's body of work, his work of repeated bodies:

> WF [William Forsythe] believes that if one would accept his casting of the entire oeuvre of AG [Antony Gormley] in a choreographic role, it would be obvious that this protracted, incremental accretion of figures and their inversions, eversions, translations: extended, compressed or otherwise formally distributed and configured into manifold orthogonal space, is one of the most original, visionary choreographic turns of our epoch.[3]

The repetition of the bodyform through Gormley's work (the 'protracted, incremental accretion of figures') will be discussed in this context with reference to the chorus of archaic ritual and ancient theatre – those originary *choreo*graphers. Yet to explore in a more sustained way how an exploration of dance can contribute to a reading of embodiment and time in Gormley's practice, let us return to first principles, the artist's studio, and the 'still point' of the work's genesis.

Describing the 'oceanic experience' of stilling the body – importantly, *his* body – to register its form in layers of plaster and gauze, Gormley invokes the potential of infinite expansion from subject-object boundaries:

> You still the body and in the process of it being concentrated on, its edges begin to break down. You're no longer sure about where something you call me, my, mine, I starts and stops and you become aware that human consciousness can be dispersed and have no edge and be a kind of field awareness.[4]

3 William Forsythe, 'Second Body', in *Antony Gormley: Second Body*, Paris: Galerie Thaddaeus Ropac, 2015, p. 93.
4 Martin Caiger-Smith, *Antony Gormley*, New York, Rizzoli, 2017, p. 260.

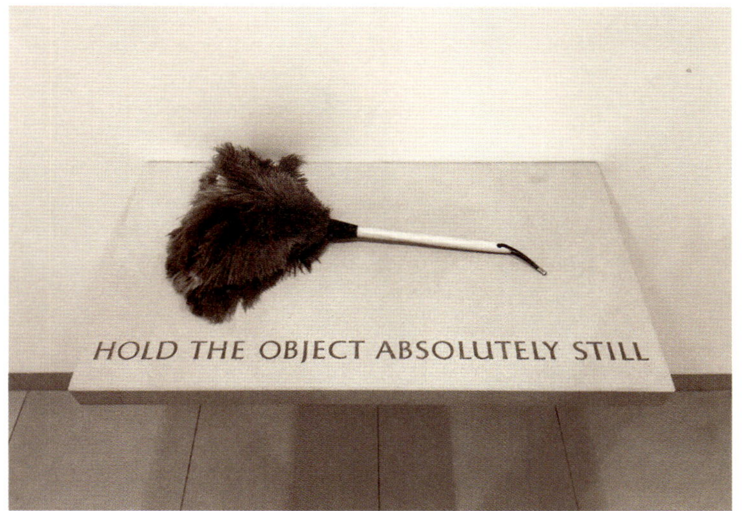

William Forsythe, *Towards the Diagnostic Gaze*, 2013
Readymade feather duster, engraved stone shelf from stone locally sourced for exhibition
5 × 80 × 45 cm

For Gormley, this process of finding stillness in the body – be it during casting or digital scanning – is crucial to the agency of his sculptures as reflexive instruments, inviting us to project ourselves into their corporeal forms and, in so doing, to experience our own being-in-the-world more deeply. André Lepecki's words on dancer and choreographer Jérôme Bel could almost refer to Gormley's works here: 'Just as [he] deploys singularity to propose how subjectivity is always a multiplicity, I would argue that he deploys stillness [...] to propose how movement is not only a question of kinetics, but also one of intensities, of generating an intensive field of microperceptions'.[5] Gormley's sculptures invite contemplation and intense physical experience of our (collective) subjecthood, our singular conditions of living within our singular bodies. Here, as so often in writing about Gormley's work, the structures of first or third person pronoun, singular or plural noun register – and falter under – the sculptures' complex ontology.

William Forsythe's own work, *Towards the Diagnostic Gaze* (2013) from his series of 'Choreographic Objects', seems to register a similar field of 'microperceptions' through an entirely different kind of 'instrument'. Here, a feather duster is presented on a stone shelf inscribed with the words 'Hold the object absolutely still'. This 'Choreographic Object' becomes, in Forsythe's words, the 'focus of human will as the viewer grasps hold of it and attempts to quiet the nervous energies of its plumes [...]. The feather duster registers the human body's every tremor and pulse'.[6] Forsythe draws attention to these micro-movements, to the ebbs and flows of the singular bodies that occupy both the social space of the gallery and the collective subjective of inhabiting a body. Of course, Gormley's sculptures – his own form of 'choreographic objects', perhaps – appear entirely still: their vibrations are barely more perceptible to the human senses than the localised vibrations of the electron field, the photon field, the up quark field, the gluon field, the muon field. Yet, for the inhabited body that encounters the bodyform, an internal pulse can be felt, seen, heard all the more strongly in the reflected stillness of the sculpture.

5 André Lepecki, *Exhausting Dance: Performance and the Politics of Movement*, New York and London: Routledge, 2006, p. 57.
6 'Choreographic Objects: William Forsythe and Emilio Montevideo in Conversation', *Mousse Magazine*, http://moussemagazine.it/choreographic-objects-william-forsythe/ [accessed 18 April 2019].

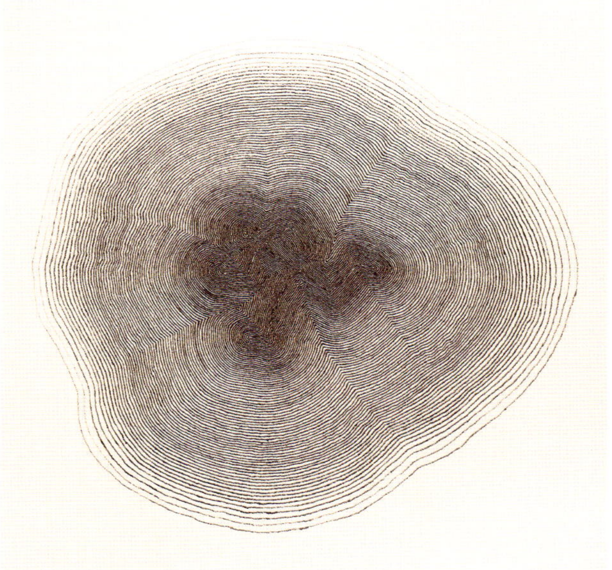

Exercise Between Blood and Earth, 1979 – 81
Chalk on wall
1.84 m (diameter)

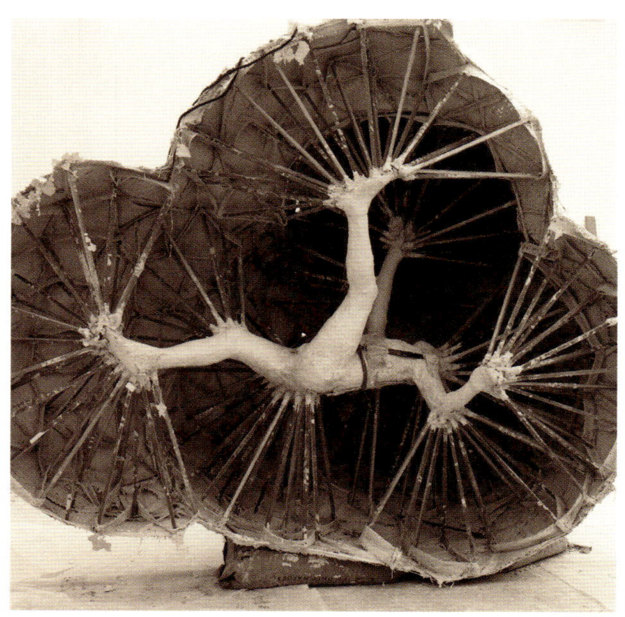

Work in progress, *Still Leaping*, 1994, at Bellenden Road studio, Peckham, London

Discussing his *Expansion Works*, Gormley wrote of his drive towards 'renegotiating the skin: questioning where things and events begin and end'.[7] In the related early drawing, *Exercise Between Blood and Earth* (1979–81), concentric lines radiate inwards and outwards from the outline of the artist's body, reflecting Gormley's earliest explorations of the cutaneous membrane as a container of energy, of potential expansion. Translated into three dimensions in the sculptural *Expansion Works*, the plaster mould registered the artist's body, arrested mid-movement, and wooden spars radiated out from its extremities – its head, hands, feet, buttocks – delineating the surface of the final cocoon-like form.

The *Extended Blockwork* sited in the *orchestra* (or, 'dancing-space') of the open-air Theatre at Delos, *Knot* (2010), echoes the idea of expansion into space around the foetal bodyforms of the early drawing and of *Expansion Works* such as *Body* and *Fruit* (1991). Where the continuous domed surfaces of this earlier sculptural pairing concealed the originary bodyform almost entirely, in *Knot* the structure of the body at the gravitational centre of the work is exposed to view. Constructed from the 'materialised pixels' – cast iron blocks – that characterise Gormley's increasing interest in abstraction, here the bodyform appears to crouch tightly, as the blocks describing its anatomical volumes extend along three axes.[8] As in the earlier *Expansion Works*, which are often shown suspended from the gallery ceiling, it seems impossible to tell here whether the primary force acting on this body is centripetal or centrifugal. The figure is held in balance; even the slightest further extension along one axis would require counterweight in order for the form to maintain its orientation. Compression and extension are suspended in finely calibrated equilibrium. *Neither from nor towards.*

When shown for the first time at White Cube, in 2010, Gormley presented the *Extended Blockworks* alongside the installation *Breathing Room III*, exploring the forms

7 See Antony Gormley's statement, 'Expansion Works, 1990–2018' on the artist's website: http://www.antonygormley.com [accessed 18 April 2019].
8 Margaret Iverson, 'Still Standing', in *Antony Gormley: Still Standing*, London: Fontanka Publications, 2011, p. 50.

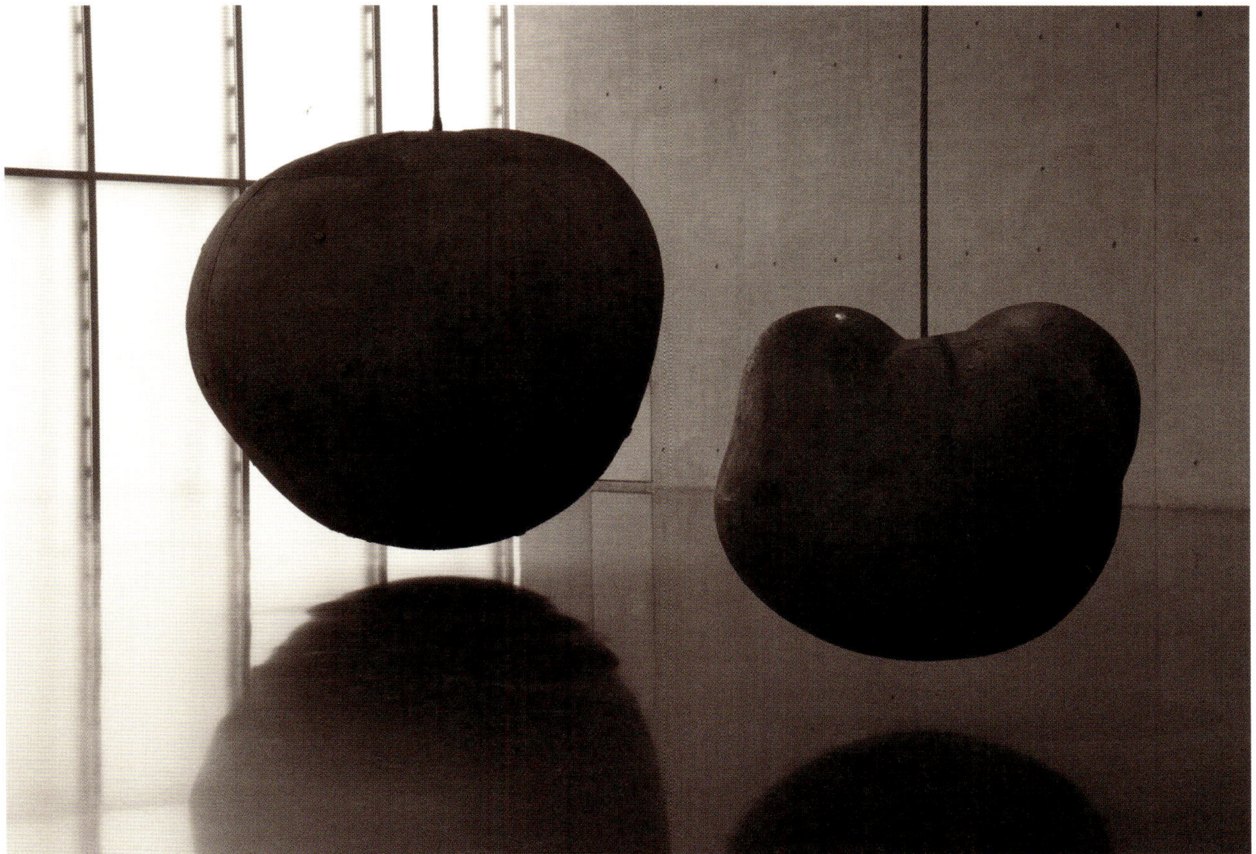

Installation view, 'Antony Gormley', Kunsthaus Bregenz, Austria, 2009, showing, left to right: *Body* and *Fruit*, both 1991/93

– and lived experiences – of human bodies in relation to the typically orthogonal stacking and cantilever structures of our built environments. There, the three axes of extension appeared as if limited by, or subservient to, the internal walls of the white cube, the potential for growth curbed by the austere architecture of the gallery. In the open-air Theatre at Delos, however, *Knot* appears almost boundless, to the left, right, front, behind, above. With the back of the figure extending such as to elevate the body 65 centimetres from the earth, even the ground seems to be activated, probing its impression of absolute, horizontal solidity within geological time.

It is as if the single figure at the centre of this dancing-space, engaged in its own *pas seul*, awaits the return of an imagined *corps de ballet* to reabsorb its virtuosity back into a narrative, back into direct relation with other bodies, into a dialogue of gesture. And yet the blocks denoting calves remain clamped to the thighs, the arms held tight around the knees. The extensions from each figure are not the limbs of the ballet dancer arrested in *arabesque*, nor the limbs of the soon-to-be-triumphant Diskobolos. The energy of the *corps de ballet*, such as it might have been, is held within this one astrolabe-like form; the stillness – of the body in casting and the iron cast as body – acts as a marker of lived time and space radiating into 'field awareness'.

As we step around *Knot*, entering into our own *pas de deux* with the work, it is only at certain points that the densely clustered blocks at its core resolve into a figure. And, just as quickly as this figure appears, it dissolves back into abstraction, its interlocking cuboids like a Suprematist painting extended into three dimensions. Encountered in the context of the ancient Greek theatre, the unstable relation between figuration and abstraction of this work finds resonance in the Apollonian and Dionysian impulses conceptualised by Nietzsche in *The Birth of Tragedy*. Within Nietzsche's decidedly metaphysical treatment of the theatre in ancient Greek culture, the Apollonian is associated with physical form, Classical sculpture and the rational individual. The Dionysian impulse, on the other hand, drives towards formlessness, chaos and, through its attendant combination of horror and pleasure, the dissolution of individual identity into a universal spiritual community – a 'field awareness' of sorts. With these principles acting, in Nietzschean tragedy, at once in competition and in mutual dependence, the abstract collective experience is condensed within, and born out of, singular form.

In an interview with Hans Ulrich Obrist, Gormley recalls the reflections of artist John Latham that 'the event of [the body-forms] being brought into the world, that moment of consciousness, was more important in a way than their material presence'.[9] Spinning this proposition round to face itself, the 'material presence' is, however, the only physical proof that the moment of focussed attention, 'the event', occurred – it is the viewer's most direct point of access to 'field awareness'. Returning to Eliot's 'Burnt Norton', we are reminded that 'Only by the form, the pattern, / Can words or music reach / The stillness, as a Chinese jar still / Moves perpetually in its stillness.'[10] As we turn about *Knot*, it is as if we trace the footsteps of ancient Delian chorus, finding for ourselves the forwards-backwards motion of *strophe* and *antistrophe* at the still point where figuration and abstraction – the 'material presence' and the 'event' – coexist.

Might we indeed imagine the sculptures dispersed across the island as a chorus of sorts, one song voiced through many bodies, many bodies cast from one man? As a cultic centre of panhellenic significance, from the archaic period Delos welcomed choruses of foreign cities to perform in the sanctuary for audiences assembled from across Ionia.[11] In the Homeric *Hymn to Apollo*, the chorus of Delian maidens performing at the cultic festival is praised for its ability to represent the voices of all peoples for its audience: 'each would say that he himself were singing, / so close to truth is their sweet song'.[12] Here, choral performance and spectatorship are set into an idealised feedback loop, in which the performers are able to represent the shared sensibility of their audience who, in turn, are able to project themselves into the frame of the performance. Little wonder that scholars have held up this passage as an important early instance of performance criticism and the reflexive potential of (proto-)theatre.[13] Ritual – whether in worship, in theatre, in a sculptural encounter – depends on this reflexive relationship between the individual and the collective.

With his rejection of 'any system that purports to encompass some ideal, some absolute', Gormley does not seek to represent the voices of all peoples; indeed, he refers to his 'voiding of the subject, of gesture, of *drama*' in his work, resistant to the

9 Hans Ulrich Obrist, 'The Tale of Trafalgar Square', in *Antony Gormley: One and Other*, London: Jonathan Cape, 2010, p. 245.
10 T. S. Eliot, pp. 181-82.
11 Edmund Stewart, *Greek Tragedy on the Move: The Birth of a Panhellenic Art Form c. 500–300 BC*, Oxford: Oxford University Press, 2017, p. 46.
12 *Hesiod, The Homeric Hymns and Homerica*, trans. Hugh G. Evelyn-White, London: William Heinemann, 1914, p. 337.
13 Anastasia-Erasmia Peponi, 'Choreia and Aesthetics in the Homeric Hymn to Apollo: The Performance of the Delian Maidens (Lines 156–64)', *Classical Antiquity* 28, no. 1 (2009), p. 67.

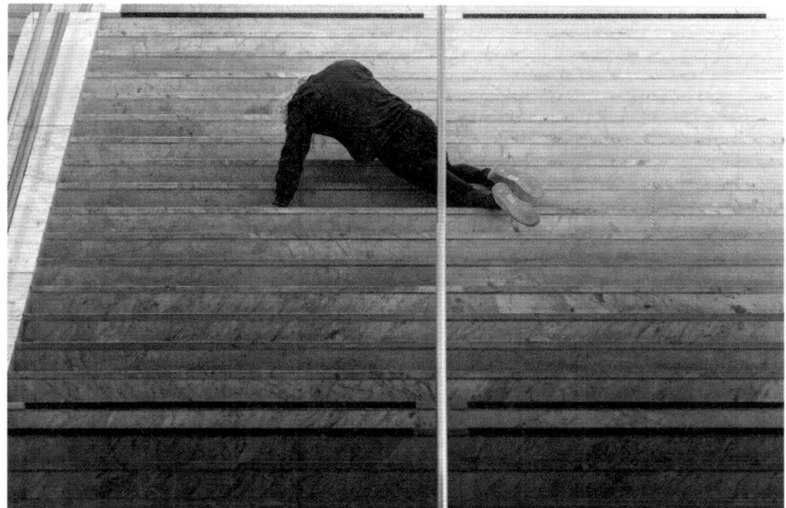

Maria Hassabi: *PLASTIC* (2015) Installation view at the Hammer Museum, Los Angeles, 2015

idea of the theatrical, the narrative, the spectacular.[14] Nonetheless, the relationship he builds between 'one body' and 'any body' speaks strongly to the idea of mutual projection of performer and spectator and his interest in 'the action of a living, willing, feeling body on other bodies' – the potential of the bodyform to *act* as a reflexive instrument – is thrown into particularly sharp relief by the setting of his sculptures in a cultic framework of such significance.[15] 'We are only just beginning to scratch at the real potential of the space of theatre, not as a space of demonstration, but of exploration,' Gormley suggests, discussing his collaborations with choreographers Akram Khan and Sidi Larbi Cherkaoui at Sadler's Wells: 'In the end it is the energy of the audience that is reflected in the energy of the dancers.'[16]

The work of artist, dancer and choreographer, Maria Hassabi seems to share much with Gormley's use of bodyforms as reflexive instruments here. Developing a language of movement that she terms the 'velocity of deceleration', Hassabi capitalises on the physical labour and charged energy of almost imperceptible movement in her performers' bodies, and the intense looking and feeling of embodiment it solicits from the viewer.[17] In Hassabi's live installation *Plastic* (2015) at the Museum of Modern Art, New York, her cast of dancers moved at an apparently glacial pace across the gallery floors and connecting staircases, shifting incrementally between postures of collapse and repose. Some visitors stooped in concern for these slumped bodies, some hurried onwards as if embarrassed at the invitation to reflect. Others stopped and allowed the performers' barely perceptible movements to come into sharp focus, allowed themselves to enter into that 'intensive field of microperceptions'. As in the encounter with Gormley's cast of bodyforms, Hassabi's sense of her dancers' 'collective resistance' to time and movement as producing a 'collective commitment to the here and now' is not the preserve of the performers alone: by slowing or stopping

14 Antony Gormley, in *Antony Gormley: Blind Light*, London: Hayward Gallery, 2007, p. 59, my emphasis.
15 Antony Gormley, in *Antony Gormley on Sculpture*, ed. by Mark Holborn, London: Thames & Hudson, 2015, p. 8.
16 Guy Cools in conversation with Antony Gormley, Sadler's Wells, 9 December 2013.
17 'Conversations: Maria Hassabi at Live Arts Week VI, Bologna', Mousse Magazine, Milan, http://moussemagazine.it/maria-hassabi-live-arts-week-vi-bologna-2017/ [accessed 18 April 2019].

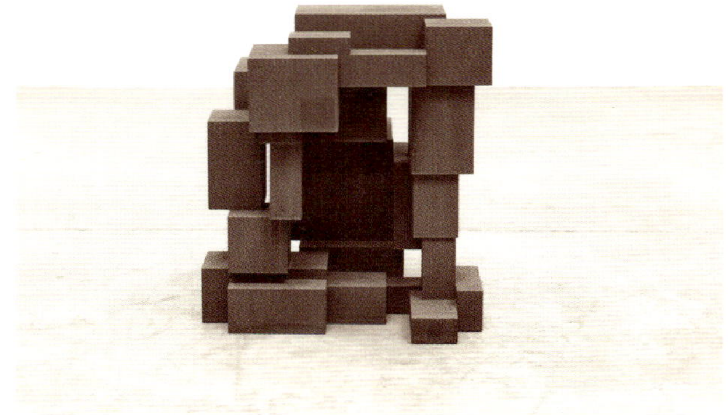

Vice II, 2015
Cast iron
66 × 59.5 × 60.5 cm

to look and to feel, the viewer also pledges commitment.[18]

If the performance of the chorus in the *Hymn to Apollo* finds resonance in the reflexive dynamic so central to Gormley's work, the chorus of captive Delian women in Euripides' *Iphigenia of Tauris* brings to the fore the quiet resistance to social and political hierarchies that runs through many of his site-responsive installations. In Euripides' penultimate episode (lines 1088 – 1152), the chorus of enslaved women, 'the plunder of oars and spears', lament their estrangement from the 'festival gatherings of the Greeks' on their island.[19] The fact that Euripides has his chorus refer so emphatically to the Delian festival during their evocation of the islands religious topography reflects the significance of the island as cultic arena. Especially following the expulsion of the Delians by Athens in 422 BC and the subsequent reinstating of the festival by the imperial powers, it acted as 'one of the most conspicuous showpieces of Athenian power, where choral and imperial policy were inextricably intertwined', the slaves of empire integrated into the mythological narrative.[20] As one of the largest trading ports of the ancient world, Delos is characterised by Strabo as being able to host the exchange of 10,000 slaves in a single day (*Geography*, 14.5.2). In this same port – some two and a half millennia later – Gormley exposes the human cost of a culture we so often hold up as foundational for our own, the shadowed underbelly of a purported Golden Age of democracy, theatre, architecture, sculpture.

Where 'the dialectic between aspirational and abject' ran through Gormley's 2015 exhibition, 'Human', at the Forte Belvedere in Florence, a similar tension emerges in the siting of work on Delos. In a vast paved area near to the Agora of the Competaliasts, thought to have been used as the slave market due to its proximity to the port, Gormley sites *Vice II* (2015). This crouched bodyform might recall the figure suspended at the core of *Knot*, but there seems to be little centrifugal energy here: the aggregation of modules curl inwards, around a void where the stomach might have been.

18 Harry Thorne, 'Maria Hassabi: Stillness is the Move', Frieze, 16 April 2018, https://frieze.com/article/maria-hassabi-stillness-move [accessed 18 April 2019].
19 Euripides, *Bacchae and Other Plays*, trans. James Morwood, Oxford: Oxford University Press, 2000, pp. 32–33.
20 Barbara Kowalzig, 'Transcultural Chorality', in *Choral Mediations in Greek Tragedy*, ed. by Renaud Gagné and Marianne Govers, Cambridge, Cambridge University Press, 2017, p. 203.

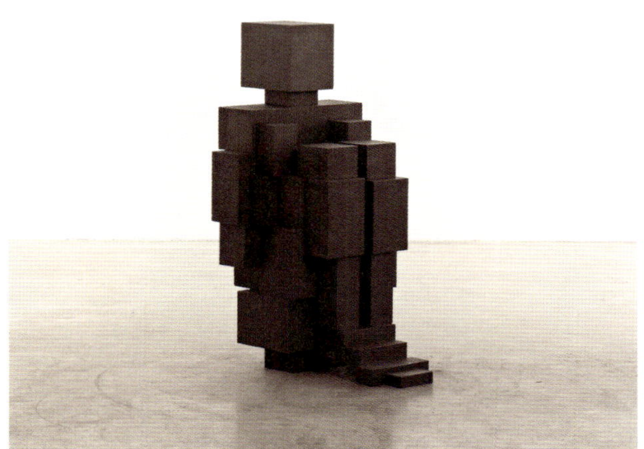

Shore, 2012
Cast iron
88 × 47 × 57 cm

In this setting, the architectonic blocks of the work rhyme with – and seem to recoil from – the fragments of pedestals and columns around the agora, remains of those monuments erected by merchants, bankers, sea captains and human traffickers of bygone days. If the title is traced back to its roots in *viere* (to bind, to twist), this *Vice* is more bound than binding, the block of the head clamped, as if in anguished introspection, between both hands. Reflecting on architecture, as Gormley does, as a second skin to the human body, the stone fragments of the ancient agora have all but subsumed the abject – and almost entirely abstracted – figure into their imperial scheme.[21]

In 'Human', the visitor ascending the staircase to the Forte Belvedere from the Boboli entrance, would have first encountered the seated figure from Gormley's *Critical Mass II* sequence, derived from his interest in the figure of the Egyptian scribe: 'one who chooses not to act in order to witness'.[22] On Delos, the scribe figure – here a blockwork entitled *Shore* (2012) – sits within the Belvedere Midas, its tightly compressed form reading almost as a silhouette against the harbour below. 'These fragments I have shored against my ruins,' wrote Eliot in the final lines of *The Waste Land*: here the words appear to echo not only through the work's title and the architectural fragments that surround it, but also through the apparent stoicism of the figure's upright, balanced, unmoved and unmoving posture.[23]

The crouching figure of *Vice II*, meanwhile, encountered moments after we step onto solid ground, seems to have witnessed too much. Setting sculpture in the Competaliast Agora, Gormley brings ancient histories of empire building and enslavement into focus; in *One & Other* in Trafalgar Square in 2009, Gormley's Fourth Plinth commission, the act of elevating living, breathing human bodies, in all the 'diversity, vulnerability and particularity of the individual in contemporary society', probed much more recent narratives of warfare, dominance and imperial expansion. One is put in mind of the woman who, participating in *One & Other*, sat similarly curled up on the 7.5-metre-high plinth, nervously observing those in the

21 W.J.T. Mitchell, 'Architecture as Sculpture as Drawing: Antony Gormley's Paragone', in *Antony Gormley: Blind Light*, London: Hayward Publishing, 2007, p. 121.
22 'An interview between Antony Gormley and Arabella Natalini', in *Antony Gormley: Human*, Florence: Forma Edizioni, 2015, p. 29.
23 T. S. Eliot, The Waste Land (1922), in *T. S. Eliot: Collected Poems 1909–62*, London: Faber & Faber, 1974, p. 69.

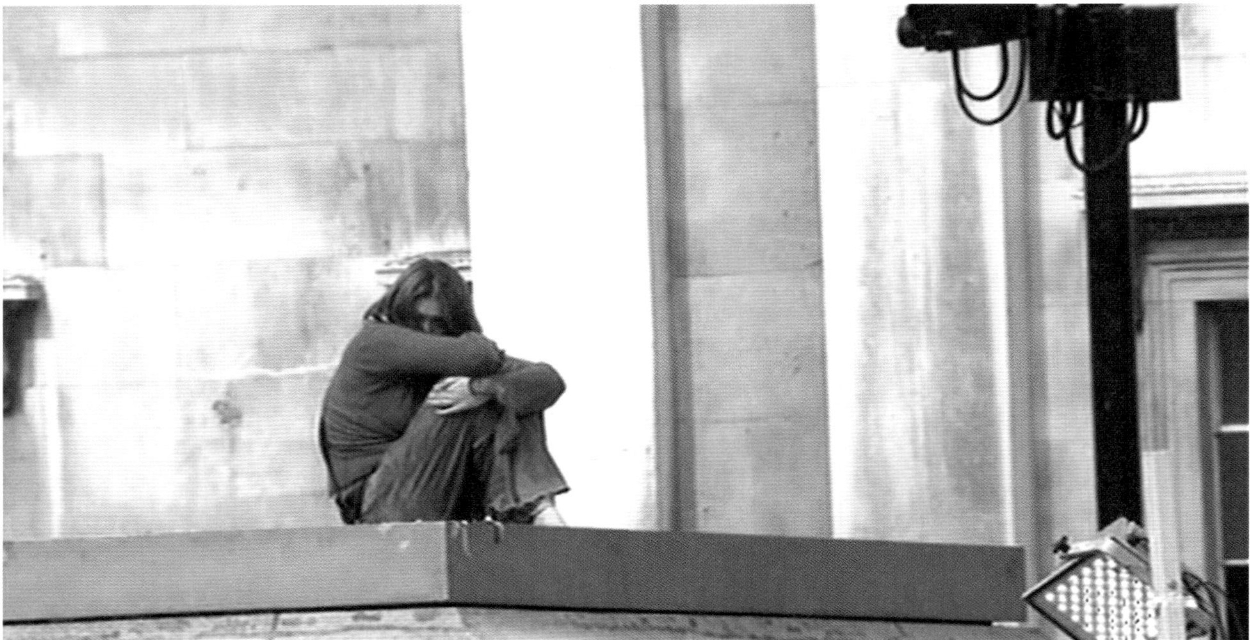

One & Other, 2009
The uninterrupted occupation of the Fourth Plinth for 100 days and 100 nights by 2,400 individuals drawn from across the UK from 6 July – 14 October 2009

The Mayor's Fourth Plinth Commission, Trafalgar Square, London

square beneath her with the intention 'to go into the fear and nervousness' as fully as she could.[24] In the siting of *Vice II* on Delos, Gormley brings agoraphobia back to its etymological roots.

Here too, Maria Hassabi's use of performing bodies seems to resonate with Gormley's siting of bodyforms, whether flesh-and-bone or cast iron, in their questioning of socio-political hierarchies. In anticipation of her presentation *Staging: Solo #2* (2018) at the Centre Pompidou, Hassabi referred to her repeated use of postures that imply "bodies falling apart – or what we call 'forgotten bodies'", those sidelined members of society who are disregarded because they fail to 'produce capital, just take up space'.[25] On Hassabi's *Plastic* at MoMA, curator Thomas J. Lax described her dancers as 'avatars of what appears to be a breakdown in a manufacturing chain'.[26] At their most abject, Gormley's sculptures could be the products of a similar such breakdown, instances of 'forgotten bodies'. Indeed, Gormley's earliest sculptural works in plaster and linen – *Figure* (1973) and *Sleeping Place* (1974) – grew from his experiences of seeing people sleeping on the railway platforms and streets of Calcutta, enveloped in cotton saris or dhotis that 'described the minimum space necessary for a person to establish shelter'.[27] Sited in the Comptetaliast Agora, haunted by the memory of one set of bodies sold to another set of bodies, the figure of *Vice II* seems to buckle under the pressure of capital, a body that would join the ranks of the 'forgotten' were it not for its value as commodity.

Discussing his site-responsive installations in Florence and on Delos, Gormley refers to his sculpture as 'a sort of acupuncture for what is there (visible and invisible)', where 'history becomes immediate and distant in equal measure through the insistent present-ness of the sculpture'.[28] There can be little coincidence that he uses

24 Claire Ross, 'Plinther Profile: No 1516 | 7 September | 12pm', in *Antony Gormley: One and Other*, London: Jonathan Cape, 2010, p. 331.
25 Harry Thorne, 'Maria Hassabi: Stillness is the Move', *Frieze*, 16 April 2018, https://frieze.com/article/maria-hassabi-stillness-move [accessed 18 April 2019].
26 Thomas J. Lax, 'Maria Hassabi: Glances', in *Maria Hassabi: Plastic*, Museum of Modern Art, New York (February 21–March 20, 2016), exhibition brochure, pp. 8–9.
27 See Gormley's statement, 'First Plaster Works' (1973), on the artist's website: http:// www.antonygormley.com [accessed 18 April 2019].
28 'The Body as Lost Subject: Conversation between Alberto Fiz and Antony Gormley', in *Antony Gormley: Time Horizon*, Milan: Electa, 2006, p. 194.

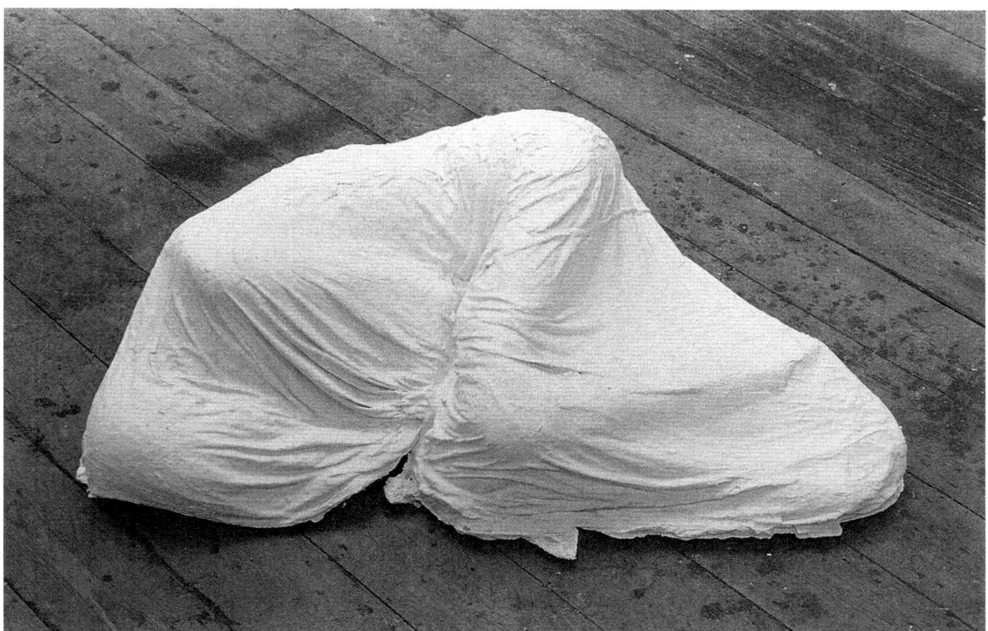

Sleeping Place, 1974
Plaster and linen
55 × 91 × 106 cm

the same metaphor with reference to post-modern dance and its relation to quotidian experience: 'a kind of acupuncture in reality'.[29] Reflecting on his interest in the work of artists such as Anna Halprin, Merce Cunningham, Simone Forti and Trisha Brown, Gormley refers to the importance of their 'looking again at the syntax of the body in space: walking, sitting, standing, and looking at it as an intrinsic emotional language without the need to carry any narrative'.[30] In their interruption of kinetics with (relative) stillness, these acts of sitting and standing demand a particularly active engagement with time, generating an 'intensive field of microperceptions' in both performer and spectator.

Anna Halprin's *Still Dance* (1998–2002) seems to resonate particularly strongly with Gormley's idea of acupuncture here. Working in collaboration with Eeo Stubblefield, Halprin performed a series of 20 *tableaux vivants* in natural environments, exploring 'the arrival at the 'still point' in which the voice of a living place is responded to by a performer'.[31] Evoking Ana Mendieta's *Silueta* series (1973–80), Stubblefield covered Halprin's naked body with clays, grasses, bark and molasses as she adopted near-motionless positions, in the presence of Stubblefield and her camera alone. 'My hope for both the performer and the viewer,' Stubblefield wrote, 'is to refine and extend the senses, to fully sense each place, triggering memories deep in the body. They are old memories and yet in their awakening comes the chance to couple again with the land'.[32] This triggering of memories 'deep in the body', and the exploration of this human body – and mind – as coextensive with the natural world, seems to share its vocabulary with Gormley's reference to his own acts of sculptural acupuncture 'revitalising the clogged energy of a site'.[33]

29 Hans Ulrich Obrist, 'The Tale of Trafalgar Square', in *Antony Gormley: One and Other*, London: Jonathan Cape, 2010, p. 244.
30 Guy Cools in conversation with Antony Gormley, Sadler's Wells, 9 December 2013.
31 Eeo Stubblefield, quoted in Helen Poynor and Libby Worth, *Anna Halprin, Routledge Performance Practitioners*, London and New York: Routledge, 2004, p. 47
32 Quoted in Arden Thomas, 'Stillness in Nature: Eeo Stubblefield's Still Dance with Anna Halprin' in Wendy Arons and Theresa J. May (eds), *Readings in Performance and Ecology*, New York: Palgrave Macmillan, 2012.
33 'An interview between Antony Gormley and Arabella Natalini', in *Antony Gormley: Human*, Florence, Forma Edizioni, 2015, p. 26.

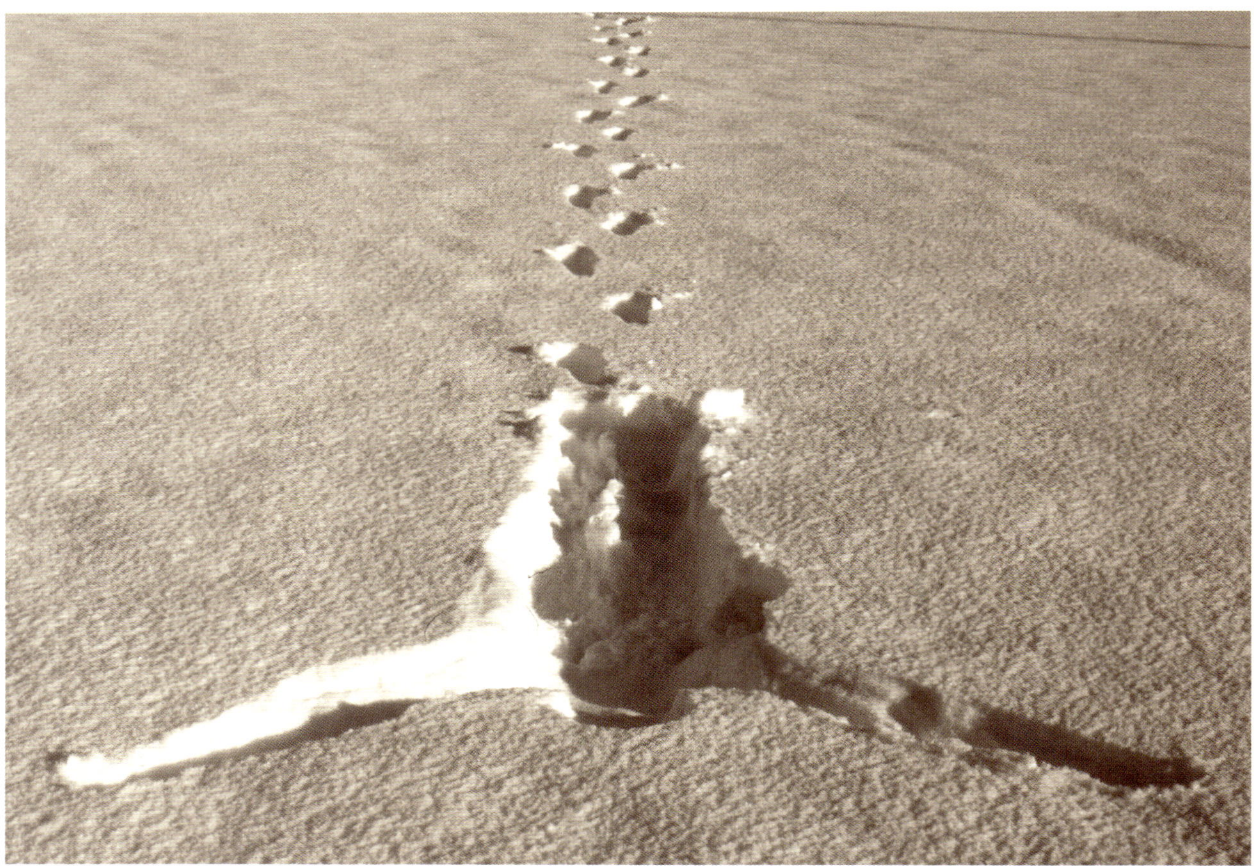

Snowfall, 1979
Temporary action,
Hampstead Heath,
London

Discussing Mendieta's 'earth-body work' in relation to his own, Gormley refers not only to her 'bringing ritual back' – which holds its own relevance in the context of Delos – but also her exploration of the body 'as a generative zone, a zone of reconciliation with the elemental, the natural, the cycles of birth and death'.[34] Mendieta's use of her own body in many of the works in the *Silueta Series* – either with her arms raised or held close to the body – find resonance even in Gormley's early photographic works. In *Snowfall* (1979), for example, Gormley captured on camera the recessed space in the snow where, moments before, his fallen body had been. Yet his siting of bodyforms in the natural landscapes and ritual spaces on Delos finds even greater affinity with Mendieta's photographs taken in the archaeological site, Yagul, in the valley of Oaxaca, Mexico, in which she used the outline of her body, rather than the body itself, as the basis of the work. 'Through my earth/body sculptures I become one with the earth', Ana Mendieta wrote in 1981: 'I become an extension of nature and nature becomes an extension of my body'.[35] This coextensive relationship between the body and the site, as in Gormley's work, involves not only the spatial but also, crucially, the temporal. With arms raised in reference to the ancient Minoan snake goddess, the biological time of Mendieta's singular – and specifically feminine – body merges with the ritual time of the static archetypal body and, in turn, with the geological time of the natural world.

34 Conversation between Antony Gormley and Martin Gayford, January 2019, unpublished transcript, Antony Gormley Studio Archive.
35 Quoted in Petra Barreras del Rio and John Perreault, *Ana Mendieta: A Retrospective*, New York: The New Museum of Contemporary Art, 1988, p. 10.

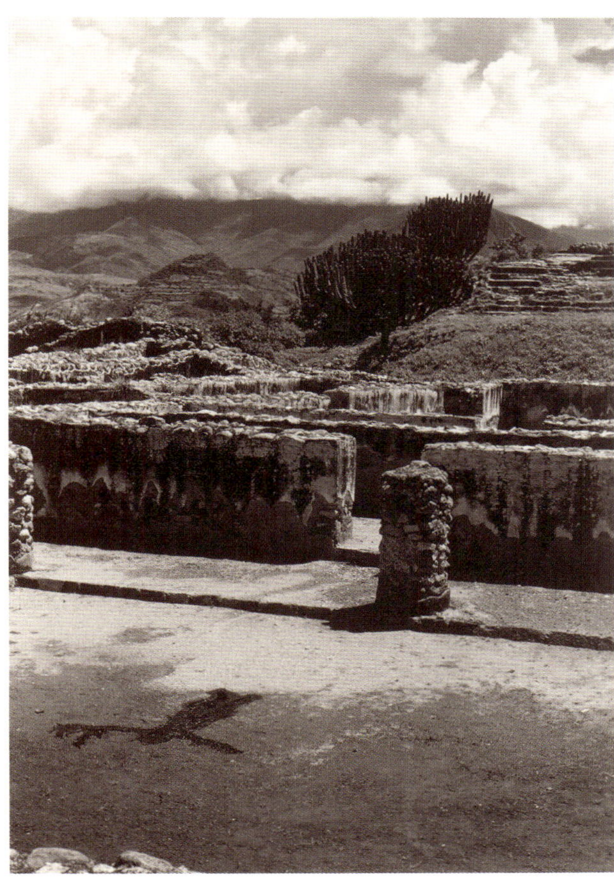

Ana Mendieta, *Untitled: Silueta Series, Mexico. From Silueta Works in Mexico, 1973-1977*, 1974

In *Exhausting Dance: Performance and the Politics of Movement*, André Lepecki borrows the language of anthropologist Nadia Seremetakis and her concept of the 'still act' to discuss the effects – and affect – of stillness in choreographed movements. For Seremetakis, the 'still act' refers to the moment in which a subject pauses and, in so doing, is able to understand – and importantly feel – the historicity of their actions:

> Against the flow of the present, there is a stillness in the material culture of historicity; those things, spaces, gestures, and tales that signify the perceptual capacity for elemental historical creation. Stillness is the moment when the buried, the discarded, and the forgotten escape to the social surface of awareness like life-supporting oxygen. It is the moment of exit from historical dust.[36]

In the context of Gormley's works on Delos, there seems to be a particular synergy between thinking of his dispersed, static bodyforms acting as 'a sort of acupuncture' and Seremetakis' image of 'the buried, the discarded, and the forgotten' being released, through the 'still act', from their 'historical dust'. To find stillness in the body – whether in casting or in the encounter with the cast – is to be confronted with one's own presence within time. Sited within the reconstituted walls of the Dionysus House, the stacked figures of the newly commissioned blockwork, *Reflect* (2017) rhyme with the reconstituted columns and with the nearby mosaic of the god of drink and dance, a composition in 'materialised pixels' from another age. As one face with two bodies – an inverted Janus – in *Reflect*,

36 C. Nadia Seremetakis (ed.), *The Senses Still: Perception and Memory as Material Culture in Modernity*, Chicago: University of Chicago Press, 1994, p. 12; André Lepecki, *Exhausting Dance: Performance and the Politics of Movement*, New York and London: Routledge, 2006, p. 15.

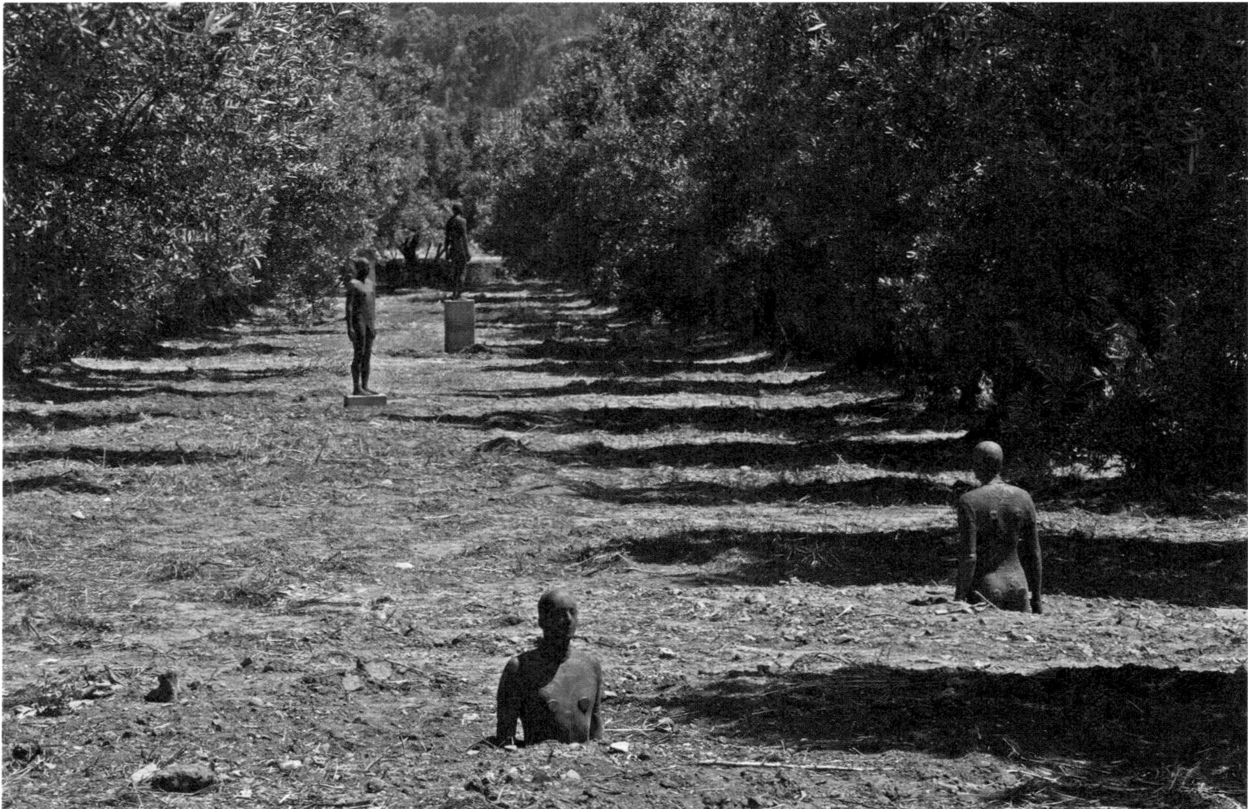

Time Horizon, 2006
Cast iron
100 bodyforms, each:
189 × 53 × 29 cm
Installation view,
'Antony Gormley:
Time Horizon',
Parco Archeologico di
Scolacium, Roccelletta
di Borgia, Catanzaro,
Italy, 2006

the head of the lower figure bends backwards, as if allowing the upper figure to gaze skywards towards its feet. While the two bodies rotate through 180 degrees, their (imagined) eyes turn towards a single point, a gravitational centre, as if, in Eliot's formulation, looking to a point '[w]here past and future are gathered'.

The 'historical dust' on Delos is, of course, every bit as physical – as geological – as it is metaphorical; Gormley's works resonate with the architectural and ritual frameworks of the sanctuary, the Theatre, even the agora, but so too do they draw attention to the natural topography of the island, sculpted by the elements over time. These cast iron figures are of the earth and of the body, given form by the very same mineral, Gormley suggests, that 'gives us our gravitational weight, gives us our trajectory through space and our magnetic field'.[37] In *Time Horizon* at the Parco Archaeologico di Scolacium, Catanzaro, Gormley dispersed these iron bodyforms across the 8.5 hectares of Roman remains, taking the mean present-day level of the earth's surface – 1.8 metres above the excavated forum – as its datum level for the heads of the sculptures. Some stood fully exposed on 2.75-metre-high plinths, others were buried to their chests or chins as if, like Winnie in Samuel Beckett's *Happy Days*, sinking in the sands of time. Where Gormley disrupted 'historical dust' in *Time Horizon* by presenting the trajectory of time as sedimentary, in Delos the placement of sculptures across the archaeological site registers his interest in the temporal more obliquely. Here, there is no fixed datum level, no single point of reference – except for the 'still point', the 'still act', of each bodyform.

37 'An interview between Antony Gormley and Arabella Natalini', in *Antony Gormley: Human*, Florence, Forma Edizioni, 2015, p. 30.

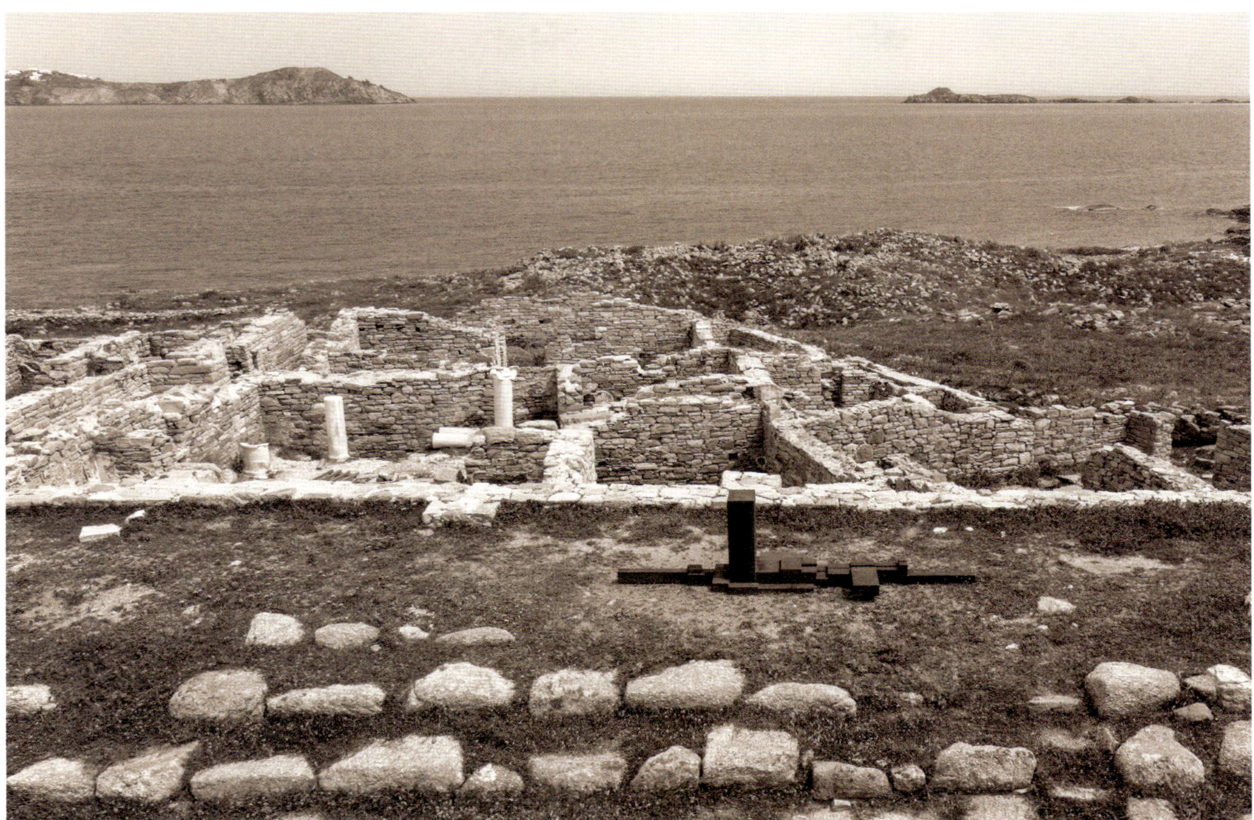

Installation view, 'Antony Gormley: SIGHT', archaeological site of the island of Delos, 2019, showing *Spread*, 2010

29 cast iron bodyforms installed across the island

Gormley speaks of the figures from *Another Time* (2011), positioned sentinel-like on the Delian coastline, as viewers and embodiments of 'the edge condition', the condition of the horizon, that limit of known time, known place, known experience. It is not only those works facing out towards, or half-submerged in the sea that seem to draw us towards the incommensurable. In some way, each face of each cuboid of each abstracted figure seems to express this same 'edge condition' – and perhaps nowhere more intensely than in the extended blockwork *Knot* and its close relative, *Spread* (2010), installed in the Stadium towards the east coast of the island. Here the blockwork lies supine, its chest extended toward the sky. Gormley refers to this work as a 'kind of anchor' for the exhibition – the first sculpture to be sited – and yet the significant weight of the work does not seem quite enough to root it to the earth.[38] 'Do not call it fixity', Eliot warned, 'where past and future are gathered'; this metric ton of iron takes on an impression of lightness in its extension towards the stratosphere, another limitless limit of our known world. 'All these obsessions I have with systems, matrices, weights and measures', says Gormley, 'are only of use in so far as they put you on that precipice or edge, or threshold – and, in the process, I hope make you feel more alive and more aware of your dancing self'.[39]

At the still point, there the dance is.

Emily Riddle is Assistant Curator at The Hepworth Wakefield, UK, and the recipient of the NEON Curatorial Award 2016

38 Conversation between Antony Gormley and the author, 21 February 2019.
39 Martin Caiger-Smith, *Antony Gormley*, New York, Rizzoli, 2017, p. 419.

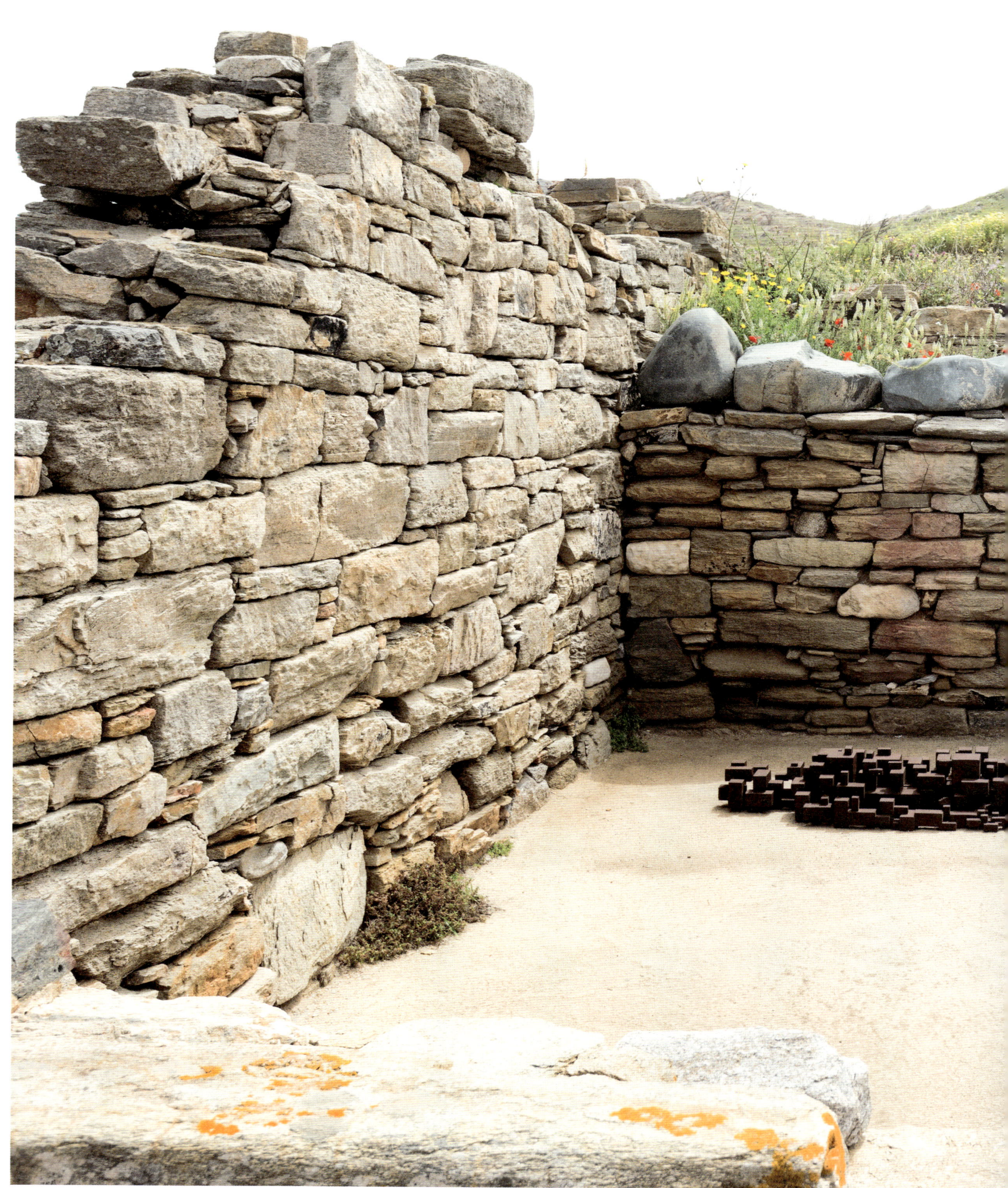

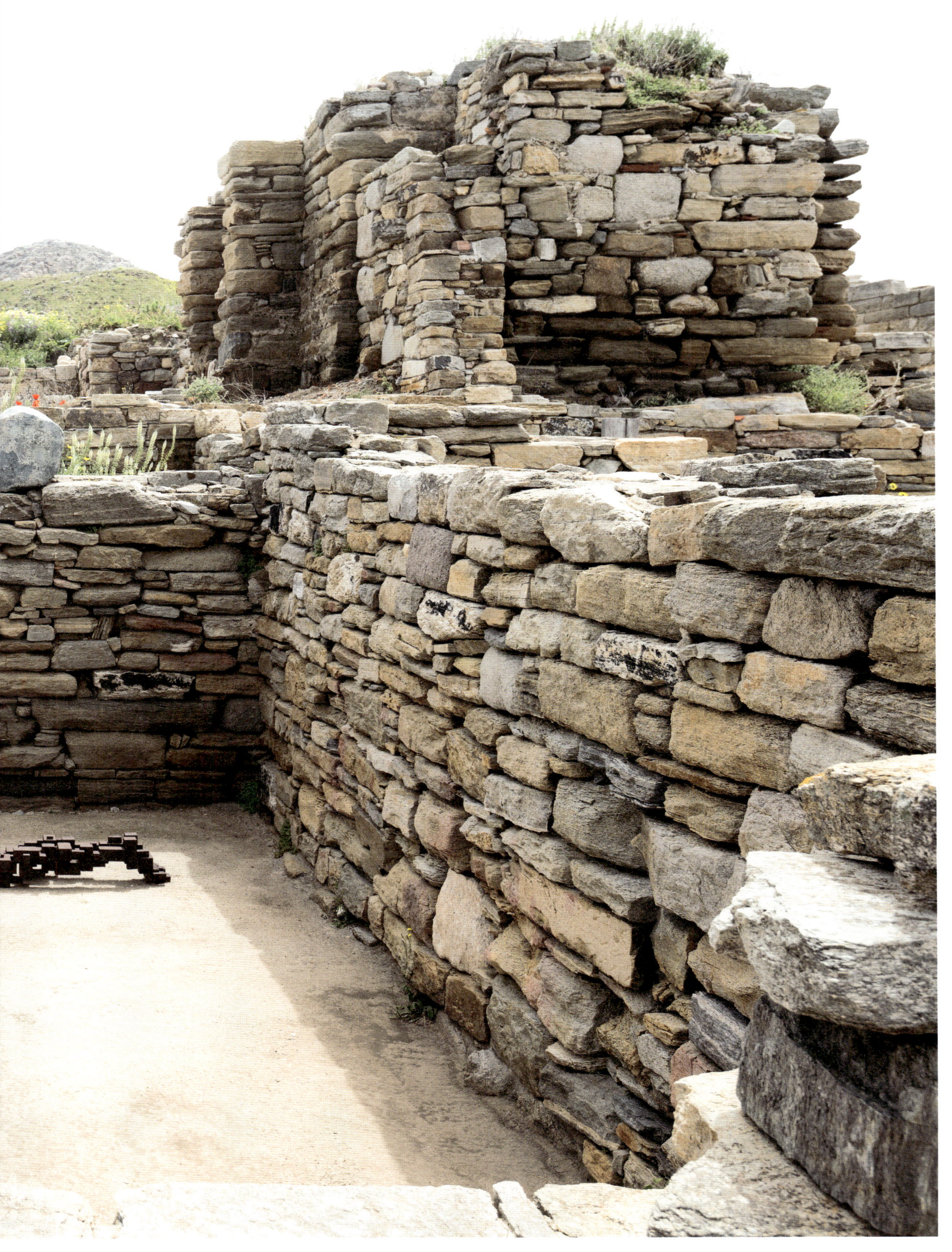

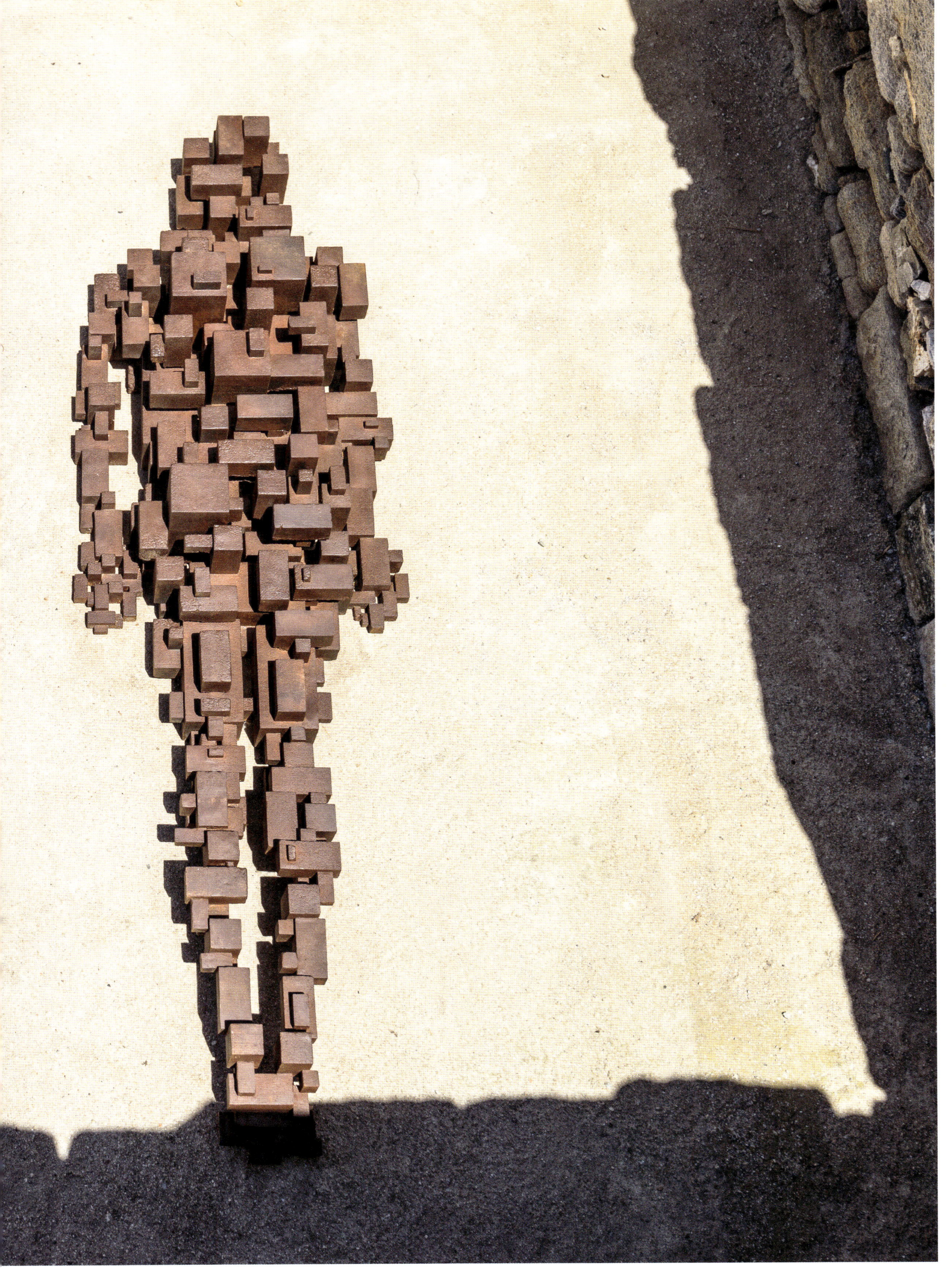

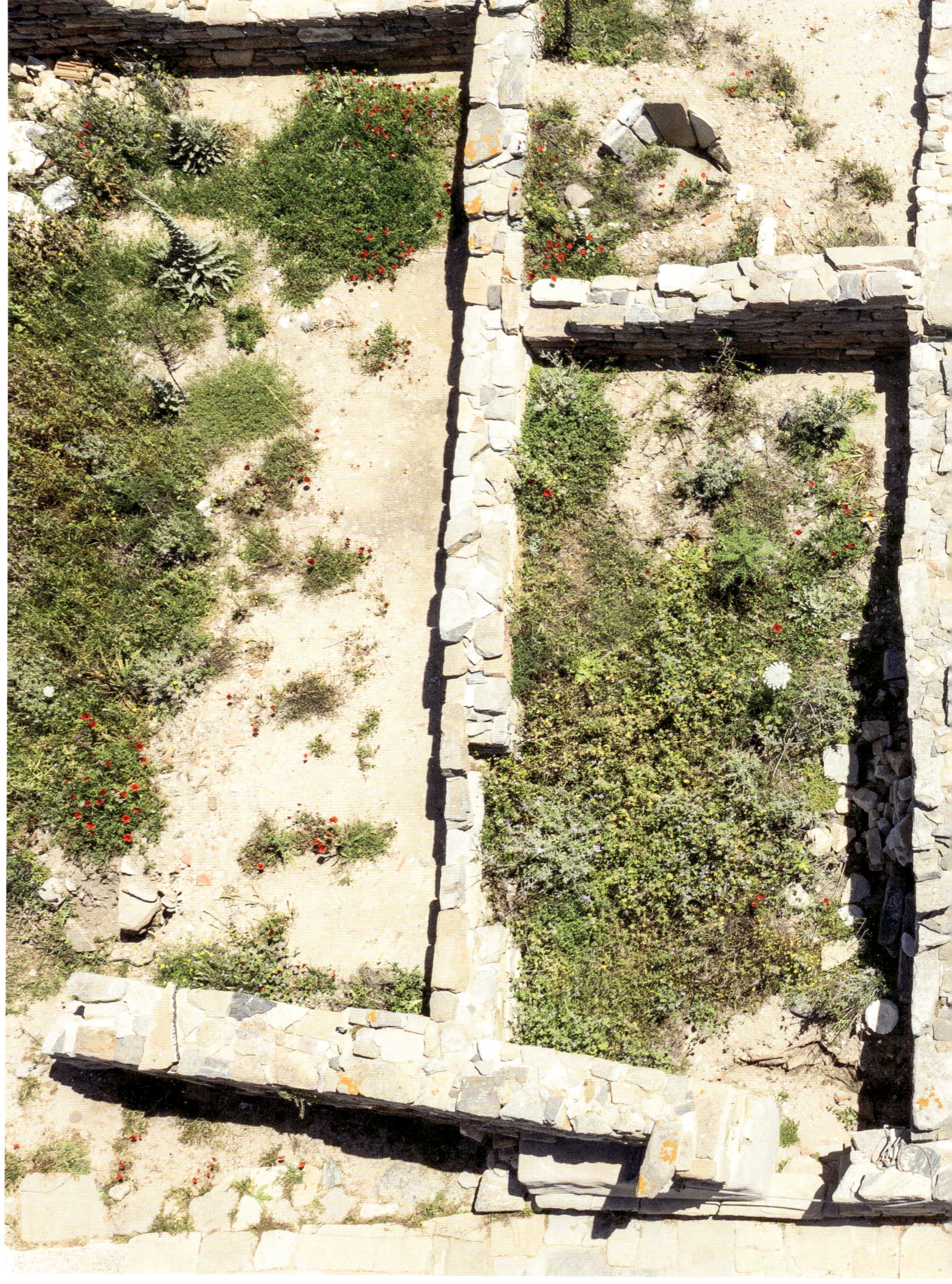

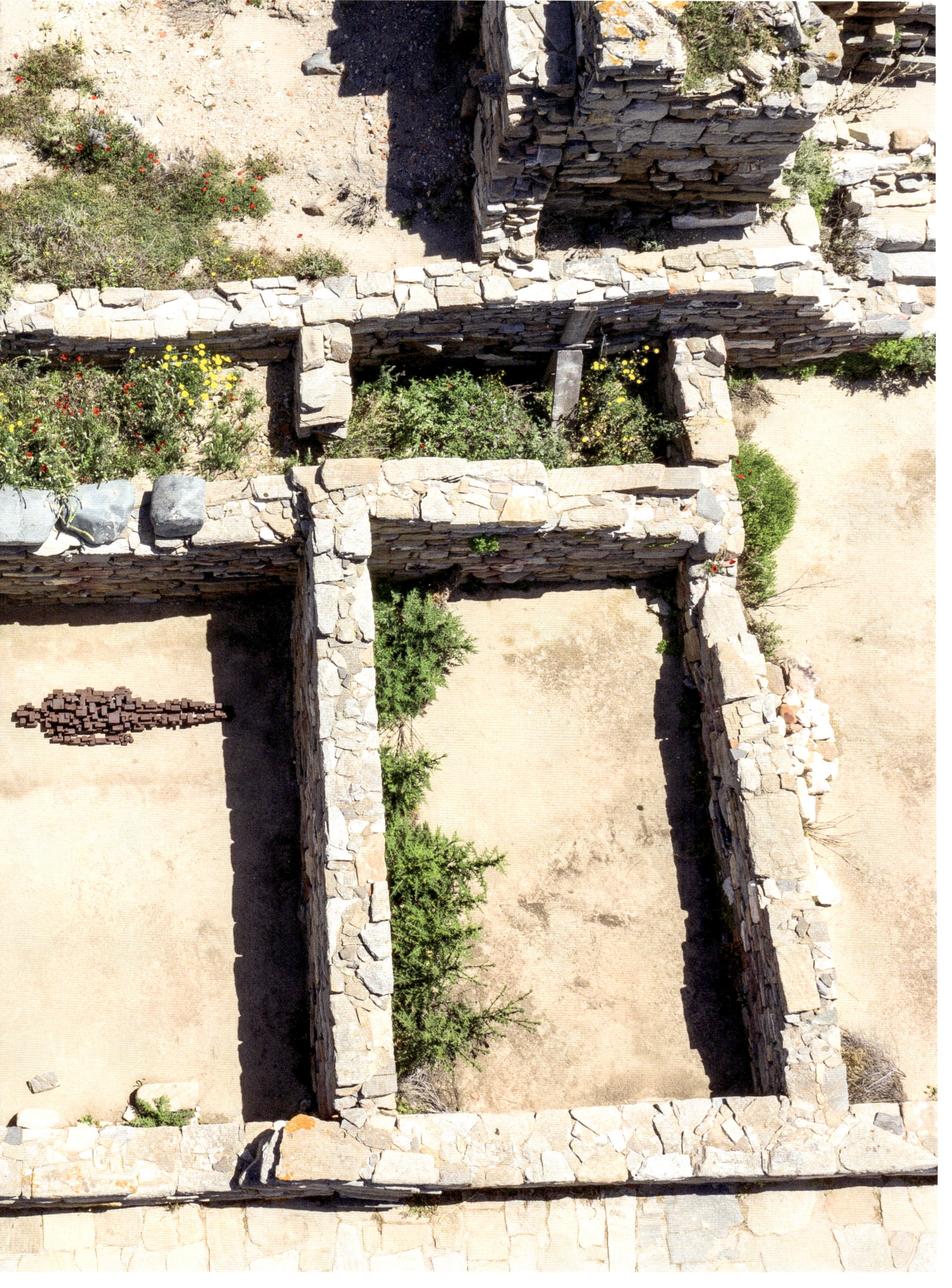

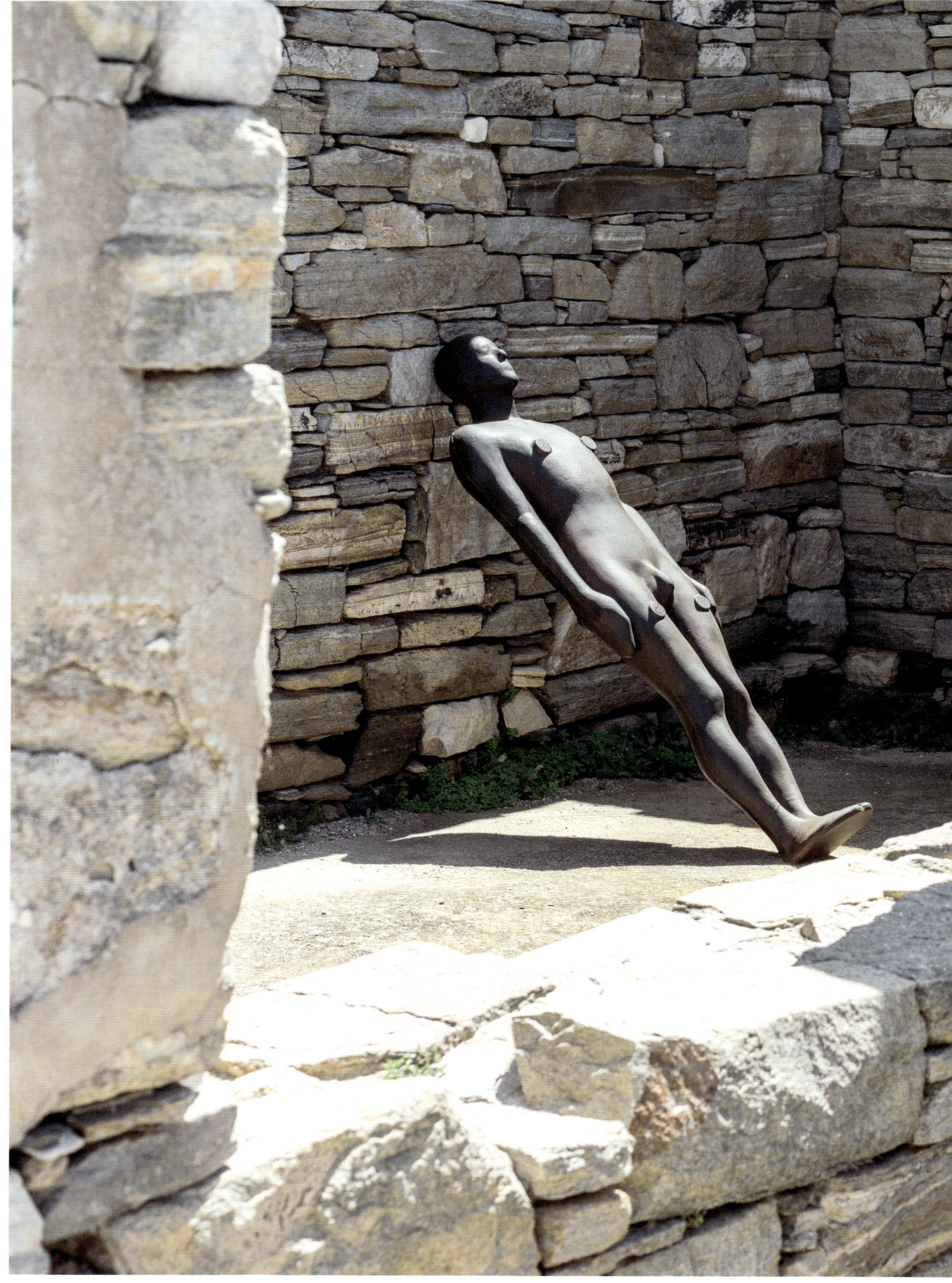

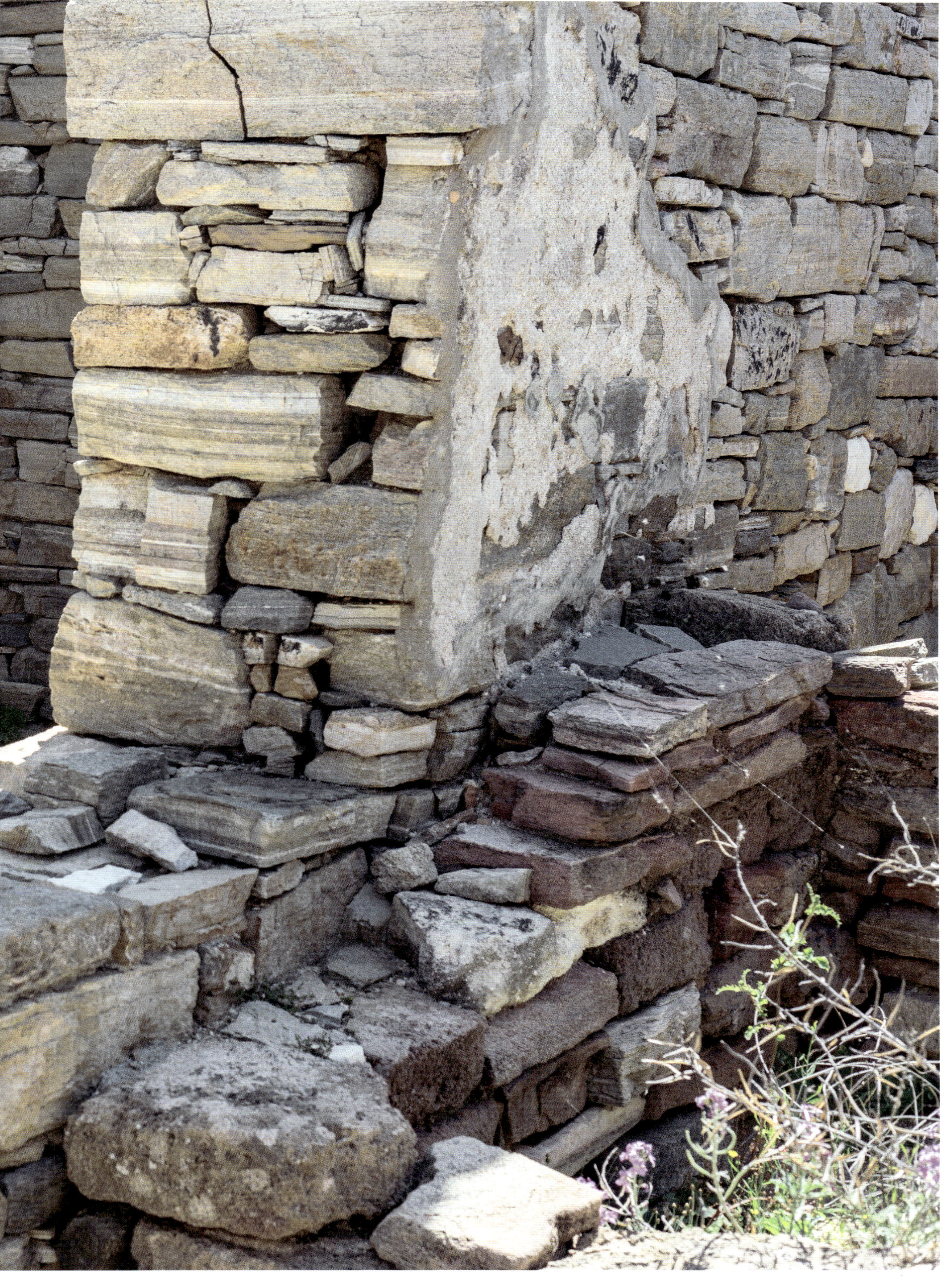

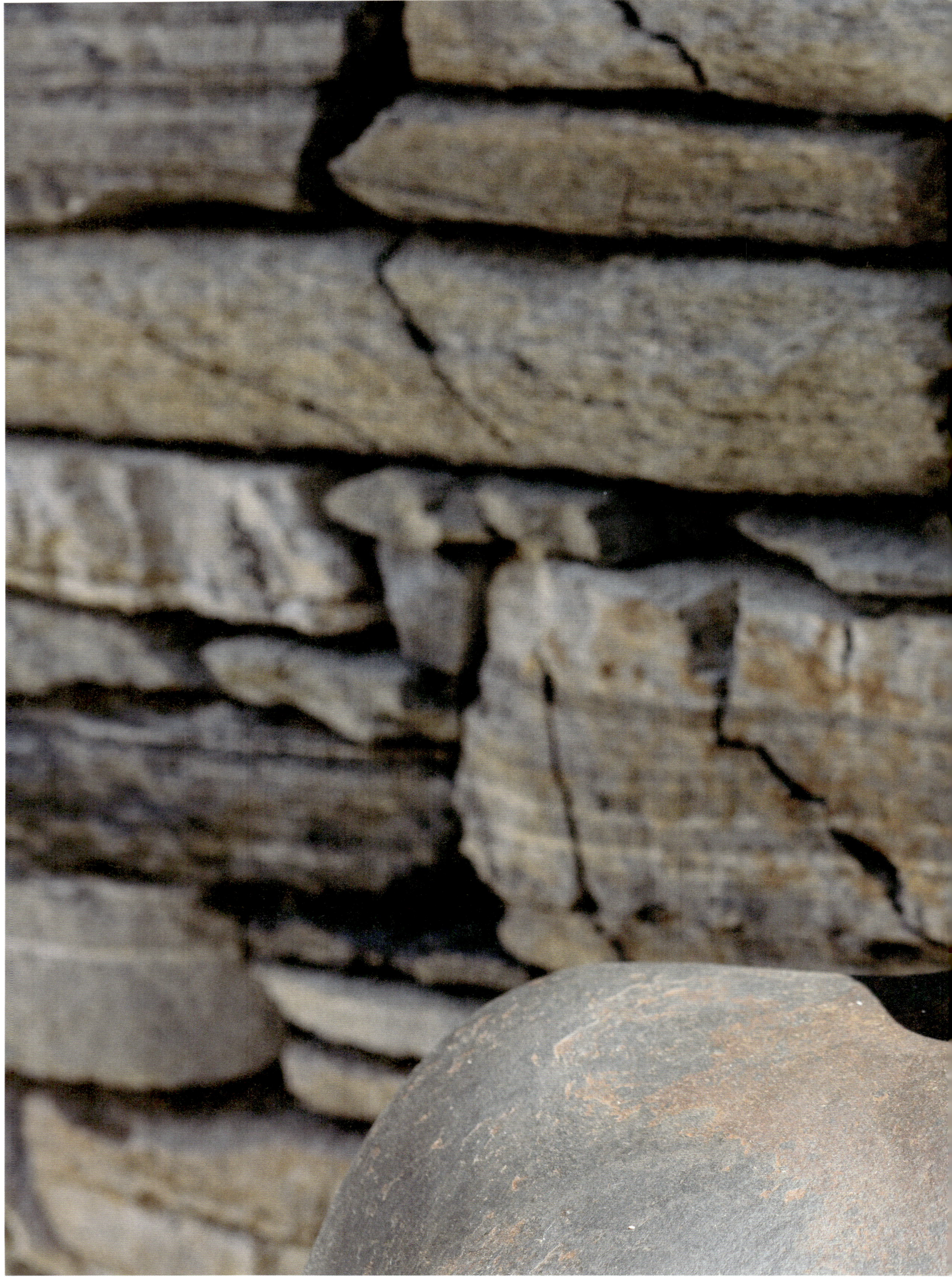

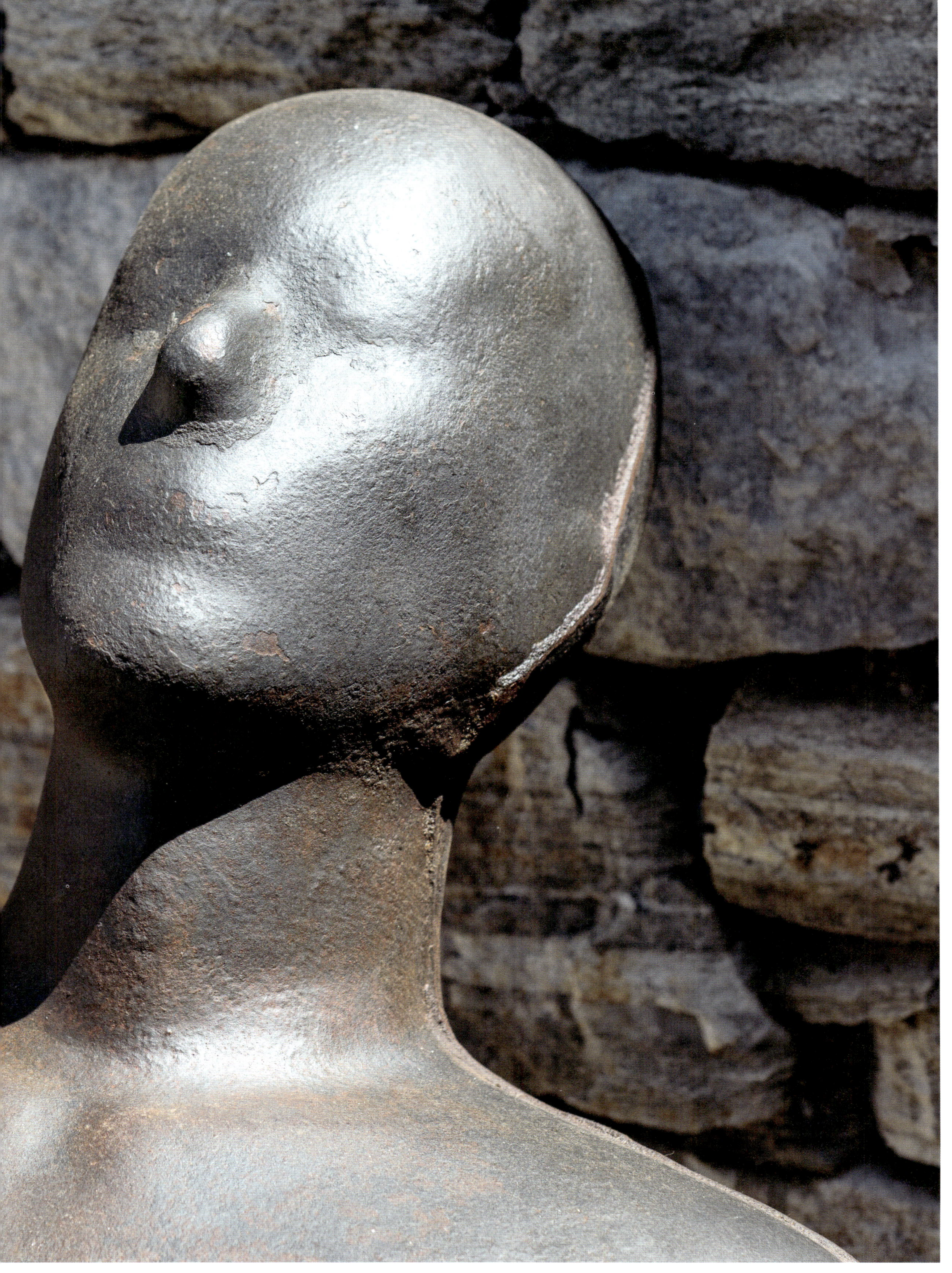

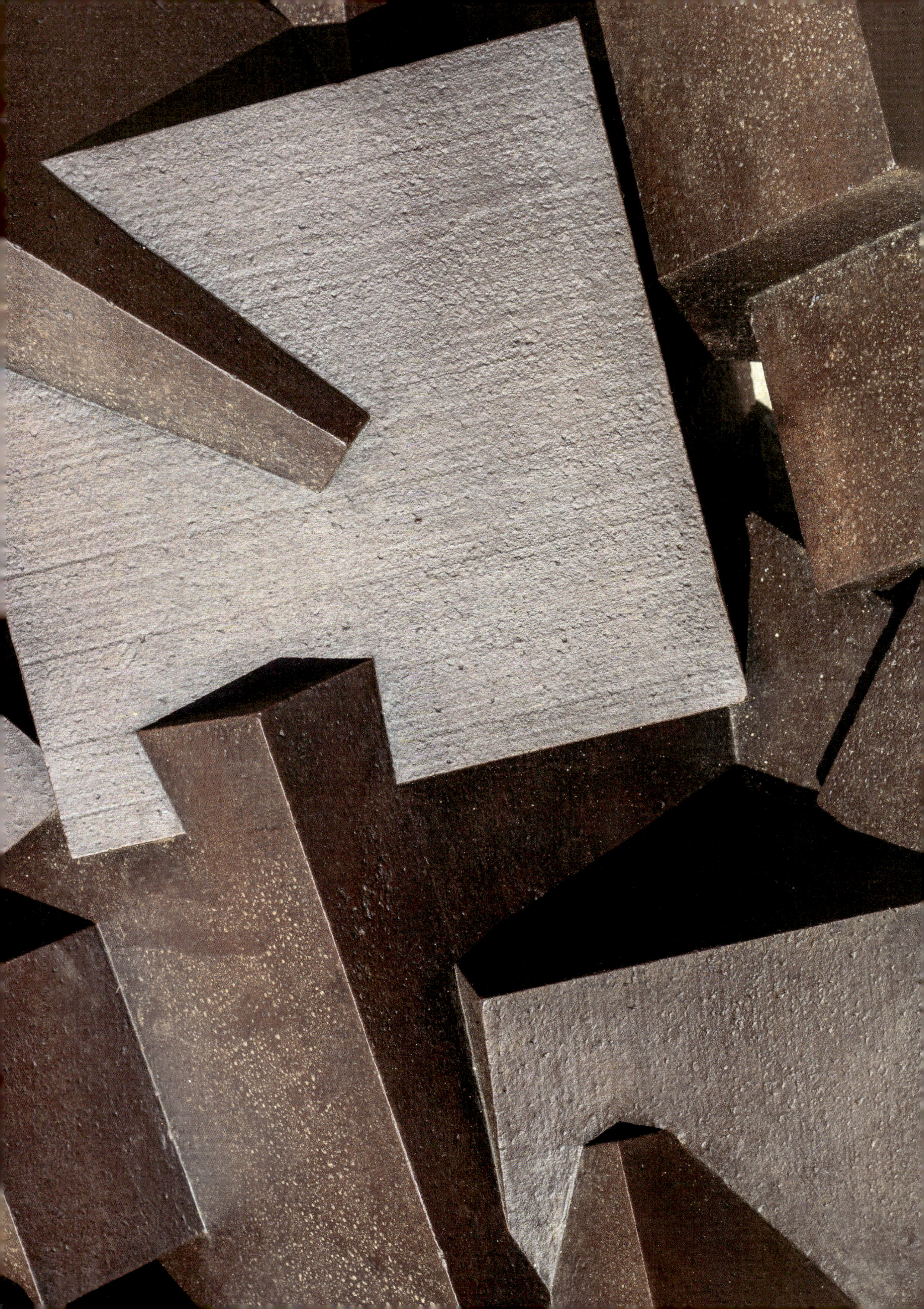

ANTONY GORMLEY IN CONVERSATION WITH IWONA BLAZWICK AND ELINA KOUNTOURI

I.B. What were your first impressions of Delos?

A.G. The thing that shocked me about it was how small, how barren, how treeless it was, but then that first impression gave way to an immediate feeling about the light and the geology. That first walk across these windswept outcrops of granite shaped by wind, sun and sea spray took me back to the time of Argos and those myths before history, as if you might expect to see a Cyclops or a three-headed monster around the next corner. That wasn't to do with the human-built structures; it was more a feeling of a concentrated time in a place where there is little to distract you other than rock, sea and sky.

I.B. What about those traces of human civilisation? Delos is quite densely populated with traces of activity – of trading, religious rituals, gymnastics and theatre.

A.G. From the top of Mount Kynthos you see the whole topography and you notice how utterly dependent on its harbours Delos was in its heyday. The archaeological site is like an amphitheatre surrounding the main harbour. This relatively small site is surrounded by this brutal, unrelenting geology. It reminds me of Pasolini's film *Oedipus Rex* and Dalí and Buñuel's *Un Chien Andalou*.

It is quite surprising that Delos is the third great sacred site of Greece, when topographically, it isn't as imposing as Naxos, Ios, Paros or Amorgos, or any of the outlying islands of the Cyclades. Yet it's the very fact that the island is so low-lying that allows it to become the turning point: in a Daoist way, it is the void at the centre of this constellation of islands around which all these myths, stories and histories circulate.

Perhaps it's the way history is written and the way that human beings make places: there must be a degree of blankness.

I.B. You're interested in deep time perhaps, rather than the fast pace of technology and culture. From 3200 BC, the human occupation of the Aegean accelerates. It has this very slow entry into occupational settlement, and then by 500 BC, it becomes the commercial centre of the ancient world. It became a hive of activity. Apparently, they could sell 10,000 slaves in one day. In the way that you've responded to Delos, it feels like you're more interested in this kind of deeper mythic time.

A.G. What I find moving is the relationship between the Hellenic and geological stories: the part to whole relationship of those shattered tors and the deconstructed geometry of the buildings. In a structure like the Grotto of Hercules, Hellenes, in the 3rd-Century BC, copied the Cyclopean architecture of Mycenae to make the roof enclosure inside a natural rock cleft, in a kind of postmodern gesture. If you stand outside the Grotto and look down, everything is laid out in front of you: the Stadium, all the *stoa*, the seven great shrines to Apollo. It is like a viewpoint from which to reflect on the human wish to impose its story and history on geological time.

I.B. And when you go inside Hercules' Grotto, you become confined by rock. You can quite easily not look out; you feel that sense of removal from society. There have always been figures that are isolated from society: seers, prophets, hermits or priests. They must be removed or remove themselves.

A.G. Yes, like Milarepa or Zarathustra...

I.B. Looking out, you are left with a reminder of the obdurate quality of nature – that it will abide while we come and go. It's astonishing that human civilisation on Delos had completely disappeared by 100 AD. It's almost a kind of Ozymandian monument, isn't it?

A.G. Yes. The magnificent buildings on Delos were very deliberately taken apart – the columns laid down on the ground and the beautifully hewn stones that formed their foundations taken away. Only ground plans of the buildings are left, the walls and pediments are laid out a stone at a time and every stone is numbered. For the archaeologists, these are literally touchstones from which they can recreate what was once there. It's an extraordinary collective act of imaginative reconstruction. I find that the most poignant and beautiful thing is that Delos is a ground plan.

I keep going back to the dialogue between the works of human kind and the work of the elements. It is, I agree, an Ozymandian, '*Look upon the works [of man] and despair!*' We know that all our structures, whether they're digital or made of calcium carbonate, can be deconstructed. And especially now, when time is speeding up and the achievability of building structures of information, at least in virtual terms, is almost limitless. To see an ancient centre as if a vast deconstructed database, with all its bits laid out and numbered, is both a message and a warning.

E.K. To what extent do you think that your works in these temples and the dwellings, and around the island of Delos, are able to act as a catalyst for the imagination?

A.G. I don't want the works brought in here to appear as if a reconstruction or re-enactment – they are from our time. I'm really interested in how they might both challenge and reconnect with the lost memory of sculpture that would have populated the site for over 500 years, without ventriloquising the life of the island back then.

In quantum time there can be no beginning. Carlo Rovelli believes that temporal sequence is a neurological human construct, and we think of the big bang as starting from a singular point, but it isn't, it's everywhere. Borges describes it very beautifully: that eternity or god is an emerging circle whose centre is everywhere, and whose circumference is nowhere. We have to think of time in that way but we're constantly projecting our dread of mortality onto time, making it into a linear construct. That's one of the challenges of taking on historical sites that are connected with historic narratives, you have to insist that these sites and the interactions with them are present stories and afford direct experience.

I.B. On the other hand, I think what's really distinct about your work for Delos compared to your other projects is that it's neither the white cube nor a *tabula rasa*, but many of your outdoor works have been in situations where there's a kind of expanse, like *Another Place* on Crosby Beach, for instance.

A.G. Yes – emptier, not inscribed.

I.B. The works in those previous situations have been like a unifying field where one reality is layered onto to another. What is distinct about Delos, and links to your exhibition 'Human' at the Forte Belvedere in Florence in 2015, is that each piece has a very particular relation to the geometries and the spatial dynamics of 29 different locations. How did you decide where each piece would go?

A.G. It's a kind of dowsing. You're moving through a landscape which already has this dialogue between human activity and the given elemental topography. It was the result of the first journey round the island. We set out towards the Stadium and the experience of the far and the near, of feeling how vistas open up and how one's relation to the horizon constantly changes were very present. That outcrop of Plakes Peak immediately caught my eye as a skyline that reveals the geology and the low-lying nature of the island itself, encouraging you to look out.

At the Stadium, the three-stepped nature of the dais (which I imagine was where the spectators stood to watch the games) and its relationship to the horizon and the sea, made me think of the work *Spread*, 2010, which is about being close to the ground. Its torso becomes a monolith that presses the chest down onto the earth. The head and the legs are extended and compliment the long, flat platform of the Stadium. I wanted it to be like a marker or an altar.

At the Gymnasium we found an empty plinth for the statue of an athlete. We know that there was a whole industry of both bronze and marble sculptures of athletes, and I wanted to put a work there that could be seen in relation to the three arches on the south side of the Gymnasium. We decided to place *Bearing III*, 1997, there, to celebrate the fact that bodies come out of bodies. It also represents a fundamental theme in my work: the connection between the darkness of the body and deep space. *Bearing III* has a sarcophagus-like lower body and its yearning, stretching neck and head have disappeared inside the genital area of a body that is crouching on the lower body's shoulders, as if giving birth. It looks up into the place of generation, as into the night sky.

From that same position you are invited to look at another work on the same axis, *Another Time XV*, 2011, standing on a bun-shaped rock, looking out to sea.

I set the terms of the show by those three works: an idea about here and there, or place-ness and distance. Notions about intimacy carried over distance by another kind of looking: an acupuncture of place.

I.B. Your work is in a context of statuary which set a paradigm for 2,000 years of sculpture and pursued a convention of authority, power, the idol, the memorial, by presenting the figure as something to be worshipped, which was separate from humans. Your work draws from that language, and yet also does the opposite. Even though it's always masculine, it isn't masculinity as a vector of power or of patriarchy, it's masculinity in a universal sense, in a humbler relation with elements and with time. There is a sense of fragility and mortality; of being simultaneous with the body of the viewer.

A.G. My return to the body in sculpture is to ask, 'what is a body?'. It starts from the notion of being uncertain about what a human body is and what it might mean. A human being is a place of becoming, it isn't an already known object.

Each sculpture is a displacement of space that looks familiar – like the space that the statue occupied but isn't a statue, nor an idealisation, a portrait or a freeze frame in a mythological or historical narrative. Nor does it underpin systems of deistic or political power. So, what is it? I am interested in the beginnings of art and that primal gesture of the standing stone. It is a marker in space, but also in time, as something that sits outside of life but has this dialogue with life. It is in no sense an equivalent for a human body, and yet there is this implicit relationship with the human body. You are drawn towards the space that the standing stone occupies, often in relation to the position of a heavenly body at the equinox. I want to replace all those burdens that the human image took on in terms of underpinning temporal or sacred power and replace the representation of stories with reflexivity.

In the context of an archaeological site, that potential for reflexivity is enormous. Delos is a place where you're left with fragments, not the whole story. The work can act like a catalyst for a reflection on the human project generally.

E.K. Bearing in mind that the space offers itself up to intense physical, spiritual and intellectual connections, on what level do you believe this installation, in a different way from exhibitions in other contexts, encourages its visitors to connect with the works within their surroundings, whether in a bodily, aesthetic or metaphysical way?

A.G. Obviously you are starting with a context rich in traces of human activity but there is something special about bringing sculpture to an island. It already has an identity in relation to its neighbouring islands and the sea. I wanted to work with the island as a 'body in relation' as much as with its historical remains and get the visitor to really move around this body and explore it physically. The sculptures could be seen as 'stations' or stops in the physical engagement of moving around the island while providing, like standing stones, markers in space. Hopefully they are also invitations to pause and in that temporal space they offer contemplative tools.

I.B. To what extent have the *kouroi* been a formal influence on your work?

A.G. For Hellenic culture, Egypt was, in a way, the classical world. They took what you see in the Tomb of Imhotep, or the Tomb of Thutmoses II: the guardian figure with one foot in front of the other and their back foot completely flat on the ground. This is not a depiction of walking but a sign of potential movement. The *kouroi* are interesting to me as the beginning of this story of the journey of Western sculpture that includes Michelangelo's *Slaves* and Bernini's *Apollo and Daphne*. That story also connects with the *Laocoon* and Gotthold Lessing's notion of the temporal: that the greatest challenge for the sculptor is to choose a narrative moment that is the product of everything that's already happened, and the seed of everything that will happen. The *kouroi* are a prophecy of the journey that Western sculpture will make, that ends with Rodin's *The Burghers of Calais*: a story that I reject. The extraordinary thing about sculpture is that it is still and silent and confronts us with our nervous movement: that's what it does best. I accept the stasis of sculpture, its gravity and remoteness; I use mass, or the lack of it, consciously.

There's a poignancy about the museum here on Delos with its blue walls, stone floor and these pale, often headless sculptures. There is a feeling that these statues are the 'orphans': the ones that didn't go to Athens, the ones that were abandoned by the Parisian archaeologists – there's something touching about that.

In a time of mass mobility, when each of us is either a tourist, a migrant or a refugee and we are all looking for distraction, sculpture can reconnect us to place and time and with the earth. The work in the museum, *Shift II*, 2000, simply lies on the floor touching the ground; it accepts entropy and gravity and hopefully encourages us to feel them.

E.K. Some people are sceptical about placing contemporary art inside the mythological site at Delos and would like to keep the site sacred, free from contemporary intervention. It is a question of how we view and how we work with our heritage. What should the relationship be between archaeological sites and contemporary art?

A.G. We cannot deny the presence of the past and must make it vibrant and relevant. The givens of the past are not fixed. Reconstruction is not the only way to approach history. The Tibetans meditate in the graveyard: an idea that is not morbid, it's about confronting time in a different way. The beauty of Delos is that these grand buildings have now literally become ground plans for an imaginative rebuilding. As such they are open to interpretation and can be a ground for new thought and feelings.

I.B. Your sculptures are composed of forms that emphasise a kind of abstract understanding of space and the architectonics of space. With the 'Blockworks' you become much more aware of the structure of the walls around you, the points of pressure and the edges of things. These works generate a zone of experience like a Euclidian plane, making you aware of all the horizontals and verticals and how the forces of entropy – the wind, the sun and the elements – act on these absolute human abstractions. Each piece engages you in that process of physical experience and conceptual thought.

A.G. I like what you just said. I like the fact that in some of the walls there are found stones: they are not dressed and made into Euclidian blocks but are boulders taken as found objects and made into a collage: a part/whole dialogue that unites the raw and the cooked. It's tempting to make the connection with Machu Picchu, but it's actually a very different kind of place-making. On Delos there is an acceptance and celebration of the predetermined nature of a large stone, which is then given a place in the construction of a perfect surface, where its flat face has a real purpose in the wall.

I also like the idea that all architecture has to have a datum base – an absolute horizontality from which to then construct the vertical. The way that we construct a world is out of bits of rock or bits of information. This is the beginning of civilisation. I am interested in the urban grid: modernism is determined by the grid – the unit, the mean, the measure – whether it's Mondrian or Carl Andre. I think Delos is a fantastic place to think about that dialogue of part to whole, and the necessary ways that human kind has found to construct a world out of chaos.

All my work plays with that idea. About a third of it accepts that the body is a found organic object that we find our existence in. A third of it says, no, the body is a construct and is subject to the same forces that we use to construct the world. Another third of the work says, no, the body is actually just energy: a system that we believe that we understand at our peril.

I accept that the body has been in art for as long as we have been conscious. The first attempts at registering it as an image are indexical. Our ancestors saw the tracks the animals left in the mud, sand and snow, they recognised that these tracks brought to mind the presence of something, and we began to make hand stencils. The original indexical image was probably the shadow: the double that has power and presence. The shadow told us something about what we already were that we didn't know. It was necessary to rethink the shadow in the hand stencils in order to make ourselves.

I was born into a body. I use it as my found object and as the lost subject of art; an investigative tool. I use my life as a test site. I use the body as an unknowable space that is connected to the shadow that I can feel from the inside. I'm not interested in the realistic portrait or in the imposition of the ideal. My work starts from the other side of appearance where the body is as unknowable as the cosmos. I feel that I have a duty to bear witness to it. There's nothing special about my body. I use it as a particular example of a common human condition. I want to use it to ask questions, not to tell stories. What is the relationship of mind to body? What is the relationship of body to space? What is the relationship of our skin to our perceptual bounding condition: the horizon?

E.K. Is there an urgency to reach out to our historical past to understand the future? Is the future reflected in this project?

A.G. All of sculpture is about the future. It asks us to think about those life forms that will follow our own: these objects, these sculptures, are industrial fossils, in other words, indexical reminders of a human moment that has been taken out of time, that then exists in space but can connect, later, with another time, with people who haven't yet been born, with life forms that we can't yet imagine. That's what I believe the power of sculpture is. It's not about decorating the world. It's not about somehow making an awesome distraction. It's a way of interrogating present time in relation to time at large.

I.B. It's interesting how your sculpture uses gesture. I mean, it's very different from looking at say, Baroque or Renaissance Italian sculpture where you might have figures wrestling with beasts or each other.

A.G. My sculptures are about being, not doing. They're not a representation of an action. They are the representation of an embodied state.

I.B. Yes, that's the perfect way to define them.

E.K. This exhibition will be viewed by thousands of people, many of whom will be visiting the ancient city without prior knowledge of your work. What would you like them to remember or think about the work? Are you hoping for a spontaneous, sensory response to the work or an intellectual one?

A.G. The sculptures are places that you can imaginatively occupy. They are empty signifiers until you give them what they lack – and they lack thought, feeling, movement – they are inert things in the world. They are invitations for you to project your feeling, your thoughts, your potential for movement. Walk around them and somehow begin to work with them. Sculpture can return you to yourself and your own first-hand experience.

I.B. You're male. The masculine figure is freighted with a history of abusive power. How do you then counter the criticism that the sculptures are a continuation of male hegemony?

A.G. Well, I would say that these works are all uncertain of their power, and they're loitering rather than representing any security about their place in the world.

I.B. Dislodging the universal as the male... Were you consciously embracing a kind of feminist critique?

A.G. I think the work is more about time than it is about sexuality. But I want the work to have a claim to truth, I accept my found gender. This is an examination of human 'being'. Mortality is more important than sexual designation. The job that I've set myself is the examination of what a human being is. I don't want to talk about something that I am not able to experience. Having said that, I'm very sympathetic to the feminist agenda and the critique of patriarchy in particular. I would say that the work has attempted to unpick the patriarchal and its rhetoric, but feel that it doesn't determine me. And I would hope that that was true of the sculpture as well. *Bearing III*, for example, addresses sexuality in terms of gestation. I tend to sidestep into other forms of generation: pathogenesis, mitosis, cell division, how a singular object reproduces by doubling itself. It plays with the mirror stage: the separation of the self and the not-self, or the notion of the anima and the id.

I.B. Your choice to work in iron, which then rusts, has often been controversial.

A.G. I've never wanted to use bronze or marble simply because they're so heavily freighted with historic statuary. I use a material that is both of the earth, but also of our time. Iron is an industrial material but at the same time, it is the core of our planetary home and gives it its specific gravity, its magnetic field, and that keeps us on our trajectory through space. Of course, it does rust, but I think the *wabi-sabi* side of the work is really important.

I.B. *Wabi-sabi*?

A.G. The Japanese principle about beauty in imperfection and the action of time on objects. We're often prejudiced against the organic response of materials to the elements, iron in particular. In Japan the relationship of material to the atmosphere – to wind, rain, sun, snow – is appreciated, is an aesthetic. That's equally important for me. When you look at most works in bronze or highly polished stainless steel, you're aware that the patinated or mirror surface is essentially an artificial creation, but these rusted works have an evolving, organic surface that is the story of their journey through time. At any time, you can decide that you're going to intervene, and you can either brush all the rust off and bring it indoors, or you can cover it with wax and oil. At a certain stage the rust does fix; it creates its own final surface; the bleeding doesn't last forever.

E.K. Similarly, the surface of the stone sculptures shows that they have a past. Even though they've only recently been positioned on Delos, the impression is that your works have been exposed to the elements over time.

A.G. The surface of the sculpture is inscribed with the journey in time. It also tells you about the way that the work is made – the rounds and squares where you see where the molten metal was introduced into the mould or where the excess metal was cut. In material terms, the work acknowledges its place in time and the history of its making. Both are very important.

E.K. It's quite an intense effort and physically exhausting for visitors to scale the 150-metre staircase up Mount Kynthos to view the works there.

A.G. Yes, but it's worth it. You see many things up there that you can't see anywhere else: the overall topography of the island, and the way that the southern end is so barren, the natural rock formations, the loose rock, the drystone walls built to contain the sheep.

I'm passionate about that staircase – you can see it clearly from the harbour. It's the most indelible mark of human intervention on the whole island. Some of those steps are cut into the rock, some of them are man-made. It connects with the prehistoric gesture of Stonehenge where blue stones from Pembrokeshire in Wales were brought to the middle of the Salisbury Plain, or to the alignments in Carnac. A wish to mark indelibly a given geology with the will of human imagination.

I put a 'Rooter' work, *Signal II*, 2018, on the landing of the staircase where it functions like an aerial against the sky. It is an invitation for you to walk up. From the top you will see the far distance marked by the mean of an *Another Time* approachable along a stony path. There are fragile little piles of stones – cairns – that people have left as their sculptural tribute to the island. Looking down, you feel that this is the place of Zeus. You see the dome of the sky, the hugeness of this earth and feel your own smallness.

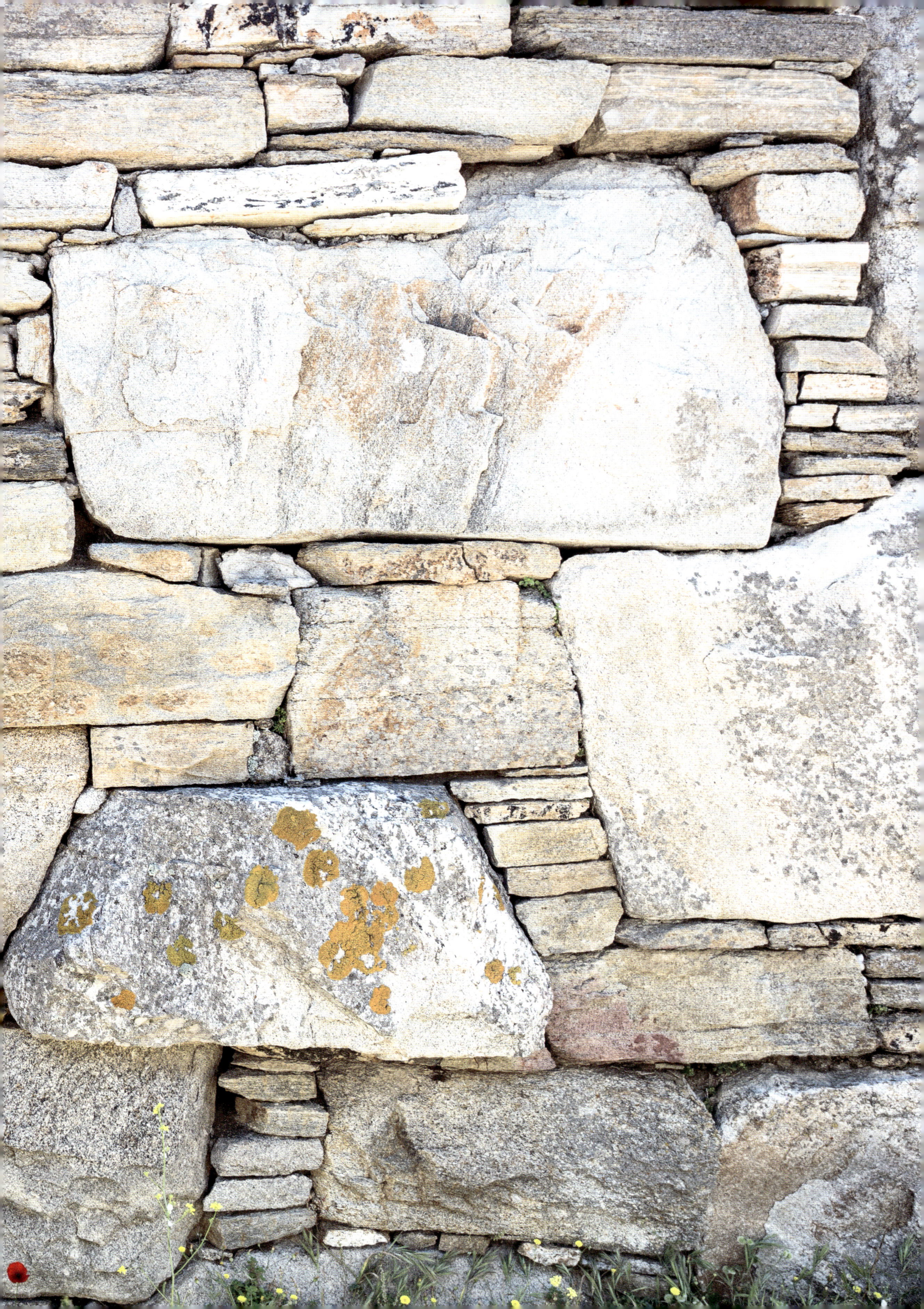

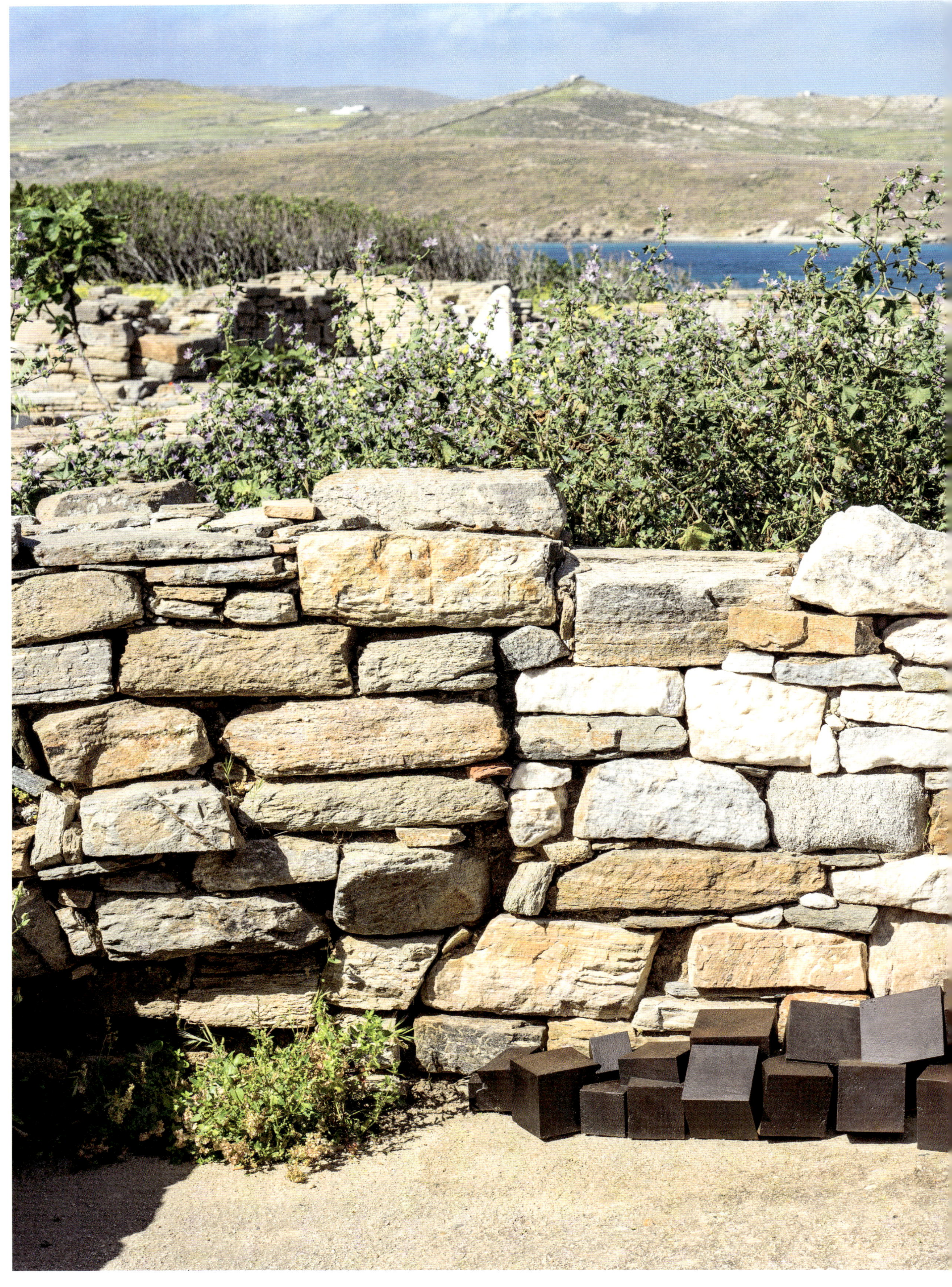

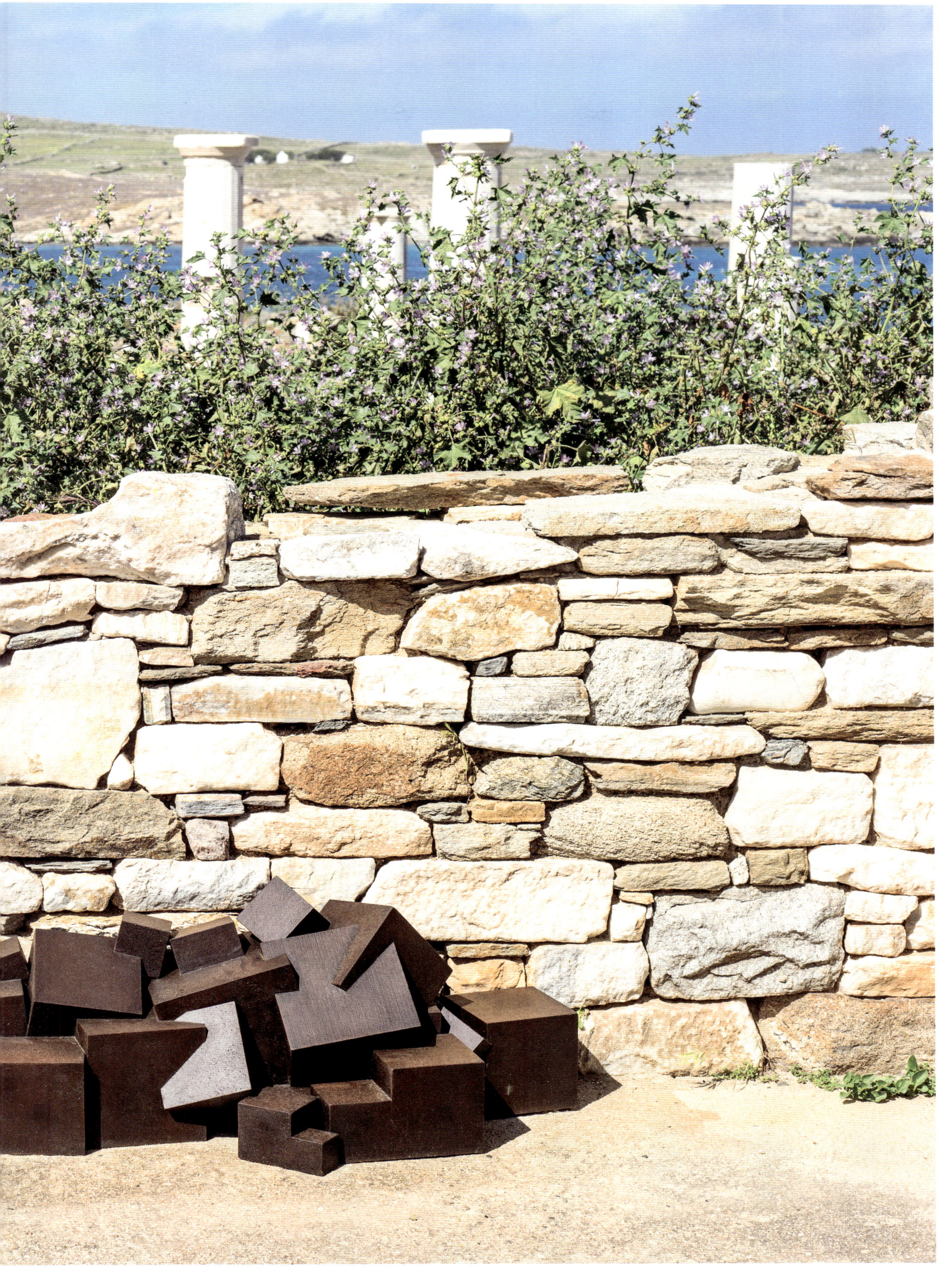

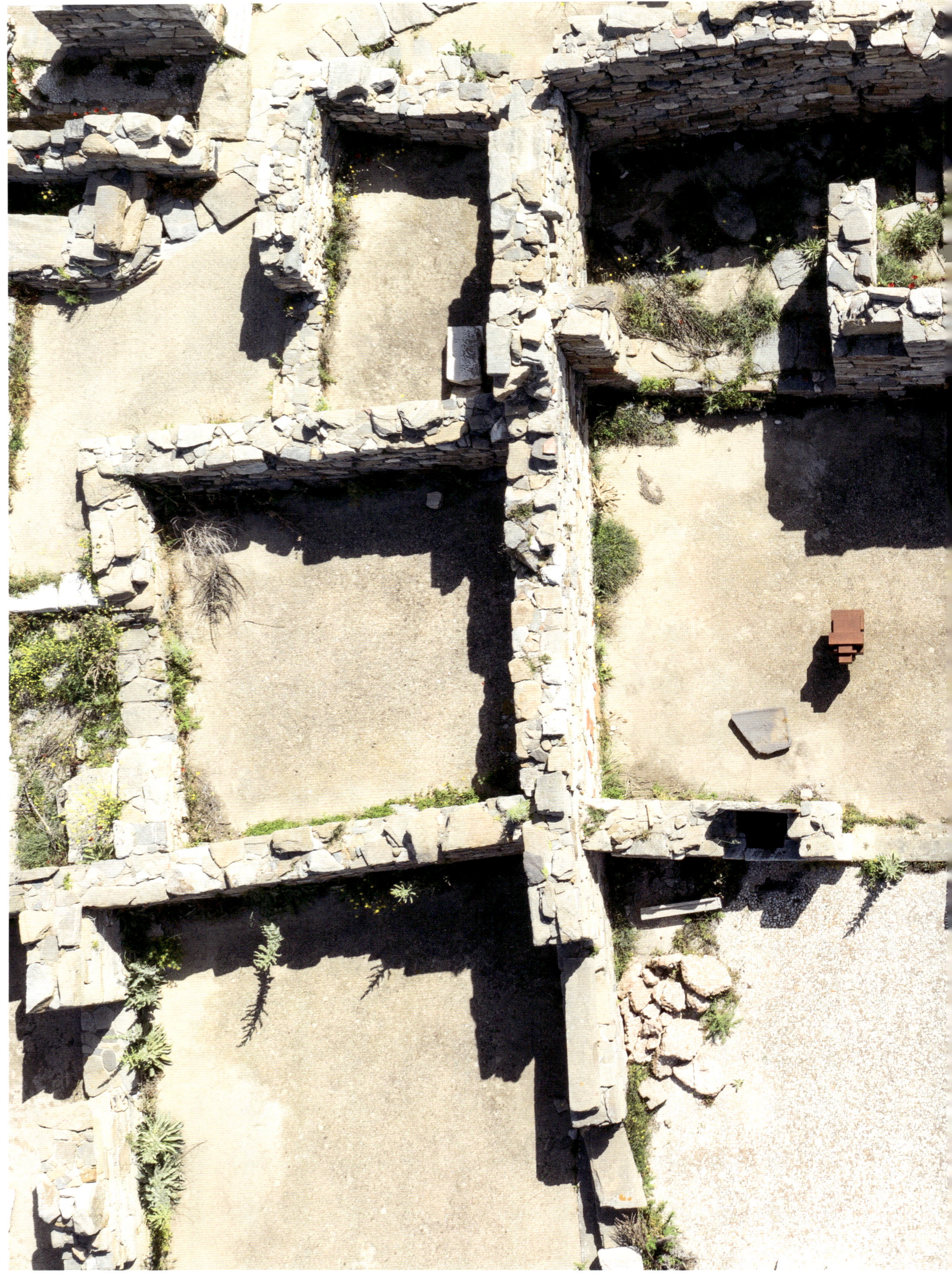

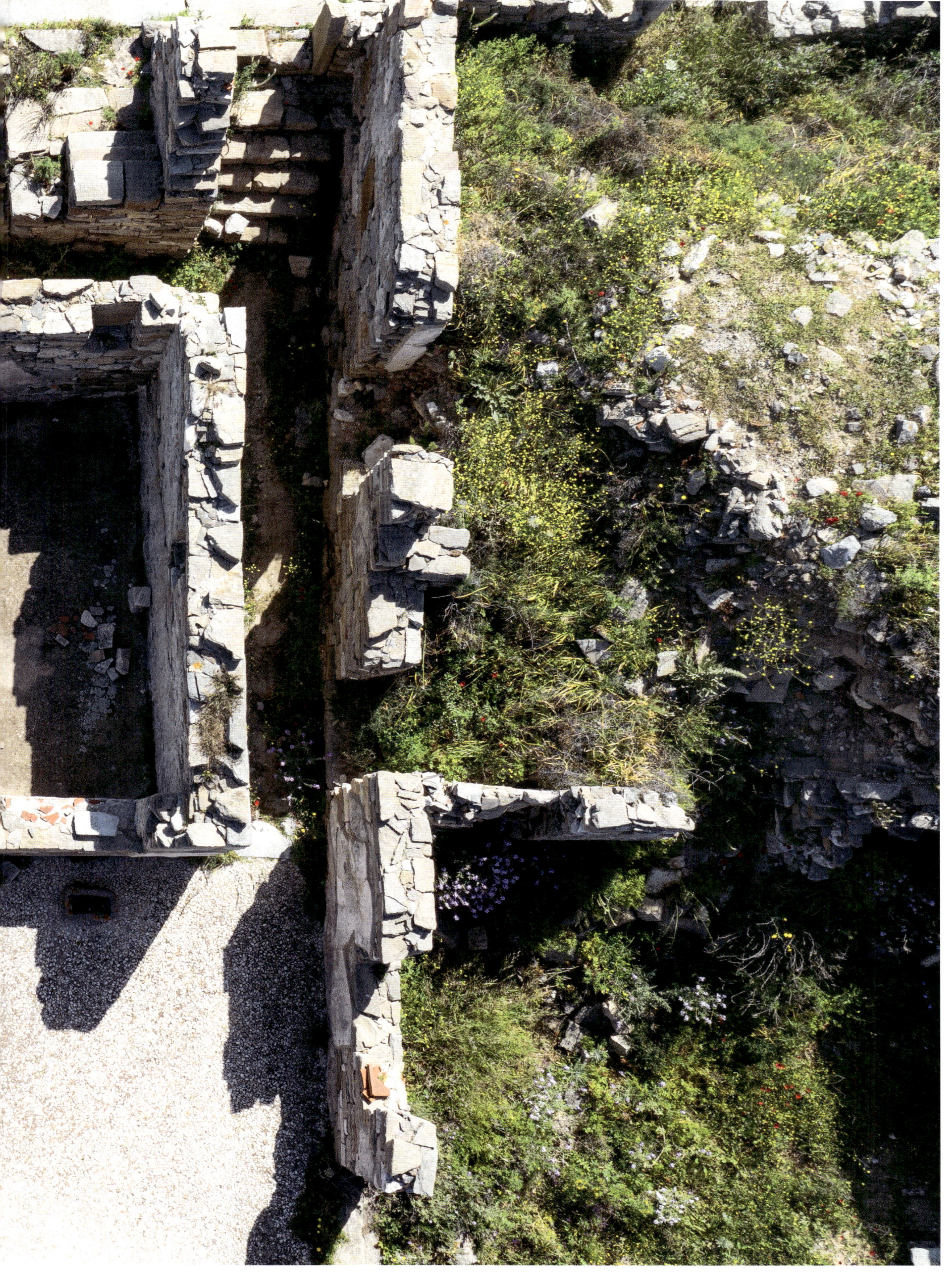

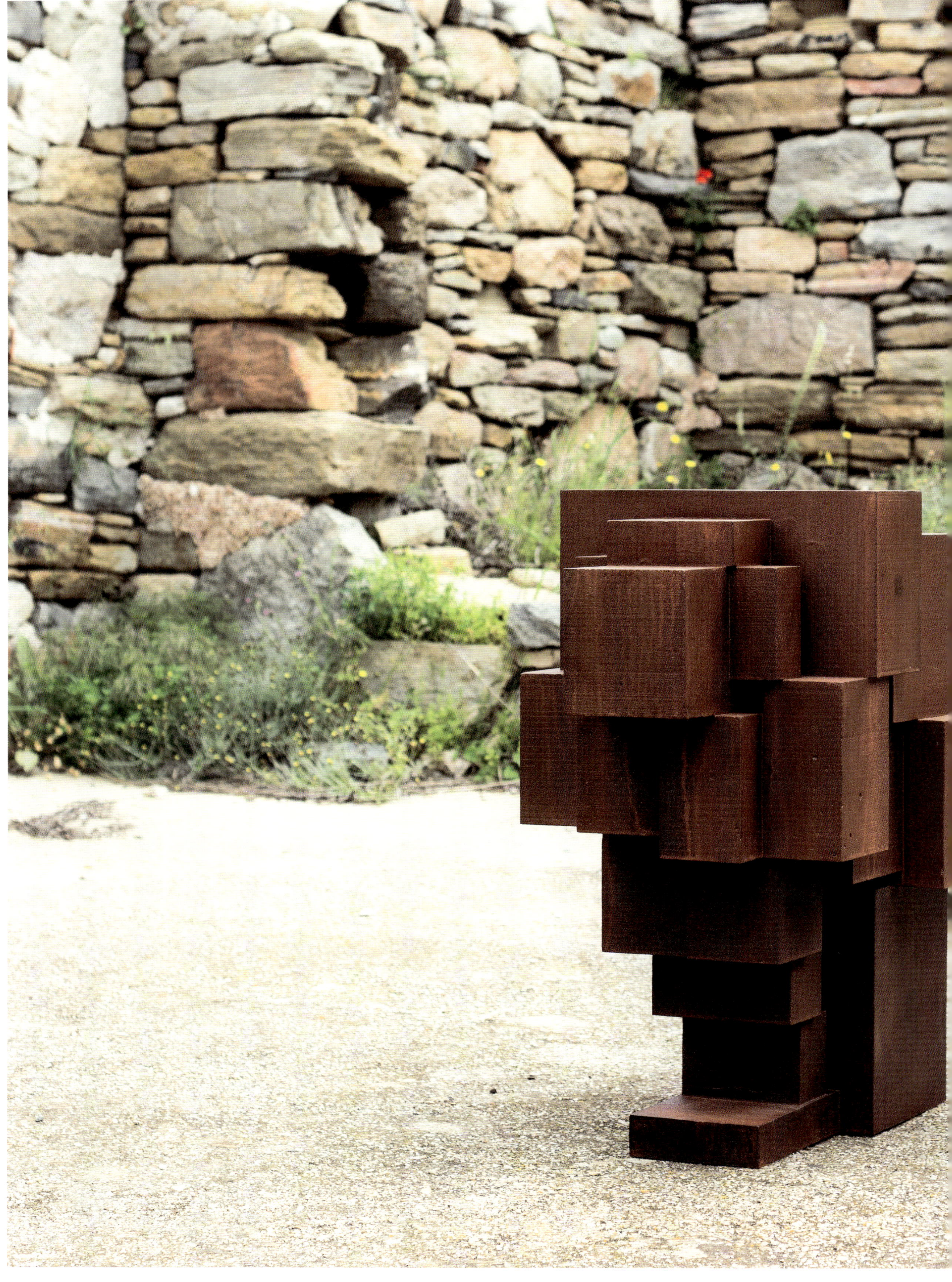

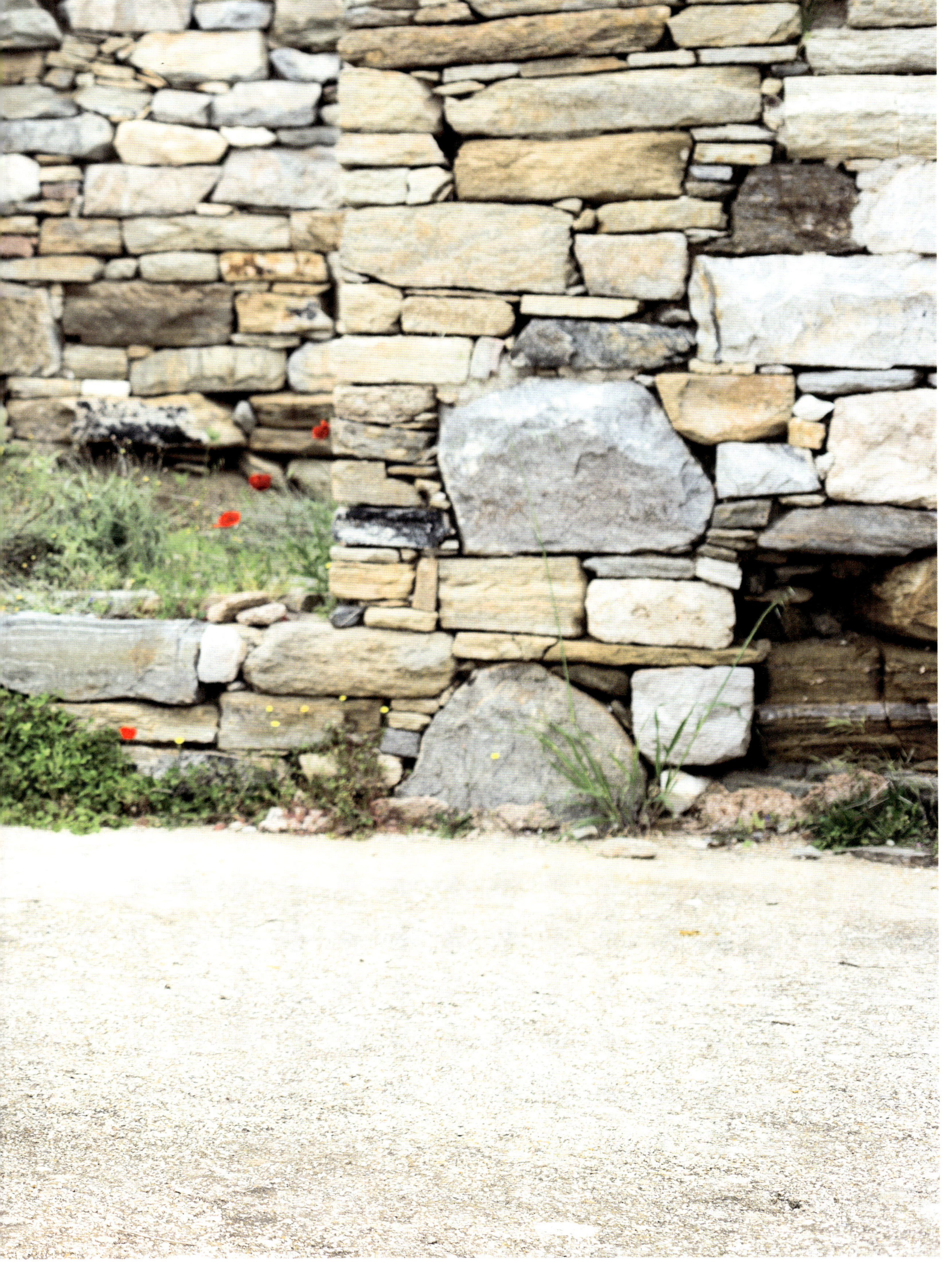

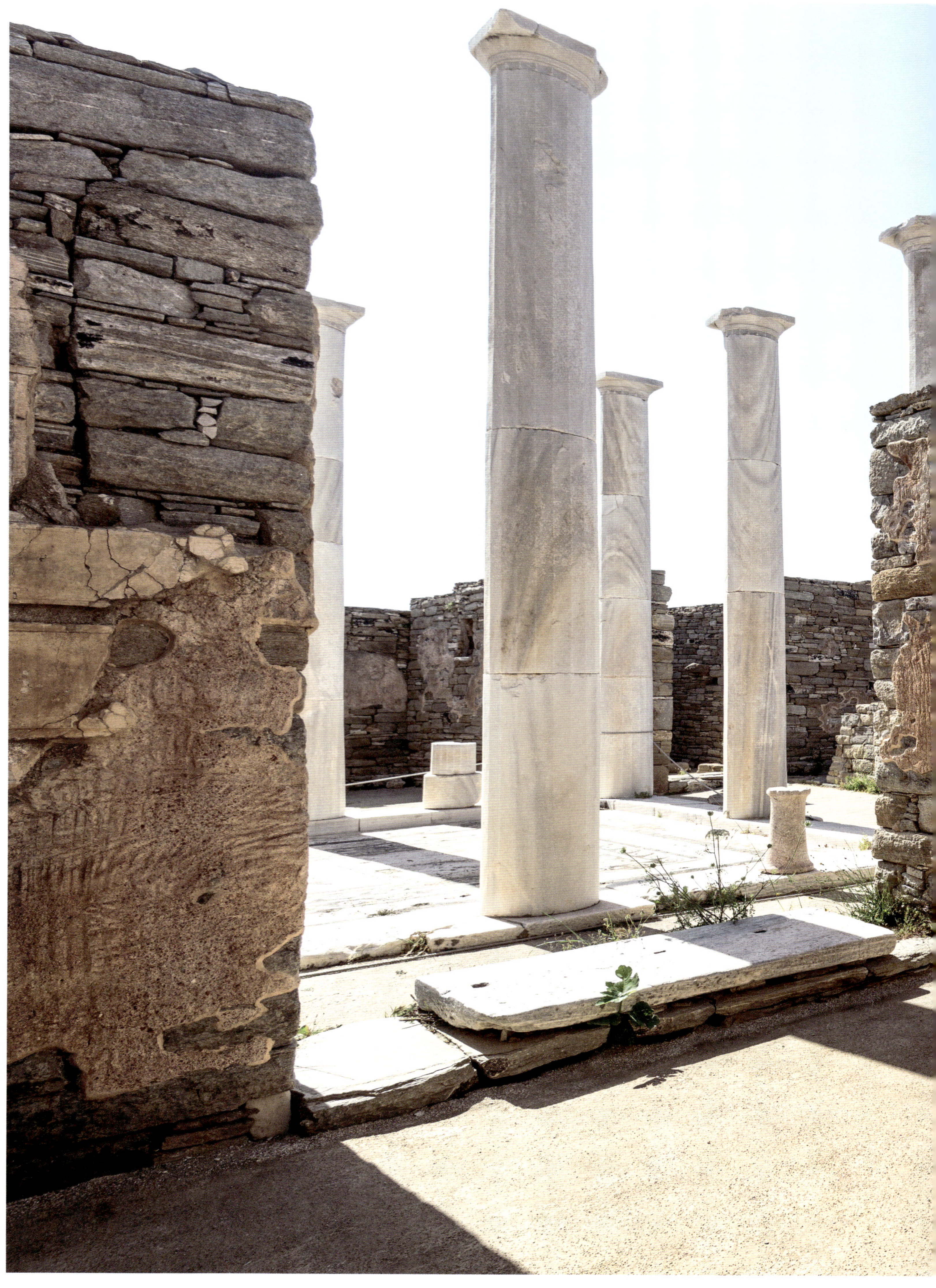

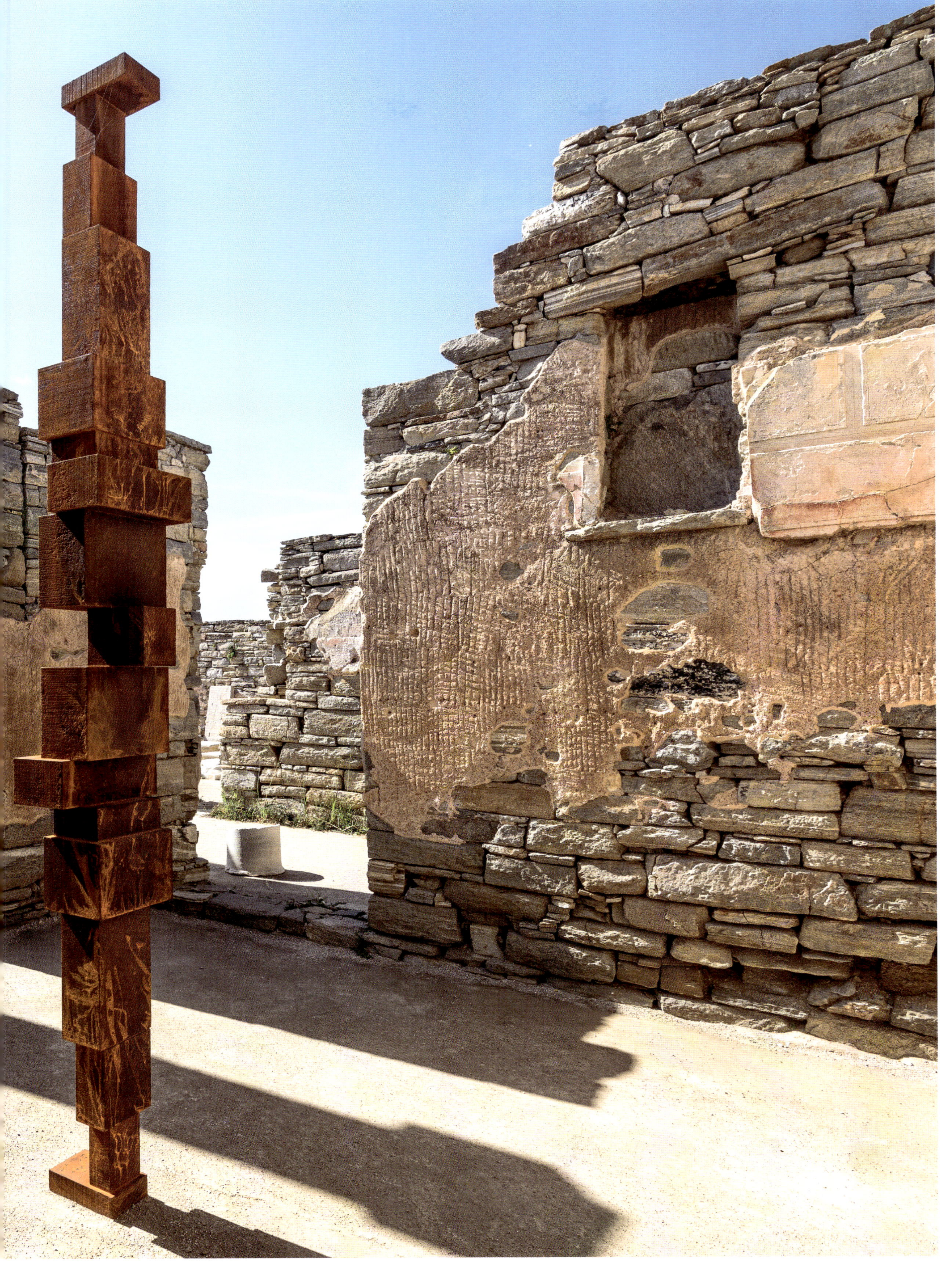

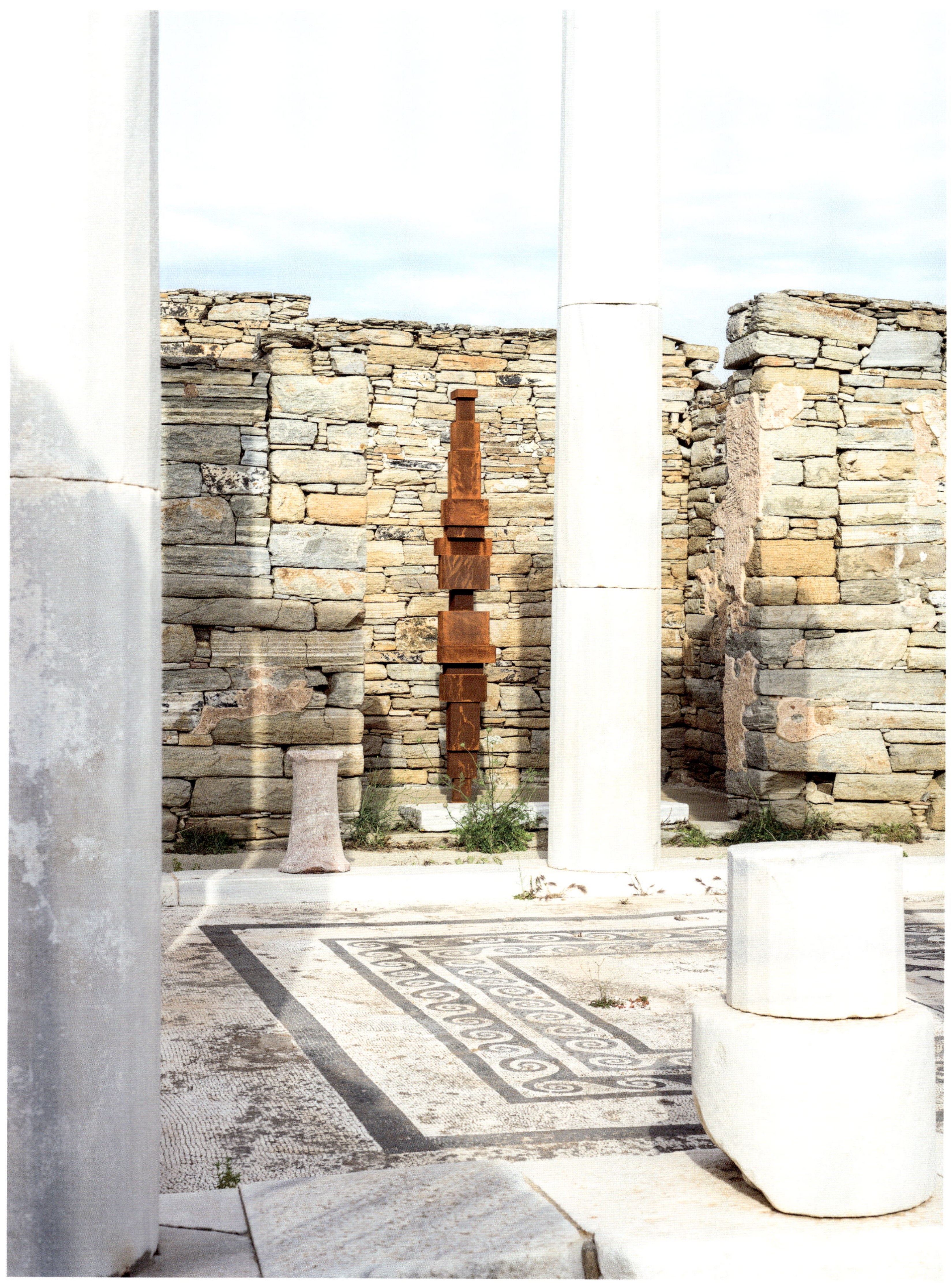

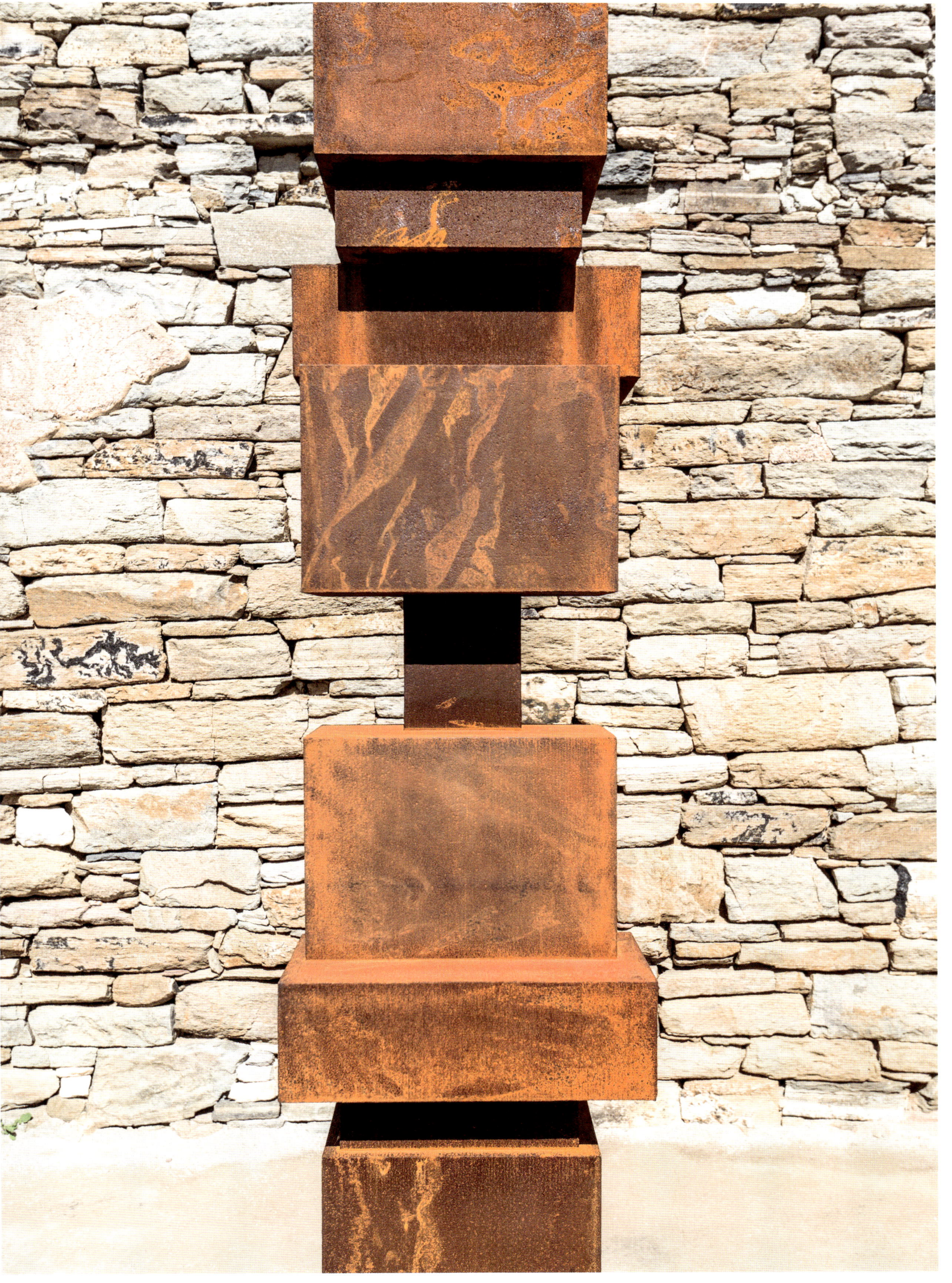

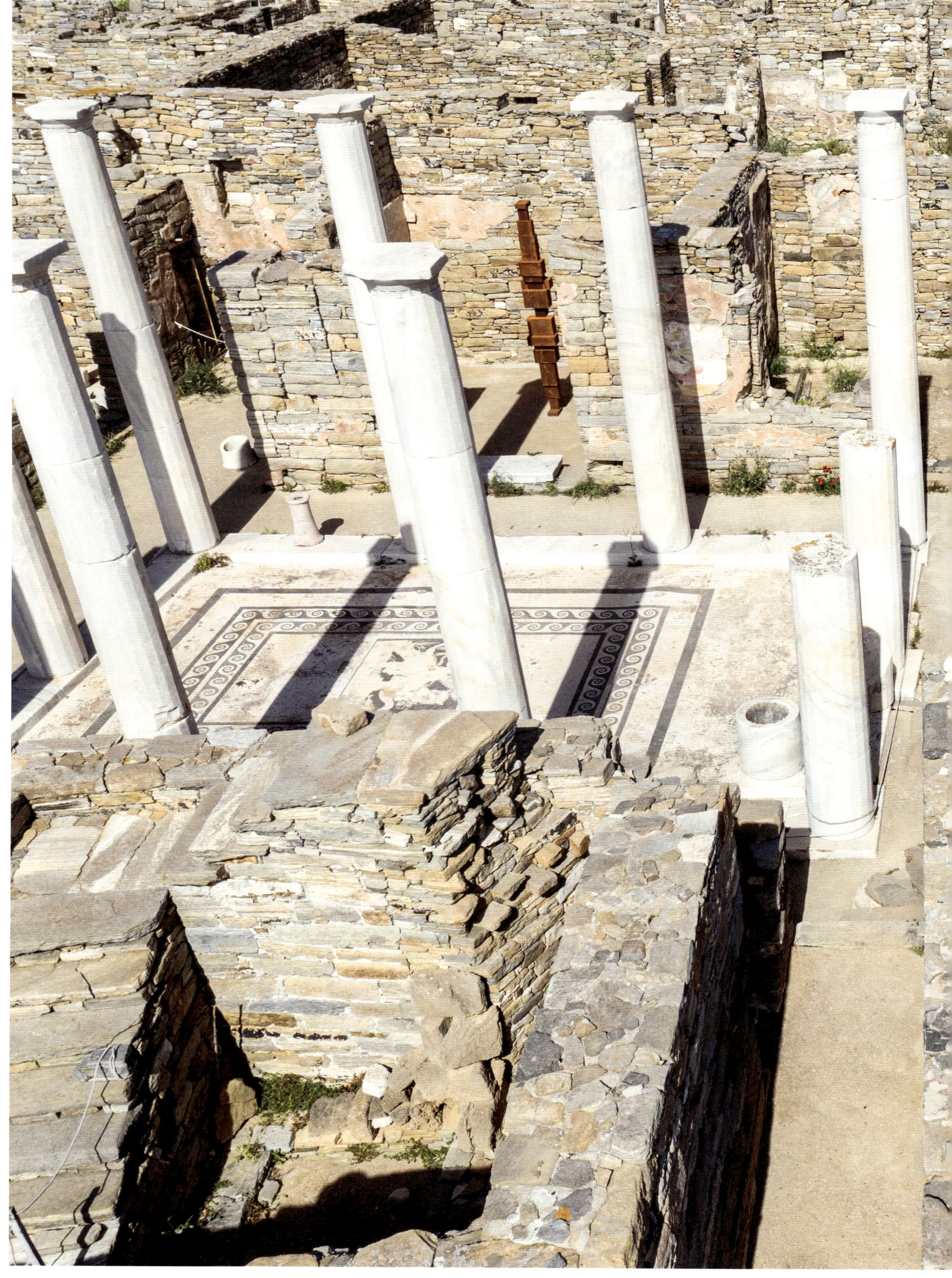

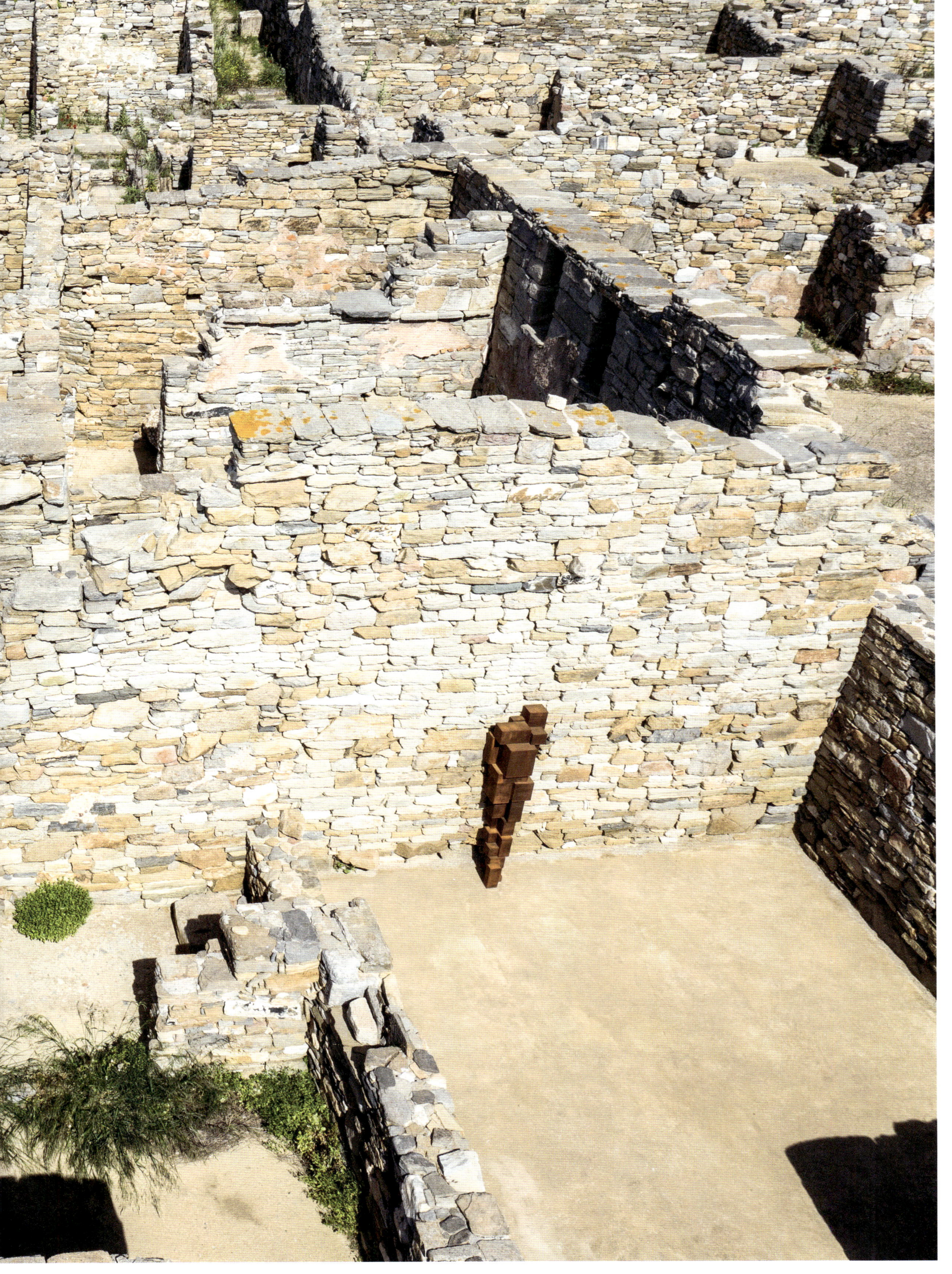

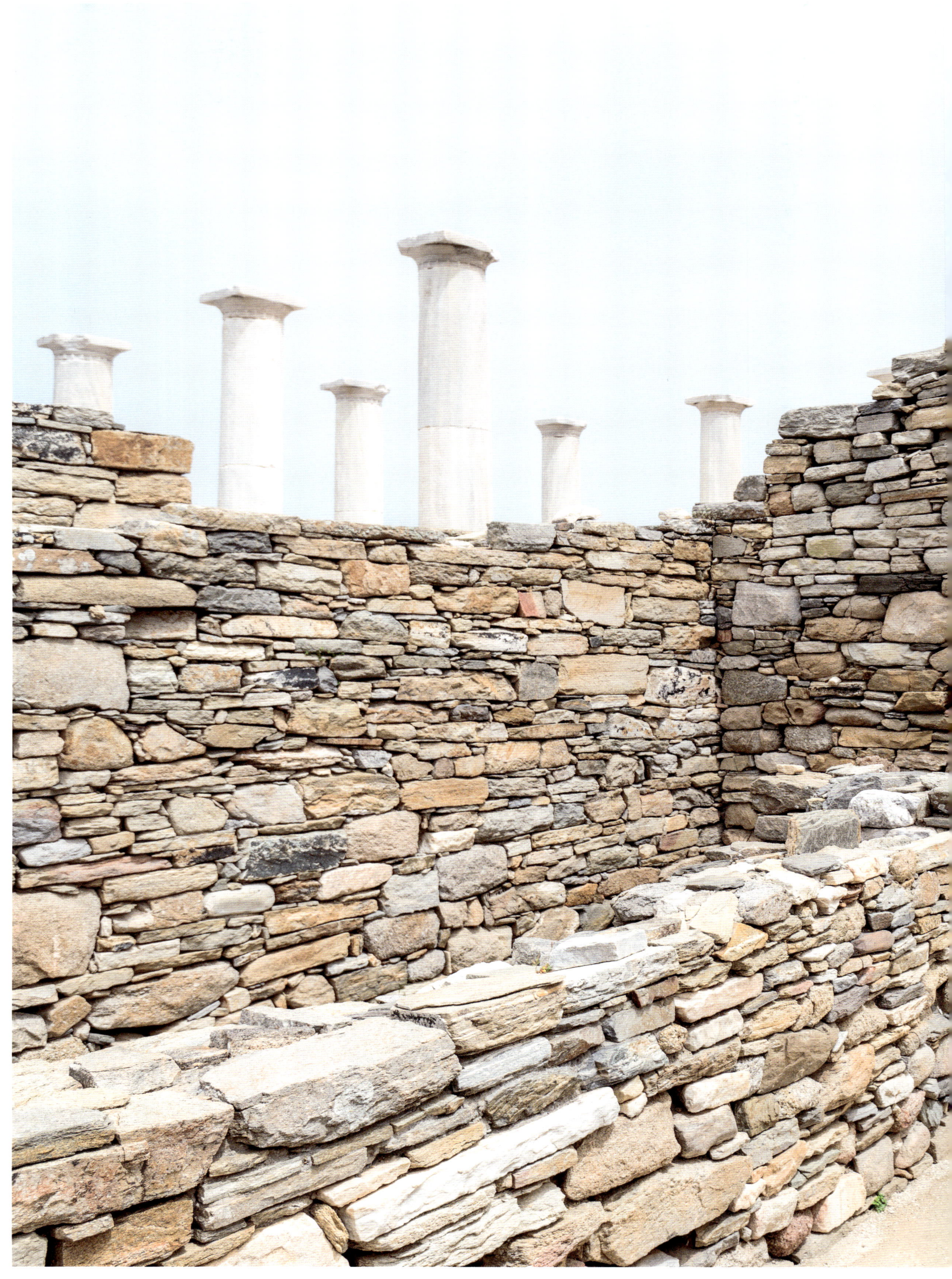

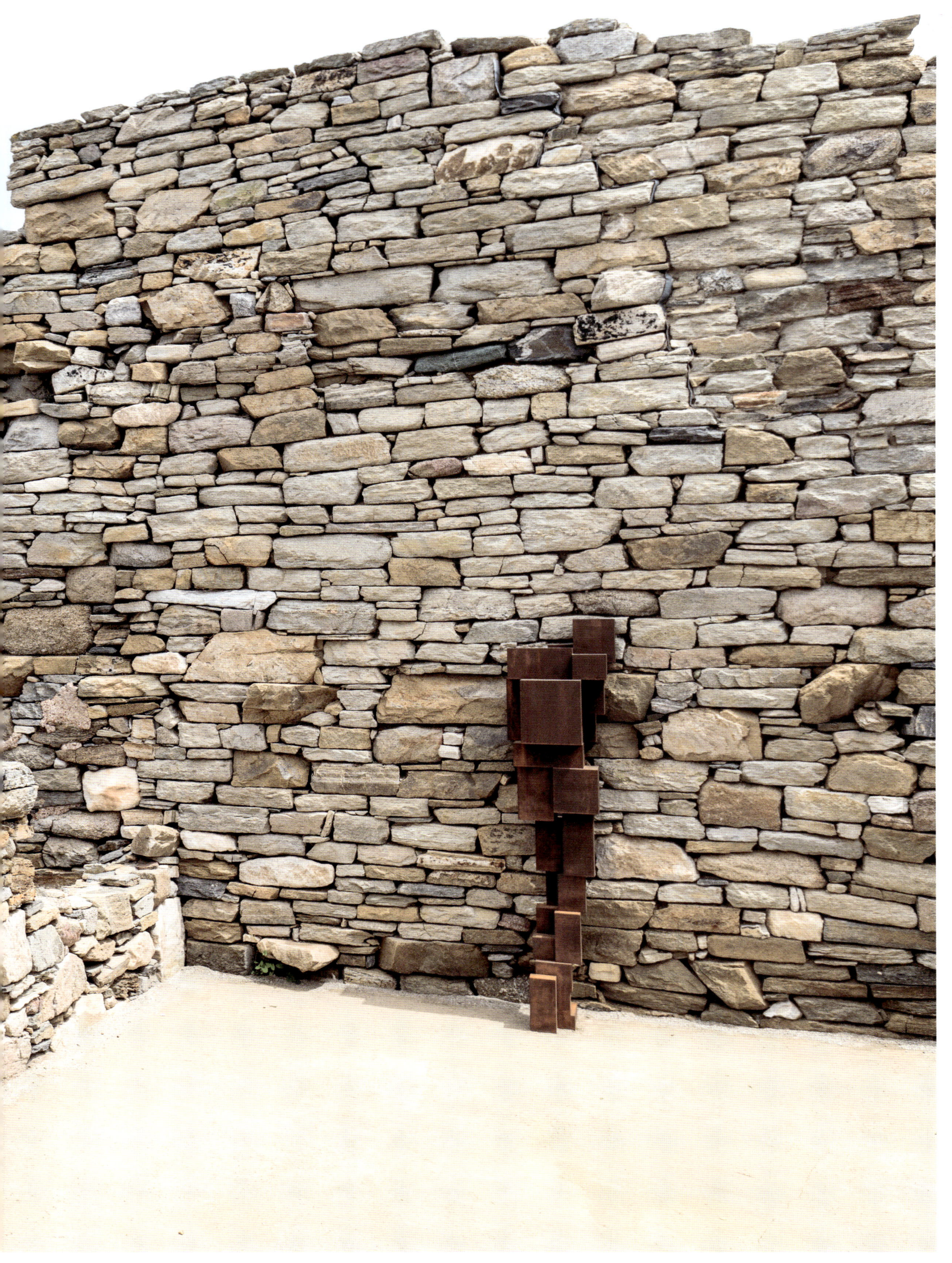

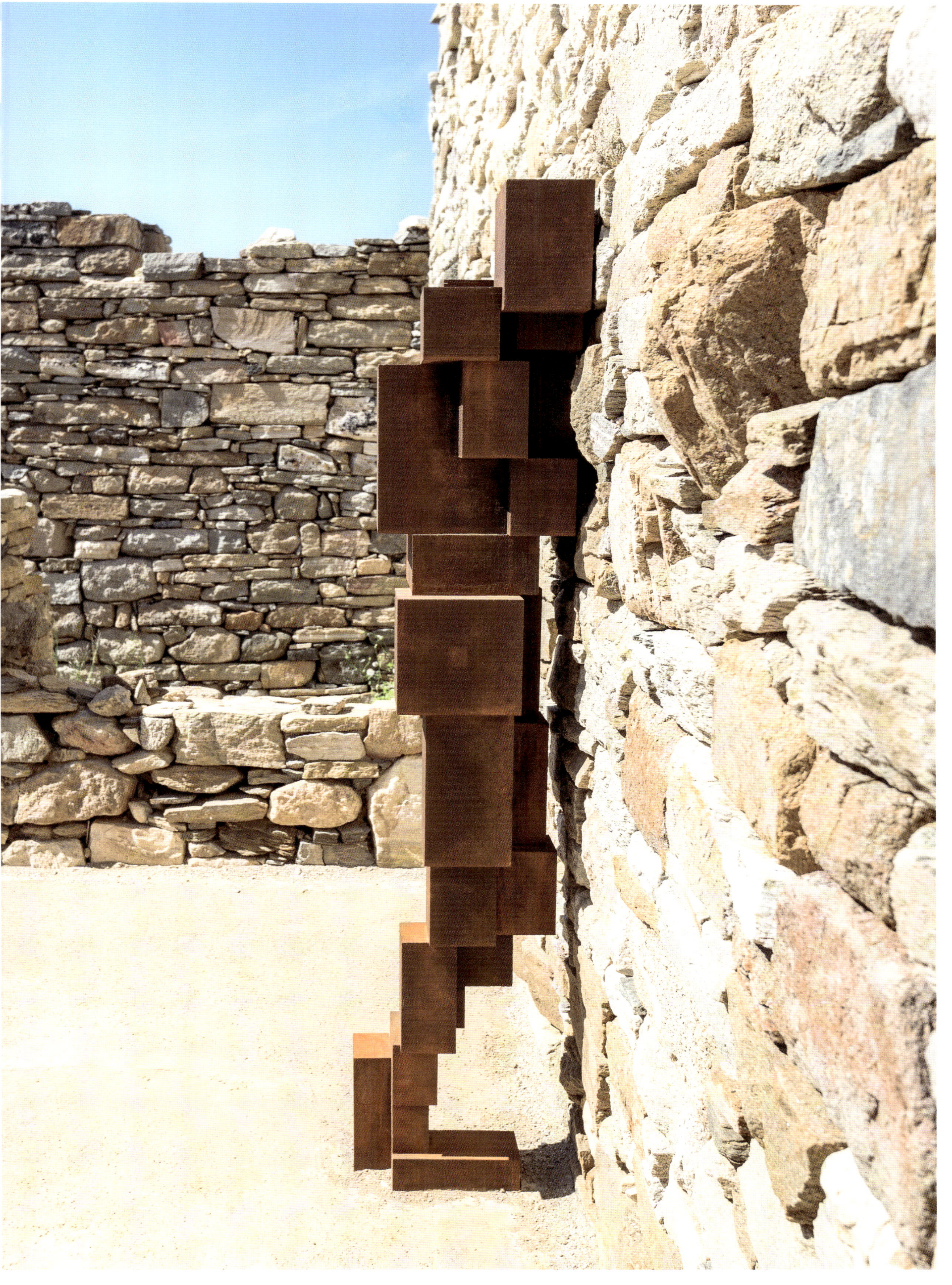

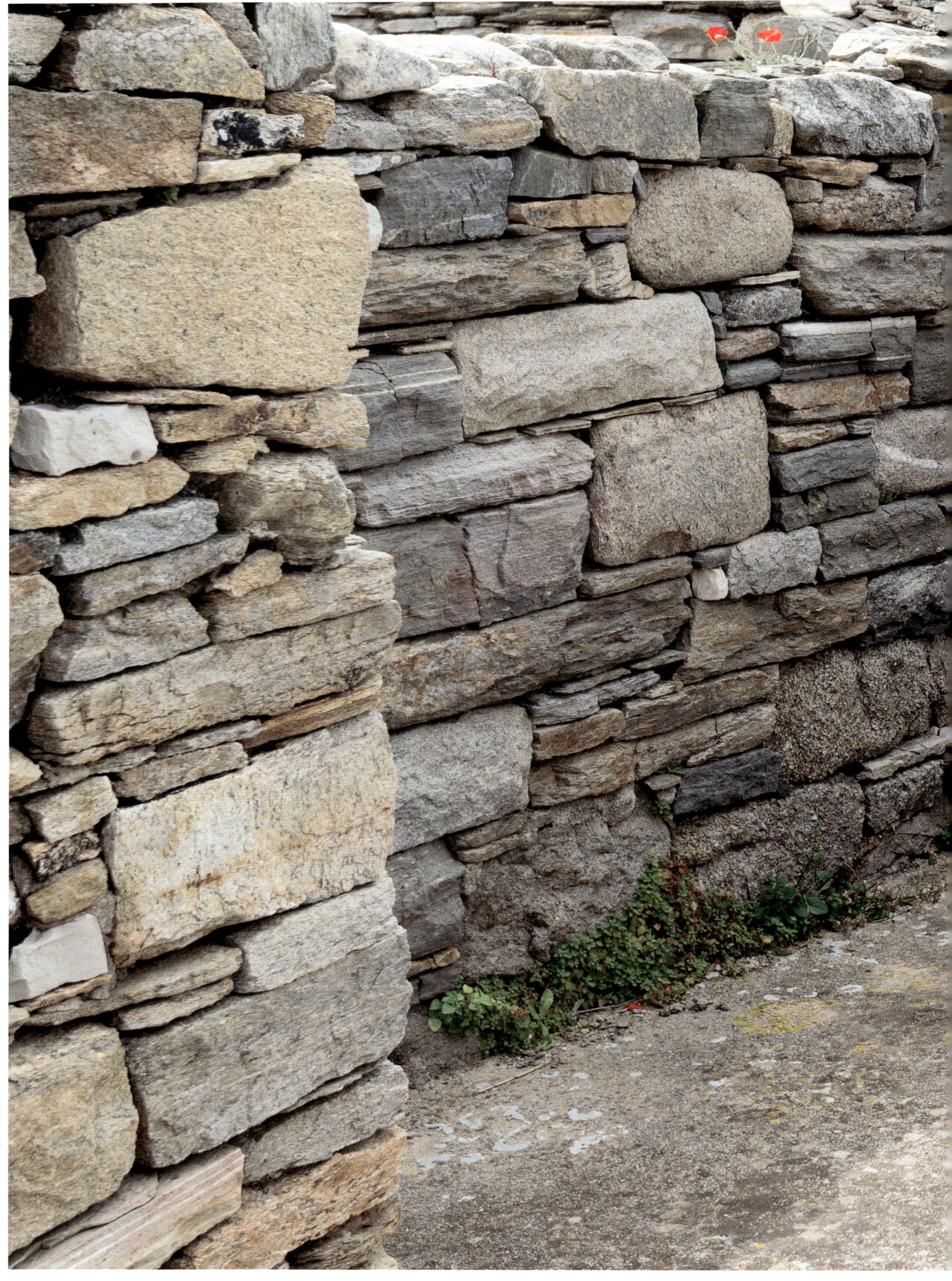

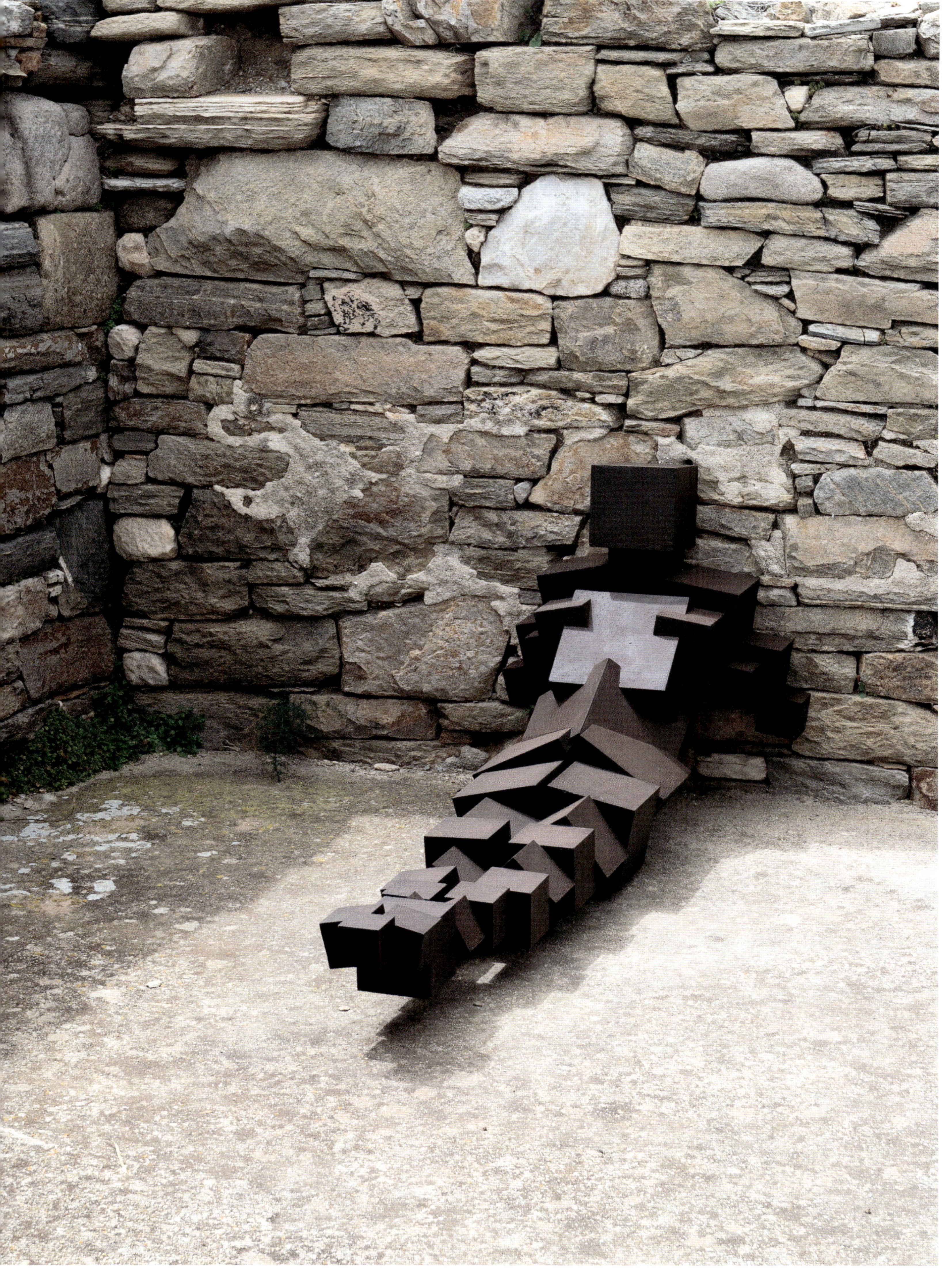

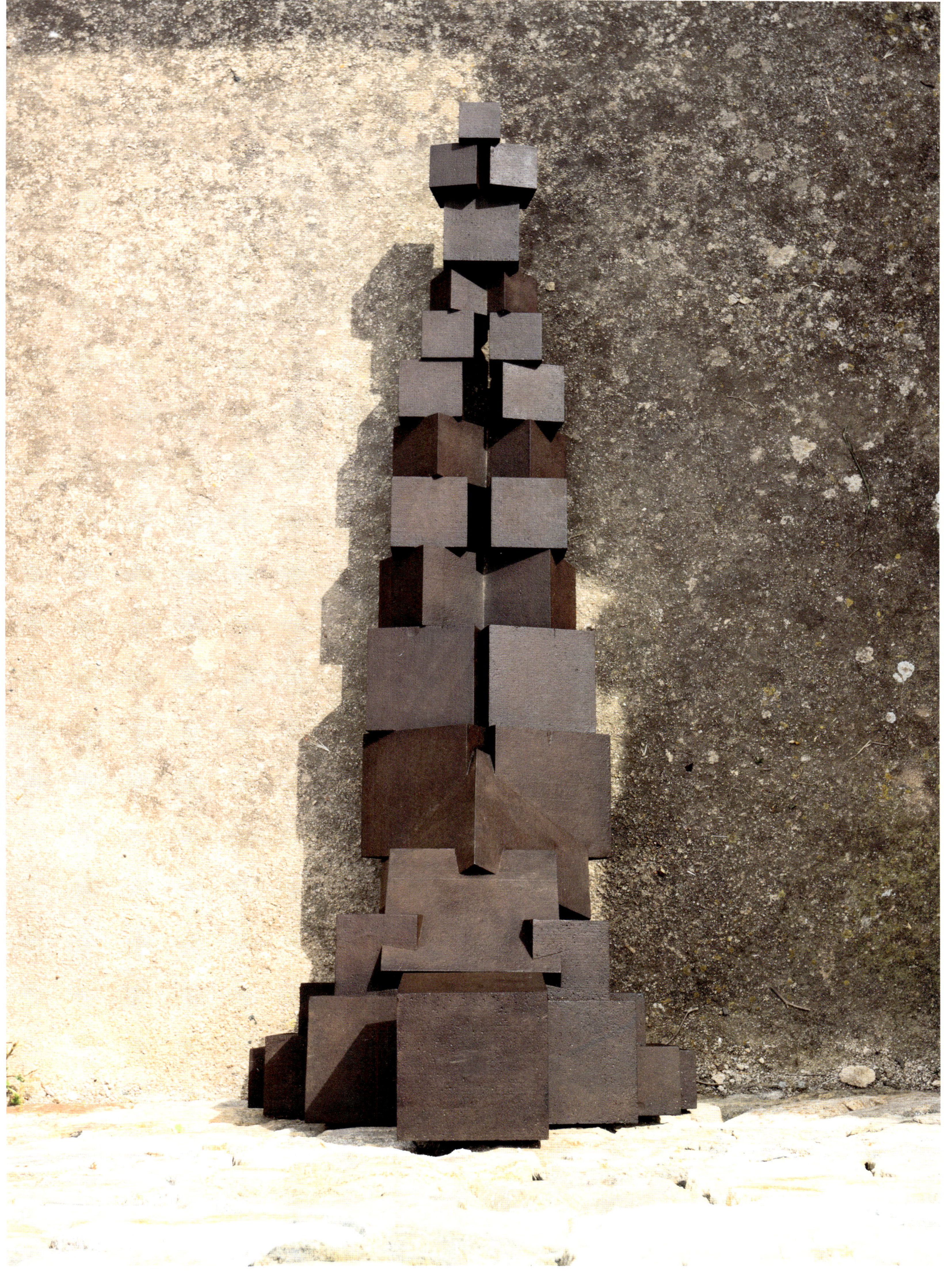

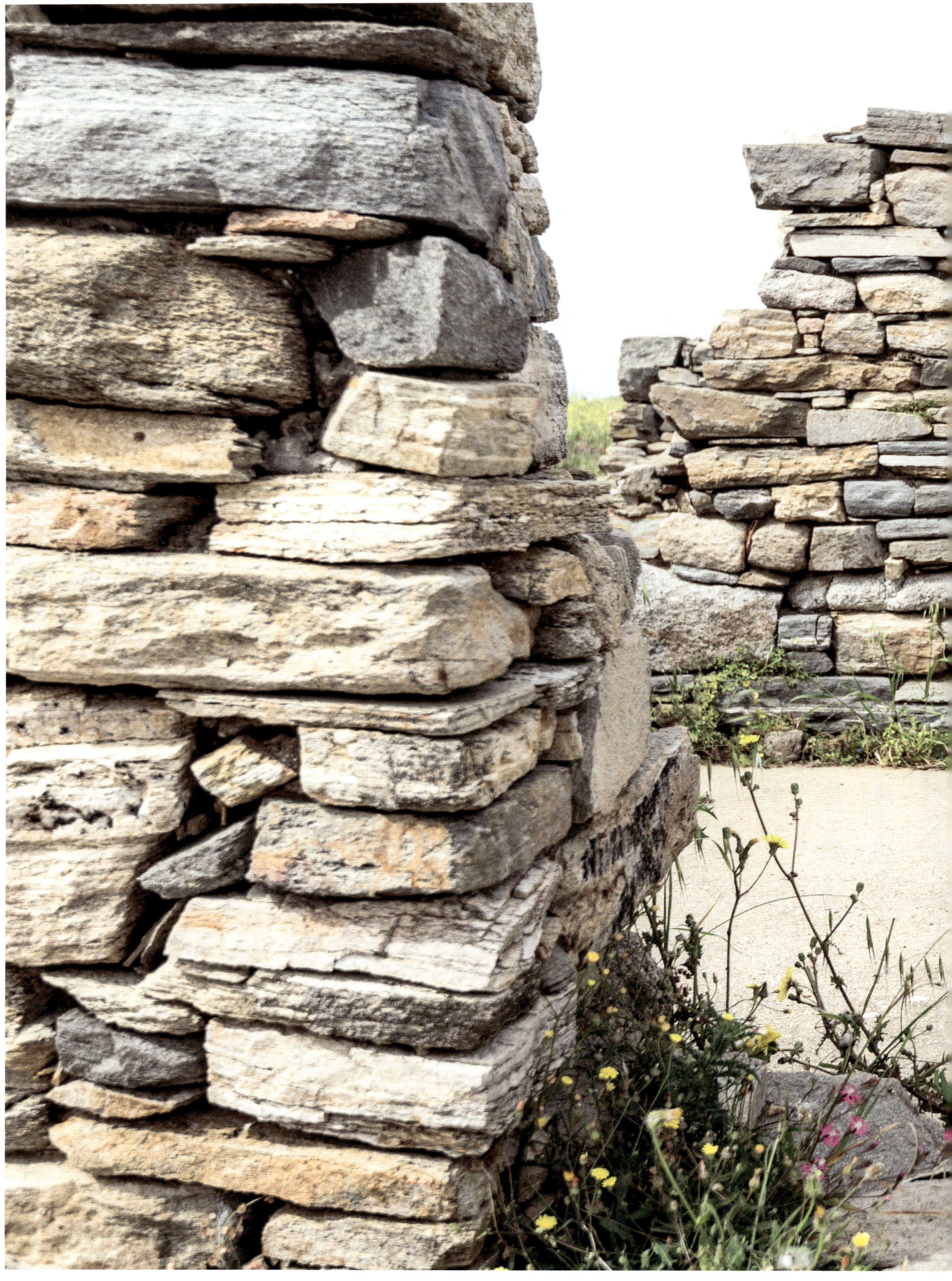

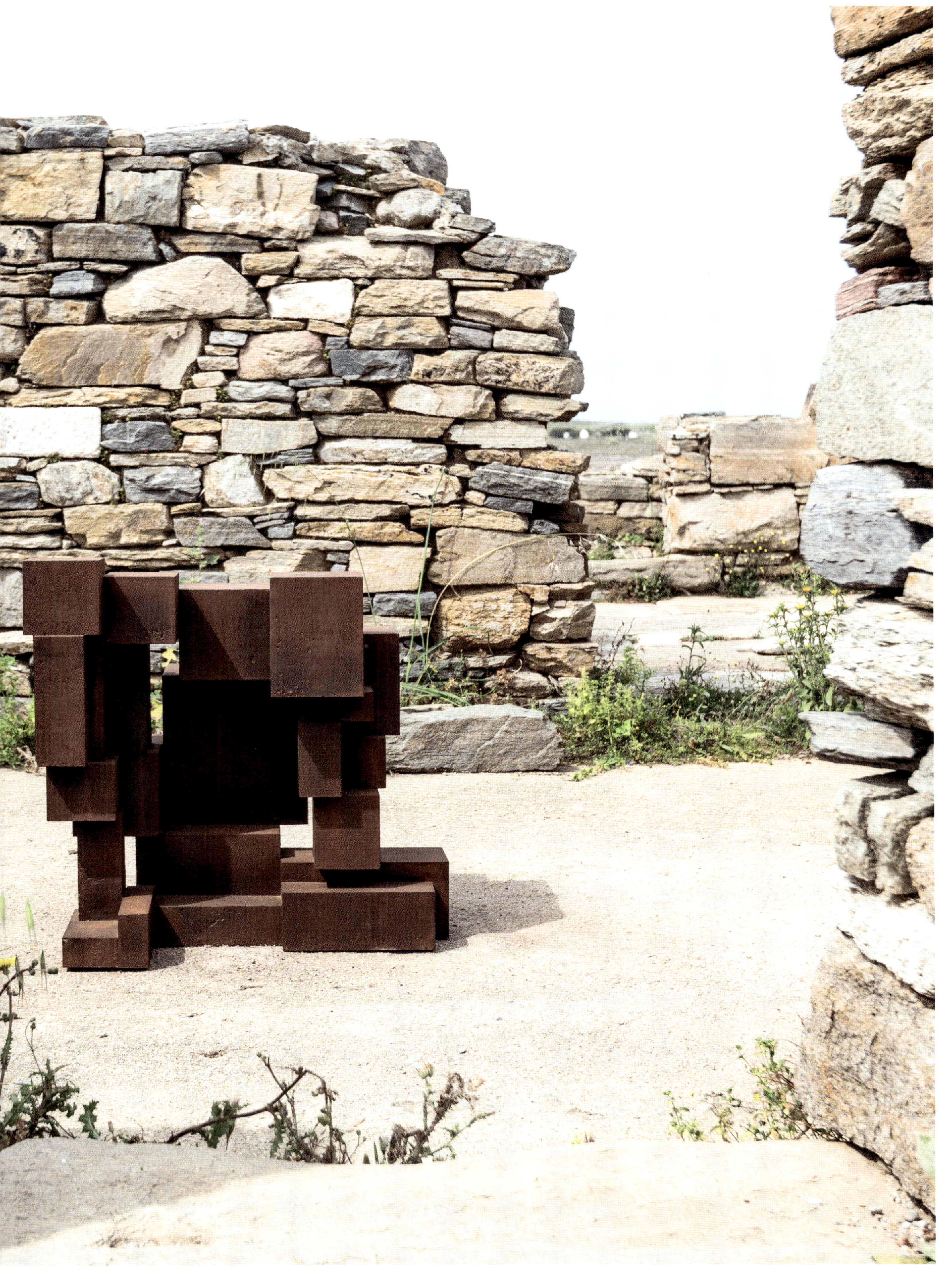

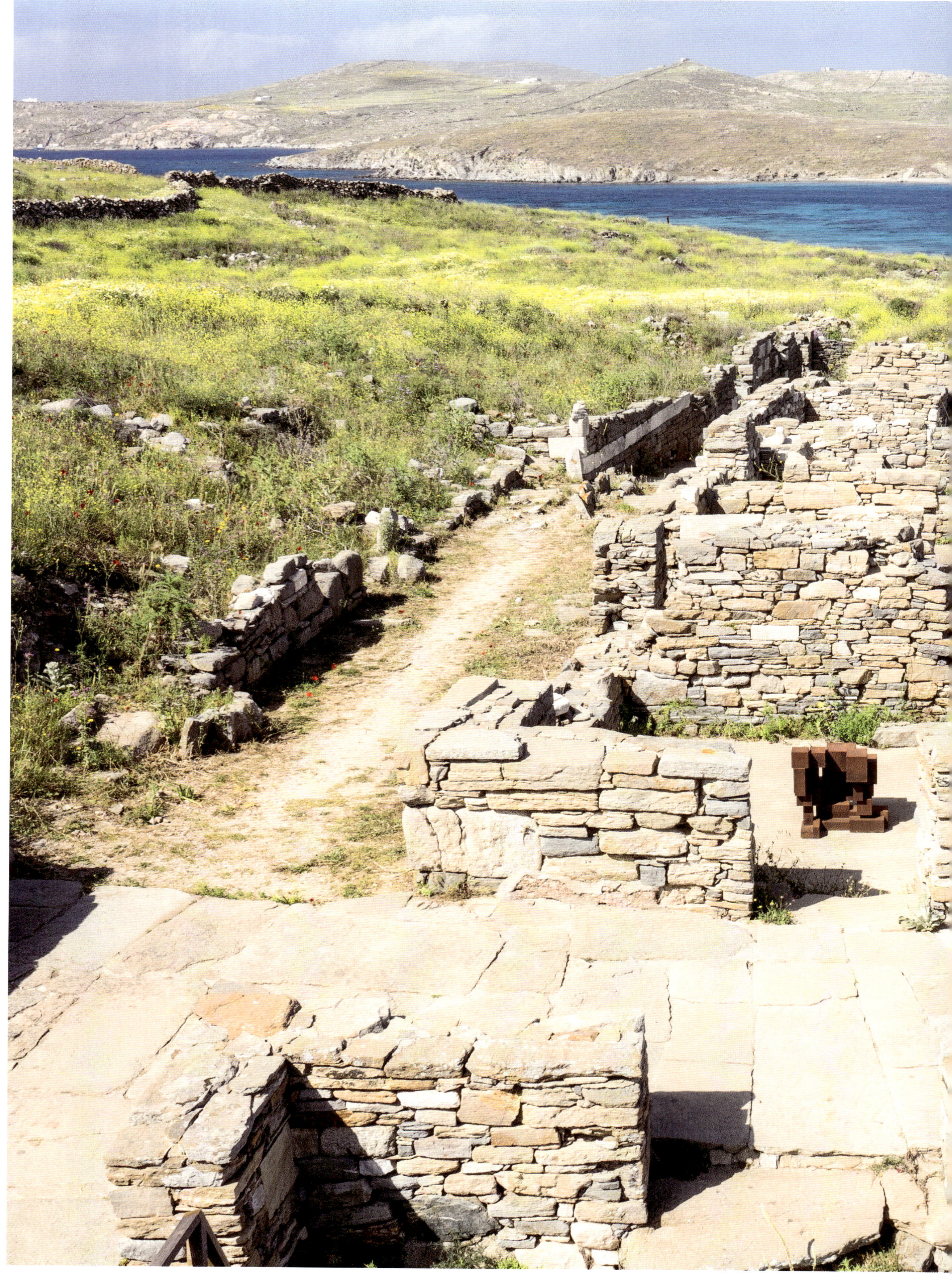

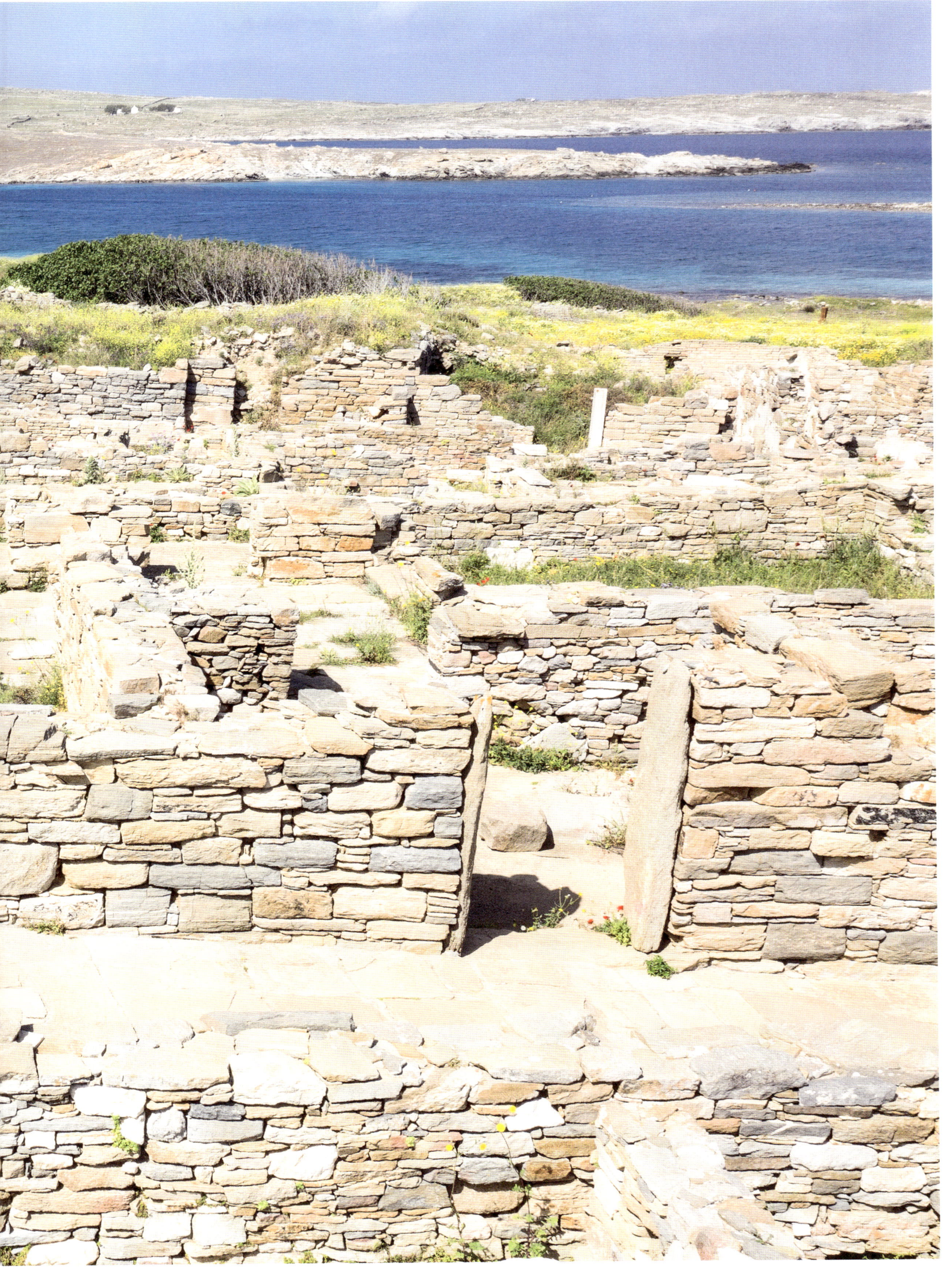

SEPARATE AND COVER: FIXING 29 SOLID CAST IRON SCULPTURES ON THE ARCHAEOLOGICAL SITE OF THE ISLAND OF DELOS

FANIS KAFANTARIS

The island of Delos has been declared a UNESCO World Heritage Site and is one of the most important and largest archaeological sites in Greece. It has an area of 3.4 sq. km. The first sporadic excavations were carried out in 1772 by the Russian army, but the first systematic excavation essentially began in 1872–73 by the French School at Athens. Archaeological research continues to this day.

How does one fix 29 sculptures made of cast iron onto an archaeological site, where the construction of supporting infrastructure and, in general, the creation of new structures falls, literally, within the realm of the exclusive action of 'archaeological' shovels? Sensing the archaeological sites as dynamic fields and networks of relationships between institutions, regulations, varying scientific disciplines and – ultimately – people, quickly paves the way for what the archaeologist Ian Hodder puts as an open question: 'how to make sense of the monuments and artefacts that survive from the enormity of the past'[1]?

There has always been interest in the material remains of human works, but their evaluation of these in the modern era has established archaeological sites as distinct geological territories. Consequently, systematic archaeological research in these sites enhanced historical links with the past, while international declarations on good practice,[2] that signify, protect and preserve archaeological sites on a material and symbolic level, were gradually proclaimed. In these positions, the concept of *Terra nullius*[3] (nobody's land) – does not exist. The repetitive clicks of the contemporary traveller's camera can prove this; the ruins

1 Ian Hodder & Scott Hudson, *Reading the Past: Current Approaches to Interpretation in Archaeology*, Cambridge, Cambridge University Press; 3rd edition, 2004, *xviii*.

2 International conventions defining fair practices with regard to cultural heritage: the *Athens Charter* (1931), the *Charter of Venice* (1964), the International Conferences in London (1969) and Valletta (1992), as well as the adoption of their declarations by the international councils and institutions that were founded, such as *ICOMOS* (1965) and *UNESCO* (1972).

3 A Latin expression meaning 'nobody's land' or 'land belonging to nobody' which derives from the term *Res nullius* used in Roman law. Here it is used to conceptually describe the safeguarding of 'archaeological' land, if not its ownership status too.

of history transform into recognisable landscapes with inherent cultural value.

For Greece, defining 'Antiquities' and founding a supervising 'Committee' to protect them could be considered a constituent element of the Greek state. Very soon after its establishment in the early 1830s, decrees were issued on the subject (in 1834 and 1836)[4], somehow fulfilling one of the Western world's wishful longings: to safeguard and preserve the connection with the classical past in its birthplace. Wide-ranging excavations commenced all over Greece in the years that followed. European Romanticism that once visited Greece with its 18th century antiquarians, returns, decades later, as archaeological missions of foreign countries.[5] Based in Athens, foreign archaeological schools were founded to officially excavate and study the Greek land – an established international archaeological asset.

Therefore, to speak about the planning process by which to install Antony Gormley's works on the archaeological site of Delos, it is difficult to not take into account all of the above; it was necessary to put together a composite project team of certified professionals and cooperate with the Ephorate of Antiquities of Cyclades regarding certain specifications and instructions. The approval of the project by the Central Archaeological Council was required, as was the implementation of the method statements[6] with the support of the archaeologists on site in Delos, while ensuring the implementation of the artist's desired aesthetic principles.

The main guideline from the Archaeological bureau was that there would be no harm to the landscape; digging was prohibited. The base on which the artworks would be fixed had to be superficial and while structurally valid, capable of distributing the weight of the artwork in a way which would not affect what lay beneath. Sheet metal plates of adequate surface and thickness and thin concrete slabs were selected. In this way – what is preserved is not only that which is seen in the archaeological site, including the shallow underwater zone around the island, but also that which is not seen within its boundaries: whatever lay hidden in the ground, unapparent, known or unknown.

Specifically, if the above had to be summarised in two words, then *separate* and *cover*, would describe the approach both structurally and aesthetically. The archaeological earth is separated from the non-archaeological, the latter limited to a ground layer only a few centimetres deep; the organic surface layer, always ephemeral.

Separate (a new soil horizon): Separating the works and their base (a base was structurally necessary in most cases) from the archaeological ground. In geology, a soil horizon is a layer parallel to the soil surface, whose physical, chemical and biological characteristics differ from the layers above and beneath. In other words, what is specified is a new layer in the stromatography of the archaeological site. The old has to be separate from the new, and the latter temporary. In practice, this includes materials

4 Reference to the first provisions 'On Antiquities' appears in the Royal Decree of 1834 and on the 'Antiquities Committee' in the Royal Decree of 1836. The institutional descriptions of 'antiquities' and 'committees' evolved and were systematically reformulated.

5 The first to be established was the French School at Athens (1846). Next came the German Archaeological Institute at Athens (1874), the American School of Classical Studies at Athens (1881), the British School at Athens (1886) and others. Today there are 17 foreign archaeological institutes operating in Greece.

6 Besides the Central Archaeological Council of the Ministry of Culture, a body responsible for the approval of the project in principle and to which a complete file was submitted for approval, it is worth mentioning all the different professions that worked on the project: Archaeologists, Architects, Civil Engineers, Antiquity and Conservators, certified art-transport companies that can work in archaeological sites, a specialised production team and special craftsmen. The plurals reflect the participation of persons with the same specialty (except archaeologists), both on the part of the Archaeological bureau and NEON, and Antony Gormley's studio, defining a strict framework of necessary-collaborating specialties and, ultimately, people.

and techniques which guarantee that any infrastructure work is fully reversible (that all can be removed without leaving any trace). This was achieved by creating a safety zone either between the artwork and the position where it is placed, or between the base of the artwork and this area: special varnish, synthetic films, geotextiles, new mortars and dry materials, as well as combinations thereof, were used. In moving the works into position, plywood was placed on top of the existing paving to avoid damaging them.

Cover: Covering the base upon which the work was fixed was necessary to achieve the desired continuity of the surface of the archaeological site; a specific landscaping direction. The method was to imitate the surrounding area of each artwork's position. In other words, where there was soil, the base of the work would be covered with soil; the rock would be covered with material that imitated the rock; an identical copy was created of an ancient column capital as was a surface resembling worn marble and even the existing cement floors would be covered with new cement. In the cases where, in combination with the way of fixing, such methods were not feasible, the creation of a small-scale stone-masonry base was chosen, the morphology of which had to resemble existing structures in the archaeological site.

But what is it that makes the fixing of Antony Gormley's sculptures on Delos different to their fixing within any other site, archaeological or not? Gormley's sculptures, in his wider practice, appear to stand without visible bases. It appears as if only gravity is at work, signifying our continuous presence on earth, as a trace of our existence on the natural and built environment where we all become eventually absent. It sets foot on the earth and remains.

With Cesare Pavese's thought, 'A true revelation, I am convinced, can only emerge from stubborn concentration on a single problem'[7] often coming to mind, the answer to the previous question may be 'Delos itself'. We realise that what makes a difference are the local geographical conditions: cultural as they are expressed and natural as they exist, which cannot be overlooked. The hills and the lowlands, the built or unbuilt routes, the sea, the waves, the isolation of the island, the geography of access, the wind, the alternating vegetation, and the birds, the quadrupeds and the reptiles among the archaeologically valuable ruins. The contemporary constructions which are built and that which is forbidden to be built; the inhabitants of the island and foreigners. The archaeological site as a landscape and as a condition of visit – day, month, year. All of the above is displayed in front of the observer's gaze, speaking silently with Antony Gormley's 29 works on Delos. There, then, the understanding of the landscape emerges perhaps as a reading anew of this significant archaeological site. On the same ground; earth and reason.

We arrived on the island at the end of January, as soon as the weather and the sea permitted it. The artwork crates were loaded in London to arrive in Athens, in Piraeus and from there they were shipped onwards to Paros, Mykonos and finally to Delos. The continuous rains had cut off easy access to the archaeological site from the dock where the boat arrived; mud.

The works and the equipment for the installation were waiting to be distributed to

7 Cesare Pavese, *Dialoghi con Leuco*, 1947, the author's foreword.

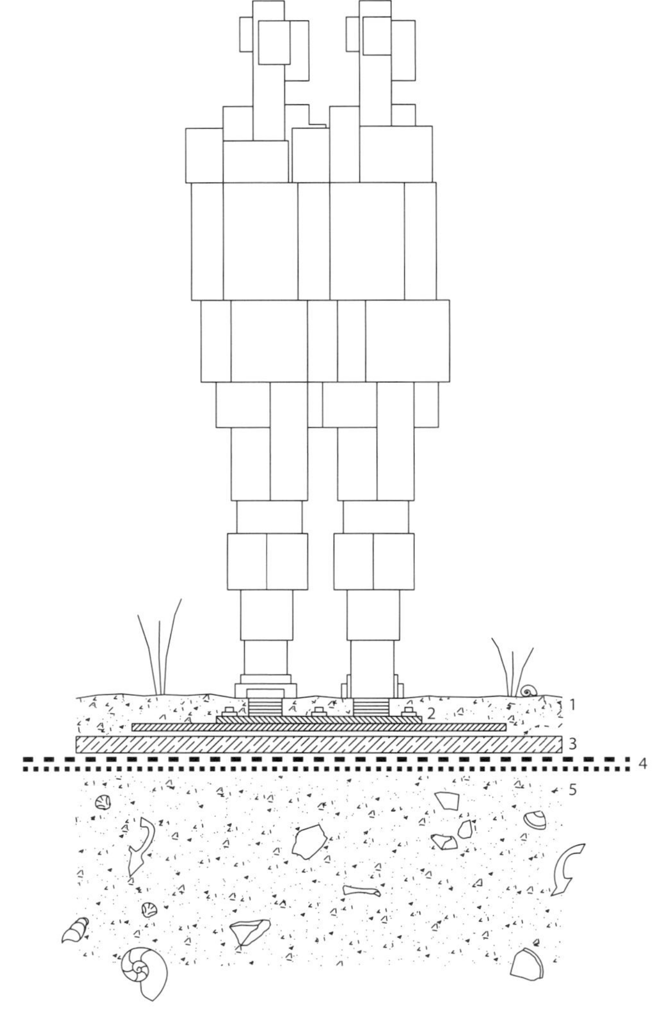

Typical fixing system
Section plan

1. Organic surface layer
2. Fixing plates
3. Cement
4. New soil horizon; protective membrane sheets
5. Archaeological earth

their locations. We set up our workshop next to the Museum. The electricity grid was limited to the museum and to the small buildings where we were staying. Keeping us company were the antiquities guards, the only inhabitants of the island. Strong people. Access to the nearest inhabited island, Mykonos, was not always feasible. Isolation.

Soon, timber decks were laid out to allow us to move over the sensitive archaeological land. All around us were the island's trademark lizards. Laden, we crossed the narrow streets of the Theatre Quarter, passing the marble thresholds of the once-inhabited ruined buildings in fear of disturbing the delicate balance of the stone walls and the marble columns. Our equipment always portable. We reached the top of Mount Kynthos. We recorded the sea level – the Mediterranean tide – and we waited for the sea to calm so that we could get to the northern cape, opposite the commercial ports. Repeatedly. For almost four months.

Air, rain, waves, clouds, sun. Intertemporal. For the artworks that had to be fixed and for us who had to fix them.

Fanis Kafantaris is Project Architect for NEON

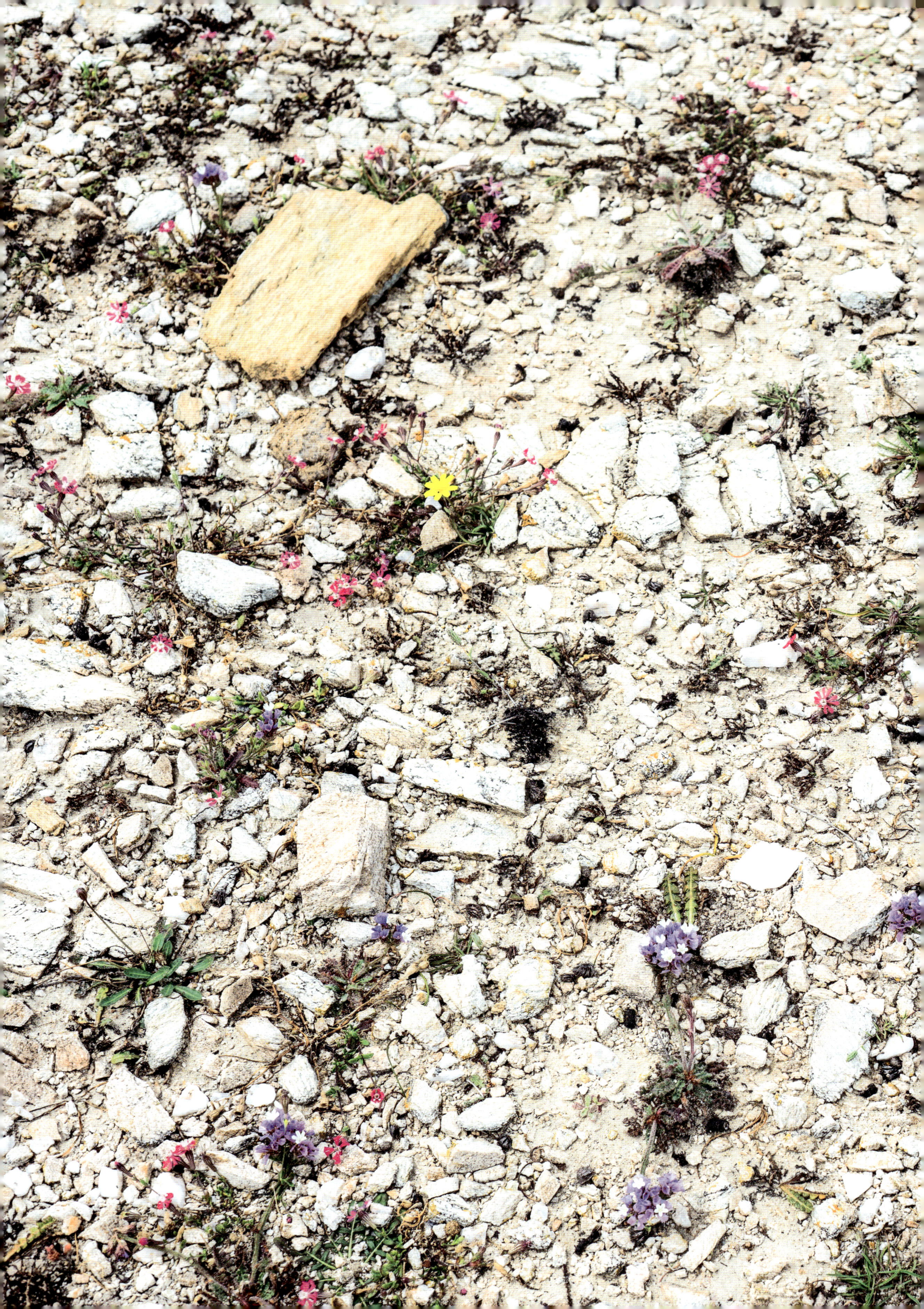

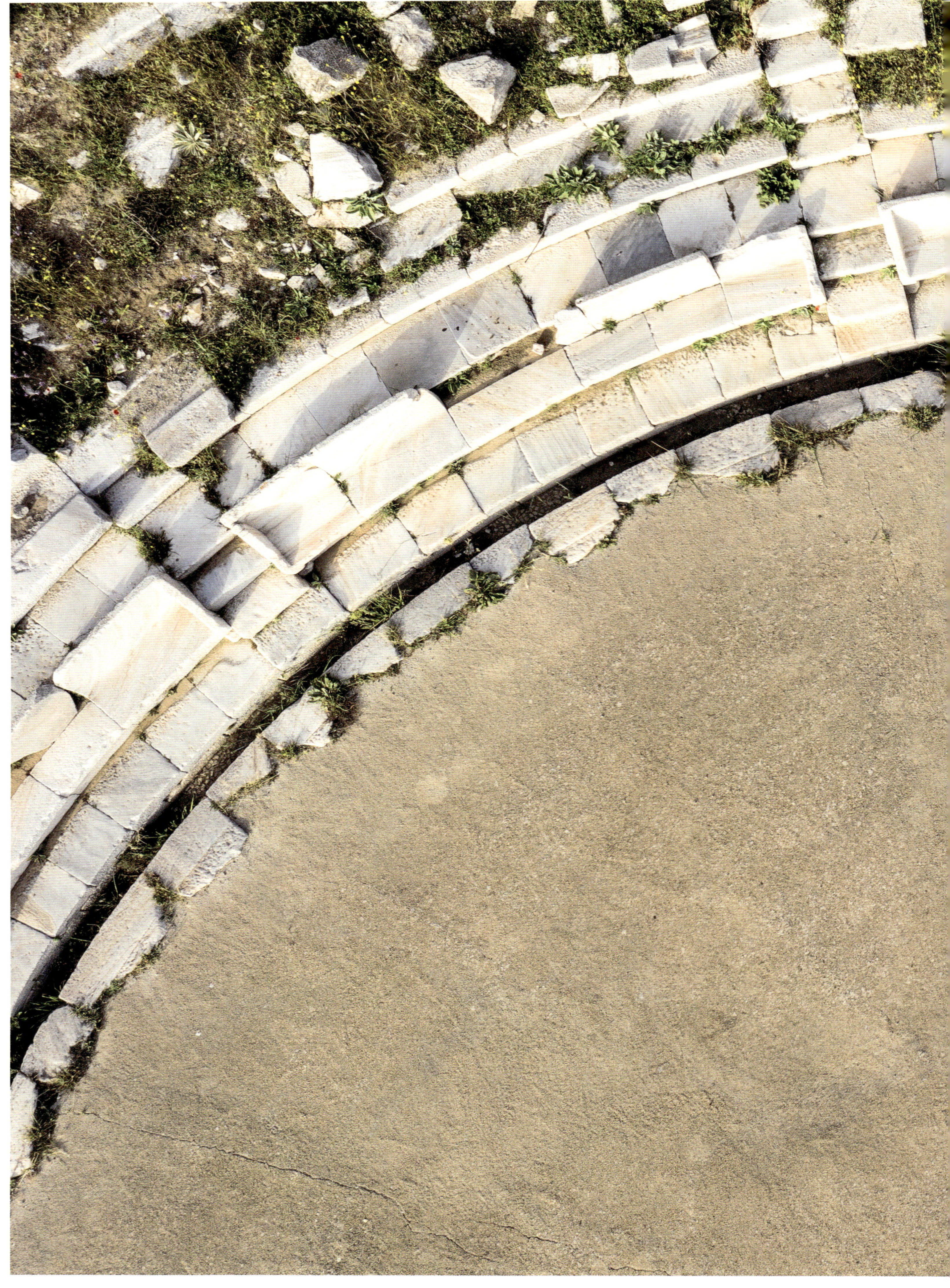

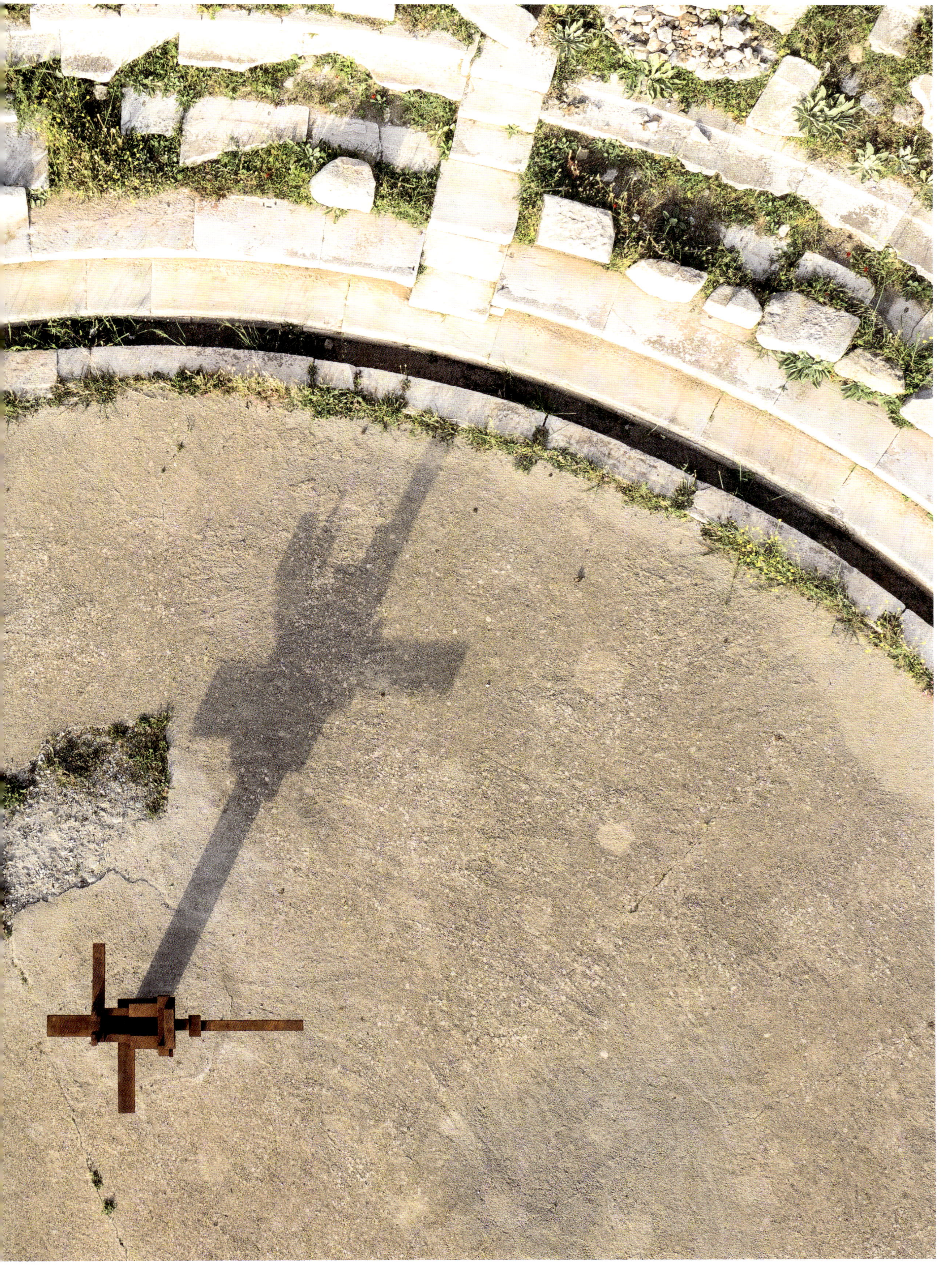

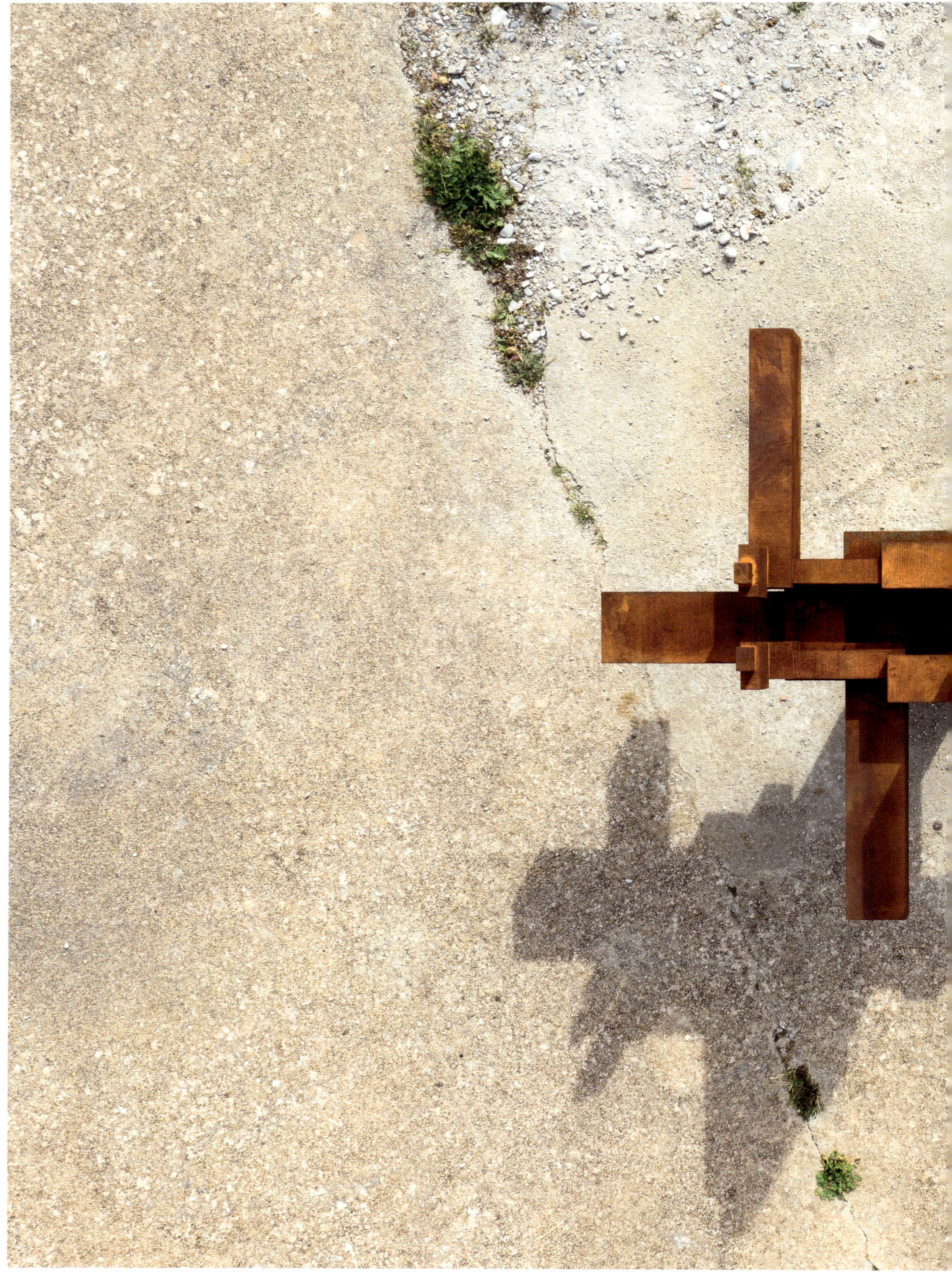

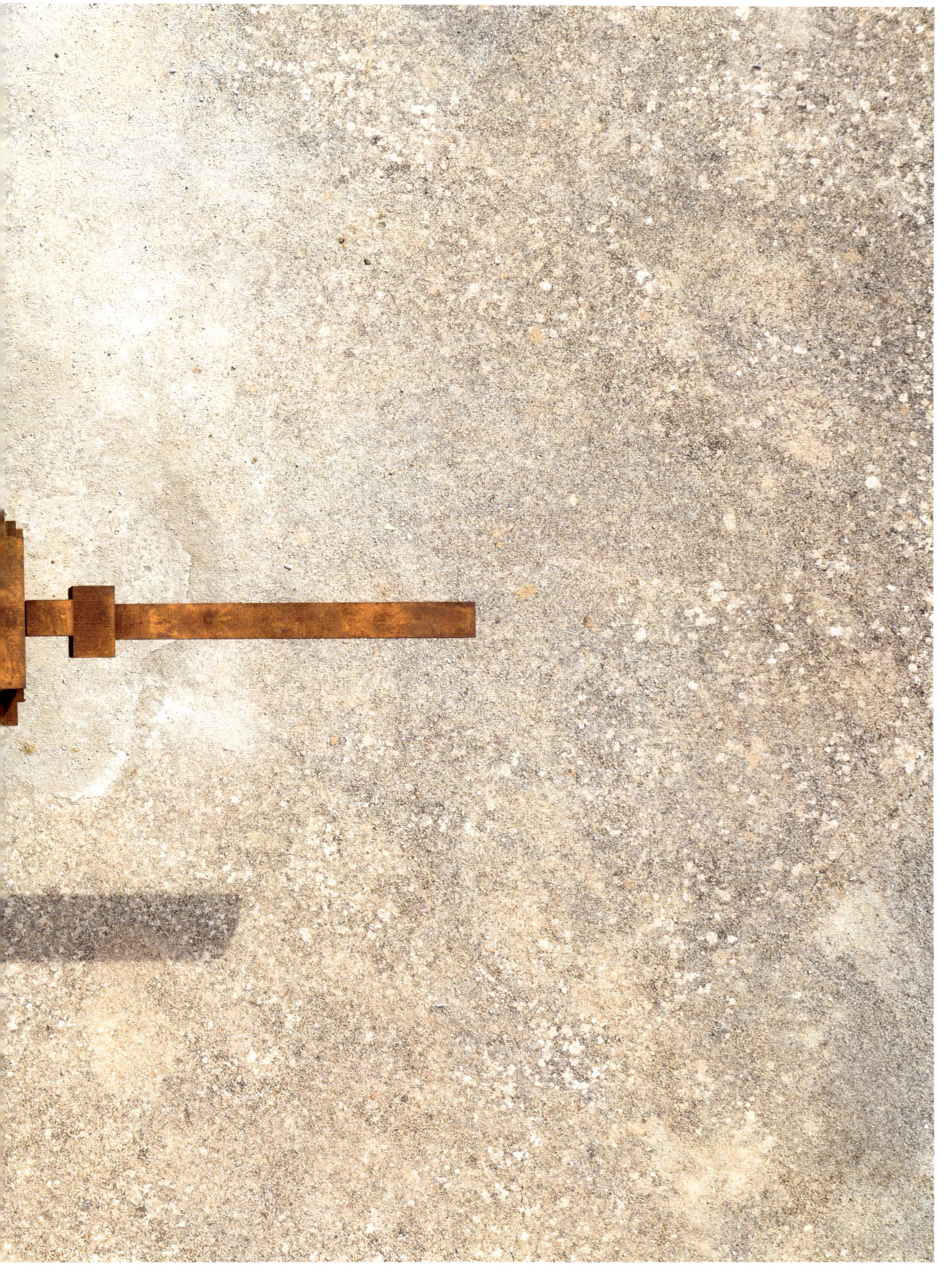

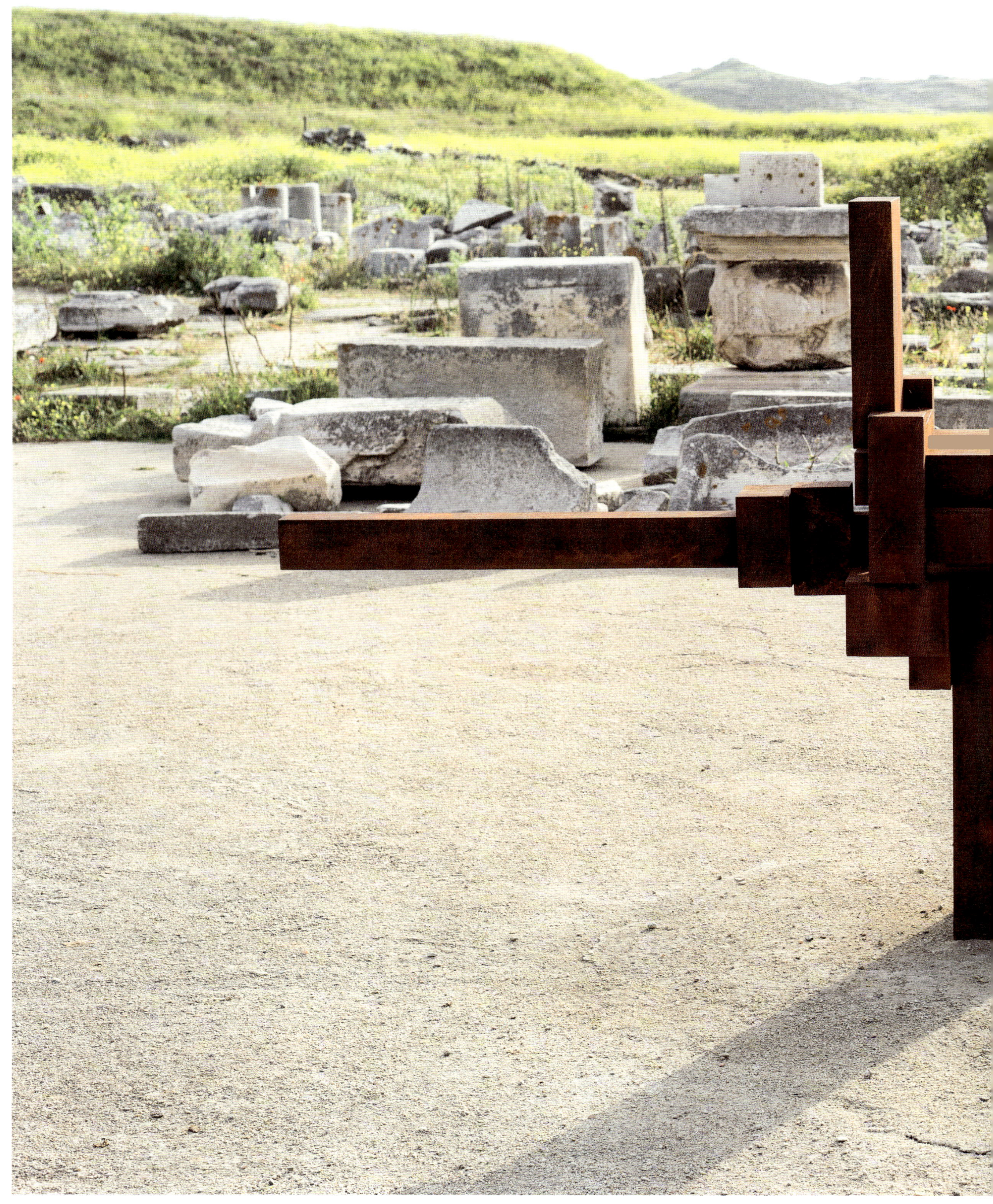

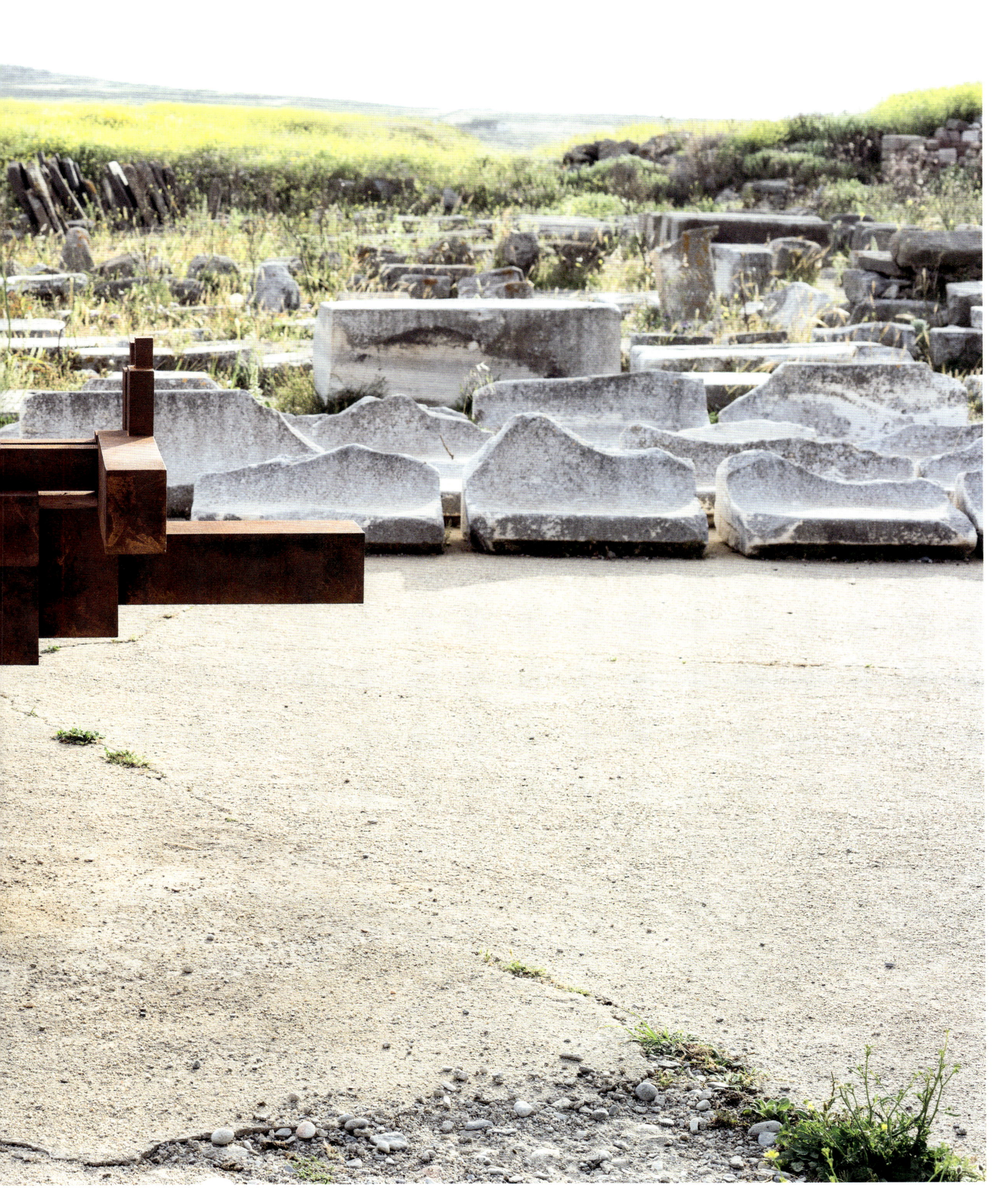

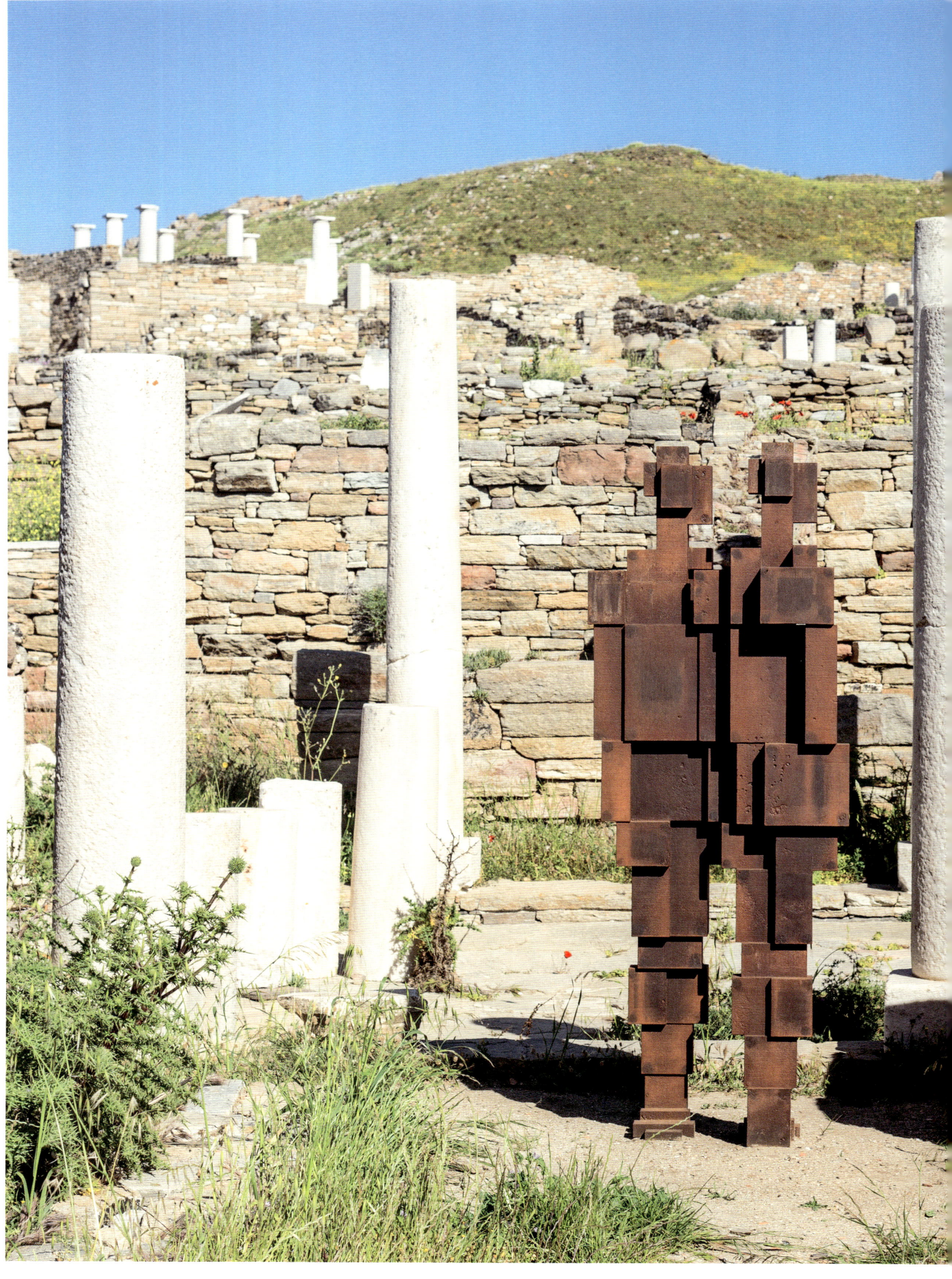

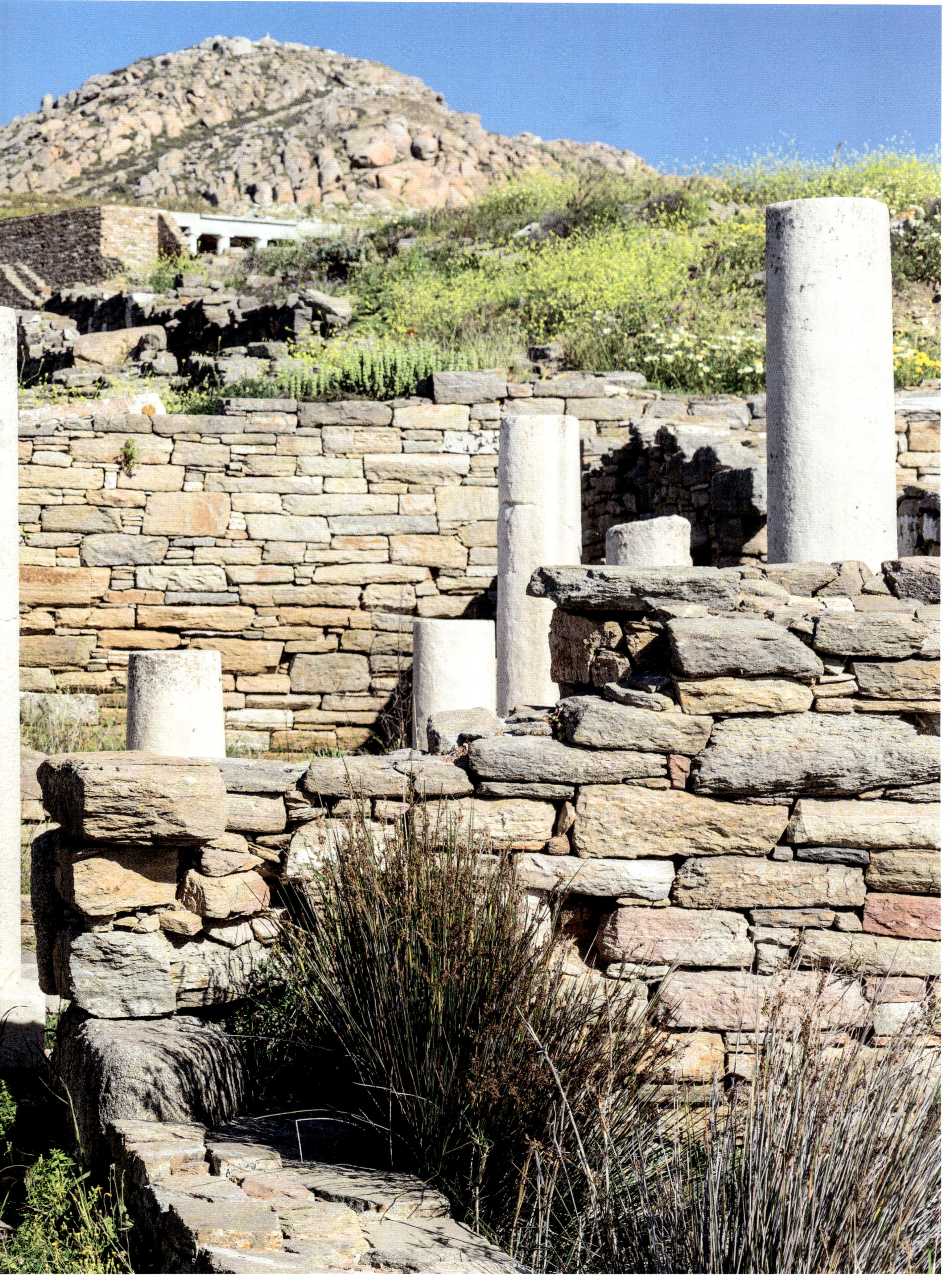

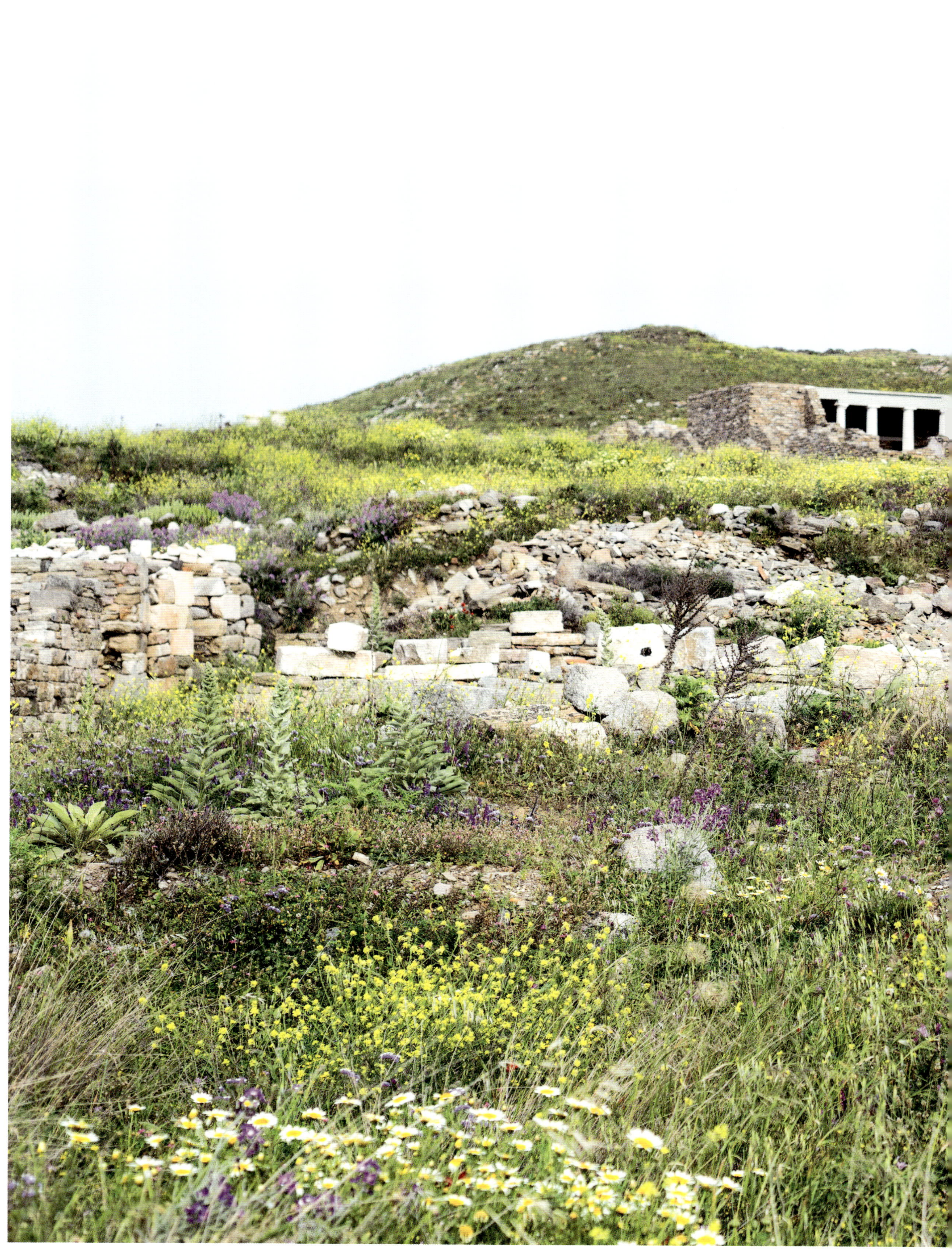

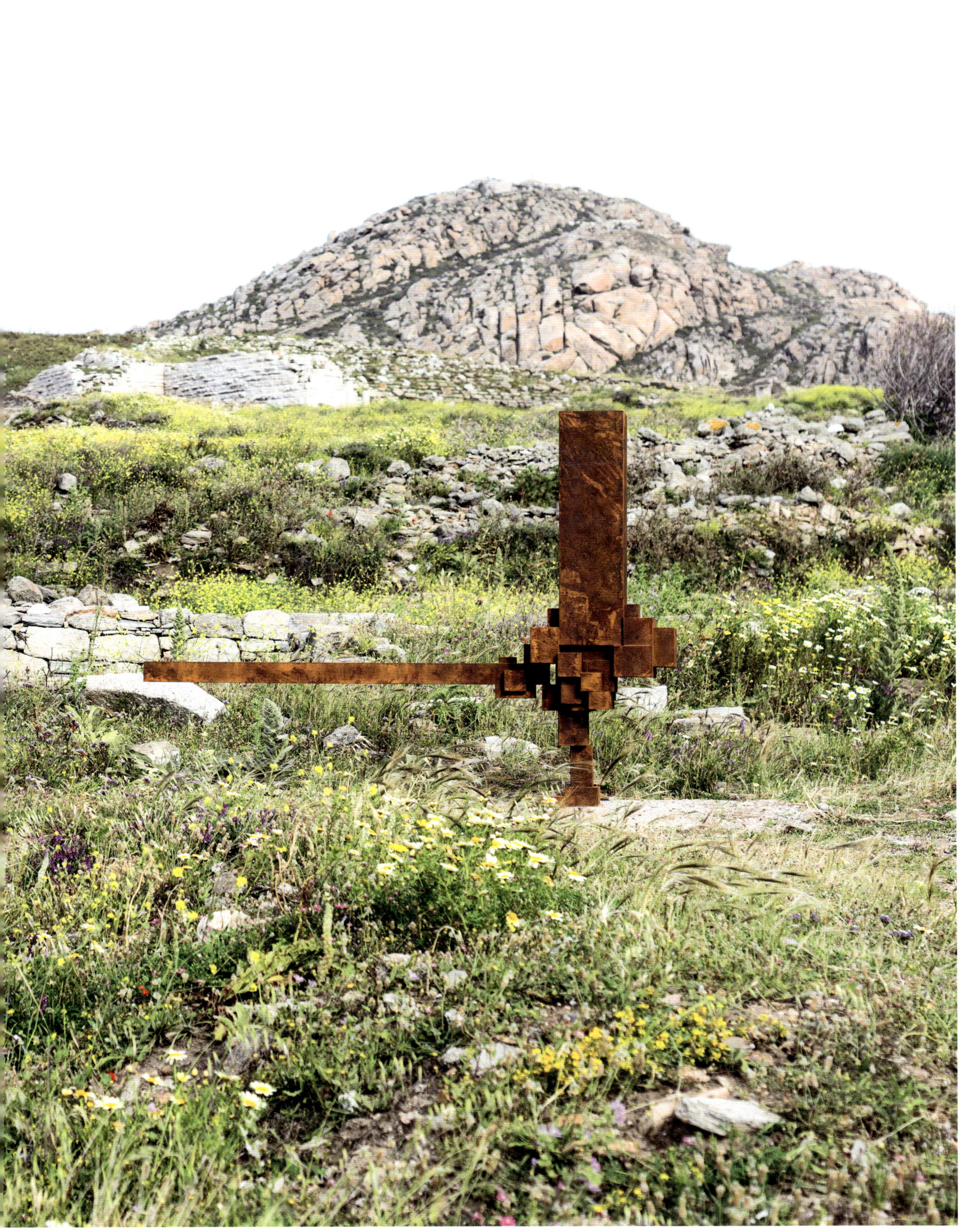

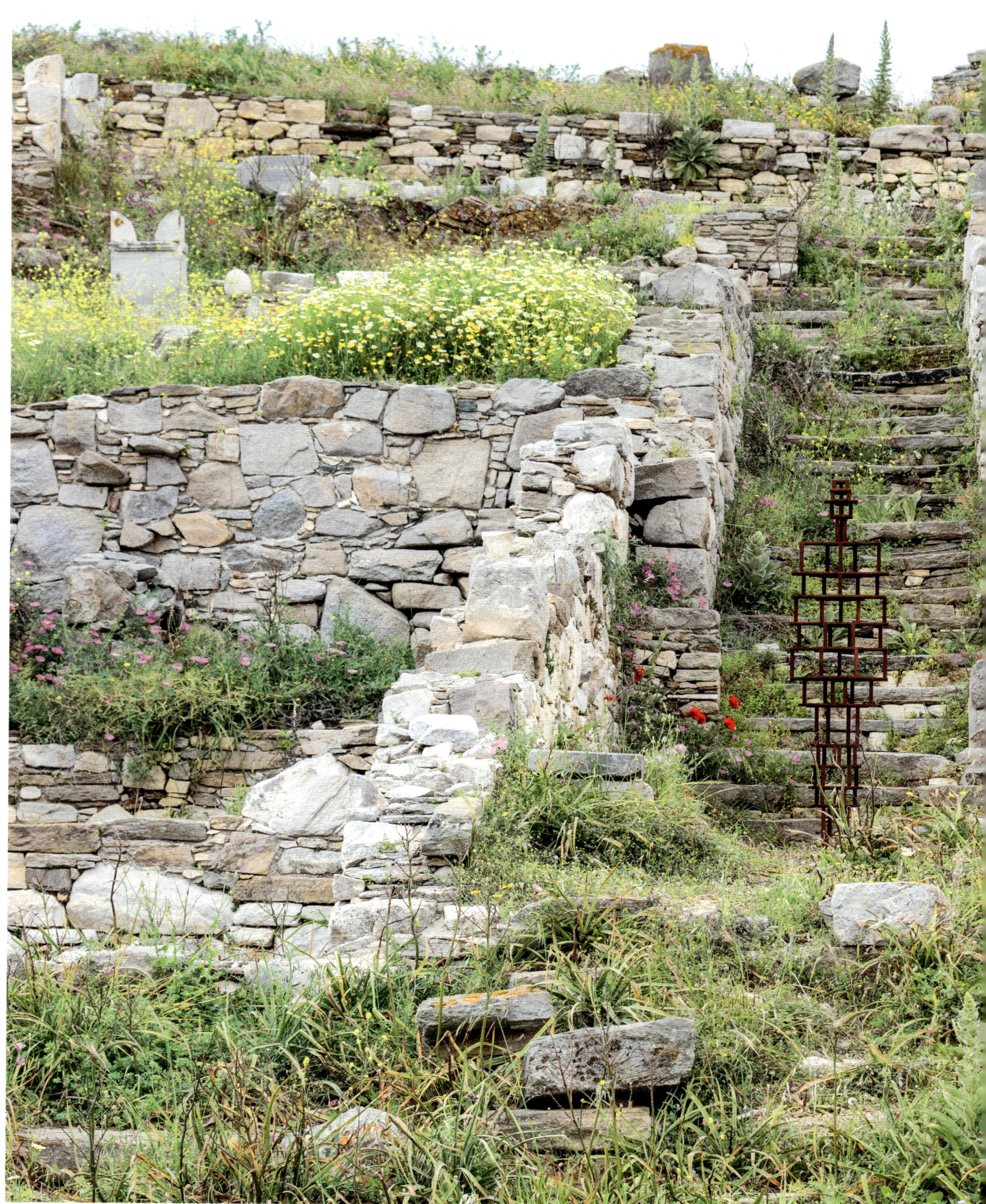

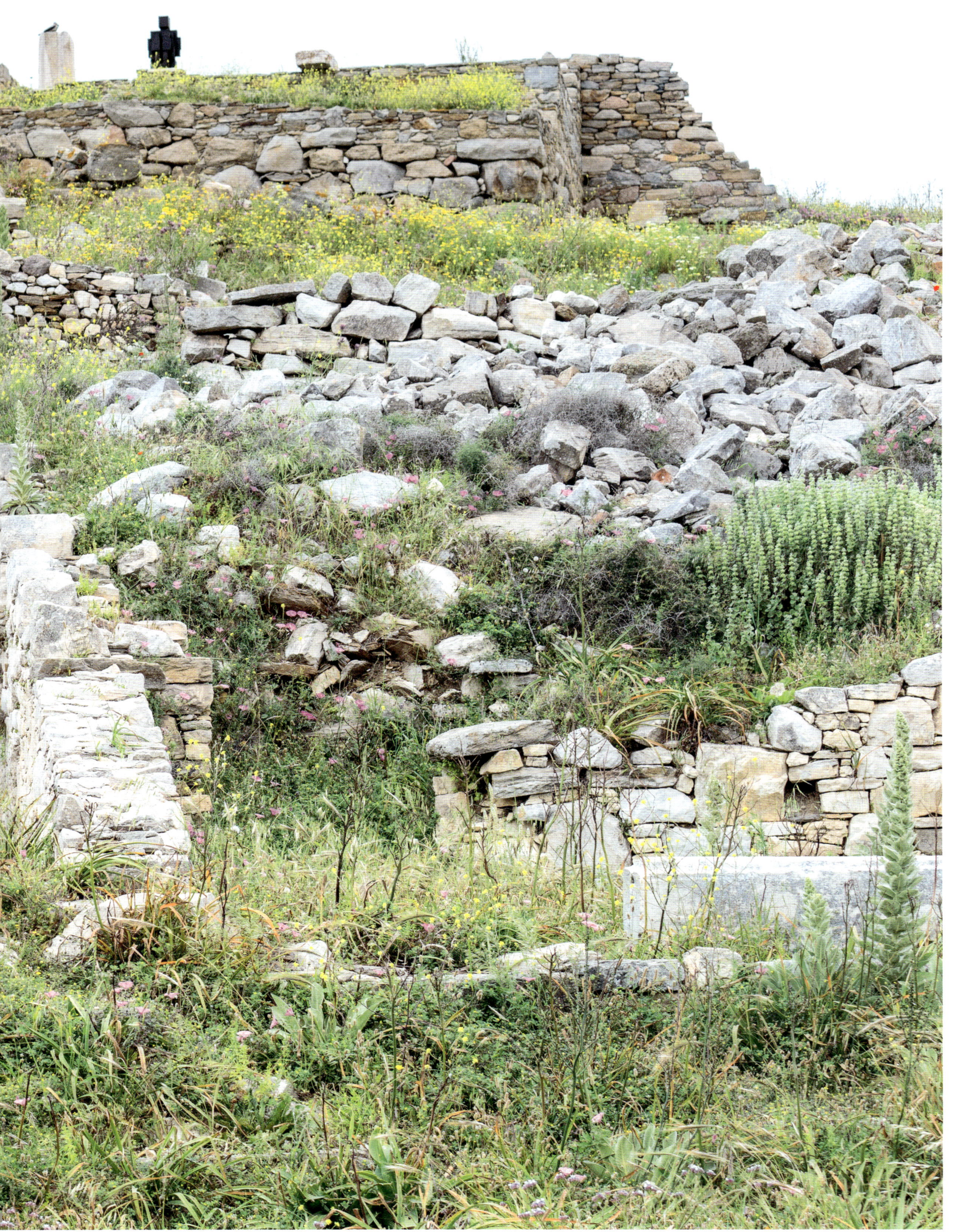

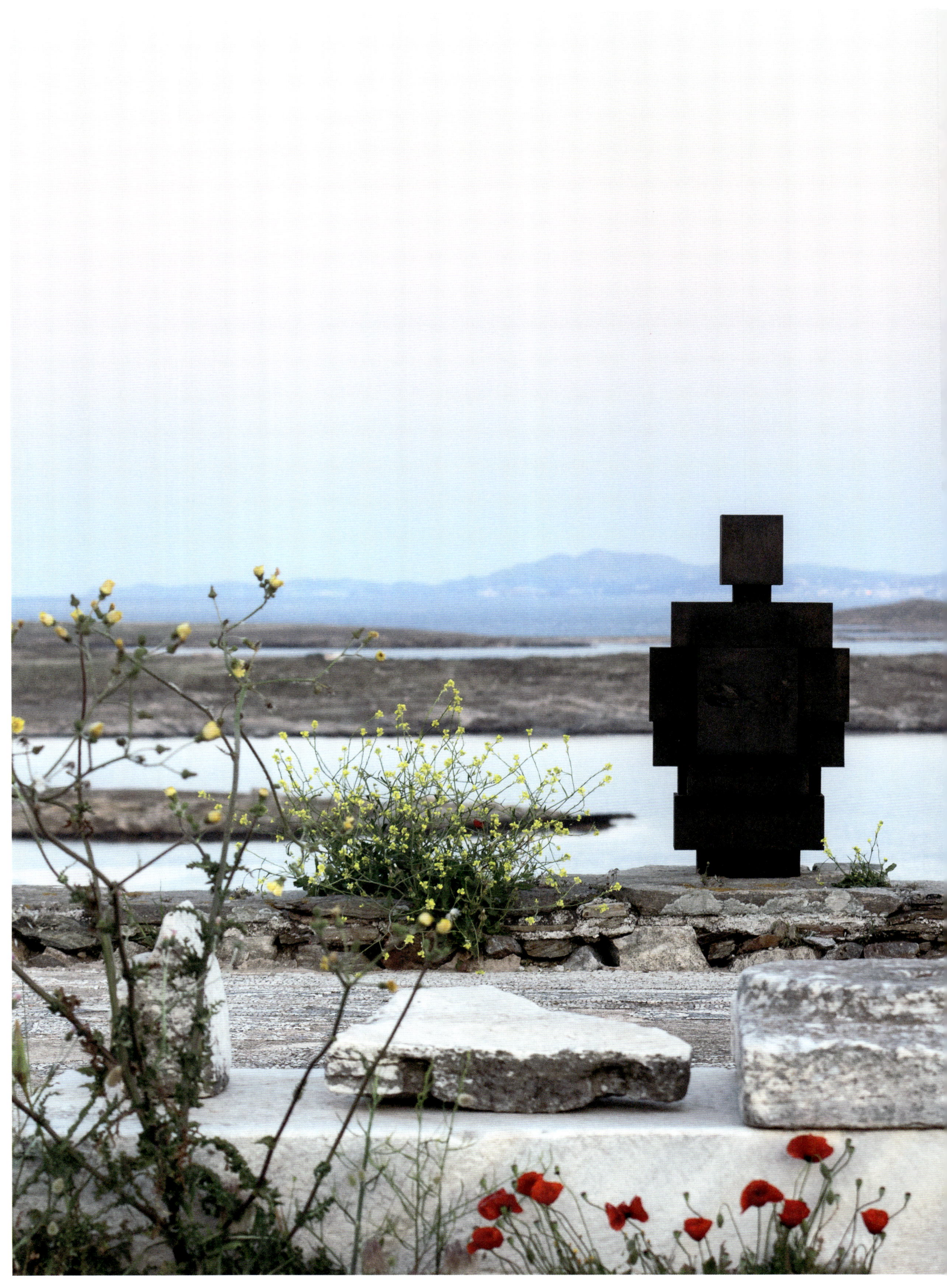

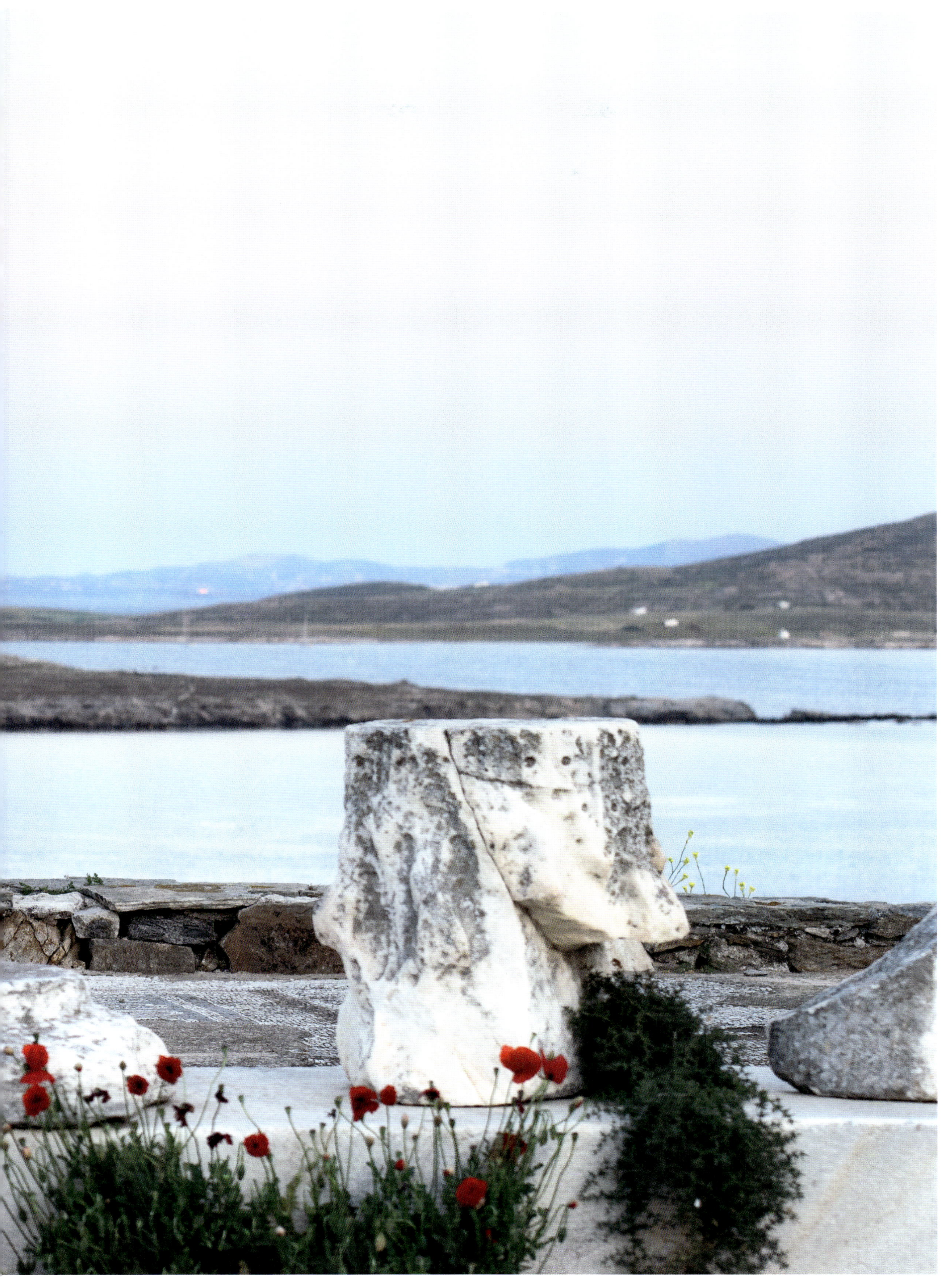

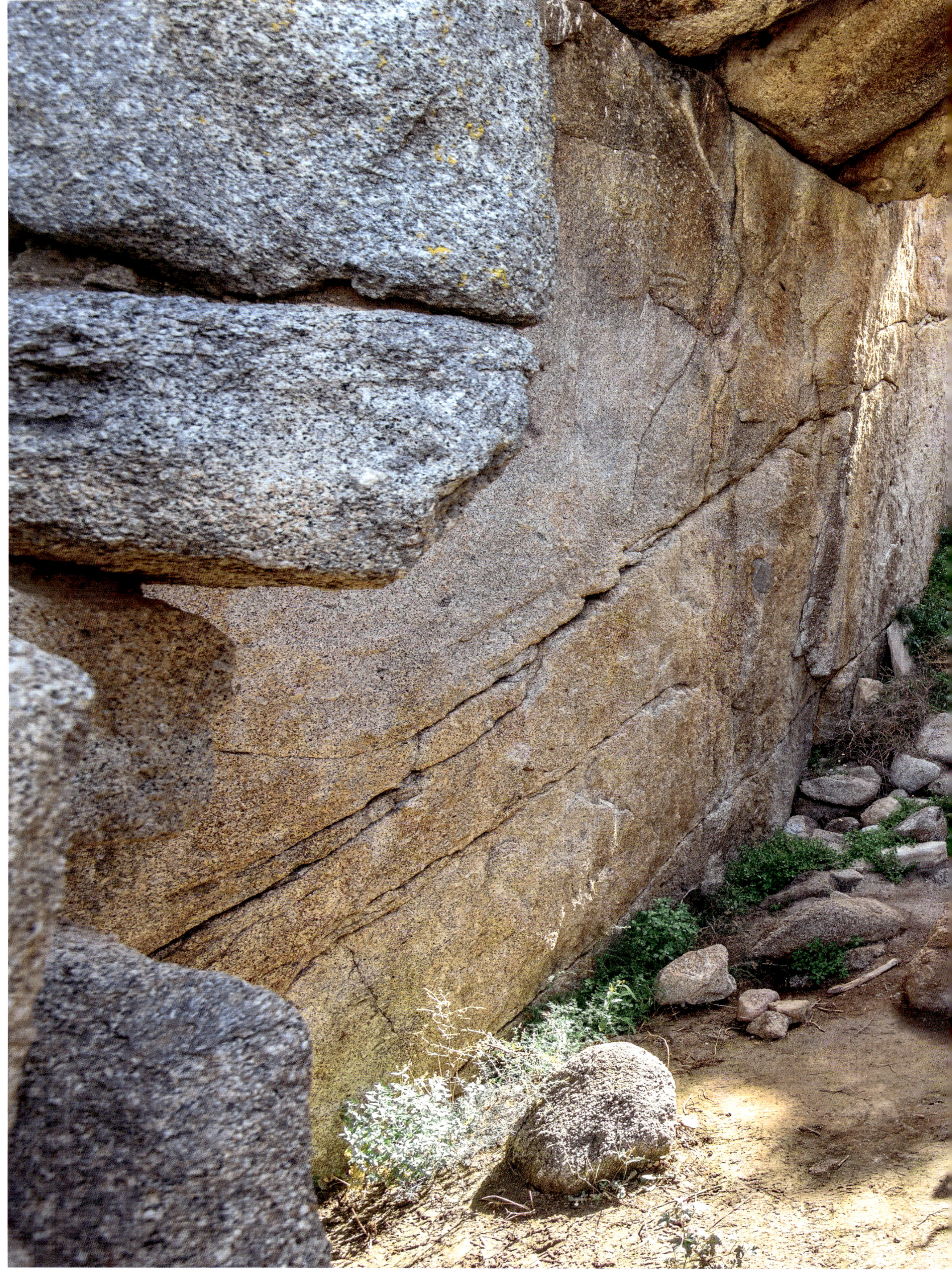

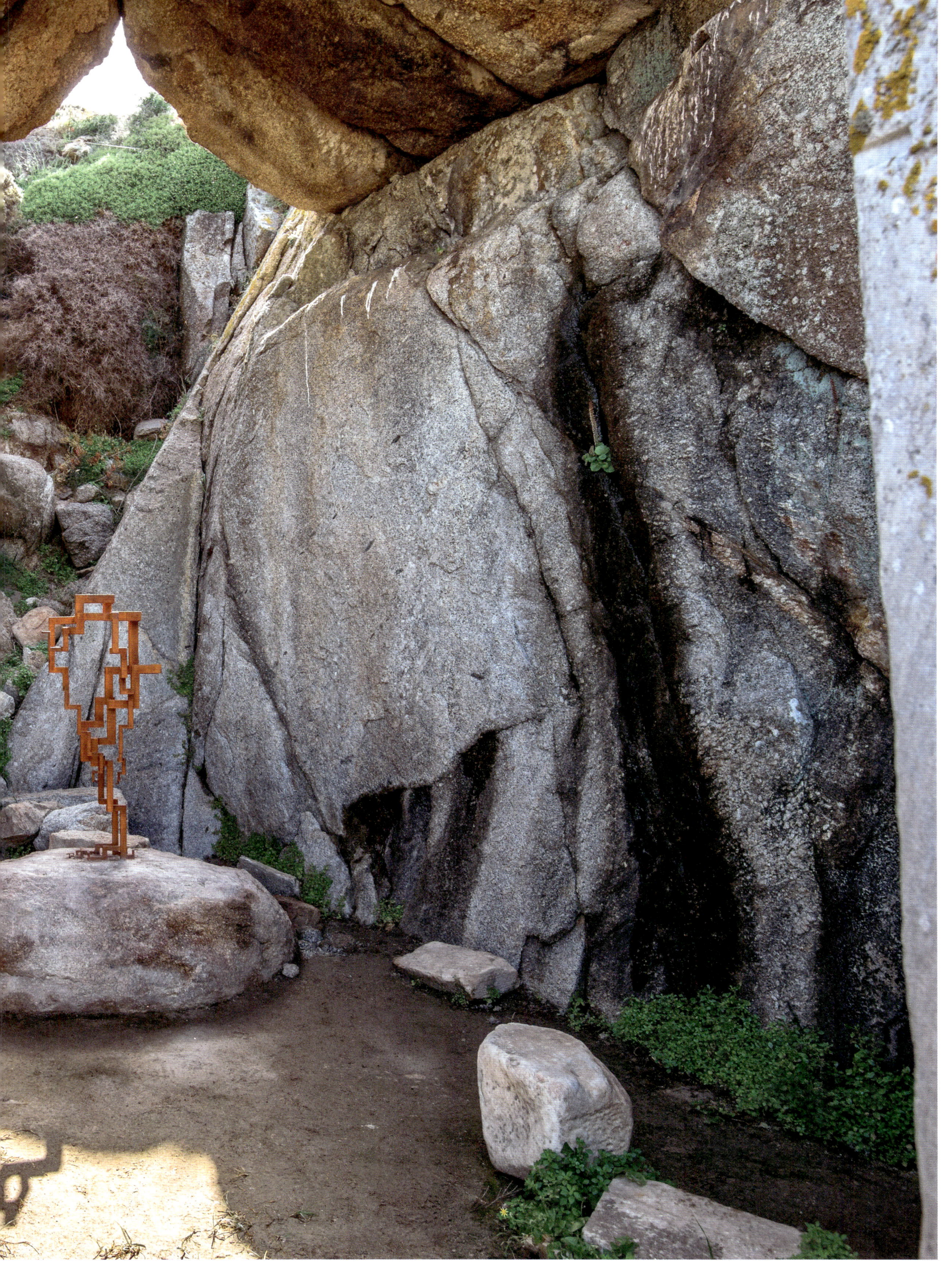

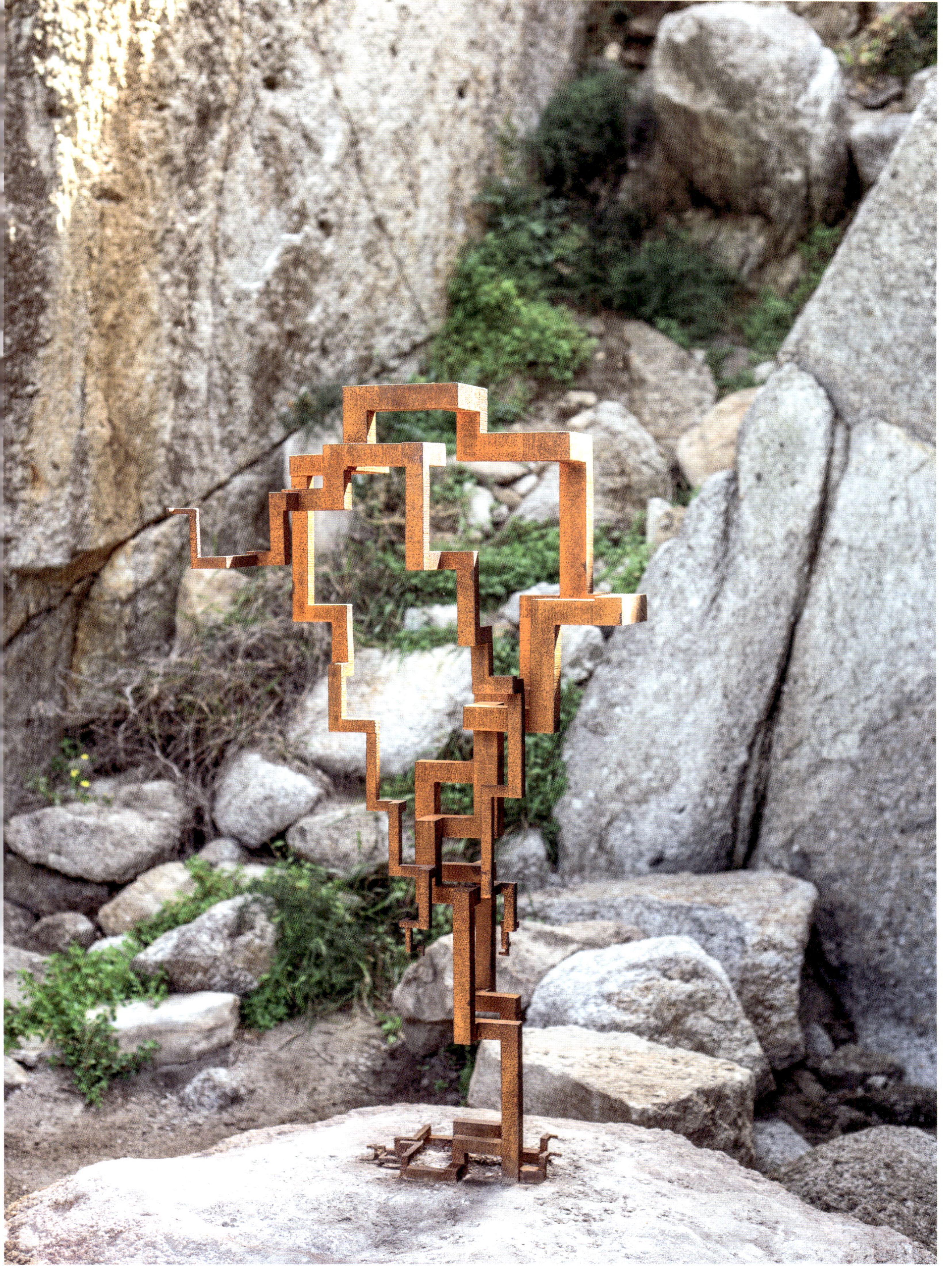

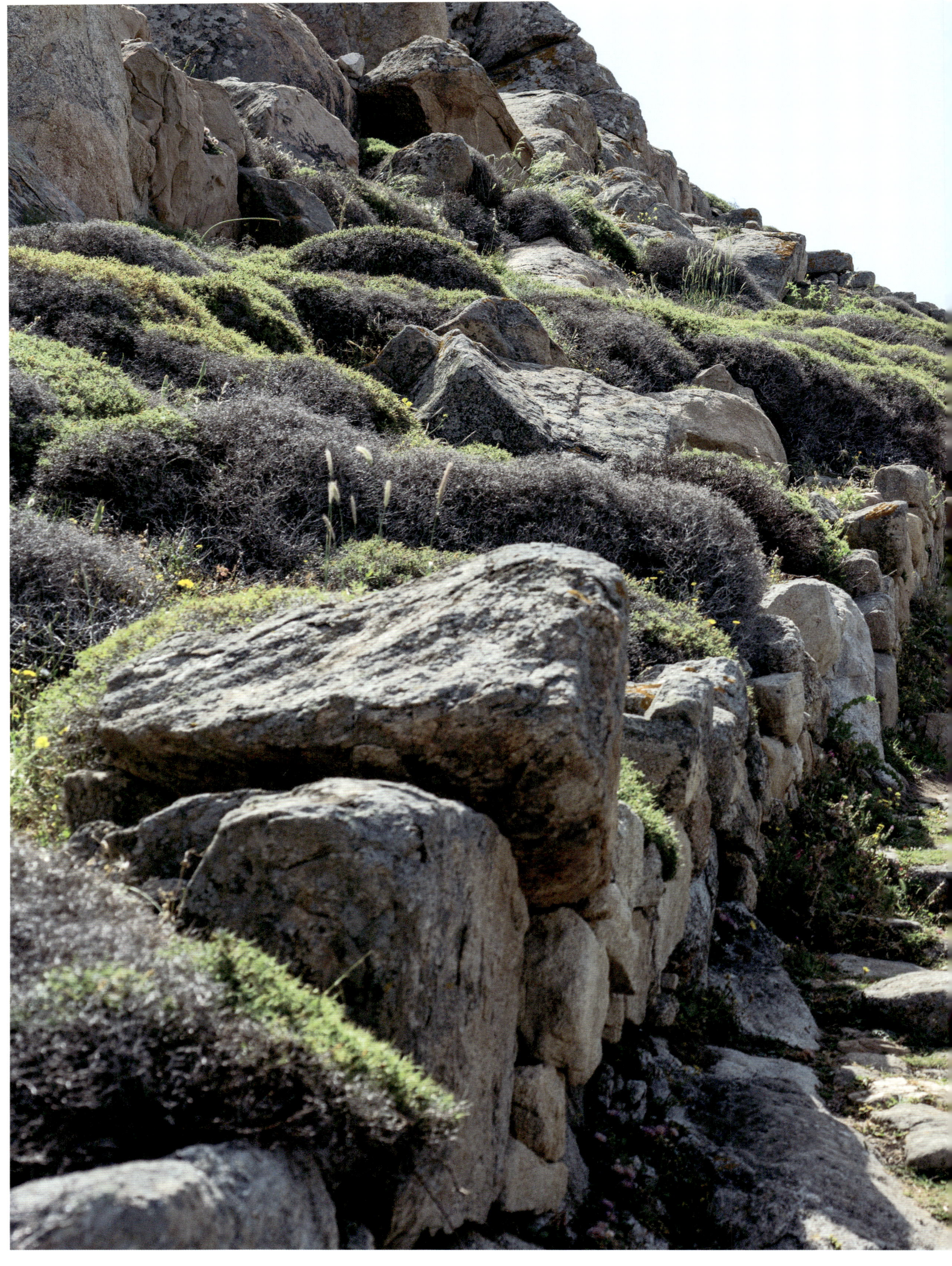

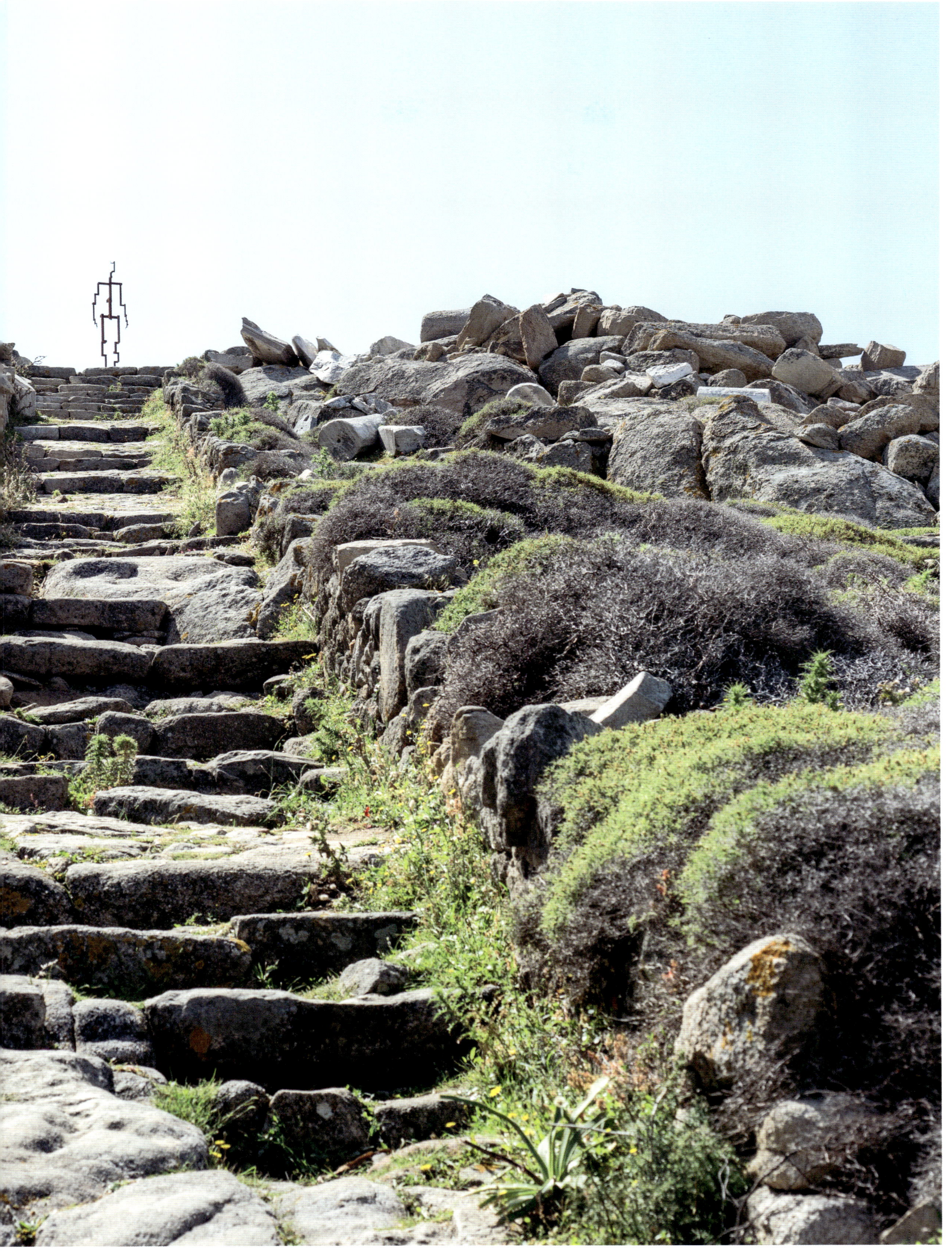

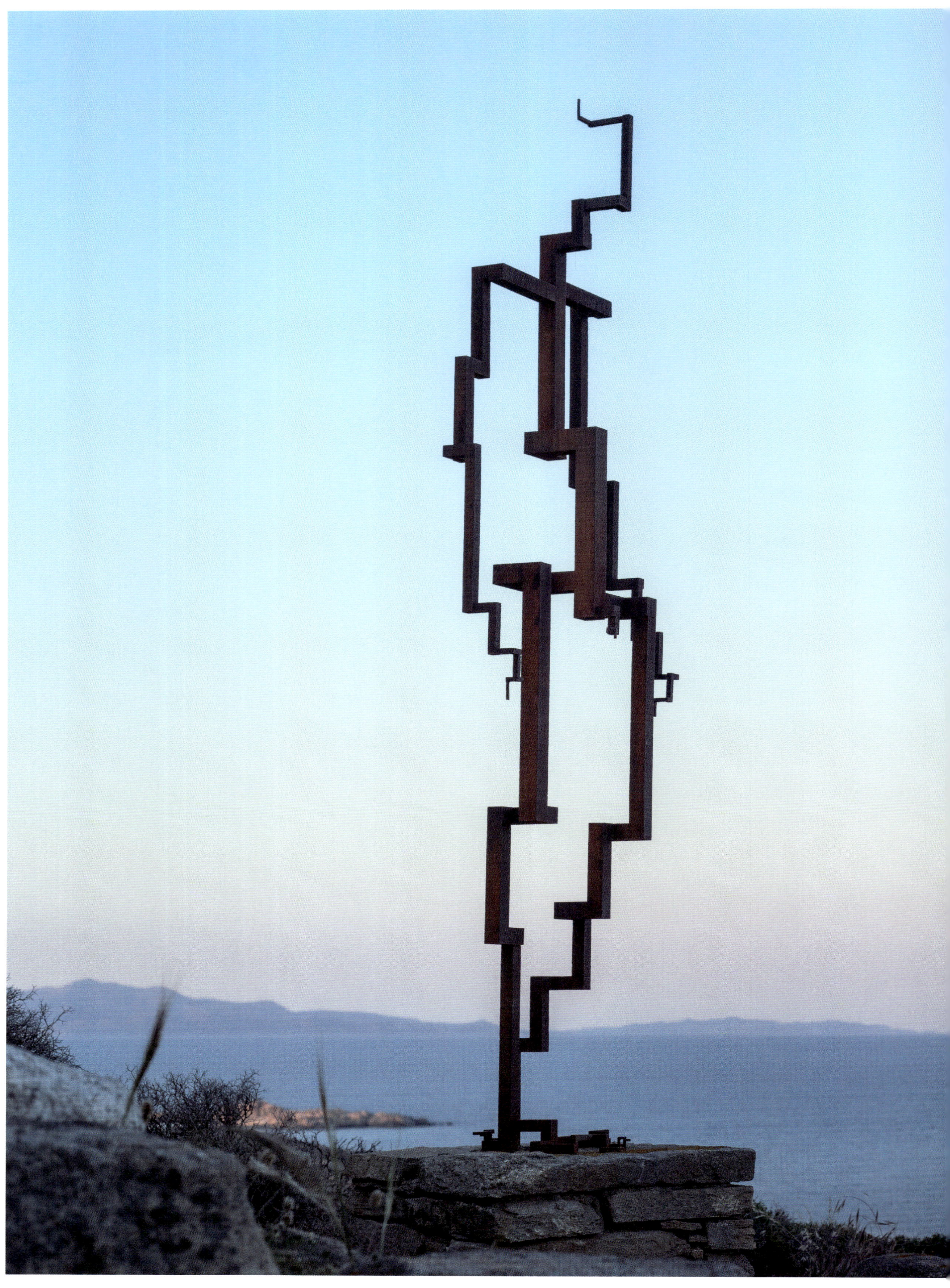

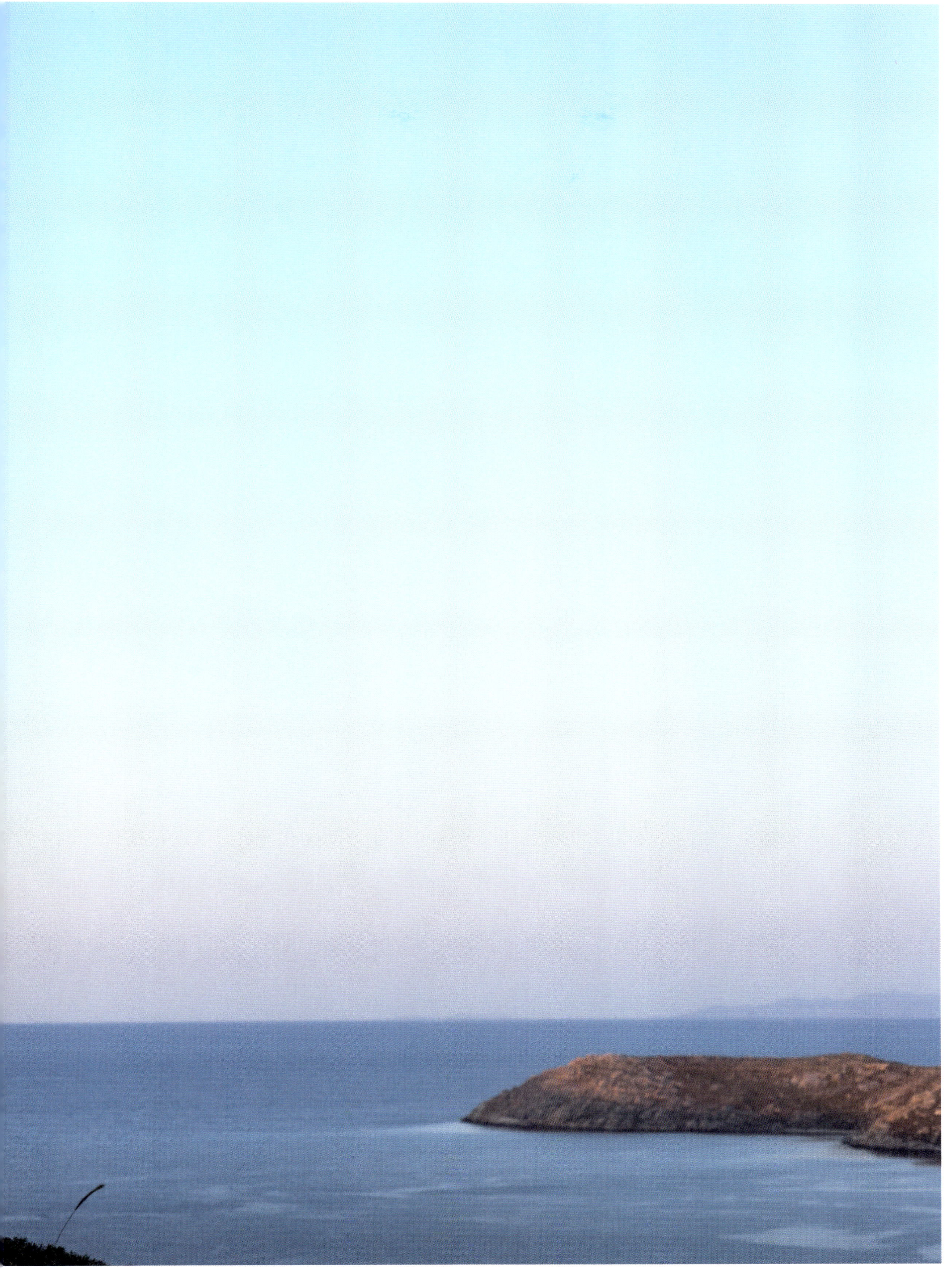

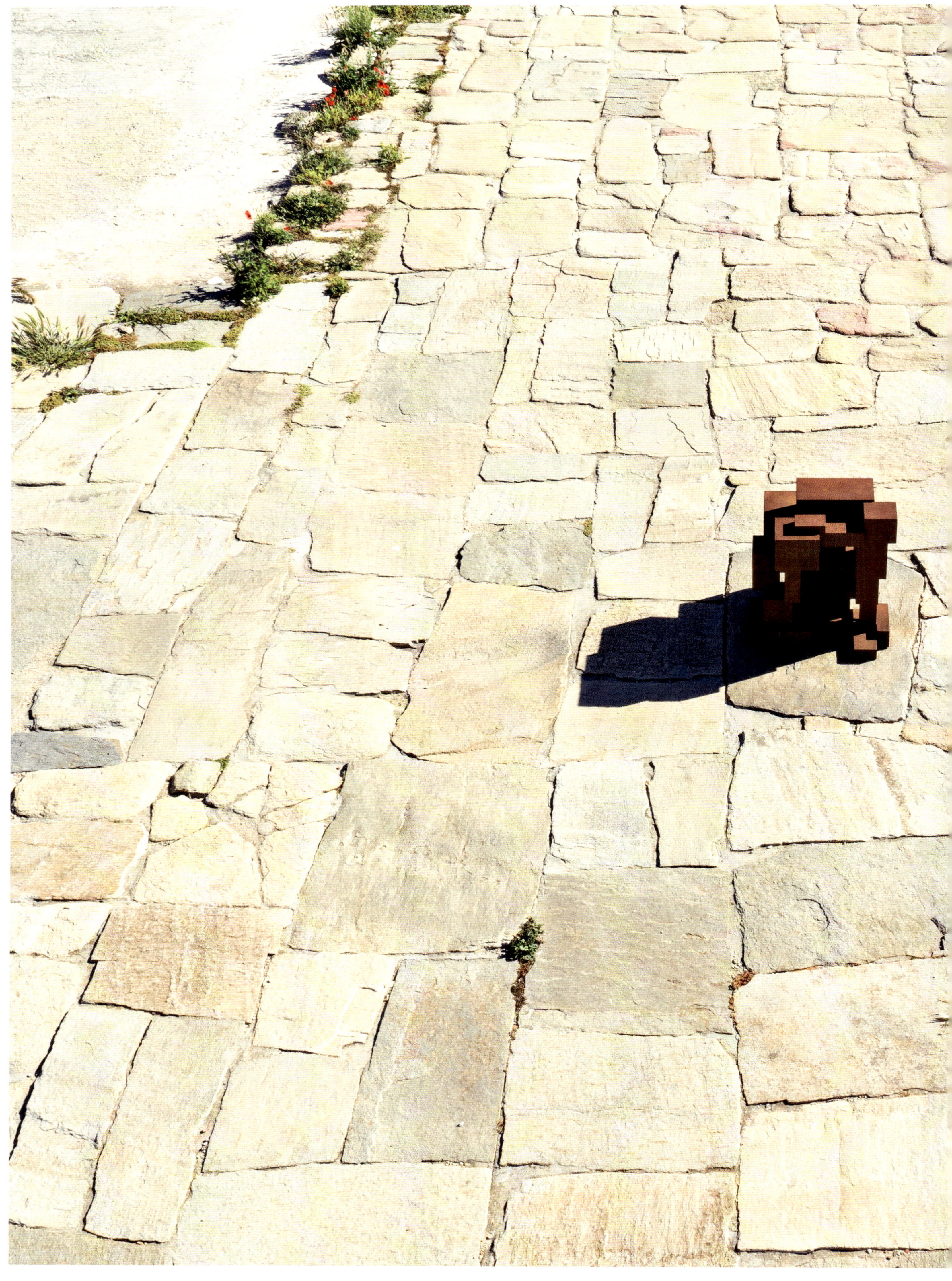

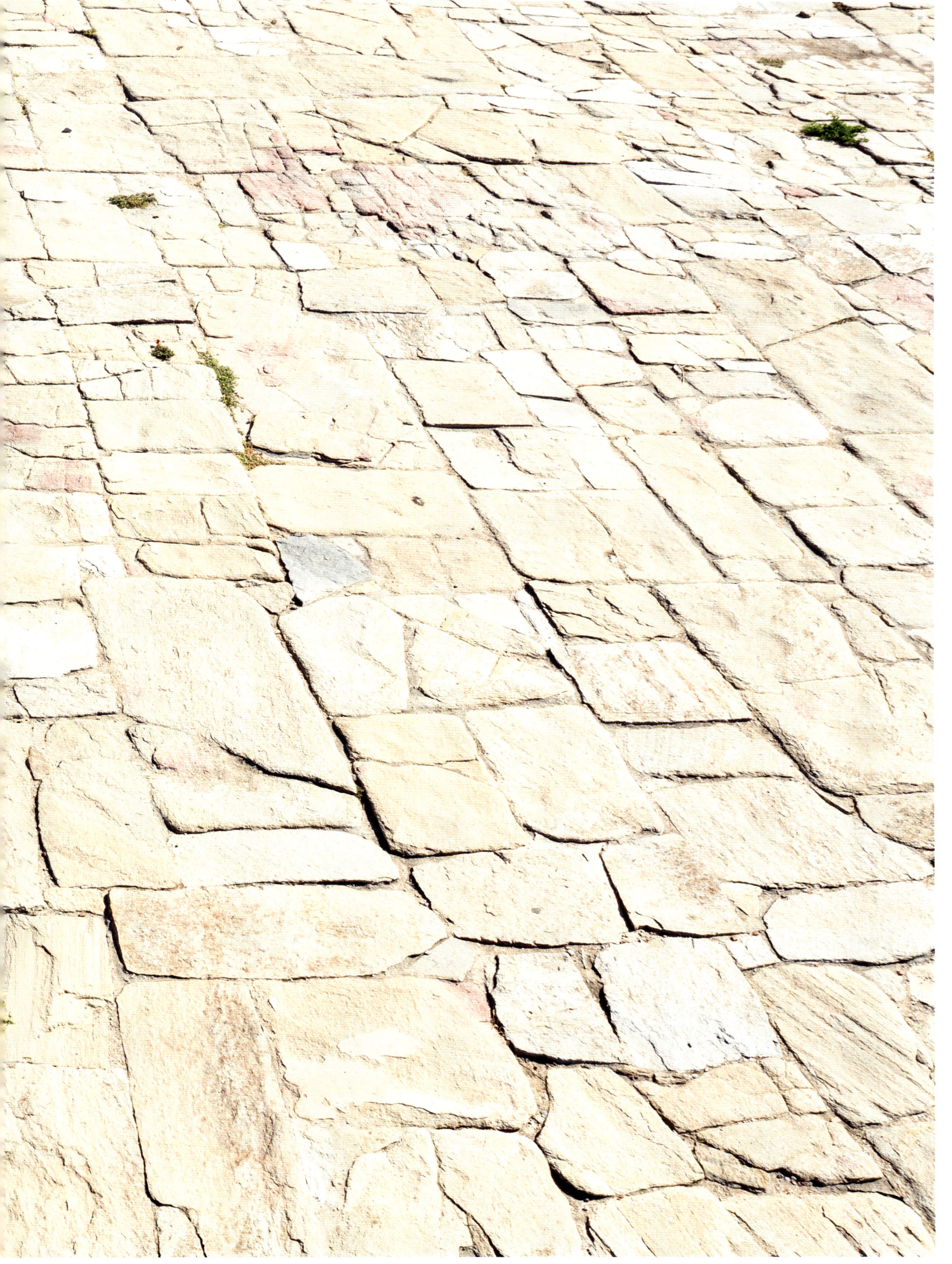

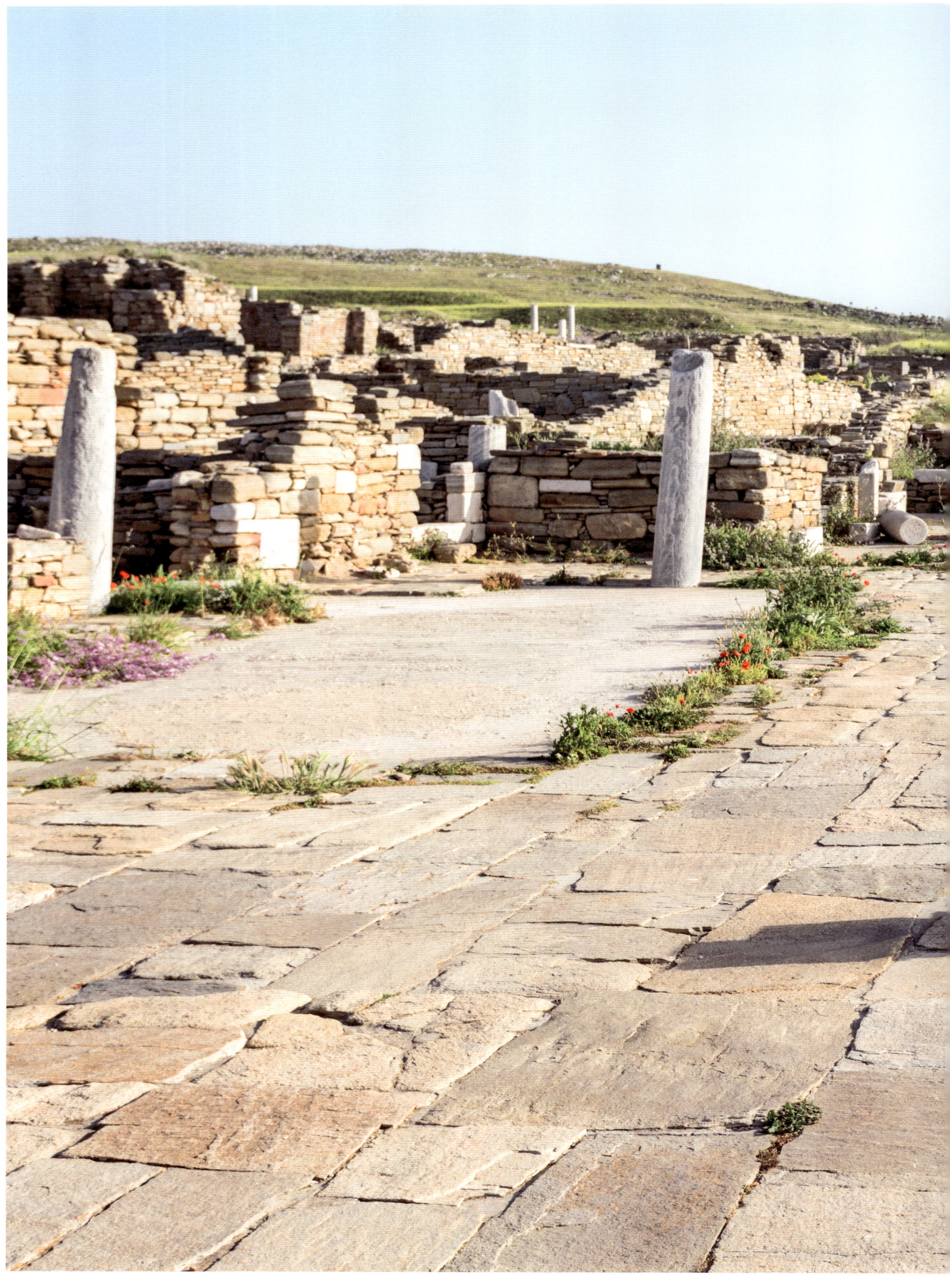

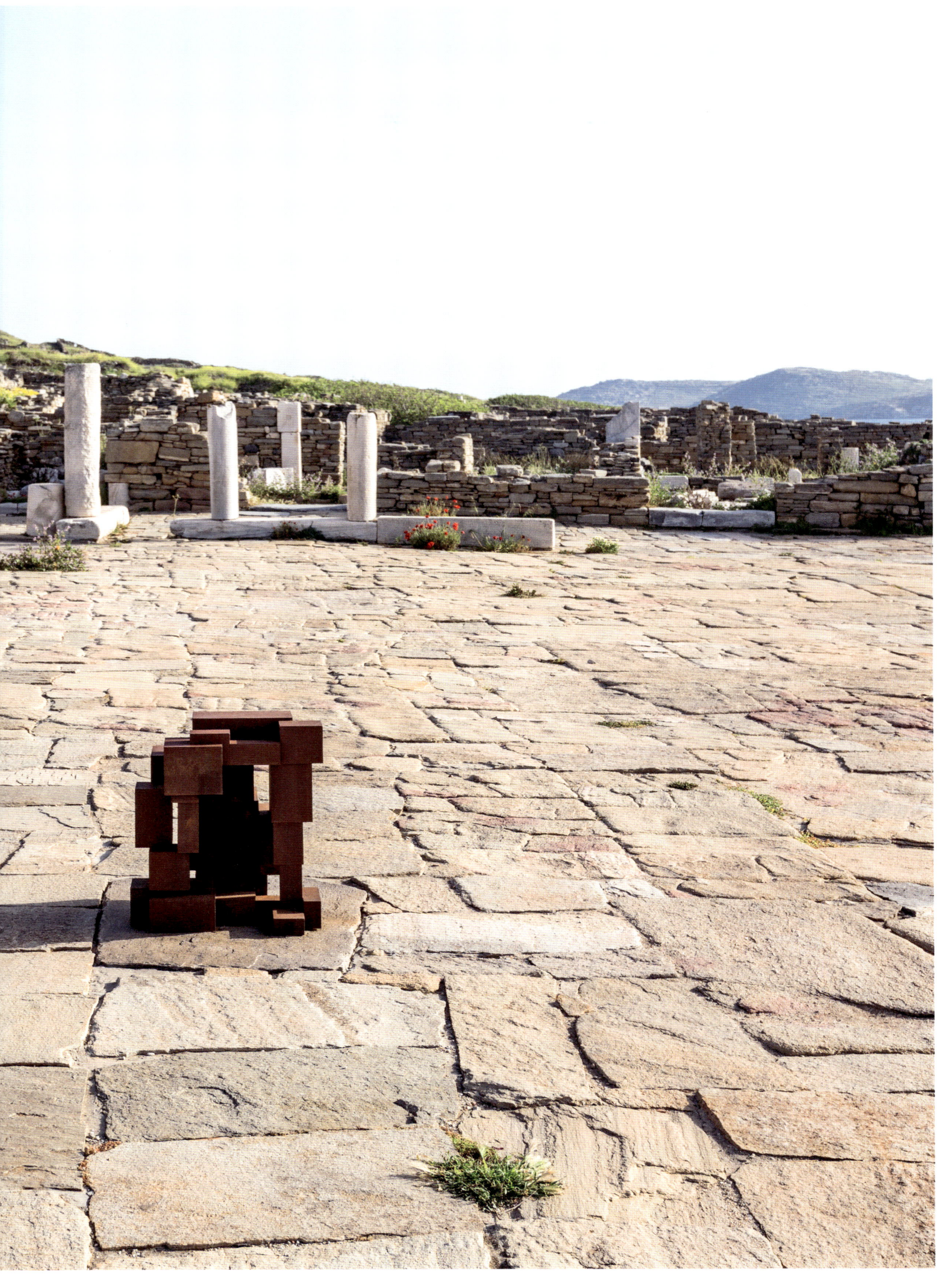

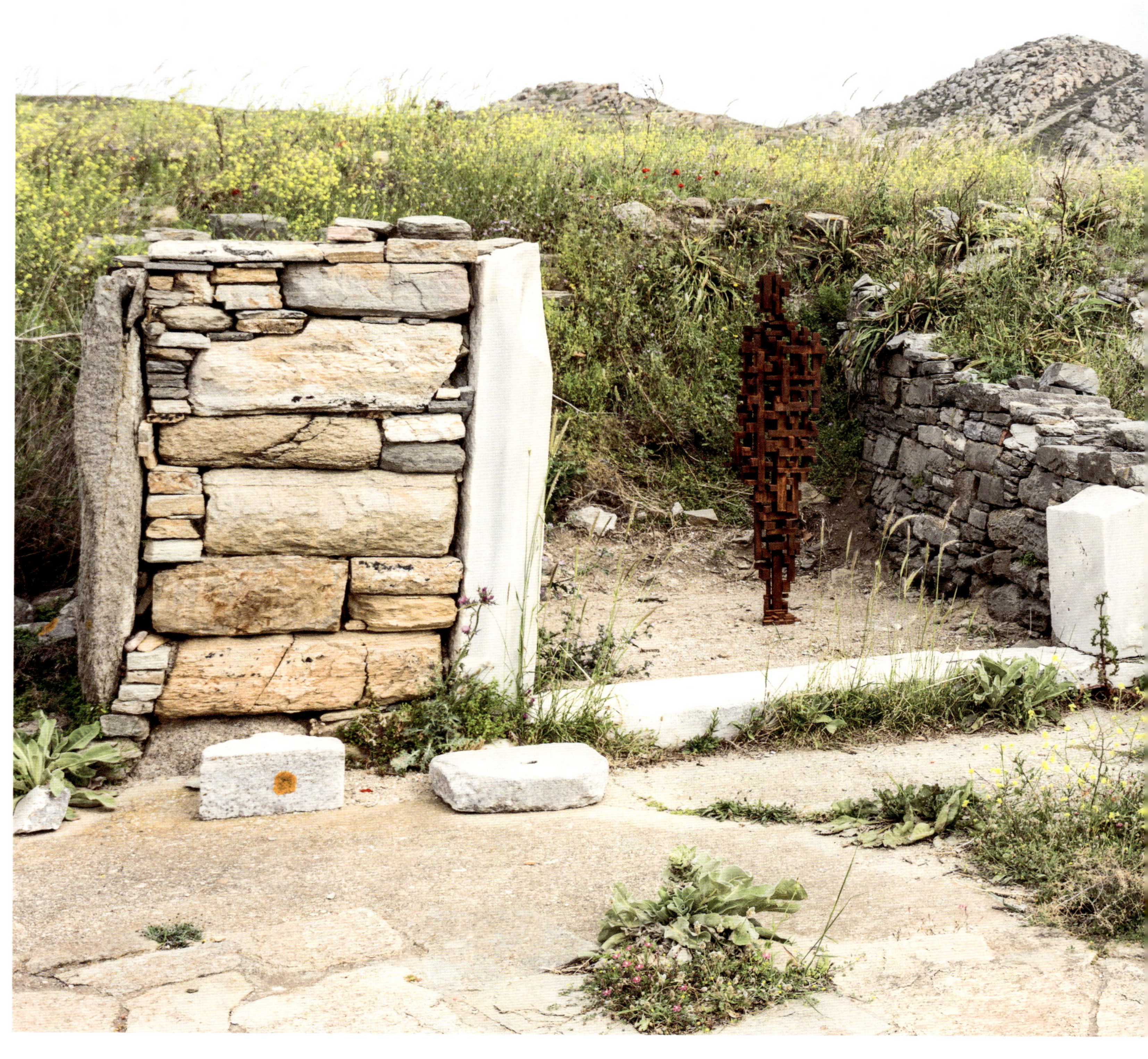

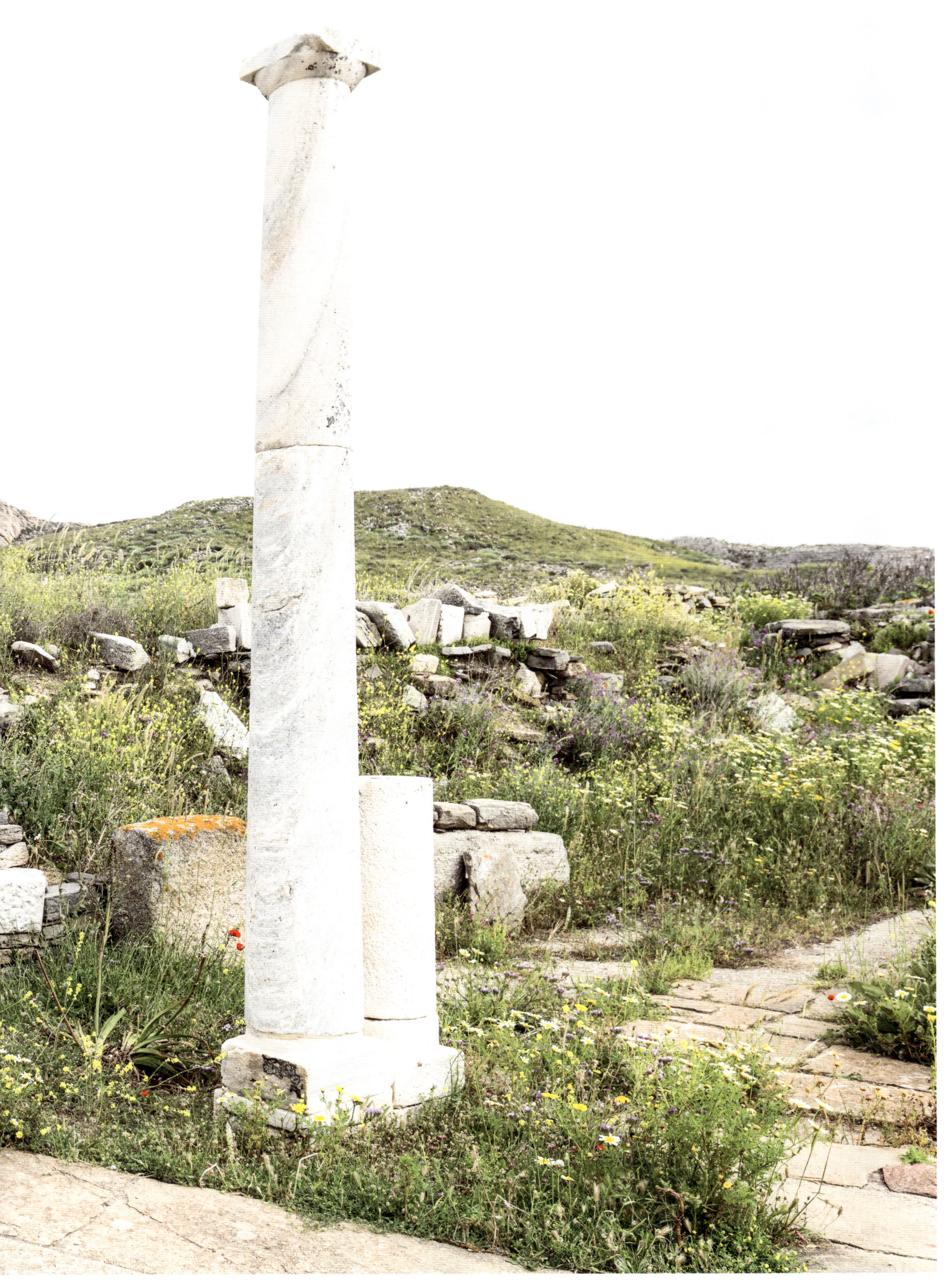

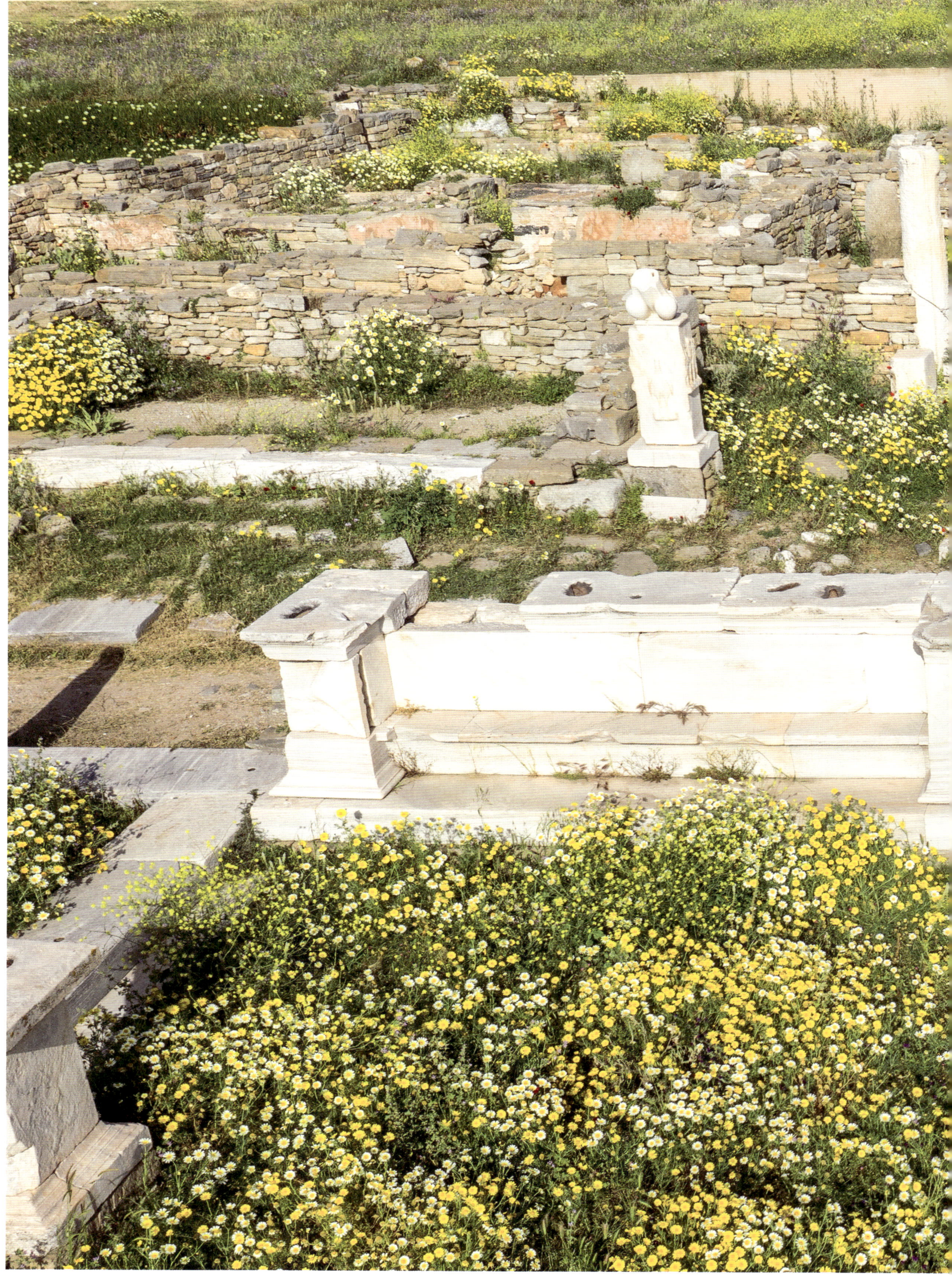

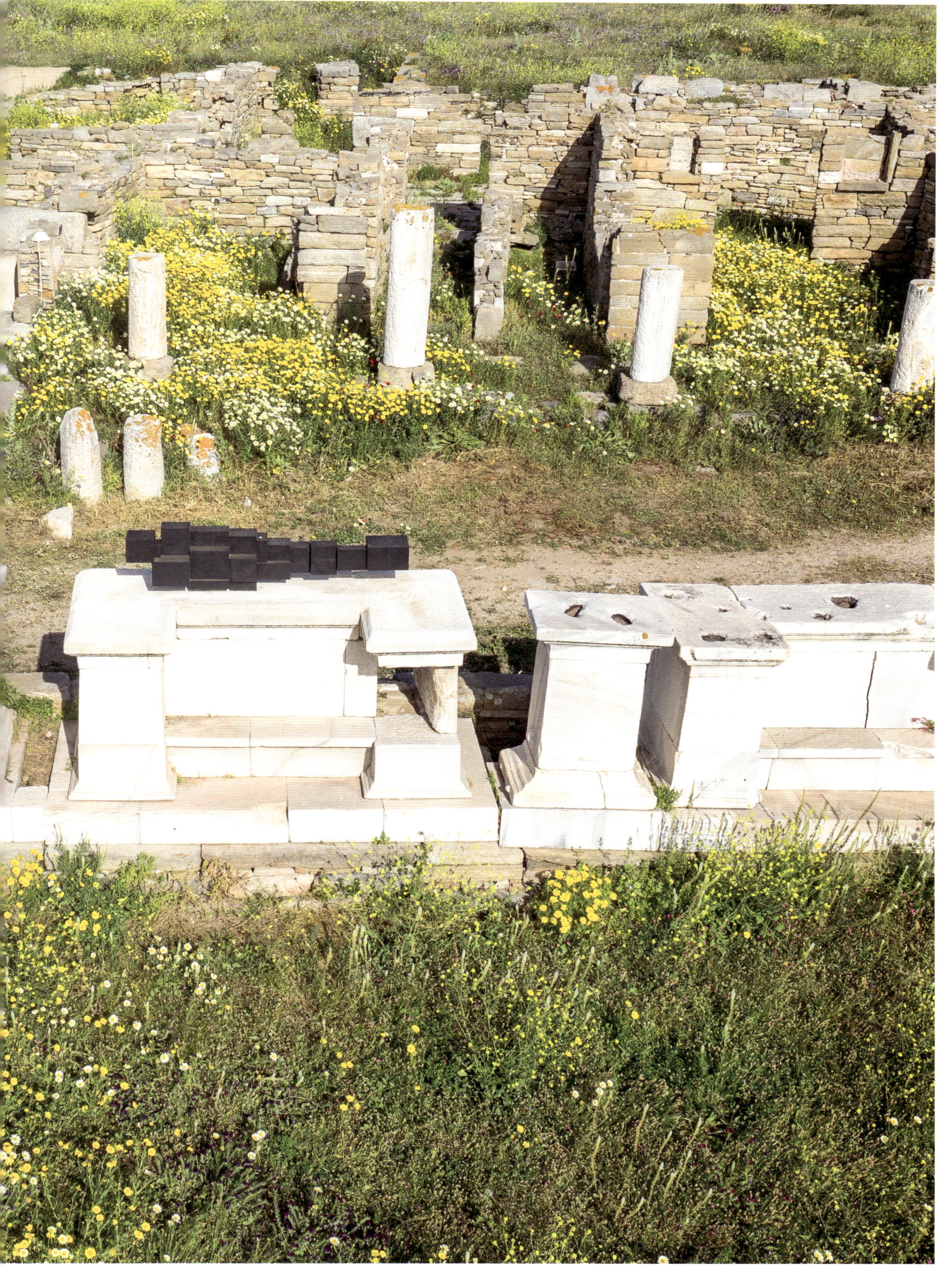

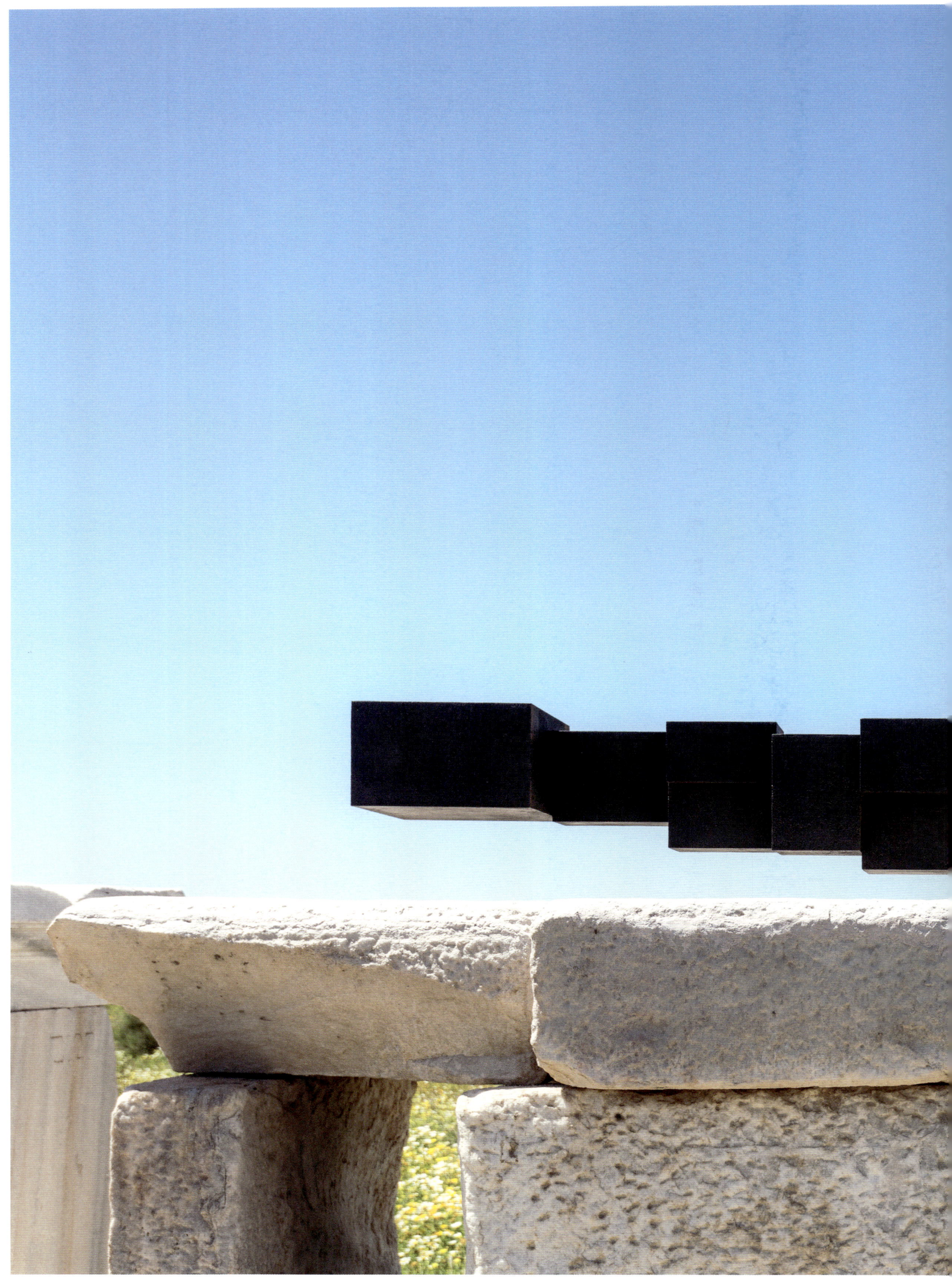

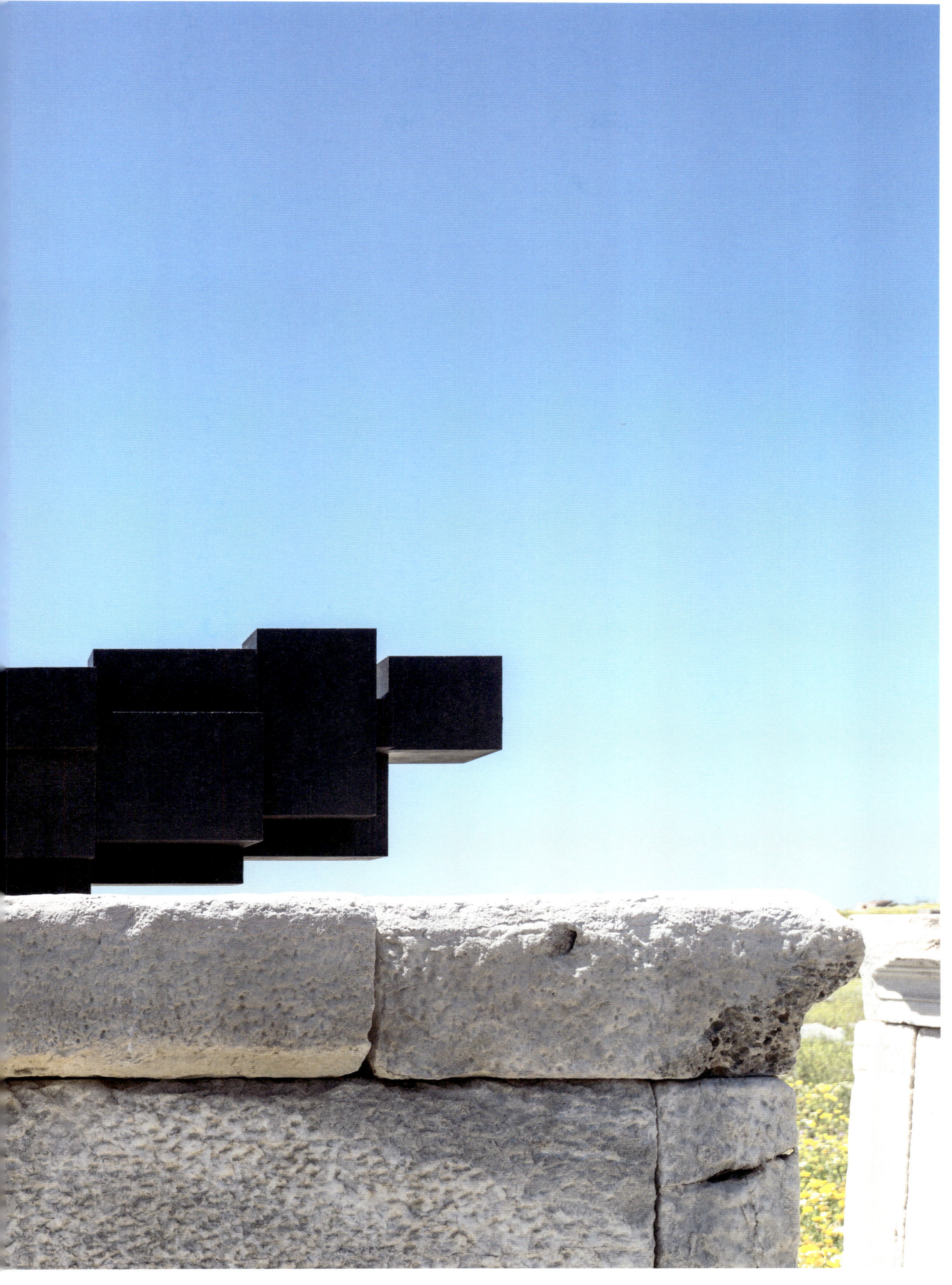

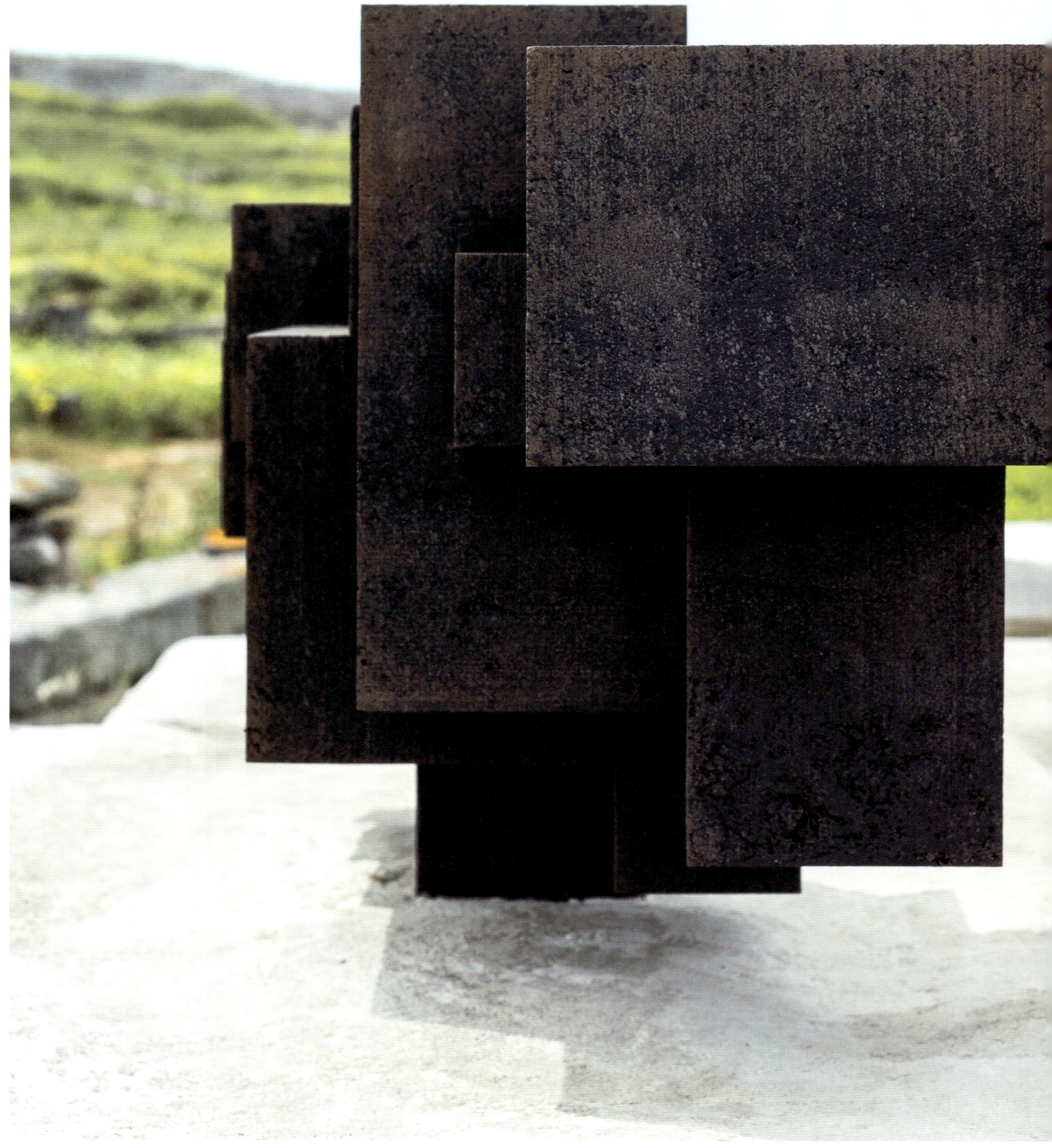

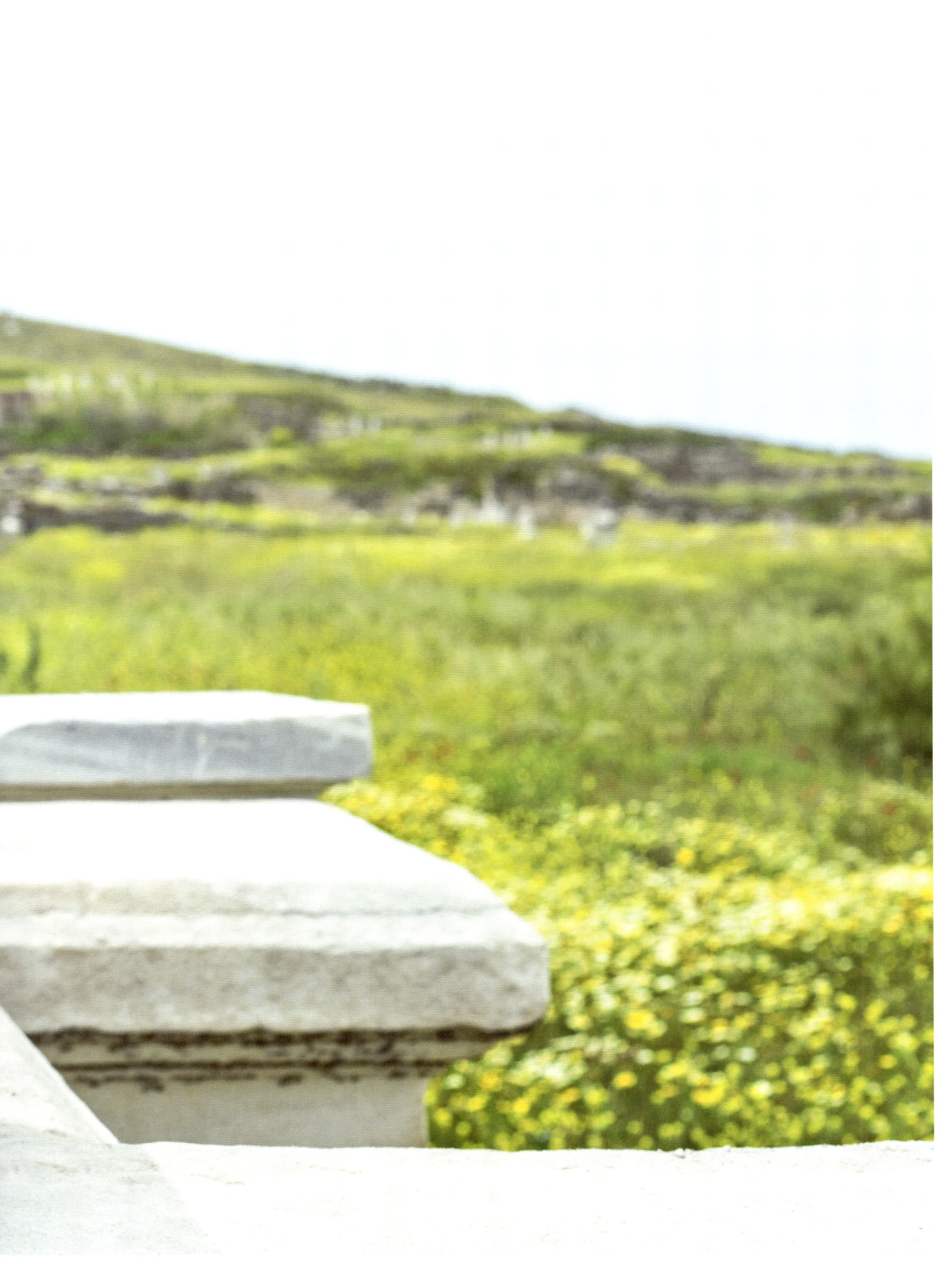

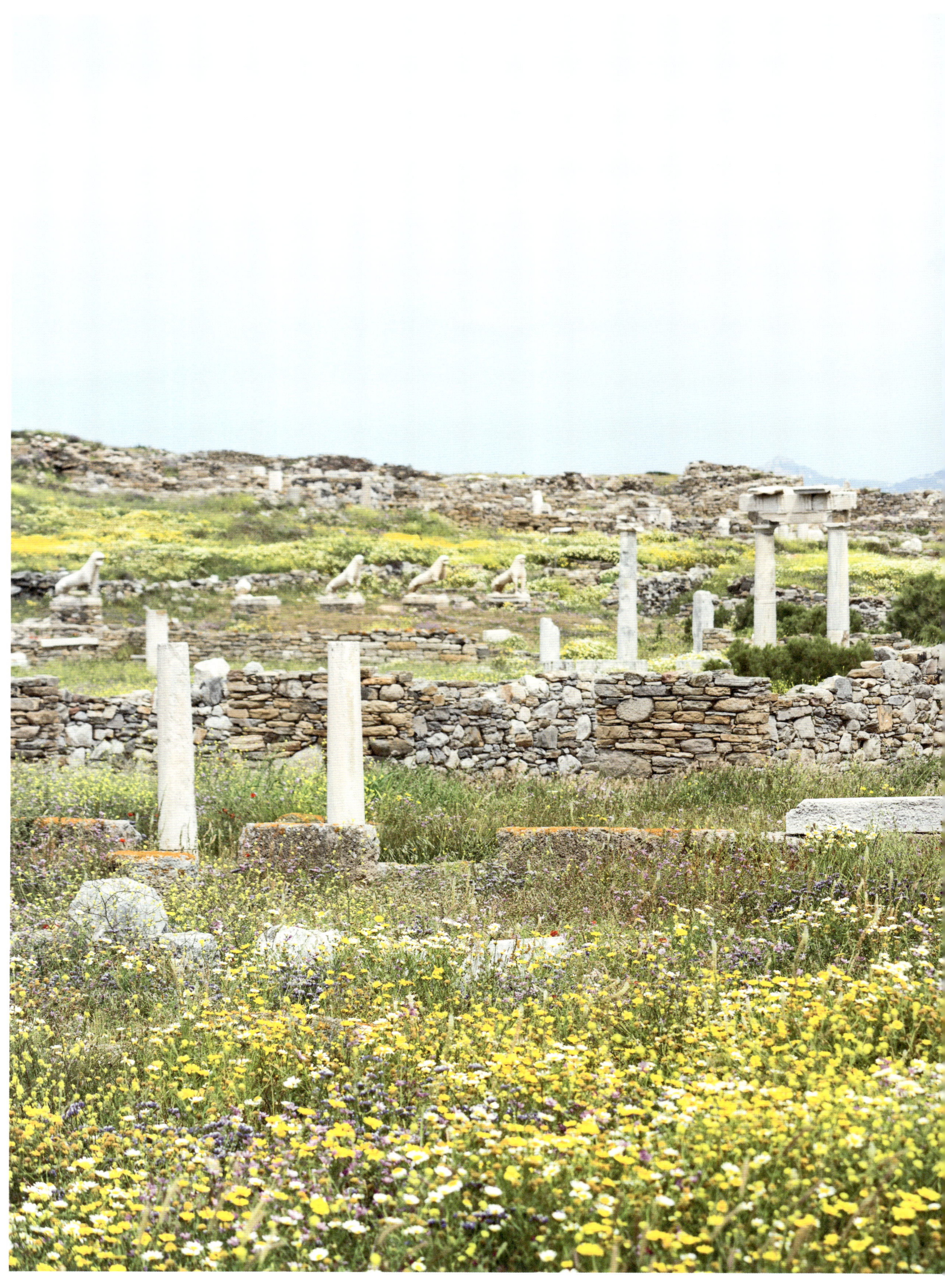

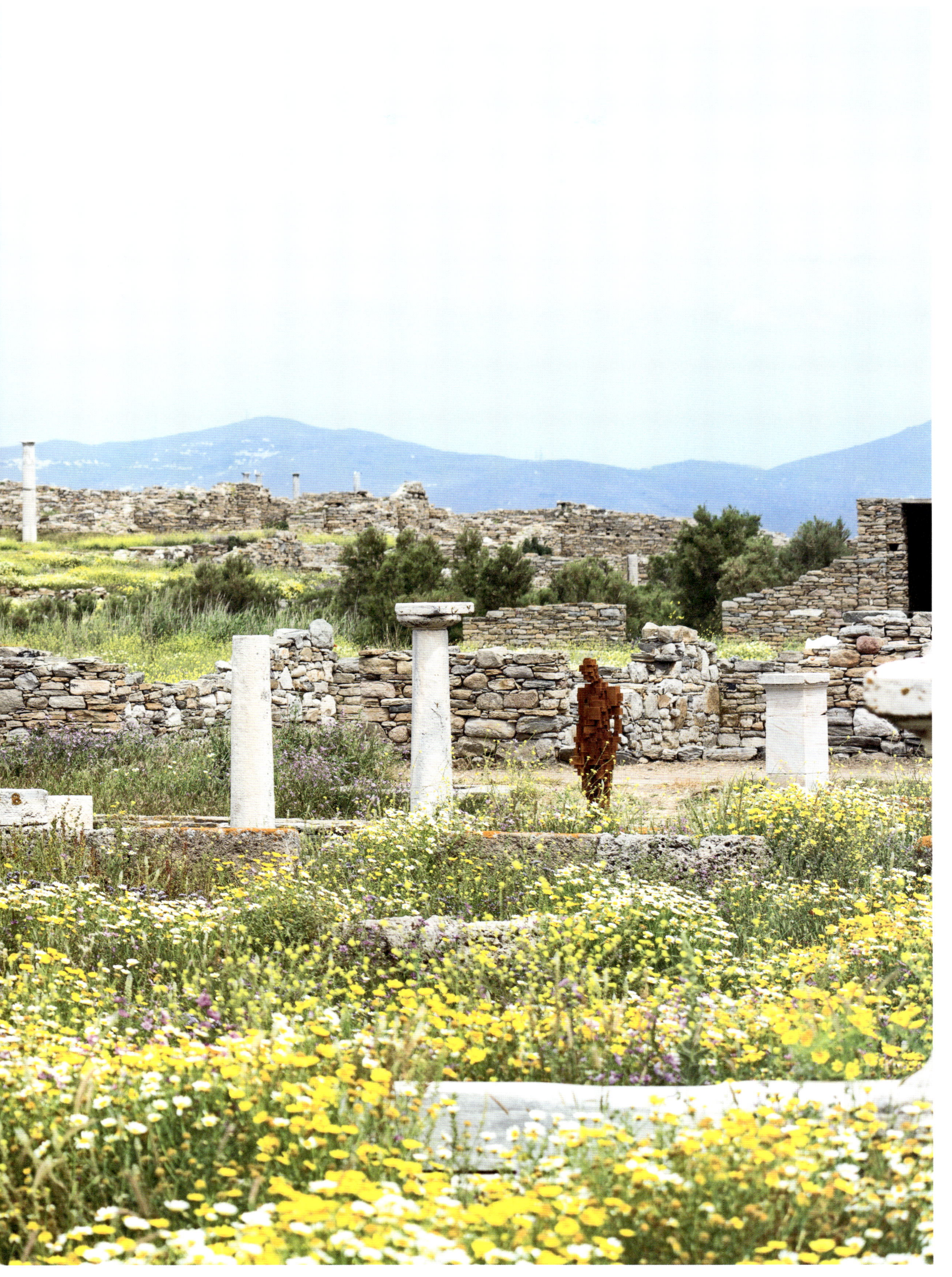

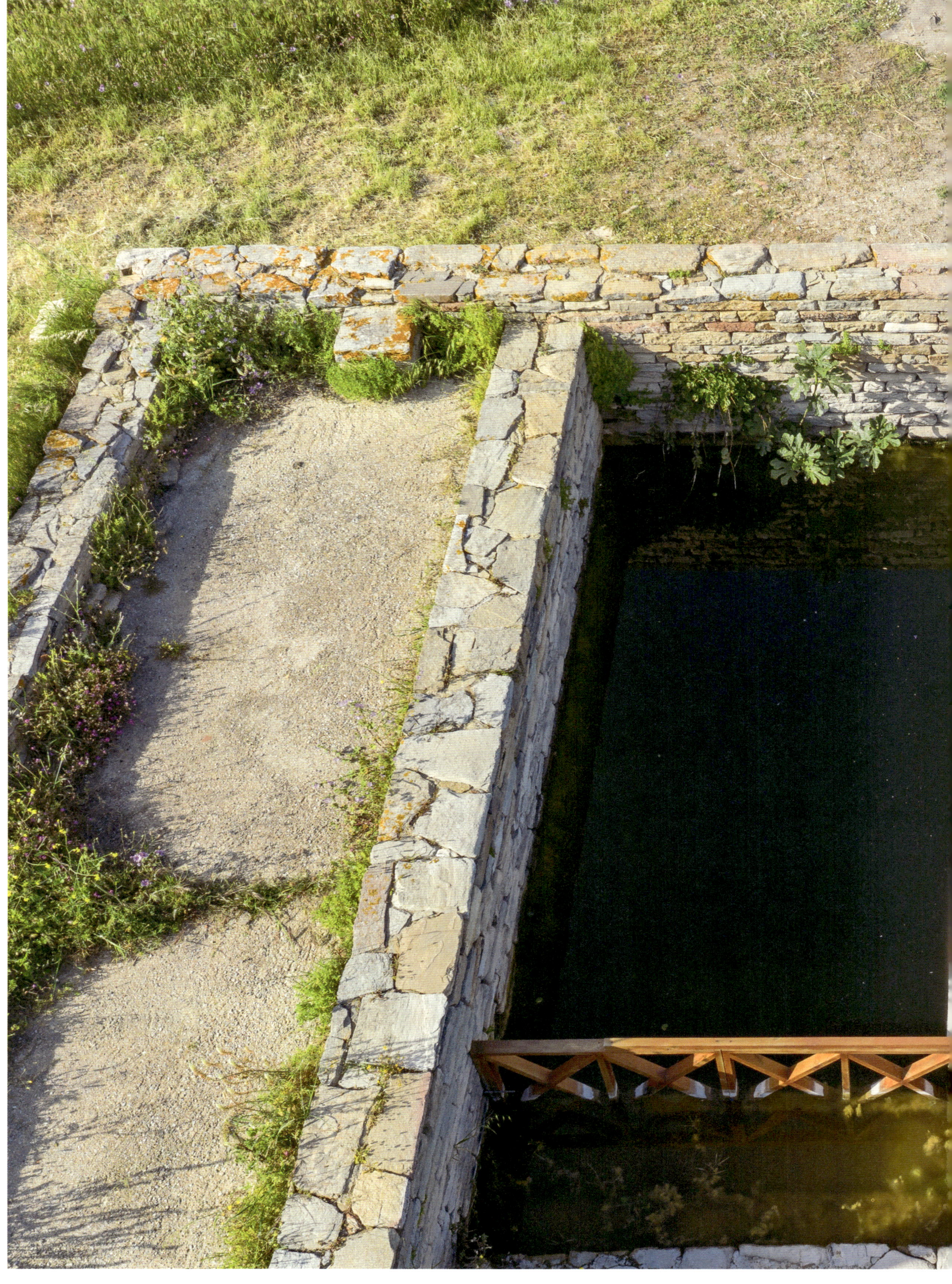

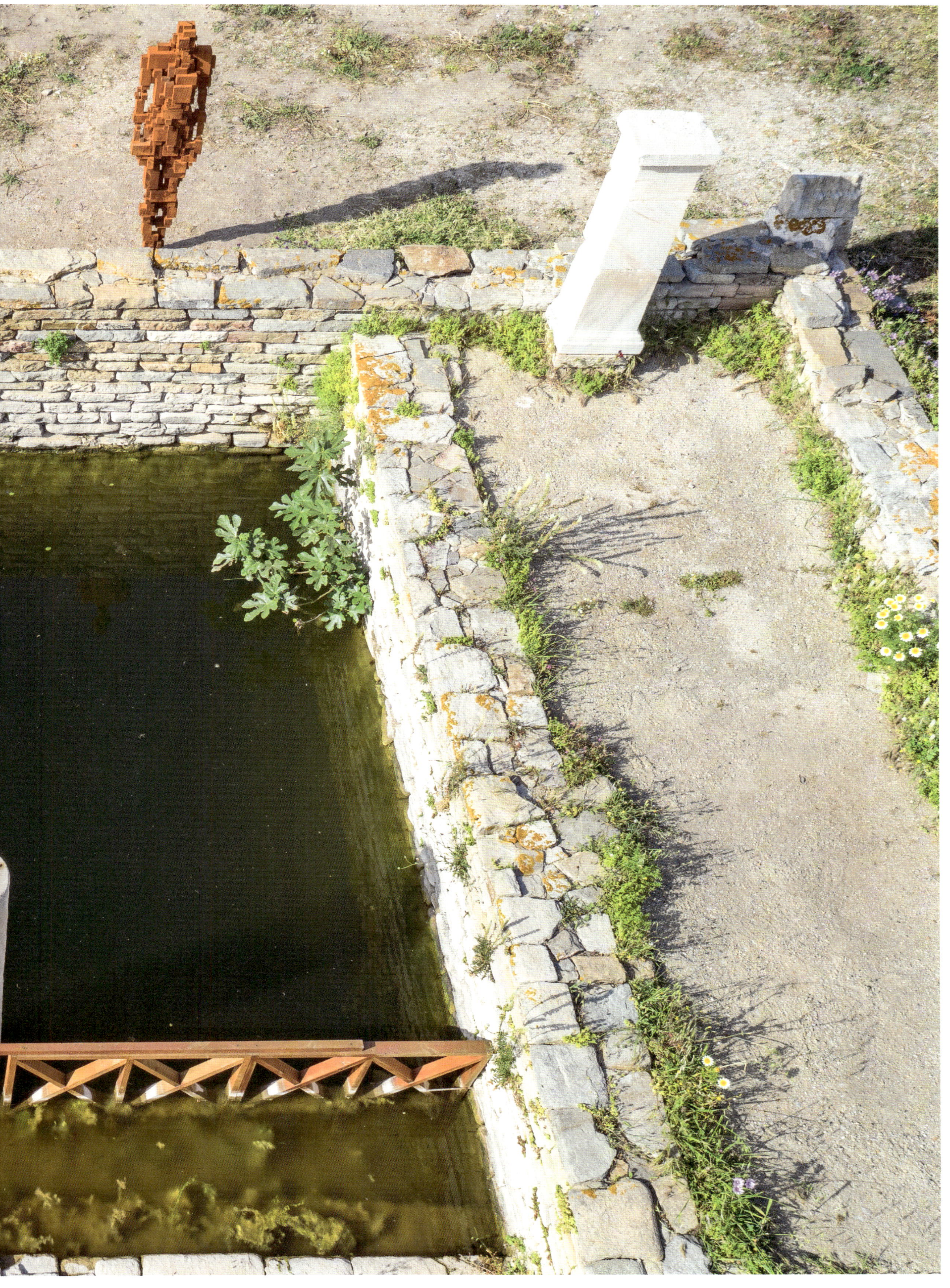

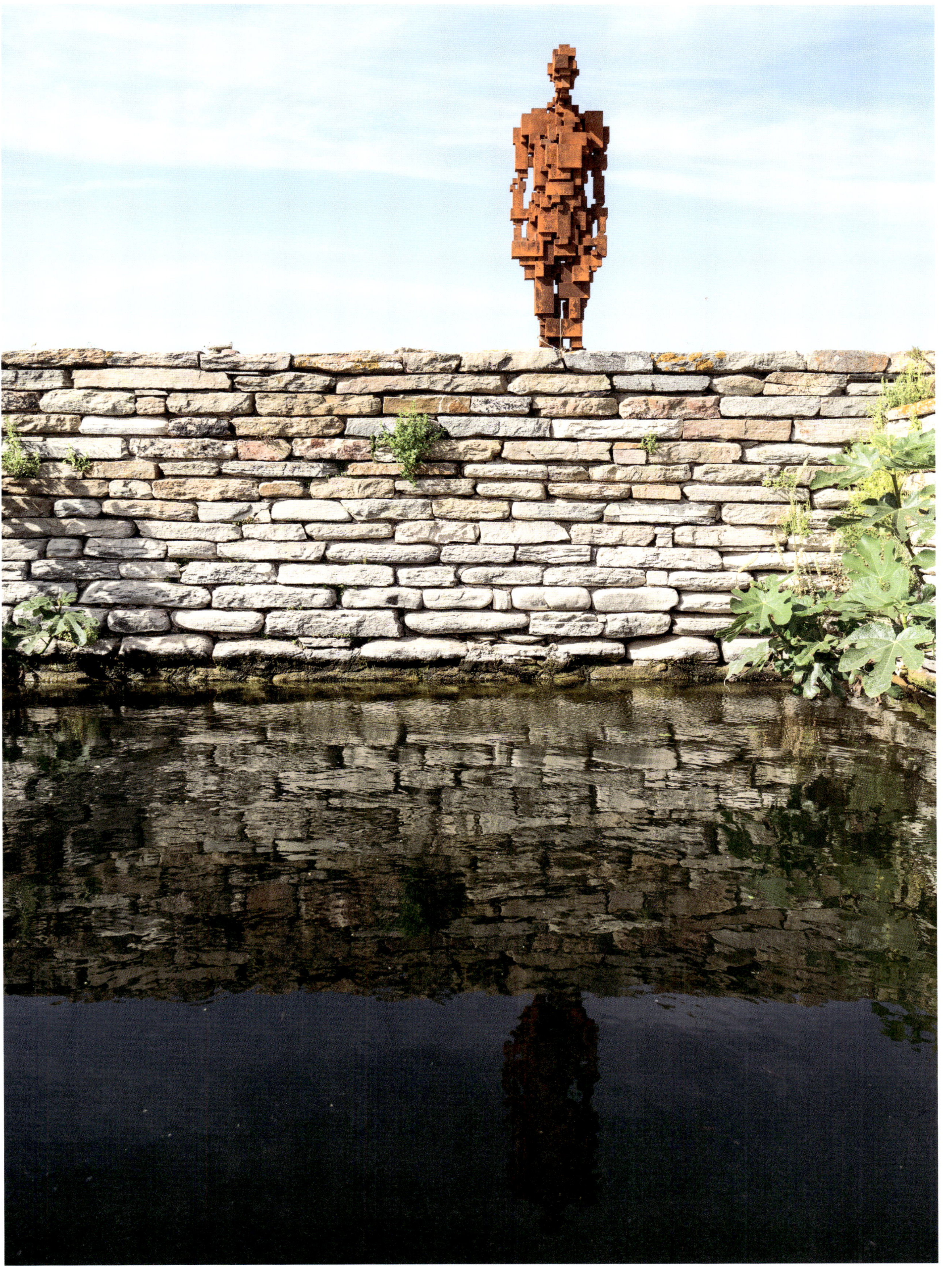

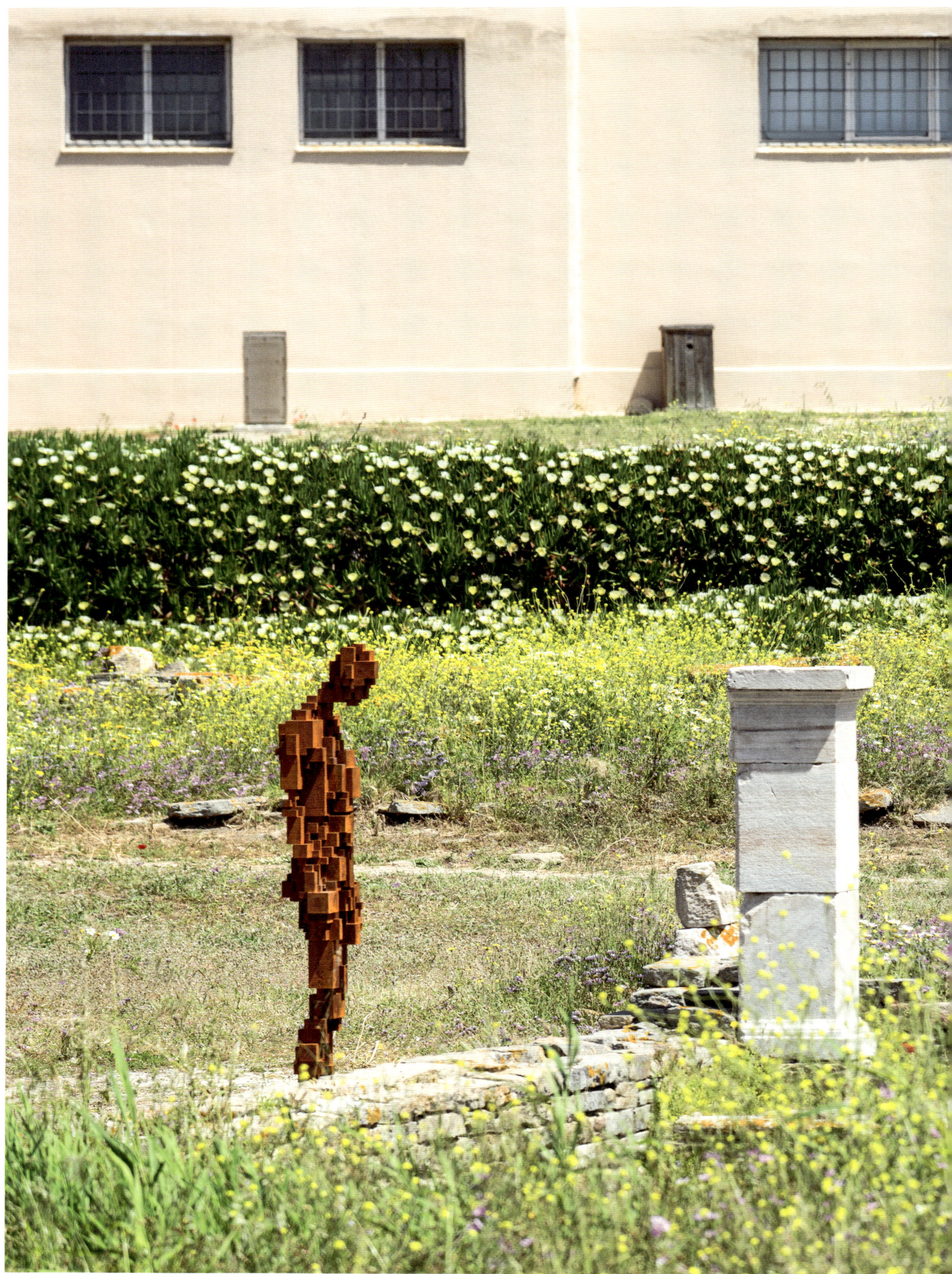

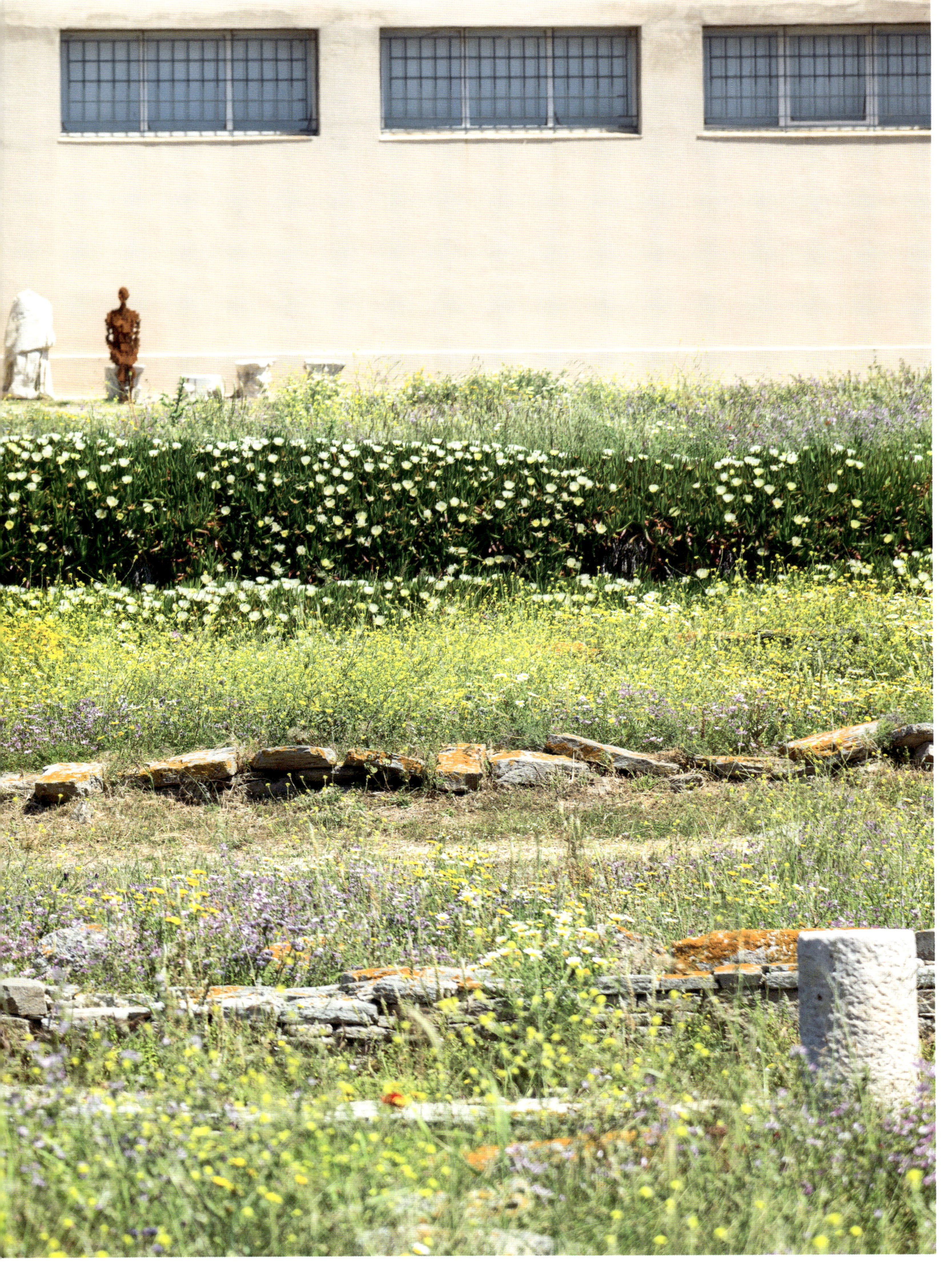

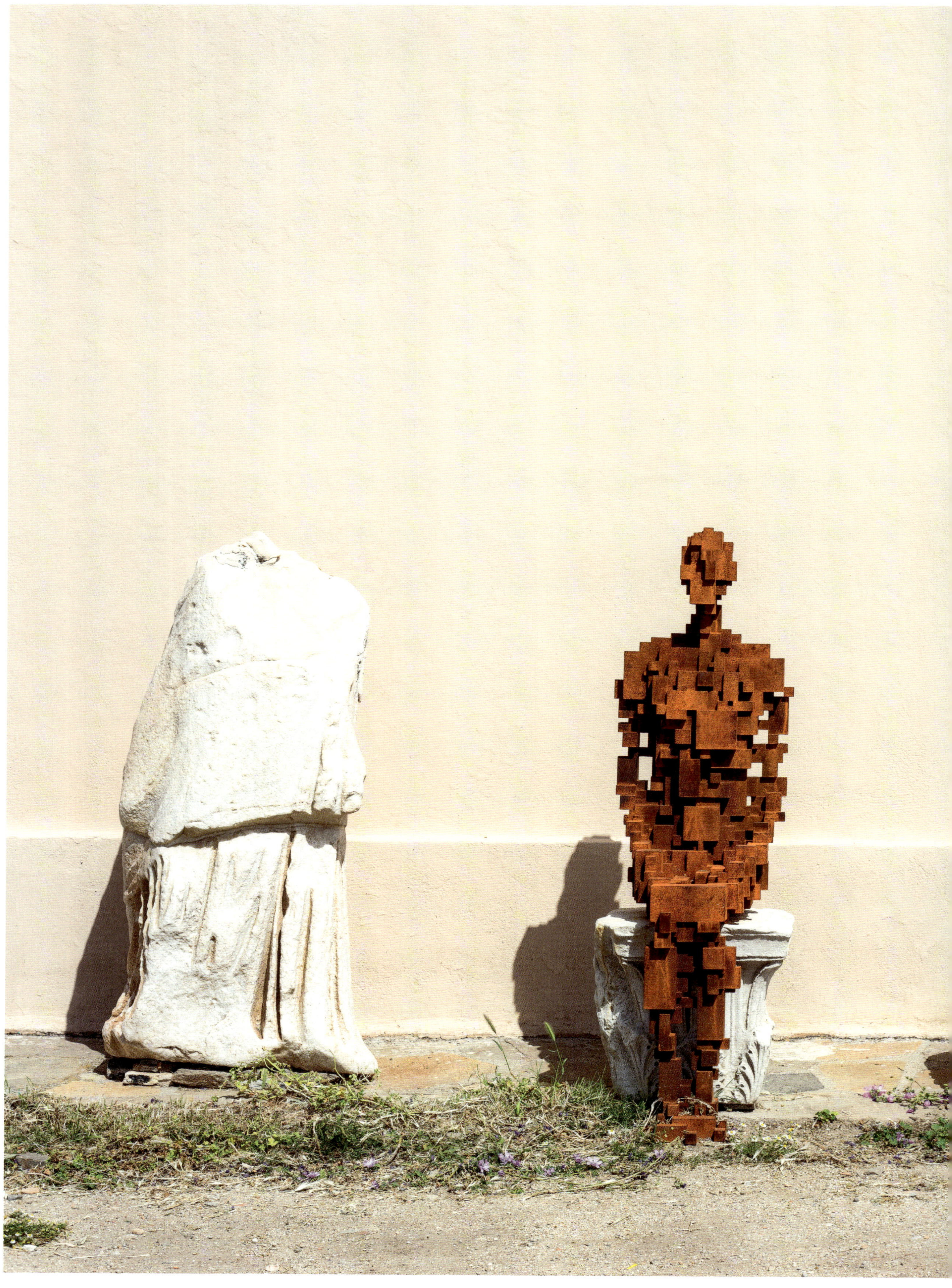

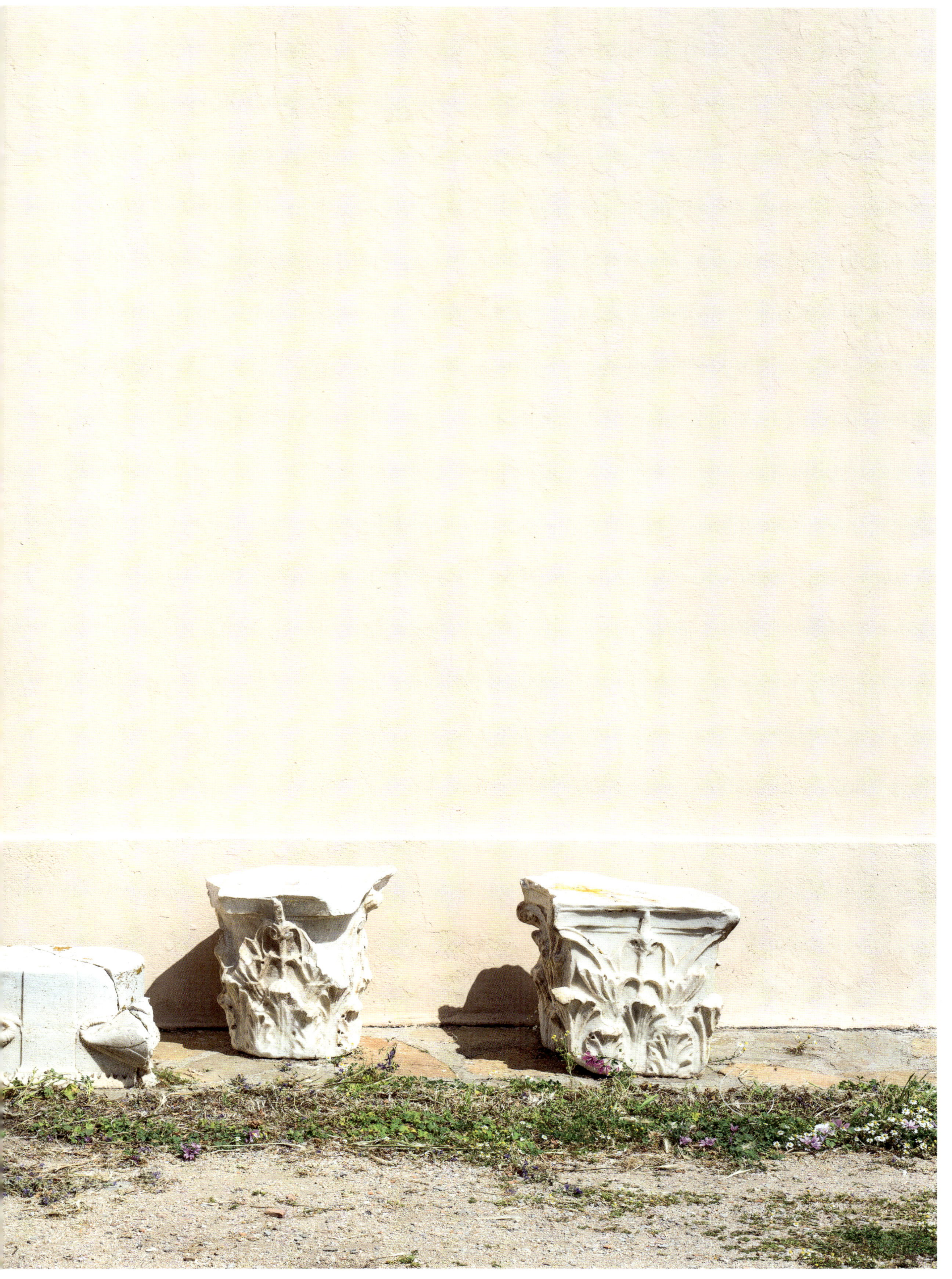

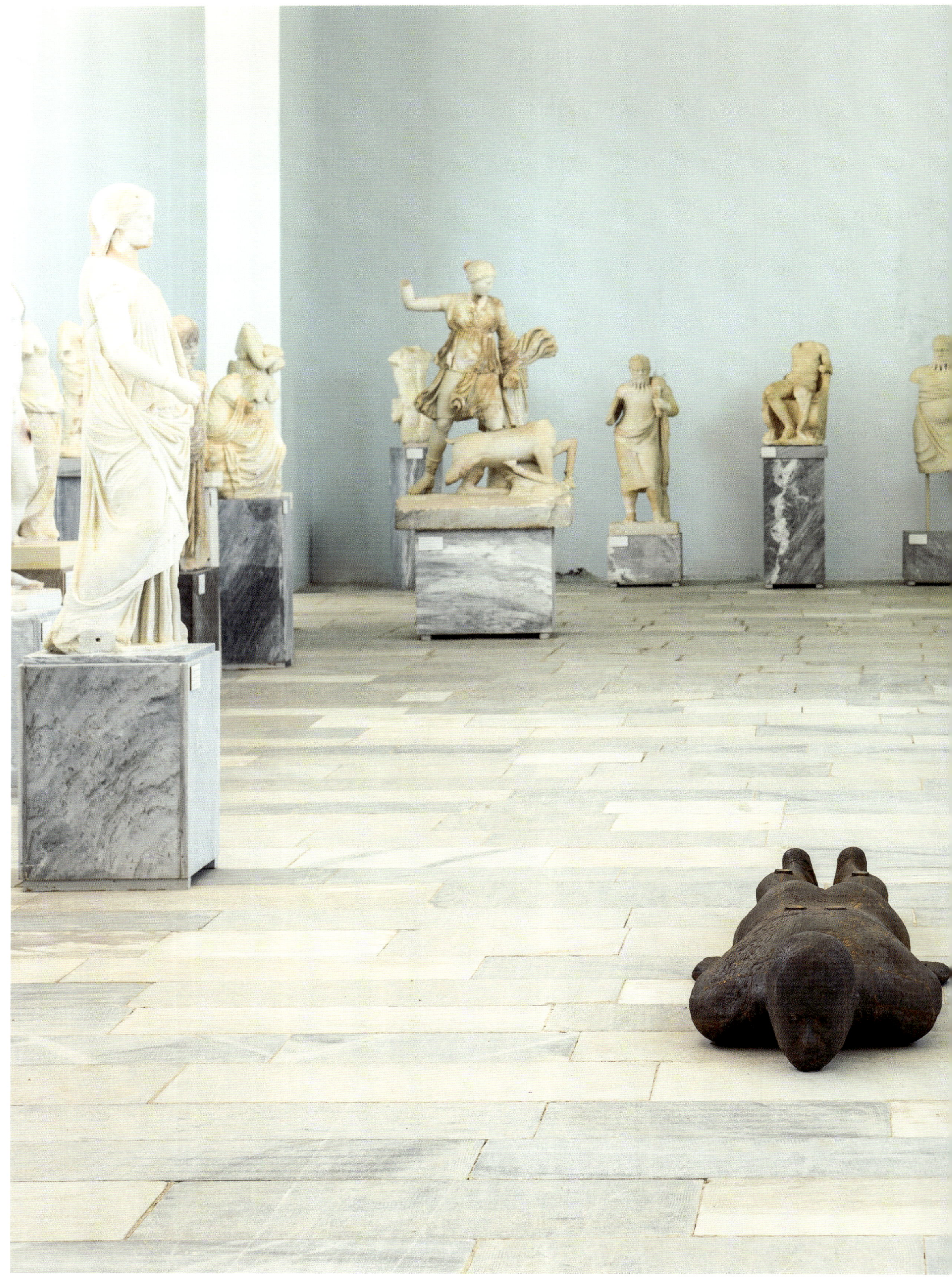

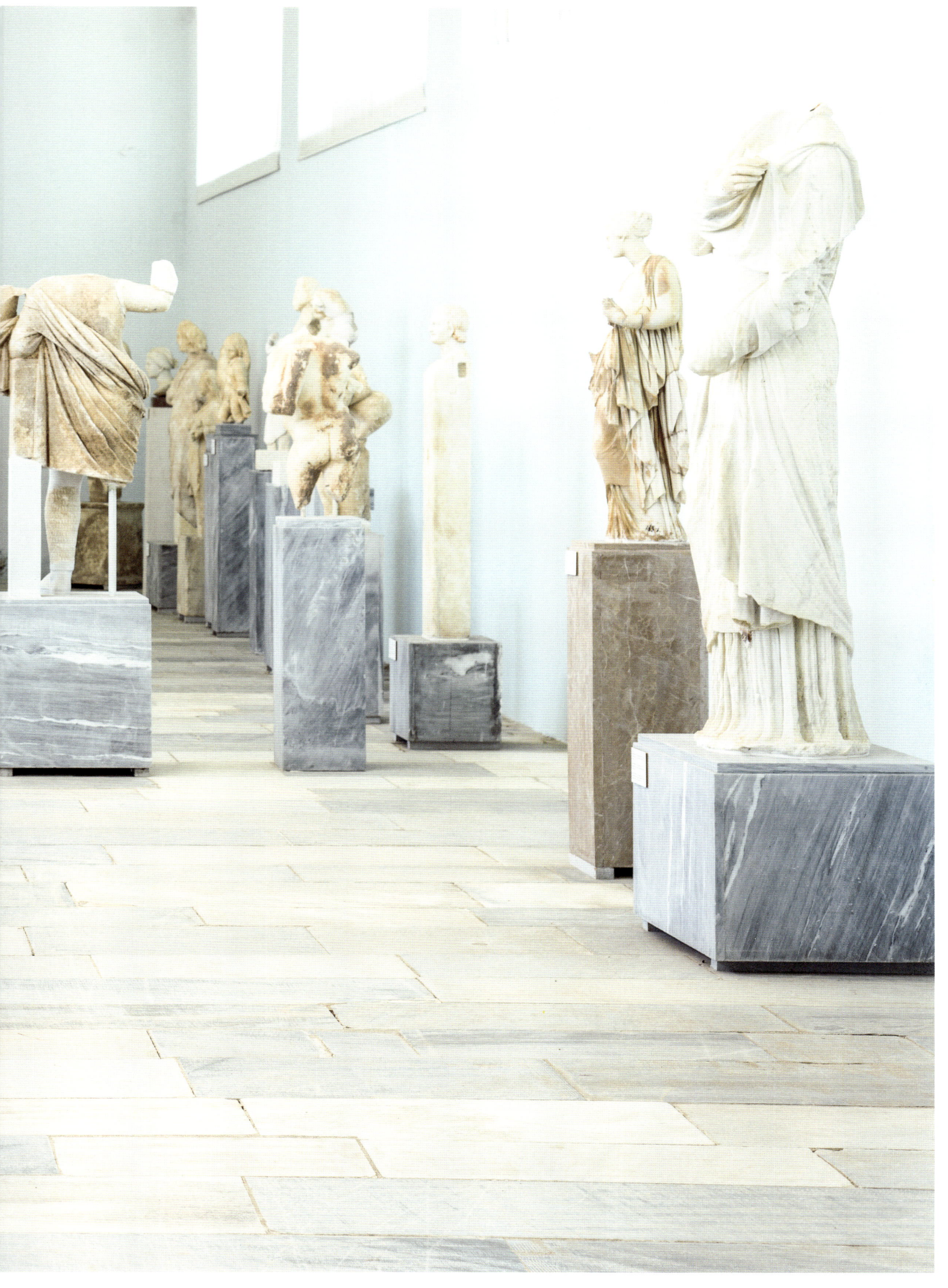

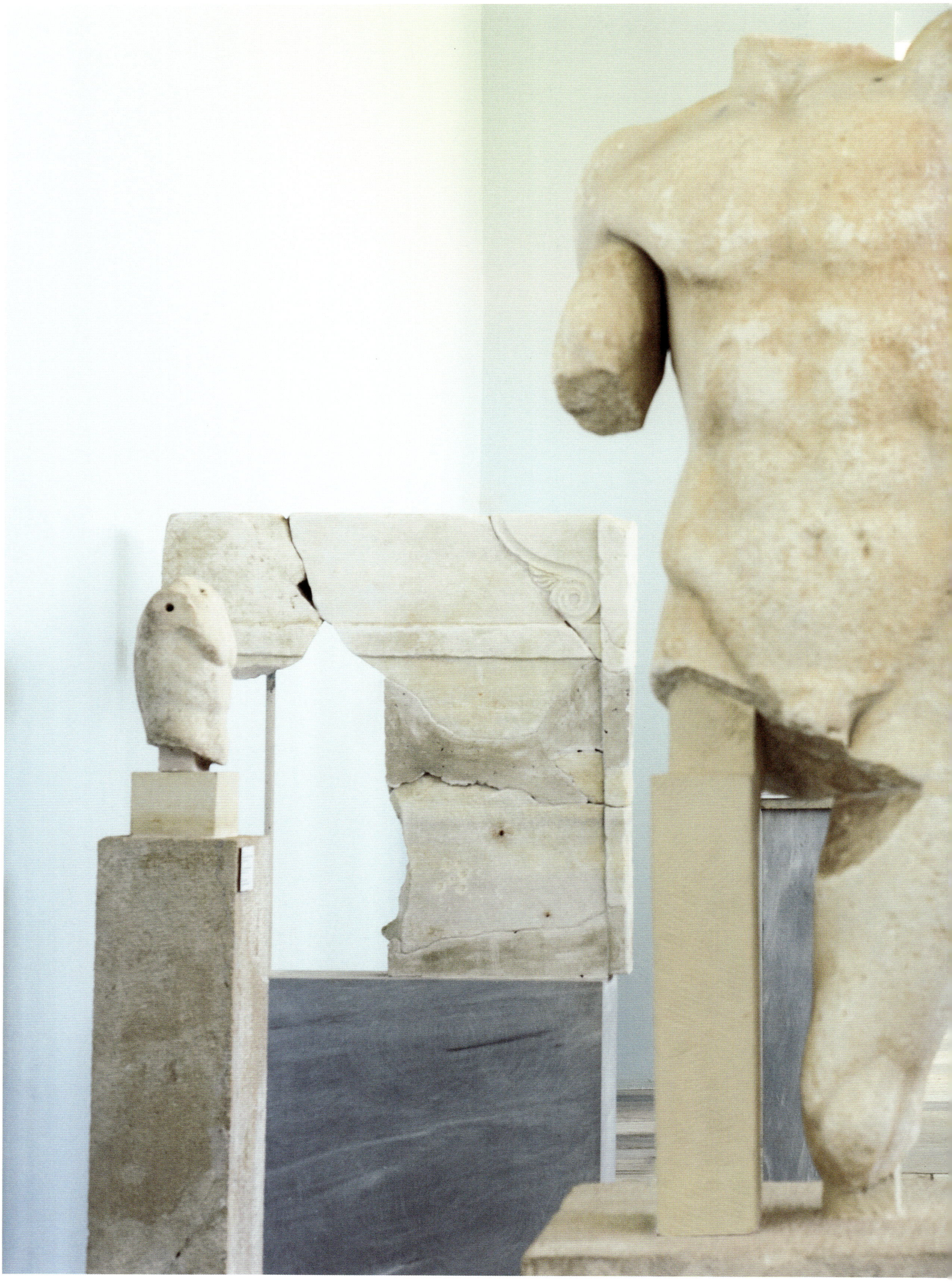

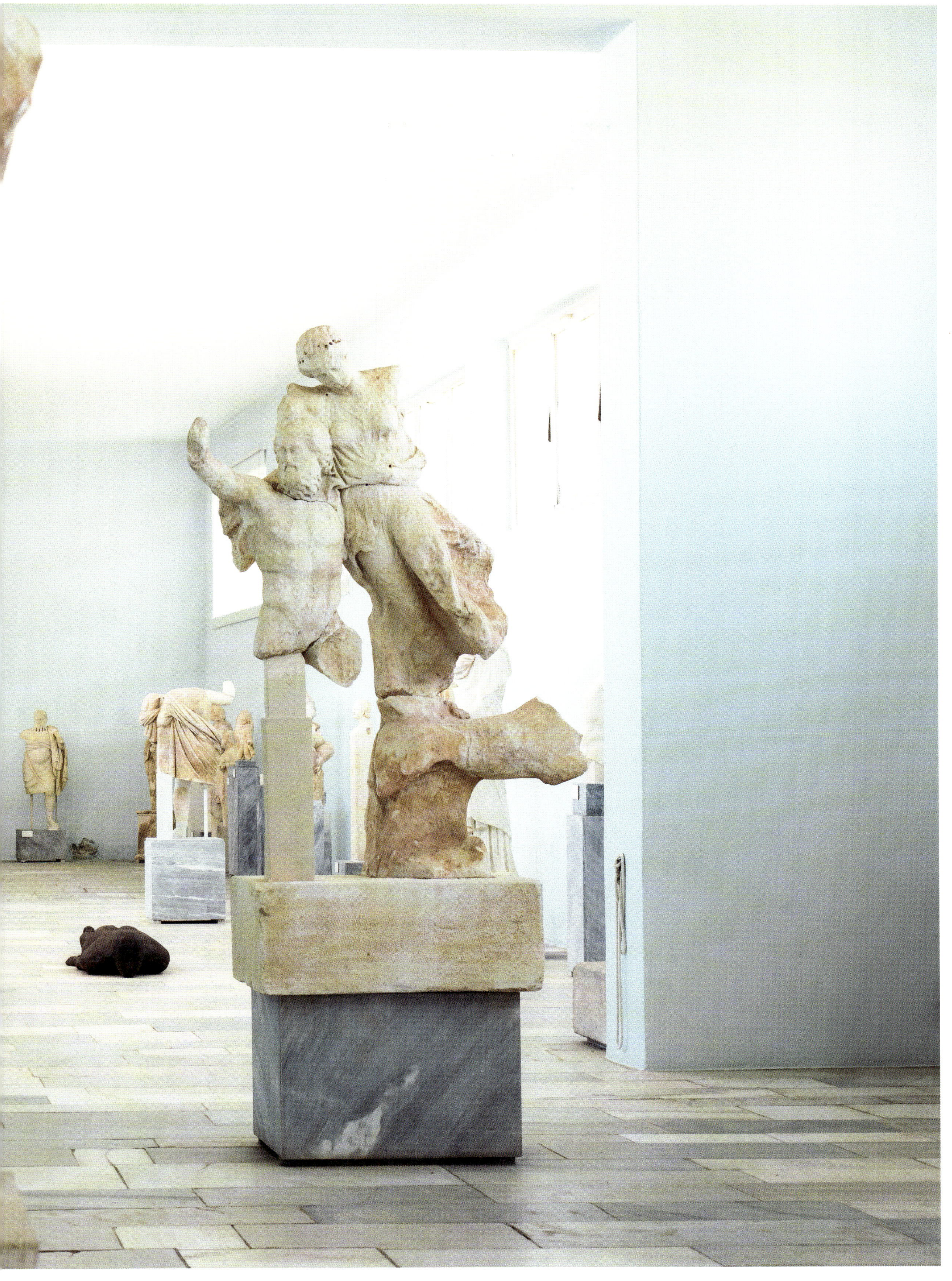

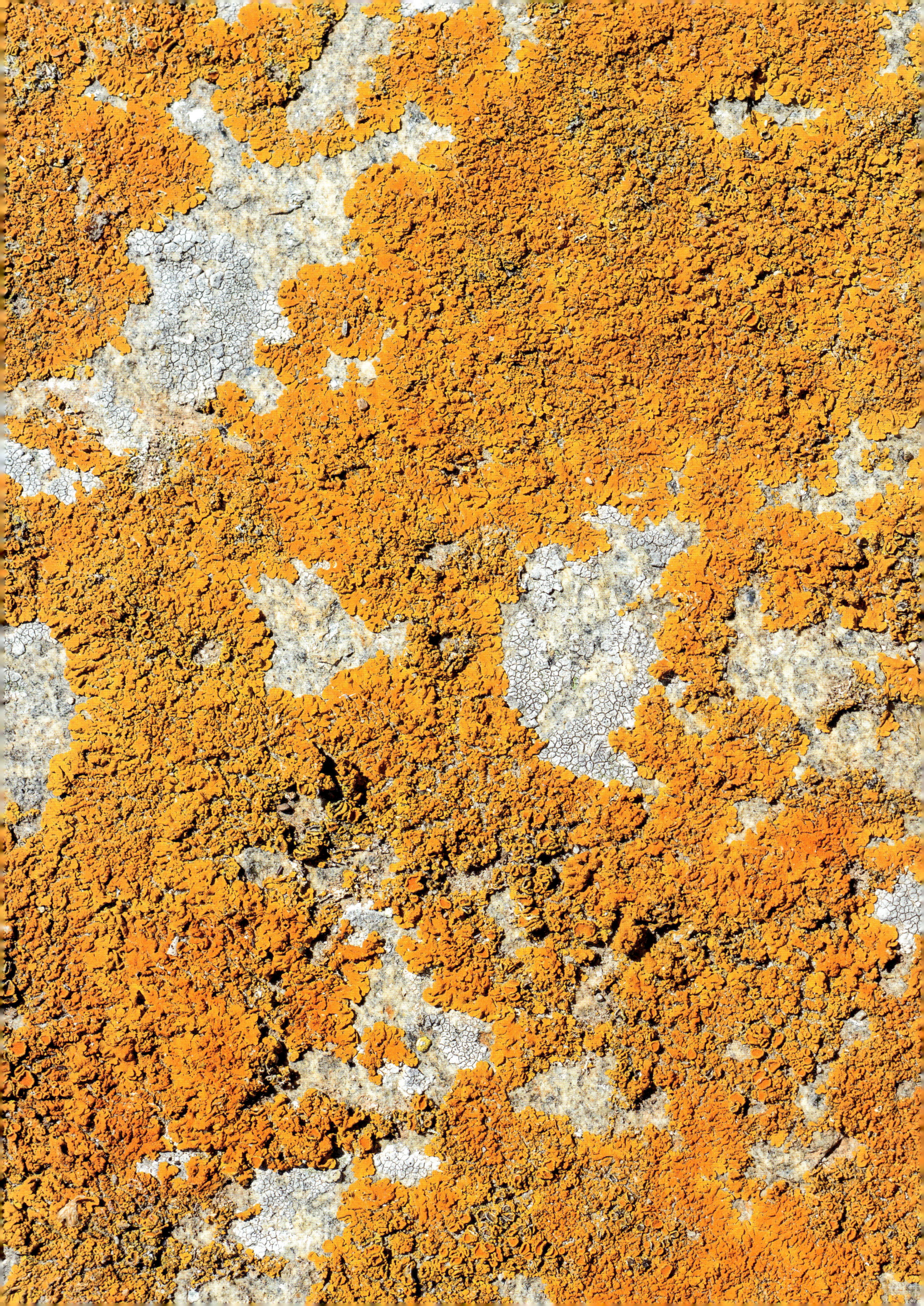

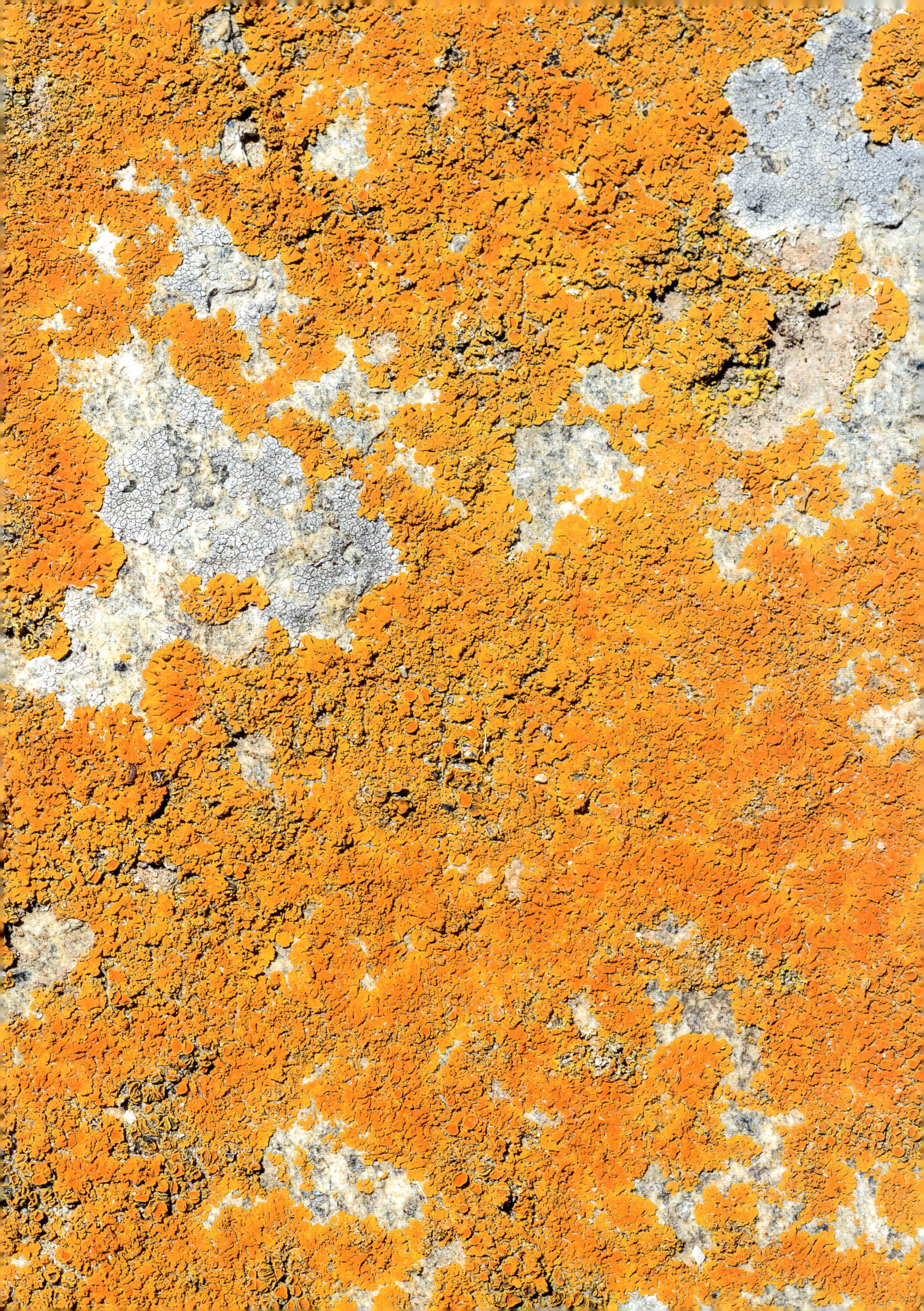

LIST OF WORKS

LIST OF WORKS

All works in cast iron

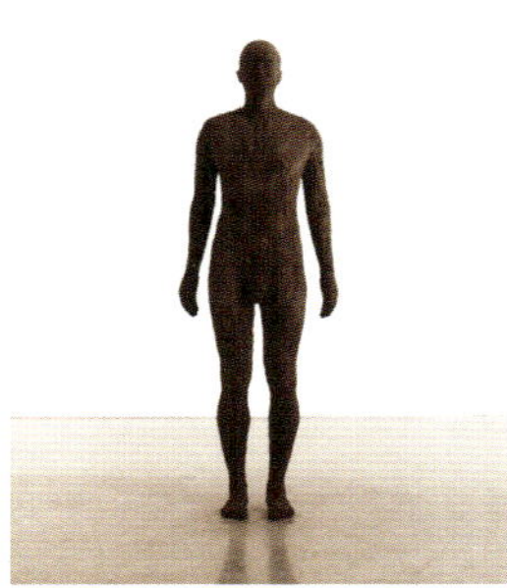

Another Time XIV
2011
191 × 59 × 36 cm
Northwest Cape
pp. 18–19, 20–21, 22–23, 24–25

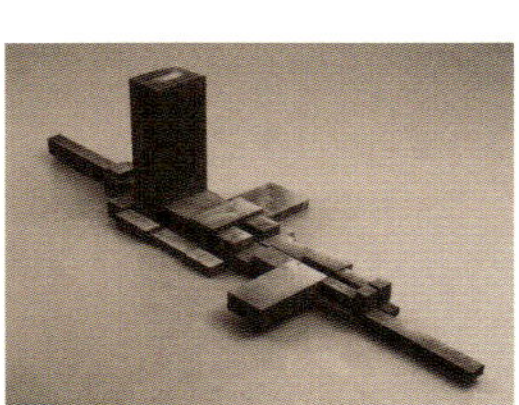

Spread
2010
87.6 × 309.4 × 106.4 cm
Stadium Quarter
pp. 48–49, 50–51, 52–53, 54–55, 73, 124 (detail)

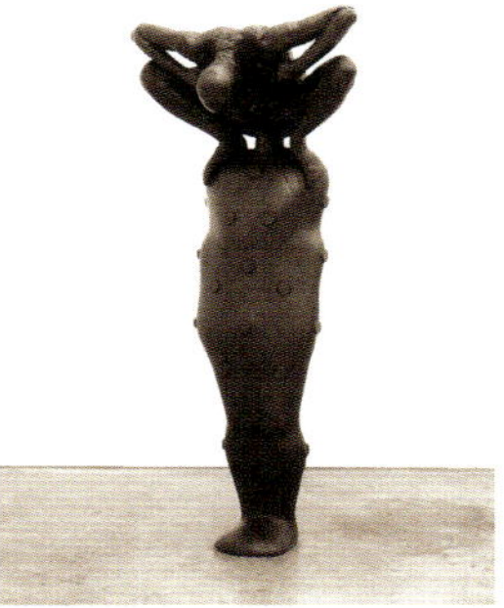

Bearing III
1997
245 × 98 × 83 cm
Stadium Quarter
pp. 42–43, 44–45, 46–47

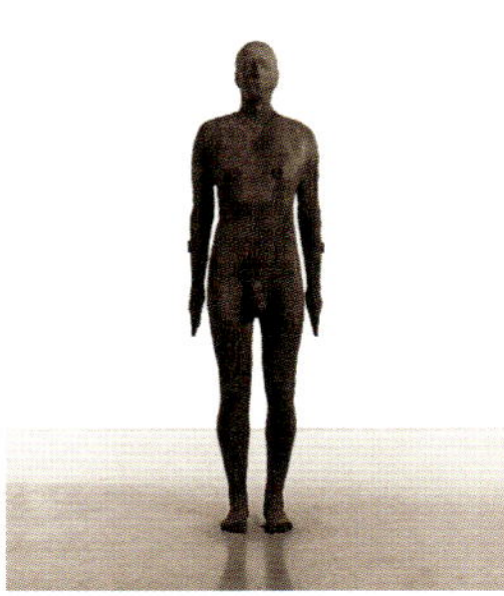

Another Time XV
2011
191 × 59 × 38 cm
Stadium Quarter
pp. 46–47, 56–57

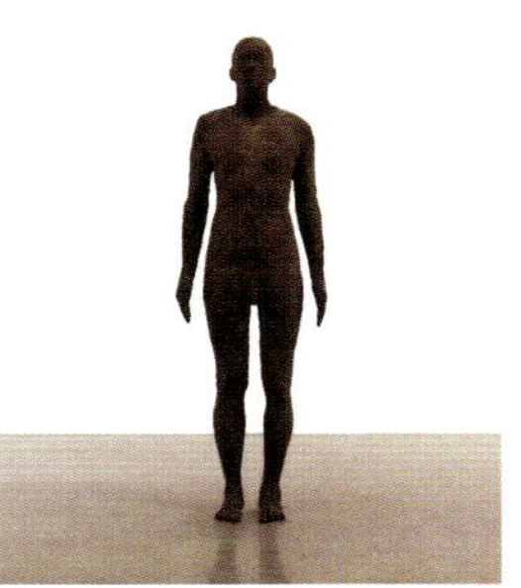

Another Time XI
2008
191 × 59 × 36 cm
Plakes Peak
pp. 32–33

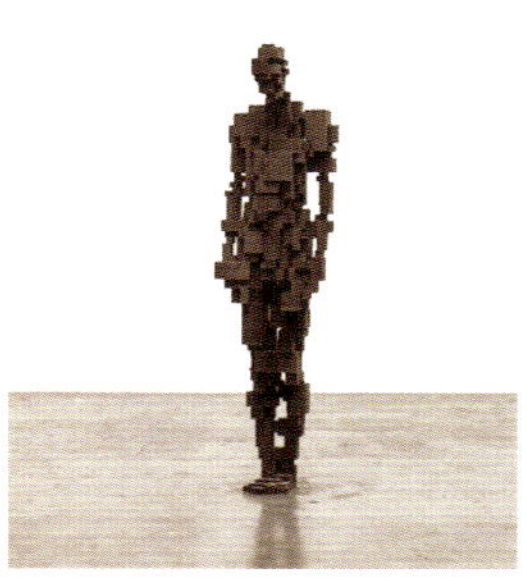

Water
2018
184.5 × 47.5 × 35 cm
Minoan Fountain
pp. 164–165, 166–167, 169, 170–171

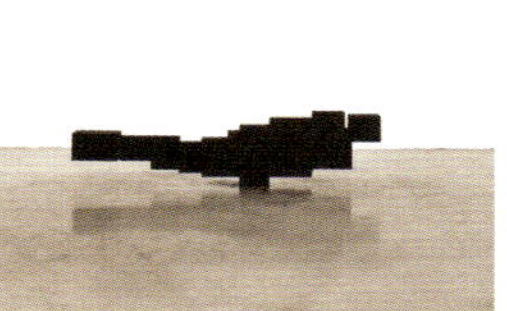

Hove
2014
50.5 × 198 × 44.5 cm
East Propylon
pp. 158–159, 160–161, 162–163

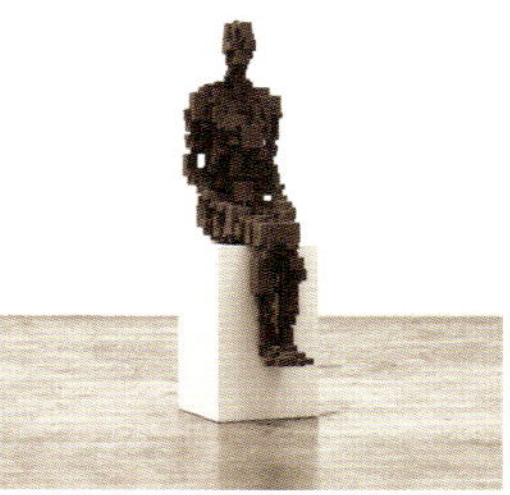

Rule
2018
149 × 45.5 × 75 cm
West wall of the Archaeological Museum of Delos
pp. 36 (detail), 170–171, 172–173

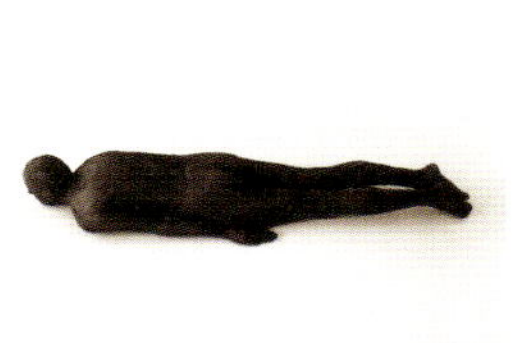

Shift II
2000
204 × 54 × 25 cm
Archaeological Museum of Delos
pp. 174–175, 176–177

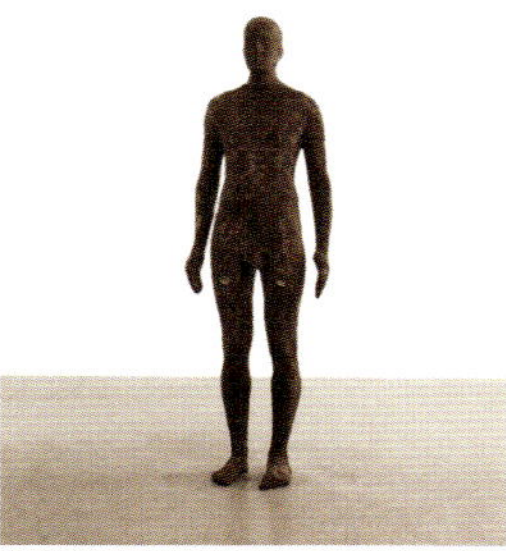

Another Time V
2007
191 × 59 × 36 cm
Entrance to the archaeological site
pp. 30–31

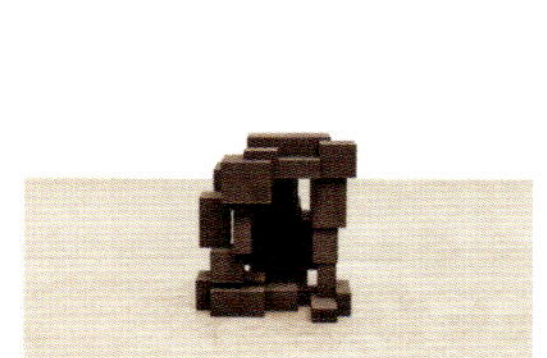

Vice II
2015
66 × 59.5 × 60.5 cm
Competaliast Agora
pp. 66, 152–153, 154–155

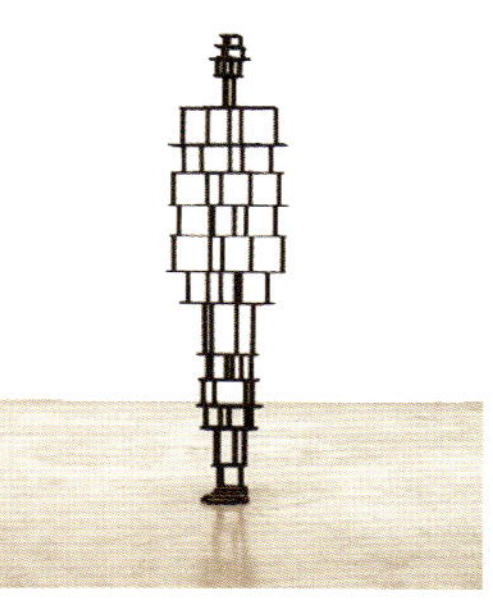

Station XIX
2014
193.8 × 48.9 × 35.5 cm
Sarapieion B
pp. 140–141

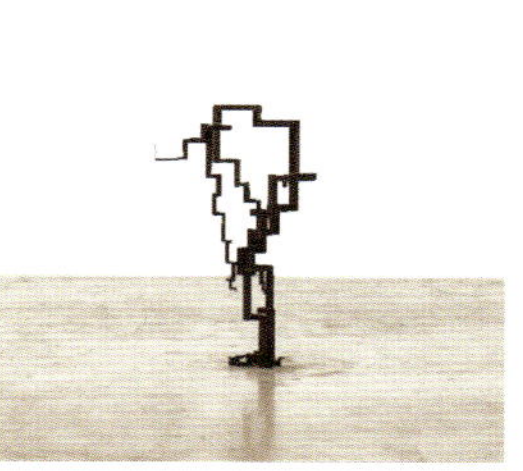

Chute II
2018
113.8 × 61.4 × 48.2 cm
Grotto Hercules
pp. 144–145, 147

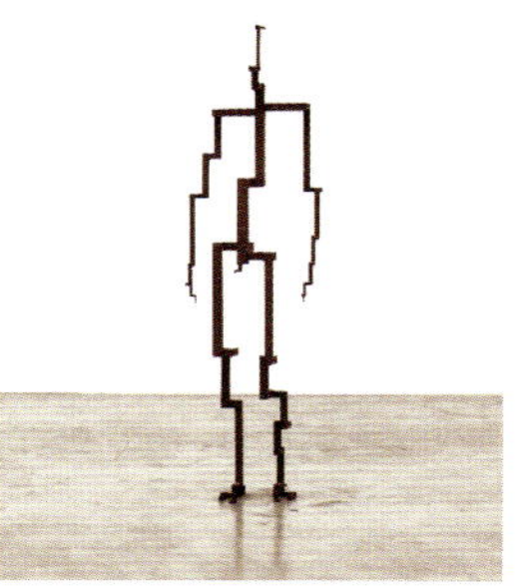

Signal II
2018
189 × 51.8 × 35.5 cm
East Stairway
pp. 148–149, 150–151

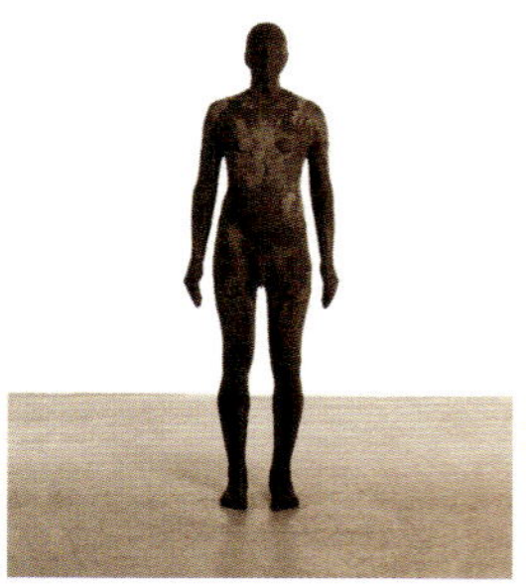

Another Time III
2007
191 × 59 × 36 cm
Mount Kynthos
pp. 34–35

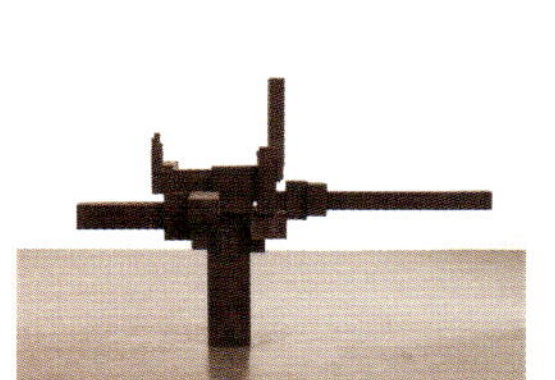

Knot
2010
129.9 × 196.7 × 129.7 cm
Theatre
pp. 2–3, 130–131, 132–133, 134–135

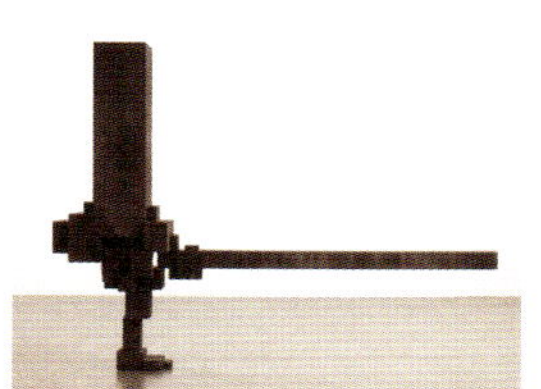

Bunch
2010
183 × 242 × 48.8 cm
Commercial Harbours
pp. 138–139

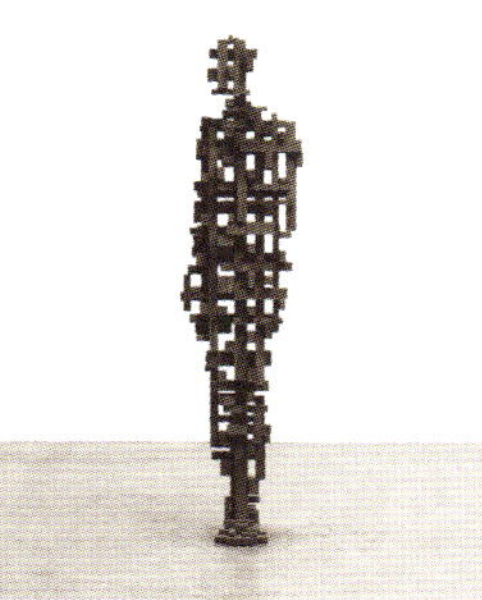

Cast III
2009
193 × 45 × 37 cm
Monument of Tritopatores
pp. 156–157

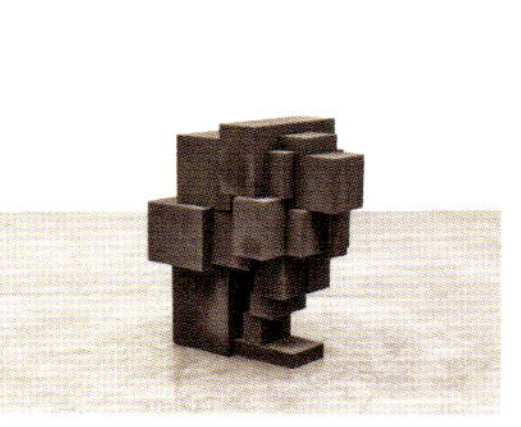

Wait
2015
80.5 × 43.5 × 68.5 cm
Theatre Quarter
pp. 100–101, 102–103

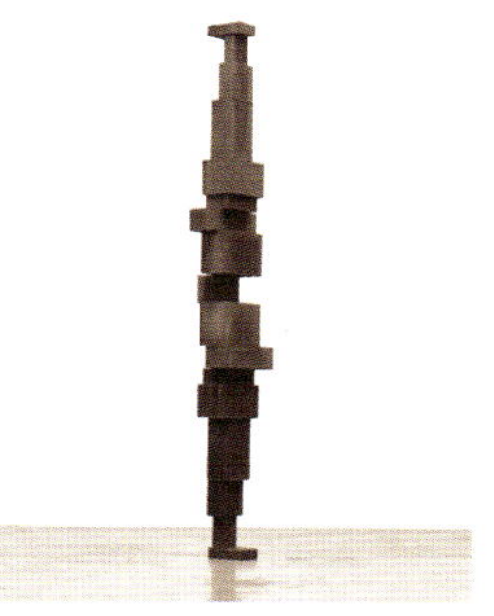

Reflect
2017
337 × 42.5 × 37.5 cm
Theatre Quarter
pp. 104–105, 106, 109, 110–111

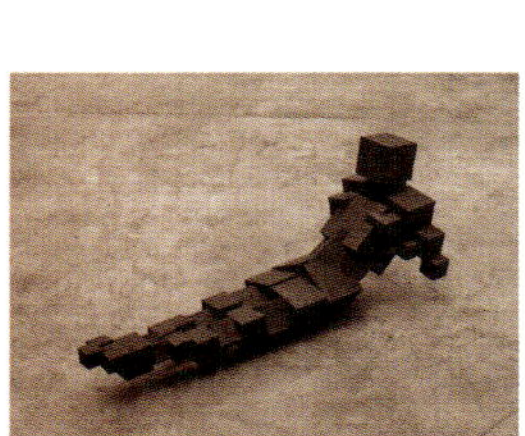

Stem
2015
74.5 × 174 × 66 cm
Theatre Quarter
pp. 116–117, 119

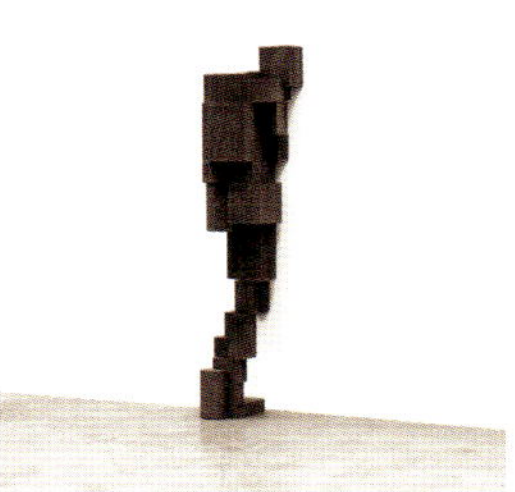

Side II
2017
167.1 × 40.5 × 33.3 cm
Theatre Quarter
pp. 110–111, 112–113, 115

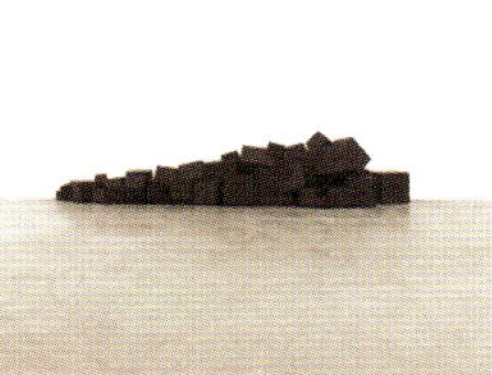

Resort IV
2013
46 × 207 × 50 cm
Theatre Quarter
pp. 86 (detail), 98–99

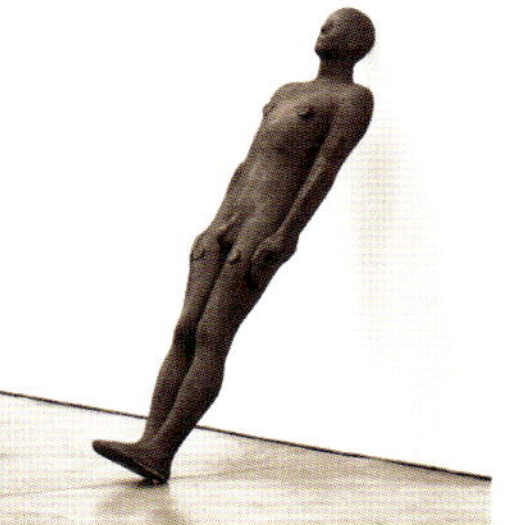

Prop
2018
195.6 × 50.8 × 40.3 cm
Theatre Quarter
pp. 82–83, 84–85

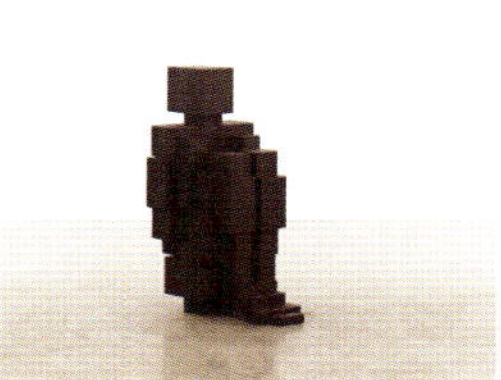

Shore
2012
88 × 47 × 57 cm
Midas Belvedere
pp. 67, 140–141, 142–143

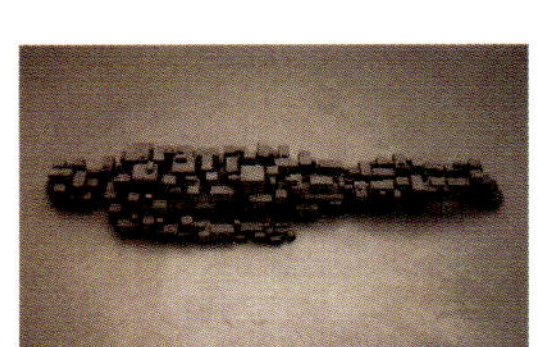

Settlement III
2005
25.5 × 210 × 62 cm
Theatre Quarter
pp. 76–77, 78–79, 80–81

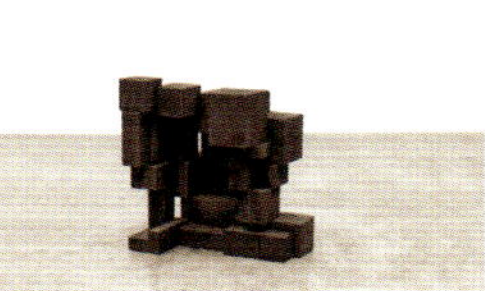

Cotch
2015
67.5 × 68.5 × 54 cm
Theatre Quarter
pp. 120–121, 122–123

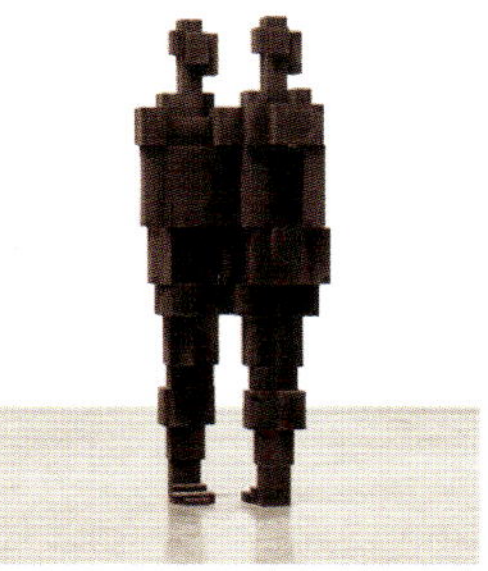

Connect
2015
192.5 × 70 × 51 cm
Commercial Harbours
pp. 136–137

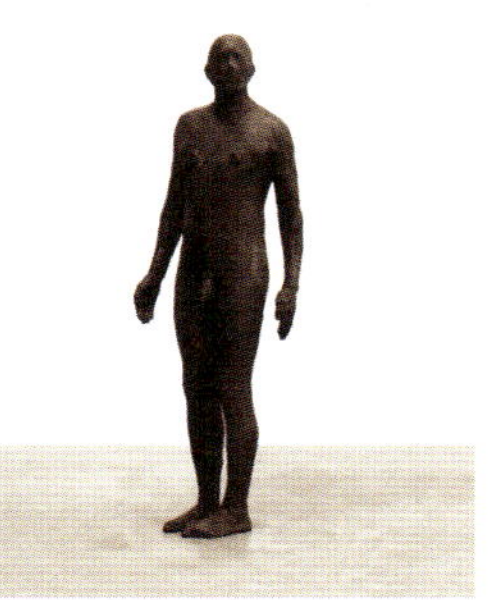

6 Times Left
2009
191 × 59 × 36 cm
Commercial Harbours
pp. 26–27, 28–29

Antony Gormley is widely acclaimed for his sculptures, installations and public artworks that investigate the relationship of the human body to space. His work has developed the potential opened up by sculpture since the 1960s through a critical engagement with both his own body and those of others in a way that confronts fundamental questions of where human beings stand in relation to nature and the cosmos. Gormley continually tries to identify the space of art as a place of becoming in which new behaviours, thoughts and feelings can arise.

Gormley's work has been widely exhibited throughout the UK and internationally with exhibitions at the Uffizi Gallery, Florence, Italy (2019); the Philadelphia Museum of Art, Philadelphia, USA (2019); Kettle's Yard, Cambridge, UK (2018); the Long Museum, Shanghai, China (2017); Zentrum Paul Klee, Bern, Switzerland (2014); Centro Cultural Banco do Brasil, São Paulo, Rio de Janeiro and Brasilia, Brazil (2012); Deichtorhallen, Hamburg, Germany (2012); The State Hermitage Museum, St Petersburg, Russia (2011); Kunsthaus Bregenz, Austria (2010); Hayward Gallery, London, UK (2007); Malmö Konsthall, Sweden (1993) and Louisiana Museum of Modern Art, Humlebæk, Denmark (1989). He has also participated in major group shows such as the Venice Biennale, Italy (1982 and 1986) and Documenta 8, Kassel, Germany (1987). A major solo exhibition of his work will be presented at the Royal Academy of Arts, London, in September 2019. Permanent public works include the *Angel of the North* (Gateshead, UK), *Another Place* (Crosby Beach, UK), *Inside Australia* (Lake Ballard, Western Australia), *Exposure* (Lelystad, The Netherlands) and *Chord* (MIT, Cambridge, Massachusetts, USA).

Gormley was awarded the Turner Prize in 1994, the South Bank Prize for Visual Art in 1999, the Bernhard Heiliger Award for Sculpture in 2007, the Obayashi Prize in 2012 and the Praemium Imperiale in 2013. In 1997 he was made an Officer of the British Empire (OBE) and was made a knight in the New Year's Honours list in 2014. He is an Honorary Fellow of the Royal Institute of British Architects, an Honorary Doctor of the University of Cambridge and a Fellow of Trinity and Jesus Colleges, Cambridge. Gormley has been a Royal Academician since 2003 and a British Museum Trustee since 2007.

Antony Gormley was born in London in 1950.

2019 *Stand*, Philadelphia Museum of Art, Philadelphia, Pennsylvania, USA

Essere, Le Gallerie Degli Uffizi, Florence, Italy (cat.)

Present, Gallery of Contemporary Art and Architecture – České Budějovice House of Art, České Budějovice, Czech Republic

Sight, presented by NEON at the archaeological site and Museum of Delos, Delos, Greece (cat.)

2018 *Earth Body*, Galerie Thaddaeus Ropac, Salzburg, Austria (cat.)

Rooting the Synapse, White Cube, Hong Kong (cat.)

Sum, National Gallery in Prague, Convent of St Agnes of Bohemia, Prague, Czech Republic

Subject, Kettle's Yard, Cambridge, UK (cat.)

2017 *Living Room*, Xavier Hufkens, Brussels, Belgium (cat.)

Co-ordinate, Galleria Continua, San Gimignano, Italy (cat.)

Being, Hall Art Foundation, Schloss Derneburg, Germany

Another Time Bordeaux, various sites, Bordeaux, France

Still Moving, The Long Museum, West Bund, Shanghai, China (cat.)

Spotlights – Antony Gormley: The Model Room 1994 –2013, Tate Britain, London

Critical Mass and Expansion Field, Changsha Museum of Art, Changsha, China (cat.)

2016 *Host*, Galleria Continua, Beijing, China (cat.)

Construct, Sean Kelly Gallery, New York, USA

Cast, Alan Cristea Gallery, London (cat.)

Object, National Portrait Gallery, London

Fit, White Cube Bermondsey, London (cat.)

2015 *Second Body*, Galerie Thaddaeus Ropac Pantin, Paris, France (cat.)

Human, Forte di Belvedere, Florence, Italy (cat.)

Land, various sites across the UK, Landmark Trust, UK (cat.)

Space Stations, Hatton Gallery, University of Newcastle, Newcastle-upon-Tyne, UK

Event Horizon, various sites, Hong Kong (cat.)

2014 *States and Conditions Hong Kong*, White Cube Hong Kong (cat.)

Another Time Mardalsfossen, Mardalsfossen, Norway (cat.)

Meet, Galleri Andersson/ Sandström, Stockholm, Sweden (cat.)

Expansion Field, Zentrum Paul Klee, Bern, Switzerland (cat.)

Sculpture 21st: Antony Gormley, The Lehmbruck Museum, Duisburg, Germany

2013 *Firmament and Other Forms*, Middelheim Museum, Antwerp, Belgium

according to a given mean, Xavier Hufkens, Brussels, Belgium (cat.)

Meter, Galerie Thaddeus Ropac, Salzburg, Austria (cat.)

2012 *Cloud Chain*, French National Archives, Paris, France

Horizon Field Hamburg, Deichtorhallen Hamburg, Germany (cat.)

Vessel, Galleria Continua, San Gimignano, Italy (cat.)

Facts and Systems, White Cube, São Paolo, Brazil

Antony Gormley – Still Being, Centro Cultural Banco do Brasil, São Paolo, Brazil (cat.)

Drawing Space, The Phillips Collection, Washington D.C, USA

Still Standing, White Cube, Hoxton Square, London

Antony Gormley – Still Being (Corpos Presentes), Centro Cultural Banco do Brasil, Rio di Janeiro, Brazil (cat.)

Two Times, The Museum of Modern Art Hayama, Japan

Bodyspace, Sean Kelly Gallery, New York, USA

Model, White Cube Bermondsey, London (cat.)

2011 *Memes*, Anna Schwartz Gallery, Melbourne, Australia (cat.)

For the Time Being, Galerie Thaddaeus Ropac, Paris, France (cat.)

Still Standing, The State Hermitage Museum, St Petersburg, Russia (cat.)

Space Station and Other Instruments, Galleria Continua Le Moulin, France (cat.)

Witness, The British Library, London, UK

2010 *Breathing Room II*, Sean Kelly Gallery, New York, USA

Event Horizon, Mad. Sq. Art, Madison Square Park Conservancy, New York, USA (cat.)

Firmament IV, Anna Schwartz Gallery, Sydney, Australia

Critical Mass, De La Warr Pavilion, Bexhill-on-Sea, UK

Test Sites, White Cube, Mason's Yard, London

Horizon Field, Vorarlberg, Austria (cat.)

Drawing Space, MACRO Museum of Contemporary Art, Rome, Italy (cat.)

2009 *Clay and the Collective Body*, Helsinki, Finland

Ataxia II, Galerie Thaddaeus Ropac, Salzburg, Austria (cat.)

One and Other, Fourth Plinth Commission, Trafalgar Square, London

Antony Gormley, Kunsthaus Bregenz, Austria (cat.)

Domain Field, Garage Centre for Contemporary Culture, Moscow, Russia

Aperture, Xavier Hufkens, Brussels, Belgium (cat.)

Another Singularity, Galleria Continua, Beijing, China (cat.)

2008 *Firmament*, White Cube Mason's Yard, London

Acts, States, Times, Perspectives, Edition Copenhagen, Copenhagen, Denmark (cat.)

Another Singularity, Galleri Andersson Sandström, Umeå, Sweden

Drawings 1981–2001, Galerie Thaddaeus Ropac, Paris, France

Between You and Me, touring: Kunsthal Rotterdam, Rotterdam, Netherlands / Musée d'Art Moderne St Etienne, France / Artium, Vitoria-Gasteiz, Spain (cat.)

Antony Gormley, touring: Museo de Arte Contemporáneo, Monterrey, Mexico / 2009 Antiguo Colegio de San Ildefonso, Mexico City, Mexico (cat.)

2007 *Blind Light*, The Hayward Gallery, London (cat.)

Spacetime, Mimmo Scognamiglio Arte Contemporanea, Milan, Italy

Bodies in Space, Georg Kolbe Museum, Berlin, Germany (cat.)

Feeling Material, Deutscher Bundestag, Berlin, Germany

Blind Light, Sean Kelly Gallery, New York, USA

Ataxia, Anna Schwartz Gallery, Melbourne, Australia

2006 *Altered States*, Galleria Mimmo Scognamiglio, Naples, Italy

Breathing Room, Galerie Thaddaeus Ropac, Paris, France (cat.)

Time Horizon, Parco Archeologico di Scolacium, Roccelletta di Borgia, Catanzaro, Italy (cat.)

You and Nothing, Xavier Hufkens, Brussels, Belgium

Critical Mass, Museo d'Arte Contemporanea Donna Regina Napoli (MADRE), Naples, Italy

2005 *Antony Gormley: New Works*, Sean Kelly Gallery, New York, USA

Another Place, Crosby Beach, Merseyside, UK

Certain Made Places, Koyanagi Gallery, Tokyo, Japan

Asian Field, ICA, Singapore (cat.)

Inside Australia, Anna Schwartz Gallery, Melbourne, Australia

2004 *Mass and Empathy*, Fundação Calouste Gulbenkian, Lisbon, Portugal (cat.)

Clearing, White Cube, London

Fai Spazio, Prendi Posto (part of *Arte 'All Arte 9*), Poggibonsi, Italy (cat.)

Unform, Yale Centre for British Art, New Haven, Connecticut, USA

Clearing, Galerie Nordenhake, Berlin, Germany

2003 *Inside Australia*, Lake Ballard, Menzies, Perth International Arts Festival, Western Australia

Asian Field, touring: Xinhuahuayuan Huajingxincheng, Guangzhou / National Museum of Modern Chinese History, Beijing / Warehouse of Former Shanghai No. 10 Steelworks, Shanghai / Modern Mall, Jiangbei District, Chongqing, China (cat.)

Standing Matter, Galerie Thaddaeus Ropac, Salzburg, Austria (cat.)

Antony Gormley, BALTIC Centre for Contemporary Art, Gateshead, UK (cat.)

2002 *Antony Gormley: Sculpture*, Centro Galego de Arte Contemporánea, Santiago de Compostela, Spain (cat.)

Antony Gormley, Xavier Hufkens, Brussels, Belgium

Antony Gormley Drawing, The British Museum, London (cat.)

Field for the British Isles, The British Museum, London

2001 *New Works*, Galerie Nordenhake, Berlin, Germany

Antony Gormley, Contemporary Sculpture Centre, Tokyo, Japan (cat.)

Some of the Facts, Tate St Ives, Cornwall, UK (cat.)

States and Conditions, touring: Orchard Gallery, Derry, Northern Ireland / Model Arts and Niland Gallery, Sligo, Ireland (cat.)

2000 *Strange Insiders*, fig-1, London

Drawn, White Cube, London

1999 *Insiders and Other Recent Work*, Xavier Hufkens, Brussels, Belgium

Field for the British Isles, Salisbury Cathedral, Salisbury, UK

Intimate Relations, MacLaren Art Centre, Barrie, Ontario, Canada

Intimate Relations, Jablonka Galerie, Cologne, Germany

1998 *Angel of the North*, Gateshead, UK

Critical Mass, Royal Academy of Arts, London (cat.)

Another Place, Stavanger, Norway

Force Fields, Rupertinum, Salzburg, Austria

1997 *Total* Strangers, Kölnischer Kunstverein, Cologne, Germany (cat.)

Our House, Kunsthalle zu Kiel, Kiel, Germany (cat.)

Another Place (part of *Follow Me: British Art on the Lower Elbe*), Cuxhaven, Germany (cat.)

Allotment, Herning Museum, Denmark

1996 *Field for the British Isles*, touring: Greenesfield BR Works, Gateshead, UK / The Hayward Gallery, London (cat.)

Still Moving, touring: Museum of Modern Art, Kamakura / Nagoya City Art Museum, Aichi / Takaoka Art Museum, Toyama / Iwaki City Museum of Art, Fukushima / Museum of Contemporary Art, Sapporo / Museum of Modern Art, Tokushima, Japan (cat.)

1995 *Critical Mass*, Remise, Vienna, Austria (cat.)

1994 *Lost Subject*, White Cube, London

Field for the British Isles, touring: Oriel Mostyn, Llandudno, Wales / Scottish Museum of Modern Art, Edinburgh, Scotland / 1995: Orchard Gallery, Derry, Northern Ireland / Ikon Gallery, Birmingham (with concrete works), UK / National Gallery of Wales, Cardiff, Wales (cat.)
Escultura, Galeria Pedro Oliveira, Porto, Portugal (cat.)

1993 *Learning to See*, Galerie Thaddaeus Ropac, Paris, France (cat.)

Testing a World View, touring: Konsthall Malmö, Sweden / Tate Gallery, Liverpool, UK / 1994: Irish Museum of Modern Art, Dublin, Ireland (cat.)

European Field, touring: Centrum Sztuki Współczesnej, Warsaw, Poland / 1994: Moderna Galerija, Ljubljana, Slovenia / Muzej Suvremene Umjetnosti, Zagreb, Croatia / Ludwig Muzeum, Budapest, Hungary / 1995: Prague Castle, Prague, Czech Republic / National Theatre, Bucharest, Romania / 1996: Arsenāls, Riga, Latvia / Museum of Contemporary Art, Vilnius, Lithuania / Art Hall, Tallin, Estonia / Magasin 3, Stockholm, Sweden (cat.)

1992 *American Field*, touring: Centro Cultural Arte Contemporáneo, Mexico City, Mexico / San Diego Museum of Contemporary Art, La Jolla, California / 1993: The Corcoran Gallery of Art, Washington DC, USA / The Montreal Museum of Fine Arts, Canada (cat.)

1991 *Sculpture*, Galerie Nordenhake, Stockholm, Sweden

American Field, Salvatore Ala Gallery, New York, USA

American Field and Other Figures, Modern Art Museum, Fort Worth, USA (cat.)

1990 *Baring Light*, Burnett Miller Gallery, Los Angeles, USA

1989 *Antony Gormley*, Louisiana Museum of Modern Art, Humlebaek, Denmark (cat.)

Sculpture, Scottish National Gallery of Modern Art, Edinburgh, Scotland

1988 *Selected Work*, Burnett Miller Gallery, Los Angeles, USA

Antony Gormley, Contemporary Sculpture Centre, Tokyo, Japan (cat.)

1987 *Drawings*, Seibu Contemporary Art Gallery, Tokyo, Japan (cat.)

Vehicle, Salvatore Ala Gallery, New York, USA

Antony Gormley, Galerie Hufkens de Lathuy, Brussels, Belgium

Five Works, Serpentine Gallery, London (cat.)

1986 *Sculpture*, Salvatore Ala Gallery, New York, USA

1985 *Drawings 1981–1985*, Salvatore Ala Gallery, New York, USA (cat.)

1984 *New Sculpture*, Salvatore Ala Gallery, New York, USA (cat.)

New Sculpture, Riverside Studios, Hammersmith / Chapter, Cardiff, Wales (cat.)

1981 *Sculpture*, Whitechapel Art Gallery, London (cat.)

Two Stones, Serpentine Gallery, London

2019 *Essere* (Florence: Gallerie degli Uffizi and Giunti); texts by Eike D. Schmidt, Luca Massimo Barbero, Shen Qilan, Renata Pintus, Max Seidel and Serena Calamai, and Antonio Godoli

2018 *Subject* (Cambridge: Kettle's Yard); text by Caroline Collier. Antony Gormley in conversation with Jamie Fobert and Jennifer Powell

Critical Mass and Expansion Field (Changsha: Changsha Museum of Art); text by Shen Qilan and a conversation between Antony Gormley and Hans Ulrich Obrist

Still Moving (Long Museum, Shanghai); texts by Pi Li and Richard Noble

2017 *Antony Gormley* (New York: Rizzoli International Publications); text by Martin Caiger-Smith

2016 *Land* (Shottesbrooke: The Landmark Trust); text by Jeanette Winterson

Field for the British Isles (London: Hayward Publishing); texts by Hugh Brody and Antony Gormley

2015 *Antony Gormley on Sculpture* (London: Thames & Hudson); texts by Antony Gormley

Human (Florence: Forte di Belvedere); texts by Dario Nardella, Sergio Risaliti, Andrew Benjamin, Mario Codognato, Antony Gormley, Arabella Natalini and Marco Casamonti

2014 *Expansion Field* (Bern: Zentrum Paul Klee); texts by Rebecca Comay, Peter Fischer and Andrew Renton

2013 *Still Being / Corpos Presentes*, 2nd ed. (São Paulo: Centro Cultural Banco do Brasil); texts by Marcello Dantas, Agnaldo Farias, W. J. T. Mitchell and Luiz Camillo Osorio. Antony Gormley interviewed by Marcello Dantas

Model (London: White Cube); texts by Antony Gormley and Michael Newman

2012 *Horizon Field Hamburg* (Cologne: Deichtorhallen Hamburg / Snoeck); texts by Stephen Levinson, Dirk Luckow and Iain Boyd Whyte

2011 *Horizon Field* (Bregenz: Kunsthaus Bregenz); texts by Eckhard Schneider, Martin Seel and Beat Wyss

Still Standing (London: Fontanka); texts by Margaret Iversen, Dimitri Ozerkov and Anna Trofimova

2010 *Antony Gormley* (London: Tate Publishing); texts by Martin Caiger-Smith

One and Other (London: Jonathan Cape); texts by Hugh Brody, Lee Hall, Darian Leader, Alphonso Lingis and Hans Ulrich Obrist

Exposure (Lelystad: The Municipality of Lelystad); texts by Karel Ankerman and Christophe Van Gerrewey

Drawing Space (Rome: Macro, Museo d'Arte Contemporanea Roma / Electa); text by Anna Moszynska. Antony Gormley interviewed by Luca Massimo Barbero

2009 *Antony Gormley* (Bregenz: Kunsthaus Bregenz); texts by Antonio Damasio, Yilmaz Dziewior, Eckhard Schneider and Marcus Steinweg

2008 *Antony Gormley* (Monterrey: Museo de Arte Contemporaneo, Mexico); texts by Jorge Contreras and Mark Cousins. Antony Gormley interviewed by Hans Ulrich Obrist

2007 *Antony Gormley* (Göttingen and London: SteidlMack); texts by Antony Gormley and Richard Noble

Antony Gormley: Blind Light (London: Hayward Gallery Publishing); texts by W. J. T. Mitchell, Susan Stewart and Anthony Vidler. Conversation between Antony Gormley, Jacky Klein and Ralph Rugoff

2006 *Intersezioni 2: Time Horizon* (Catanzaro: Parco Archeologico di Scolacium, Roccelletta di Borgia); texts by Bruno Corà, Alberto Fiz, Maria Grazia Aisa and Colin Renfrew

2005 *Inside Australia* (London: Thames & Hudson); texts by Anthony Bond, Hugh Brody, Shelagh Magadza and Finn Pederson

2004 *Mass and Empathy* (Lisbon: Fundação Calouste Gulbenkian); texts by Paolo Herkenhoff and Maria Filomena Molder. Antony Gormley interviewed by Jorge Molder

Broken Column (Stavanger: Wigestrand Forlag in cooperation with Rogaland Museum of Fine Arts); edited by Jan Inge Reilstad; texts by Stephan Bann, Trond Borgen, Kjartan Fløgstad and Siri Meyer

2003 *Asian Field* (London: The British Council); texts by Hu Fang and Richard Noble. Antony Gormley interviewed by Sui Jianguo

Domain Field (Gateshead: Baltic Centre for Contemporary Art); text by Darian Leader

2002 *Antony Gormley* (Santiago de Compostela: Centro Galego de Arte Contemporánea); texts by Lisa Jardine and Michael Tarantino. Antony Gormley interviewed by Enrique Juncosa

Antony Gormley Drawing (London: The British Museum); text by Anna Moszynska

2001 *Some of the Facts* (St Ives: Tate St Ives); texts by Iwona Blazwick, Stephen Levinson and Will Self

States and Conditions (Derry: Orchard Gallery); texts by Caoimhín Mac Giolla Léith, Brendan McMenamin and Declan McGonagle

2000 *Antony Gormley* (London: Phaidon Press); revised edition with an additional essay by W. J. T. Mitchell; Antony Gormley in conversation with E. H. Gombrich. Texts by Antony Gormley, John Hutchinson and Lela B. Njatin. Antony Gormley interviewed by Declan McGonagle

1999 *Total Strangers* (Ostfildern: Edition Cantz); texts by Antje von Graevenitz and Ingrid Mehmel. Antony Gormley interviewed by Udo Kittelman

Gormley / Theweleit (Kiel: Kunsthalle zu Kiel and Cuxhaven Kunstverein); three-way discussion between Antony Gormley, Monika Kubale-Theweleit and Klaus Theweleit. Introduction by Hans-Werner Schmidt

1998 *Making an Angel* (London: Booth-Clibborn Editions); texts by Gail-Nina Anderson, Stephanie Brown, Beatrix Campbell, Neil Carstairs, Antony Gormley and Iain Sinclair

Critical Mass (London: Royal Academy); Antony Gormley interviewed by George Benjamin

1996 *Still Moving: Works 1975–1996* (Tokyo: Japan Association of Art Museums); texts by Stephen Bann, Daniel Birnbaum, Antony Gormley, Tadayasu Sakai and Kazuo Yamawaki

1995 *Critical Mass* (Vienna: Stadtraum Remise); text by Andrew Renton. Antony Gormley interviewed by Edek Bartz. Excerpts from Crowds and Power by Elias Canetti

1994 *Field for the British Isles* (Llandudno: Oriel Mostyn); texts by Lewis Biggs, Caoimhín Mac Giolla Léith and Marjetica Potrc

1993 *Field* (Montreal and Stuttgart: The Montreal Museum of Fine Arts / Oktagon); texts by Antony Gormley, Thomas McEvilley, Gabriel Orozco and Pierre Théberge

Antony Gormley (London: Tate Gallery Publications); texts by Stephen Bann and Lewis Biggs. Antony Gormley interviewed by Declan McGonagle

1992 *Learning to See: Body and Soul* (Tokyo: Contemporary Sculpture Centre); text by Masahiro Ushiroshoji

1991 *Field and Other Figures* (Texas: Modern Art Museum of Fort Worth); texts by Richard Calvocoressi, Antony Gormley and Thomas McEvilley

1987 *Five Works* (London: Serpentine Gallery / Arts Council of Great Britain)

1984 *Antony Gormley* (Milan / New York: Salvatore Ala Gallery); text by Lynne Cooke

AUSTRALIA

Inside Australia, 2003
Lake Ballard

BELGIUM

Another Time XVI, 2012
Knokke

FRANCE

Open Space, 1991/94
Place Jean Monnet, Rennes

Passage, 2000
Caumont, Picardy

Cloud Chain, 2012
French National Archives, Paris

GERMANY

Out of the Dark, 1987–88
Martinsplatz, Kassel

Steht Und Fällt, 2001
Jakob-Kaiser-Haus,
Dorotheenblocke, Berlin

Mark II, 2014
Erzdiözese München, Munich

Bare V, 2014
Erzdiözese München, Munich

ITALY

Fai Spazio, Prendi Posto, 2004
Poggibonsi

Seven Times, 2006
Catanzaro, Calabria

JAPAN

Mind-Body Column, 2000
Osaka

Here and There, 2002
Izumi City Plaza, Osaka

Another Singularity (Japan), 2009
Tokamachi City, Niiigata Prefecture

Another Time, 2013
Kunisaki Peninsula, Kyushu

NETHERLANDS

Exposure, 2010
Lelystad

NEW ZEALAND

Stay, 2014
Avon River, Christchurch

Stay, 2014
Arts Centre, Christchurch

NORWAY

Havmann, 1994
Mo i Rana

Place of Remembrance, 2000
Oslo

Broken Column, 2003
Stavanger

Standing Matter XVII, 2008
Lillehammer

PORTUGAL

Rhizome II, 1998
Parque Das Naçoes, Lisbon

SINGAPORE

Drift, 2009
Marina Bay Sands

SOUTH KOREA

Bearing III, 1997
Tongyoung City

SWEDEN

Here and Here, 2001
Höganäs

A Sculpture for the Subjective Experience of Architecture, 2008
Kivik

UK

Two Stones, 1979–81
Kent History and Library Centre,
Maidstone

Still Falling, 1983
Tout Quarry Sculpture Park, Dorset

Untitled (Listening), 1985
Maygrove Peace Park, London

Sound II, 1986
Winchester Cathedral

Sculpture for Derry Walls, 1987
East Wall, Derry

Iron:Man, 1993
Victoria Square, Birmingham

Angel of the North, 1998
Gateshead

Quantum Cloud, 2000
Greenwich, London

Planets, 2002
The British Library, London

Making Space, 2004
Heart Science Centre, Harefield

Another Place, 1997
Crosby Beach, Merseyside

You, 2005
The Roundhouse, London

Resolution, 2005
Shoe Lane, London

Another Time XI, 2008
Exeter College, Oxford

Plant, 2002
MacDonald Institute for
Archaeological Research, Cambridge

Another Time X, 2008
Maggie's Centre, Dundee

6 Times, 2010
Edinburgh

Transport, 2010
Canterbury Cathedral, Canterbury

Witness, 2011
The British Library, London

Another Time XVI, 2012
Limehouse Reach, London

Room, 2014
Beaumont Hotel, London

Grip, 2014
Saddell Bay, Mull of Kintyre

Connect, 2015
Holland Park School, London

USA

Habitat (Anchorage), 2010
Anchorage, Alaska

Chord, 2015
MIT, Cambridge, Massachusetts

NEON is a nonprofit organisation that works to bring contemporary culture closer to everyone. It is committed to broadening the appreciation, understanding and creation of contemporary art in Greece and to the firm belief that this is a key tool for growth and development. NEON, founded in 2013 by collector and entrepreneur Dimitris Daskalopoulos, breaks with the convention that limits the contemporary art foundation of a collector to a single place.

NEON's space is the city. It acts on a multitude of initiatives, spaces and civic and social contexts. It seeks to expose the ability contemporary art has to stimulate, inspire and affect the individual and society at large. NEON constructively collaborates with cultural institutions and supports the programs of public and private institutions to enhance increased access and inventive interaction with contemporary art.

The Ephorate of Antiquities of Cyclades constitutes a Directorate of the Hellenic Ministry of Culture and Sports. It is responsible for all the material remains that have been brought to light or are preserved in the territory of the island complex of the Cyclades. These evidences of human presence date back to Early Prehistory and continue until the establishment of the Modern Greek State, in AD 1830. Such a broad chronological context incorporates many different expressions of the cultural heritage of the area: archaeological sites, monuments, castles, traditional settlements and of course a whole world of movable finds and relics that are selectively presented in the Ephorate's museums and collections.

During the recent years, the Ephorate of Antiquities of Cyclades has developed an extensive action plan aiming to manage the voluminous cultural capital under its responsibility. The protection and the thorough documentation of the archaeological, architectural, and historical data of the monuments are the primary, essential act of this initiative. Having successfully attracted important donations and funding through competitive European programs, the Ephorate is working towards the conservation, restoration, and promotion of important archaeological sites and monuments. The work of the Ephorate is also focused on communicating its work, engaging with the local community, keeping an active presence in international scientific and museological fora, and implementing new ways of expression. In line with these efforts, this summer the Ephorate opens up towards the world of contemporary art, wishing to underline the revitalizing force of the form and timeless inspiration, and the need for a dialogue between the 'established' past and contemporary artistic expression.

It was a waking dream and a great honour to be invited to the Cyclades to do a project. I had never been to Delos before and it stung me with its concentrated beauty.

I want to thank Dimitris Daskalopoulos for his vision in enabling this, Iwona Blazwick for inviting me and Elina Kountouri for having faith in what sculpture can do.

It has been an amazing experience working with Fanis Kafantaris and his excellent team: Effie Syrigou, Gina Tsilimpi, Irene Kalliga, Irini Kiachtypi, Nafsika Papadopoulou, Irini Svolakou, Christos Stefanidis, Vasiliki Tsiropoulou, Christodoulos Zafiridis, Ioannis Serekas and Anastasios Dafnis. The going was not easy but in spite of rain and storm, high winds and a flooded site, their professionalism and determination prevailed.

I feel gratitude to Demetris Athanasoulis who allowed all of this and championed the potential of a dialogue between ancient marble and cast iron.

The work displayed at Delos is the result of close collaboration with Adam Humphries, Ashley Hipkin, Giles Drayton and Ocean Mims at the studio, who have all individually overseen the evolution of the sculptural languages exposed to the Aegean light. Ocean greatly enjoyed the experience of working closely with the NEON team on the island.

The studio team is brilliantly managed by Tamara Doncon and the works packed and transported under the care of Anna McLeod. A project of this complexity is not possible without the extraordinary planning and support of the wider studio: Philip Boot, Ruby Brown, Ondine Gillies, Alice O'Reilly, Ella Bucklow and Lucy Page all helped with its coordination. The catalogue production has been a wonderful collaboration between Alkistis Dimaki, Andrew Spyrou and Dimitra Chrona at NEON and Rosalind Horne at the studio. Kobi Benezri's elegant and evocative design compliments Oak Taylor-Smith's exceptional photography and the texts, including an insightful essay by curator Emily Riddle.

I am indebted to my gallery for their support of this project: Jay Jopling, Daniela Gareh, Susanna Greeves and Alexander Flint of White Cube who worked tirelessly to make this show on the mythical island of Delos a reality.

Antony Gormley

The island of Delos resonates deep in the Greek psyche. Through the exhibition and now this publication, we were honoured to share its historical and mythical significance with a worldwide audience, marking the start of a new era of collaboration between our ancient past and contemporary art.

In undertaking such a challenge, I couldn't have wished for a more sensitive artist to work with than Antony Gormley who, both personally and through his sculptural work, deeply understood the context of Delos and the opportunity for gradual change. I am forever indebted to Antony for accepting the invitation and for making all of us revisit Delos and our humanity.

Bringing the exhibition into being in an archaeological site was an exciting, thought-provoking and often demanding experience. Every step – from sketching the earliest plans, to the winter and spring installation of Antony's singular sculptures, to visitor-filled summer months on Delos and, finally, the poignant removal of the sculptures after the exhibition had closed – has brought revelations and possibilities to explore and hurdles to overcome.

SIGHT could not have been accomplished without the enthusiasm, dedication, commitment, professionalism and hard work of a large number of people.

Thank you to the early believers of the project, in particular Iwona Blazwick with whom I was privileged to co-curate the exhibition. I am also very grateful to our partners in this extraordinary endeavour, Demetris Athanasoulis who enabled the exhibition to take place by having the vision and generosity to grant us permission to hold it on Delos, along with the Central Archaeological Council of Greece.

My thanks to Maria Koutsoumpou, Themis Vakoulis and Stefanos Keramidas, archaeologists for the Ephorate of Antiquities of Cyclades, and all the staff of the archaeological site and Museum on the island of Delos for their constructive collaboration. Thank you to Christos Stefanidis and Spyros Maroudas and their teams for working patiently and carefully, often battling howling winds and driving rain, to install the sculptures on Delos.

To my team at NEON I extend my gratitude and heartfelt thanks for their steadfast commitment throughout such an intellectually and technically demanding project. To my friend Mania Xenou who gave me invaluable guidance and support throughout the project. To my team based on the island: Fanis Kafantaris who created the architectural drawings from which we planned the exhibition and who later supervised the installation; Tasos Dafnis, associate architect and site supervisor; Konstantinos Toumbakaris, civil engineer; Christodoulos Zafeiridis, assistant site engineer; Effie Syrigou, production coordinator; and Gina Tsilimbi, production assistant.

At NEON's Athens headquarters exhibition manager and project leader Irene Kalliga brought the whole plan together assisted tirelessly by Irini Kiachtypi. Irini Svolakou and Nafsika Papadopoulou organised the NEON events on Delos that will remain imprinted on our memories and the memories of our visitors for years to come. Malvina Deligianni prudently ensured our digital profile was accurately updated, and Maria Tavlariou assisted with events and office administration and elements of this catalogue. Thank you also to Nikolaos Kappas and his excellent financial team for facilitating the whole process.

It has been a pleasure to get to know the team at Antony Gormley's studio who worked thoughtfully and diligently to make the exhibition happen – Studio Manager Tamara Doncon; Anna McLeod; Ocean Mims; Ella Bucklow; Ondine Gillies and Alice O'Reilly.

Thank you to Efi Lazaridou, Calum Sutton and Melissa Emery who brought the exhibition to the attention of the world's press. I would also like to thank Lilette Botassi, Panayotis Kravvaris and their team for the wonderful digital documentation of the exhibition. This beautiful catalogue was designed by Kobi Benezri and produced by Dimitra Chrona. It could never have reached the page without the coordination skills of Alkistis Dimaki and Andrew Spyrou and creative input from Rosalind Horne. My thanks to Emily Cloney and Alexis Kalofolias for their thoughtful comments and edits.

My personal thanks also go to Vicken Parsons who has enthusiastically supported the whole project and has become a true friend.

And finally, I am, as always, deeply indebted to Dimitris Daskalopoulos, the founder of NEON, without whose financial, intellectual and emotional generosity this extraordinary exhibition would never have become a reality. His belief in the ability of art to change lives is our inspiration. He has certainly done so for Delos and for our shared history.

Elina Kountouri,
Director NEON

Setting up a contemporary art installation on Delos in a way that respects the material and intangible value of an archaeological site which is inscribed on the World Heritage List and plays an emblematic role in Greek institutional memory, required that its conception, its design and its creation be worked out to the last detail and that all involved rise to the occasion. The enormous administrative difficulties in setting up the installation on an uninhabited island exponentially increased the project's difficulty.

Its ultimate success is due to the exemplary collaboration and contribution of all those involved, whom the Ephorate of Antiquities of Cyclades gratefully acknowledges: Antony Gormley who incorporated his creations into the Delian landscape with the utmost respect. The staff of NEON and especially its founder Dimitris Daskalopoulos, the exhibition's curators, and especially the organisation's Director Elina Kountouri, for her decisive input towards the selection of the artist and the realisation of a demanding project. Thanks are also due to the Central Directorates of the Ministry of Culture for supporting the proposal and to the Central Archaeological Council for accepting it. Lastly, the exhibition would not have been possible without the invaluable input of the entire staff of the Ephorate of Antiquities of Cyclades, and in particular Stefanos Keramidas, under whom the collaboration between the Ephorate and NEON began in 2018; Themis Vakoulis who was responsible for setting up the installation on Delos; and the Ephorate's permanent and temporary staff on the island which took on the task of realising and running the exhibition.

Dr. Demetris Athanasoulis,
Director, Ephorate of Antiquities of Cyclades

CREDITS

EXHIBITION

Curators:
Iwona Blazwick OBE, Director, Whitechapel Gallery
& Elina Kountouri, Director NEON

Project management:
Irene Kalliga

On-site production coordination:
Effie Syrigou

Project architect & site supervisor:
Fanis Kafantaris, *Architect NTUA*

Associate architect & site supervisor:
Anastasios Dafnis, *Architect NTUA*

Assistant site engineer:
Christodoulos Zafiridis, *Architect NTUA*

Structural study:
Konstantinos Toumpakaris, *Civil Engineer NTUA*

Production:
Irini Kiachtypi, Gina Tsilimbi

NEON team:
Malvina Deligianni, Nafsika Papadopoulou,
Irini Svolakou, Maria Tavlariou

Head of artwork installation,
transport & maintenance on Delos:
Christos Stefanidis, *Conservator of Antiquities & Works of Art*

Installation team:
Konstantinos Koniaris, Dimitris Melissas-Baltzis, Georgios Papanikolaou, Vasiliki Tsiropoulou (*Conservators of Works of Art*), Athanasios Georgalas, Euaggelos Mpousoulas, Ioannis Serrekas

Cast construction:
Athanasios Gritzapis, Christos Stefanidis

Artwork transportation:
MOVE ART S.A.

Exhibition visual identity:
SCHEMA – Dimitra Chrona

Photography:
Oak Taylor-Smith

Filming:
Inkas Film Productions &
Panayotis Kravvaris, *Film Director*

Insurance:
Peter Milne at Cambridge Art Insurance

Press:
Melissa Emery and India Roche at Sutton;
Efi Lazaridou at Reliant Communications

Translations:
Alexis Kalofolias (*English to Greek*),
Mary Kitroeff (*Greek to English*)

Antony Gormley Studio

Vale Royal: Eduard Barniol Ferreres, Kerrie Bevis, Isabel Bohan, Philip Boot, Jamie Bowler, Ruby Brown, Ella Bucklow, Tamara Doncon, Danny Duquemin-Sheil, Sam Ford, Ondine Gillies, Rosalind Horne, Fred Howell, Adam Humphries, Gethin Jones, Pierre Jusselme, Bryony McLennan, Anna McLeod, Ocean Mims, Philippe Murphy, Lucy Page, Alice O'Reilly, Maria Ribeiro, Alice Steffen; *Hexham Studio*: Cat Auburn, Oliver Beck, Sacha Delabre, Pauline Elliott, Ashley Hipkin, Emily Iremonger, Mike Pratt, Matthew Young; *Hexham Studio Castings*: Chris Bell, Mick Booth, Ben Bryant, Max Condren, Rory Coulson, Stewart Creek, Jessica Freeman, Carmine Fortini, Daniel Jackson, Joe McDonough, Carol Robson, Stephen Tiffin, Zachry Vernon

Ephorate of Antiquities of Cyclades Team

Director - General coordination:
Dr. Demetris Athanasoulis, *Ephor*

Installation coordinator:
Dr. Themistoklis Vakoulis, *Archaeologist*

Supervising conservator:
Giannis Staikopoulos, *Head of the Department of Conservation of Antiquities*

Architects:
Dimitra Mavrokordatou, Konstantina Kouli

Archaeologist:
Maria Koutsoumpou

Delos staff:
Nikos Chatzioannou, Stella Georgala, Katerina Karali,
Irene Kazinaki, Panagiotis Xipteras

CATALOGUE

Editors:
Alkistis Dimaki & Andrew Spyrou (NEON)
Rosalind Horne (Antony Gormley Studio)

Assistant proofreader (Greek)
Maria Tavlariou

Translation:
Alexis Kalofolias (*English to Greek*)
Mary Kitroeff (*Greek to English*)

Photography:
Oak Taylor-Smith

Catalogue design:
Kobi Benezri Studio

Production:
SCHEMA – Dimitra Chrona

Printed by:
Fotolio & Typicon, Greece

Typeface:
LL Brown (Lineto.com), Kobi Benezri Garamond

Paper:
GardaPat KIARA, 135 gsm

Distributed by Thames & Hudson Ltd
181A High Holborn, London WCIV 7QX
www.thamesandhudson.com

Published by:
NEON

NEON, Amarousiou-Chalandriou 89, Athens, 15233, Greece
NEON.org.gr

ISBN: 978-618-81565-4-8

PHOTOGRAPHIC CREDITS

Oak Taylor-Smith: cover, 2–3, 17, 18–36, 41–58, 73–86, 97–124, 129–179

Elfi Tripamer: 60

Julian Gabriel Richter: 61

Markus Tretter: 63

Thomas Poravas. Courtesy of the artist, Maria Hassabi. Thank you to The Breeder, Athens: 65

Stephen White: 62, 66, 67, 182–183

Courtesy skyArts: 68

© The Estate of Ana Mendieta Collection, LLC. Courtesy Galerie Lelong & Co.: 71

Peppe Avallone: 72